A PEOPLE'S HISTORY OF THE FRENCH REVOLUTION

A PEOPLE'S HISTORY OF THE FRENCH REVOLUTION

Eric Hazan

Translated by David Fernbach

VERSO
London • New York

Avec le soutien du

Ouvrage publié avec le concours du Ministère français chargé de la culture – Centre national du livre

This work was published with the help of the French Ministry of Culture – Centre national du livre

This English-language edition published by Verso 2014

First published as *Une histoire de la Révolution française*

1 3 5 7 9 10 8 6 4 2

Verso
UK: 6 Meard Street, London W1F 0EG
US: 20 Jay Street, Suite 1010, Brooklyn, NY 11201
www.versobooks.com

Verso is the imprint of New Left Books

ISBN-13: 978-1-78168-589-1 (HB)
eISBN-13: 978-1-78168-590-7 (US)
eISBN-13: 978-1-78168-675-1 (UK)

British Library Cataloguing in Publication Data
A catalogue record for this book is available from the British Library

Library of Congress Cataloging-in-Publication Data

Hazan, Éric.
[Histoire de la Révolution française. English]
A people's history of the French Revolution / Eric Hazan ; translated by David Fernbach. – English edition.
pages cm
Includes bibliographical references and index.
ISBN 978-1-78168-589-1 (hardback : alk. paper) – ISBN 978-1-78168-590-7 (ebook)
1. France–History–Revolution, 1789-1799. I. Fernbach, David, translator. II. Title.
DC148.H2913 2014
944.04–dc23
2014013303

Typeset in Adobe Garamond by Hewer Text UK Ltd, Edinburgh, Scotland
Printed in the US by Maple Press

Contents

Preface

Up till now I have always avoided that particular exercise in writing known as a preface, foreword or introduction, but this time, for a subject like the French Revolution, a few explanations are necessary.

As to the reasons that impelled me to such an undertaking: this was originally intended as a short book for friends of mine, especially the younger ones, who have only a vague memory of the Revolution from school, a confusing mixture of blood and boredom. But I soon realized that a short book would not have conveyed the voices of its leading figures, or addressed the more complicated questions, in a way that might arouse such readers' interest and hopefully their enthusiasm. Space was needed, a good deal of it.

Once I had reframed my project accordingly, however, another question arose: was an autodidact like myself capable of this larger and more ambitious work? Could I follow in the footsteps of Michelet, Jaurès or Mathiez, not to say of lesser historians, without inviting ridicule? And now that the book is finished, I still don't know the answer.

What I have tried to do, at all events, is present a *narrative* of the French Revolution: the fourteen chapters follow one another chronologically without digressions, something that has not always been easy, as revolutionary time is prone to sudden accelerations when events pile up one on top of the other, and a certain amount of artifice is needed to present them in some kind of order. The narrative form is a montage that tightly links the two great revolutionary stages, that of the elected assemblies and that of the people – high eloquence and the rumbling that acts as its basso continuo, and becomes so powerful at times that nothing else is heard.

I have tried not to show the Revolution as a chiefly Parisian phenomenon. We see the people of Strasbourg storming their city hall, Marseille patriots rebelling against Parisian domination, workers of Lyon, peasants burning châteaux, requisitioning barges of grain and punishing hoarders. And even on the Paris scene, we see people from the provinces send delegations and messages to the Assembly, indicating that they understand the issues involved and share in their risks.

The book does not maintain a single focal length. I have passed quickly over the most famous episodes and slowed down on the problematic moments, without drawing conclusions or summarily judging between possible interpretations. In the case of certain events and individuals, I have paused for a time in a kind of extended parenthesis or excursus, so as to freely offer my personal interpretation.

I have avoided any reference to the twentieth century, the Bolshevik Revolution and the various 'totalitarianisms'. The French Revolution is not the matrix of anything else, and readers are sufficiently grown-up to make the connections without every 't' having to be crossed. Similarly, I have not discussed in detail the debates among historians – an interesting subject, but one for another book.

As readers will see, this work contains a large number of direct quotations. There are two reasons for this. The first is that, on consulting the sources, it turns out that the most famous speakers sometimes said something different from what is generally attributed to them. The second is that in the time of the Revolution language was a thing of great beauty, poised between irony and effusion, harshness and tears. There seemed no point in citing such speeches indirectly, when the words actually pronounced had a poetic force that's quite rare in politics.

Finally, though I have done my utmost to remain faithful to what are called the facts, I do not claim that this book is objective. I hope on the contrary that it will stoke a flare of revolutionary enthusiasm, at a time when the prevailing tendency is more towards relativism and derision. In the words of Saint-Just: '*Unhappy are those who live in a time when persuasion is a matter of smartness of wit.*'

ACKNOWLEDGEMENTS

Thanks first of all to my scholarly friends Florence Gauthier and Yannick Bosc, who had the patience to read and comment on my manuscript. Their expert criticisms and suggestions were a great help in giving this book its final form. My daughter, Karine Parrot, read it in a 'faux-naïve' fashion, which helped me avoid being awkward, obscure or obvious in several places. Many thanks also to Alain Badiou and Jean-Christophe Bailly for their advice, to Sebastian Budgen for the recondite references he pointed out to me, to Patrick Charbonneau for the Hölderlin poem, and finally to Sabrina and Cléo who put up with me throughout this long work.

CHAPTER I

How Things Stood

France under Louis XVI

The king, he said, was the most generous of princes, but his generosity could neither relieve nor reward everyone, and it was only his misfortune to be amongst the number.

– Laurence Sterne, *A Sentimental Journey through France and Italy*

A needless revolution?

Whatever the title we give it, this first chapter is very far from being merely a backdrop set up before the start of the action: what is at stake here is a choice between two contrasting views of the French Revolution. For a whole lineage of historians stretching from Tocqueville to Furet, the substance of what is generally seen as the revolutionary upheaval was already under way, if not completed, by the end of the Ancien Régime. An American-style revolution, calm and democratic, would have led to the same end result, while avoiding sound, fury, and the guillotine: 'The Revolution finished off suddenly by a convulsive and painful effort, without a period of transition, throwing caution aside and without any consideration, what would have automatically been finished gradually and by slow degrees.'[1]

1 Alexis de Tocqueville, *The Ancien Régime and the French Revolution*, London:

And in his commentary on Tocqueville, Furet argues that the Ancien Régime was already dead: 'The revolutionary consciousness, from 1789 on, was informed by the illusion of defeating a state that had already ceased to exist.'[2] He reaches the following verdict, where paradox verges on absurdity: 'nothing resembled French society under Louis XVI more than French society under Louis-Philippe.'[3]

Tocqueville emphasizes the modernization already under way in France in the 1780s. He explains how centralization was established on top of 'a diversity of rules and authorities, a tangle of powers' that were the debris of the feudal order. At the summit was the royal council, which was the supreme court of justice as well as the higher administrative authority, and 'subject to the king's approval [had] legislative powers; it could debate and propose most laws; it fixed levies and distributed taxes'.[4] Internal affairs had been entrusted to a single individual, the controller-general, who 'gradually monopolized the management of all affairs involving money – in other words, the whole public administration'. In the provinces, in parallel with the governors – an honorary and remunerative office – the *intendant* was 'the sole representative of the government' in his sphere. Under him, the *subdélégués* represented the central power in the small constituencies that were attributed to them. In short, 'we owe "administrative centralization" not to the Revolution or the Empire, as some say, but to the old Regime.'[5]

This point of view was adopted by Taine ('for it is the Monarchy, and not the Revolution, which endowed France with administrative centralization')[6] and subsequently by Furet ('the administrative state and the egalitarian society whose development was the main achievement of the old monarchy . . .'[7]).

Penguin, 2008, p. 34.

2 François Furet, *Interpreting the French Revolution*, Cambridge: Cambridge University Press, 1981, p. 25.

3 Ibid., p. 24.

4 Tocqueville, *The Ancien Régime*, pp. 46, 47.

5 Ibid., p. 58.

6 Hippolyte A. Taine, *The Ancient Regime: The Origins of Contemporary France*, vol. 1, Teddington: Echo Library, 2006, p. 67.

7 Furet, *Interpreting the French Revolution*, p. 22.

Such presentations invite the question: how could such a well-oiled administration disappear at the first shock, evaporating without resistance in the summer of 1789? Elements of an answer can be found in the picture drawn by Albert Mathiez:

> Confusion and chaos reigned everywhere . . . The controller-general of finances admitted that it was impossible for him to draw up a regular budget owing to the absence of a clearly defined financial year, the vast number of different accounts, and the absence of any regular system of accountancy. Everybody kept pulling in a different direction . . . One minister would protect the *philosophes* while another was persecuting them. Jealousies and intrigues were rife. Their chief aim was not so much to administrate as to retain the favour of their master or of those about his person. The interests of the public were no longer protected. The divine right of absolutism served as an excuse for every kind of waste, arbitrary procedure, and abuse. And so the ministers and *intendants* were generally detested, and, far from strengthening the monarchy, the imperfect centralization which they represented turned public opinion against it.[8]

Here we have no longer a needless revolution but an inevitable one.

The peasantry

In describing French society of the 1780s, it is customary to follow the divisions made in the Estates-General – nobility, clergy, and Third Estate. This has a certain logic, provided we keep in mind that these 'orders' were not compact and homogeneous blocs, as the train of events would very shortly demonstrate.

The Third Estate made up the great majority of the 27 or 28 million inhabitants of France. 'What is the Third Estate? Everything',

8 Albert Mathiez, *The French Revolution*, New York: Russell and Russell, 1962, p. 10.

Sieyès wrote in January 1789.[9] But this celebrated dictum should not lead us to forget that 'Third' was not a name but a number,[10] and that this 'everything' was made up of very different groups that would each play their part in the course of the Revolution.

Among these groups, by far the most numerous was the peasantry; the number of Louis XVI's subjects that lived on the land is estimated at 23 million. In the years leading up to the Revolution, however, the forms of landed property and cultivation underwent significant change.

For centuries, the lord's *seigneurie* had been made up of two parts: the *réserve*, land over which the lord enjoyed exclusive rights, and the *censive*, where rights were divided between lord and peasants; the latter paid a *cens* to the lord – who was most often noble, but could also be ecclesiastical or a commoner – but they could not be expropriated, and transmitted their tenure to their heirs. Alongside the *seigneuries* were communal lands that were the collective property of the village community: woods, pastures, and cultivated fields whose products were divided (unequally) among its members.

From the 1760s onward, the ideas of the Physiocrats and English influence began to change the old French system in depth.[11] In England, from the start of the century, the nobility had carried out a major reallocation at the peasants' expense, dividing up the common lands (enclosure) and creating big farms from which the landlords drew rental income. The same logic was at work in France, but with too great a delay to have given rise as yet to major upheavals. The

---

9 Emmanuel J. Sièyes, 'What is the Third Estate?' in *Political Writings*, Indianapolis: Hackett Publishing, 2003. This famous phrase is stated in the 'plan of this work' with which Sieyès began his pamphlet: 'The plan of this work is quite simple. There are three questions that we have to ask of ourselves: 1. What is the Third Estate? – *Everything*. 2. What, until now, has it been in the existing political order? – *Nothing*. 3. What does it want to be? – *Something*' (p. 94).

10 ['Tiers État' is an archaic form for what would be called '*troisième état*' in contemporary French. – Translator]

11 Georges Lefebvre, 'La Révolution française et les paysans' [1932], *Études sur la Révolution française*, Paris: Presses Universitaires de France, 1954, pp. 338–67; Florence Gauthier, 'Une révolution paysanne. Les caractères originaux de l'histoire rurale de la Révolution française, 1789–1794', in R. Monnier (ed.), *Révoltes et révolutions en Europe et aux Amériques*, Paris: Ellipses, 2004, pp. 252–82.

lords tried to appropriate the commons (especially woods for hunting) and increase their reserve at the expense of the *censive*: the *cens*, being monetary, was constantly devalued along with the currency, whereas the rent from leasing out land – for farms or sharecropping (*métayage*) – was far more advantageous.

On the eve of the Revolution, a large proportion of cultivators rented from landowners the soil that they tilled. Some of these were farmers, others sharecroppers. The latter, Arthur Young explains, are 'men who hire the land without ability to stock it; the proprietor is forced to provide cattle and seed, and he and his tenant divide the produce; a miserable system, that perpetuates poverty and excludes instruction'.[12] This 'miserable system' prevailed in the poorest regions, such as Brittany, Lorraine, and the centre and south of the country. Even among the farmers, there were great differences of condition: the exploiters of large cereal farms in the Paris basin and the north had nothing in common with the small farmers of the *bocage* or the mountain regions.[13]

Those who worked the land were not always tenants. Over the course of the century, many peasants became owners of land, and it is estimated that before the Revolution they possessed a third of the total cultivable area – a proportion that varied according to the region, being low in the rich wheat-growing lands and high in those provinces where cultivation was hardest. At the top of the ladder a prosperous peasantry began to form; these grew rich with the rise in commodity prices, as their production gave them a surplus to sell

---

12 *Arthur Young's Travels in France during the Years 1787, 1788, 1789*, Cambridge: Cambridge University Press, 2012, p. 18.

13 Even in the most fertile regions, farming conditions were very restrictive. David Andress gives the example of a contract signed (with a cross) at Villefranche-de-Lauragais, in the plain south-east of Toulouse, in 1779. The farmer had to supply the landlord with thirty-six hens at Christmas, the feast of St John and All Saints' Day, and 600 eggs over the course of the year; he undertook to buy and raise pigs, geese, ducks and turkeys, and to give half of all these to the landlord when they were fat enough to be sold; he had to obtain seed and other inputs needed for cultivation; he was charged with supplying the landowner with hay and straw for the animals, and to pay from his own pocket the excess required if his own production was not sufficient. The lease was signed for one year and was not automatically renewable. David Andress, *The French Revolution and the People*, London and New York: Hambledon Continuum, 2004, pp. 6–7. [*Bocage* is a mix of woodland and pasture characteristic of many regions in northern France. –Translator]

over and above family subsistence. This stratum of well-to-do peasants was not very large: most peasant proprietors possessed a small parcel that barely allowed them to lead a self-sufficient existence. They were often obliged to seek additional income from rural industry, or to go and work elsewhere as seasonal labourers.

No matter what their condition, the peasants were subject to taxes: the *taille* to the state, the *dîme* to the Church, and seigniorial dues to the lord. In Tocqueville's *The Ancien Régime and the French Revolution*, the first chapter of Book II is entitled 'Why feudal rights had become more hated among the people of France than anywhere else'. Jaurès explained this as follows:

> There was not one action in rural life that did not require the peasants to pay a ransom. I shall simply cite with no further commentary: the right of *assise* over animals used for ploughing, the right of seigniorial ferries for crossing rivers, the right of *leide* that was imposed on goods at markets and stalls, the right of seigniorial police on minor roads, the right of fishing in rivers, the right of *pontonnage* on small watercourses, the right to dig wells and manage ponds . . ., the right of *garenne*, with only the nobles allowed to keep ferrets, the right of *colombier* which gave the lord's pigeons the peasant's grain, the right of fire, *fouage* and chimney which imposed a kind of building tax on all the village houses, and finally the most hated of all, the exclusive right to hunt . . . Feudal rights thus extended their clutches over every force of nature, everything that grew, moved, breathed; the rivers with their fish, the fire burning in the oven to bake the peasant's poor bread mixed with oats and barley, the wind that turned the mill for grinding corn, the wine spurting from the press, the game that emerged from the forests or high pastures to ravage vegetable plots and fields.[14]

In the books of grievances for the Estates-General, hatred of seigniorial rights is a constant, and at the time of the Great Fear of summer

14 Jean Jaurès, *Histoire socialiste de la Révolution française* [1900–03], Paris: Éditions sociales, 1969, vol. 1, pp. 76–7.

1789, when the châteaux were stormed, this was above all, as we shall see, in order to destroy the documents that set down the origin of these rights.

Not all rural inhabitants, however, were subject to this. The great mass of those who were neither farmers nor sharecroppers nor proprietors, those who had nothing but their own hands, could only complain of the confiscation of common land, the suppression of free pasturage and the right of gleaning that took away from them the little that remained of the primitive communism of the countryside. These labourers, *manouvriers* as they were called, migrated to find work on a seasonal basis. When the countryside did not provide this, they sought employment in small rural industries – textiles above all, wool and linen in the north, silk in the south – or else they went to work in the city as builders, hawkers, chimney sweeps or water-carriers. The border is vague between these migrants and the tens of thousands of vagabonds and beggars who tramped the roads throughout the country, accompanied by their women and children.

Most historians see the situation in the French countryside as having improved in the course of the eighteenth century, and it is true that this period no longer saw famines of the kind experienced at the end of Louis XV's reign, when thousands of peasants died of hunger. Yet dearth remained common, and when several bad harvests came in a row, the *soudure* – between June and October – remained a critical time, with infant mortality in particular reaching horrific levels.

Above all, such improvements as there were failed to benefit everyone. Those who had no land, or not enough, were often reduced to the condition that Arthur Young described around Montauban:

> The poor seem poor indeed; the children terribly ragged, if possible worse clad than if with no cloaths at all; as to shoes and stockings they are luxuries. A beautiful girl of six or seven years playing with a stick, and smiling under such a bundle of rags as made my heart ache to see her: they did not beg, and when I gave them any thing seemed more surprised than obliged. One third of what I have seen of this province seems uncultivated, and nearly all

of it in misery. What have kings, and ministers, and parliaments, and states, to answer for their prejudices, seeing millions of hands that would be industrious, idle and starving, through the execrable maxims of despotism, or the equally detestable prejudices of a feudal nobility. Sleep at the Lion d'Or, at Montauban, an abominable hole.[15]

Financiers and businessmen

'The three estates that make their fortune in Paris today are the bankers, lawyers and builders', Louis-Sébastien Mercier noted in his *Tableau de Paris*.[16] The second half of the eighteenth century saw a transformation of Paris, with new districts springing up both on the right bank (the Chaussée d'Antin, among others) and the left (the extension of the faubourg Saint-Germain). The city's population was estimated at six to seven hundred thousand, the largest in Europe after London. France's other great cities shared in the same expansion: Lyon, Bordeaux and Marseille passed the 100,000 level before the Revolution.

At the apex of this urban population were the financiers. These were above all the *fermiers généraux*, who had bought the office of collecting for the state all indirect taxes – *aides*, *gabelle*, tobacco and stamp duty – as well as customs duties on all goods and commodities that entered the cities. It was the Ferme-Générale that collected duties at the fifty-five barriers of the new wall built around Paris between 1785 and 1788 under the direction of Claude-Nicolas Ledoux – hence its name, 'the wall of the Farmers-General'. This oligarchy (there were forty members of the Ferme-Générale) had up to 25,000 employees for collecting taxes and suppressing contraband; they were not royal officials, but acted in the name of the king and could send smugglers to the galleys or even the gibbet. Half of the state's receipts passed through the hands of the Ferme-Générale,

15 *Arthur Young's Travels in France*, p. 125.
16 Louis-Sébastien Mercier, *Tableau de Paris* [1781–8], Paris: Robert Laffont, 1990, p. 75.

and its members, who were in effect the king's bankers, built up immense fortunes. They also built up a major capital of popular hatred, and many of them ended on the guillotine.

In high society, the farmers-general rubbed shoulders with bankers, arms suppliers and stock-exchange speculators, as shareholding companies were proliferating at this time – including the Compagnie des Indes, the Compagnie des Illuminations (street lighting), the Compagnie d'Assurances sur la Vie et contre l'Incendie (life and fire insurance), the Compagnie des Eaux de Paris (water), and the Compagnie des Carrosses de Place (carriages for hire).

It was the financiers rather than the nobility who now built the finest *hôtels* in Paris, such as that of the farmer-general Marin de la Haye, with a hanging garden on its roof where two little Chinese bridges crossed a stream that distributed water to the building's bathrooms;[17] or the extraordinary Hôtel Thélusson – built by Ledoux for the widow of the Genevan banker who had been Necker's first patron – 'made of an immense hemispheric gallery through which could be seen a circular colonnade raised on bosses of sharp rock, interspersed with bushes'.[18] In these dwellings and the follies they had built outside the big cities, the financiers socialized with the enlightened nobility; they had the same advanced opinions as the nobles, read the same books, married their daughters and shared their mistresses, and many were in due course ennobled themselves.

Finance was concentrated in Paris, just as were the property-owners who lived off their rents – ground rent or rent of buildings, but, above all, interest on state borrowing (the '*rentes sur l'Hôtel de Ville*'). In Necker's accounts presented in 1789, the public debt had grown to more than four billion francs, of which around a half was held by 'rentiers', increasingly worried and hostile to the government as they risked being ruined by the unmitigated state bankruptcy that looked set to be the result of the financial crisis.

Merchants and manufacturers, for their part, were divided between

---

17 This *hôtel* still exists, on the corner of the rue Caumartin and the boulevard de la Madeleine.

18 Memoirs of the marquis de Crécy, cited in Michel Gallet, *Claude-Nicolas Ledoux*, Paris: Picard, 1980, p. 196.

Paris and the provinces. At the end of the Ancien Régime, some cities were enjoying strong economic expansion: Bordeaux and Nantes, thanks to trade with the American colonies, including the slave trade; Marseille, where shipbuilders had a stranglehold on exports to the Levant; and the textile towns that were thriving – wool and cotton in Normandy and the Nord, silk in Lyon and Nîmes, bonnet-making in Champagne, cloth in Languedoc . . .

As for industry in the modern sense, it was still in its early stages. The Compagnie des Mines d'Anzin (a joint-stock company, like almost all businesses of this type) that exploited the coal mines around Valenciennes was an early pioneer, along with the 'fire machines' at Le Creusot and the Dietrich foundries in Lorraine.

Artisans

The greater part of manufacturing production still came from the immense artisan sector. The system of corporations, with its rigid hierarchy of masters, journeymen and apprentices, had been abolished shortly before the Revolution. In February 1776, Turgot, the controller-general and a convinced Physiocrat, suppressed the corporations by royal edict. From now on, 'everything in Paris was free. All trades and skills were open to all. You could wake up as a tailor, baker, locksmith or whatever you liked. Some narrow minds who saw nothing large, however, found this system monstrous. They claimed that class and corporation were rooted in nature.'[19]

In May 1776, however, Turgot was dismissed and the corporations re-established, though now in a very different form. They were concentrated (reduced in Paris from 100 to forty-four) and strictly controlled by the police and the state bureaucracy. All that was needed to become a master was to pay the requisite taxes; the status

19 Jean-Louis Soulavie, *Mémoires historiques et politiques du règne de Louis XVI*, Paris, 1801, vol. 3, p. 123. Quoted in Steven L. Kaplan, *La fin des corporations*, Paris: Fayard, 2001. The joy of the *compagnons* freed from the tutelage of the masters found expression in song: 'Tomorrow it's up to us, as free as we please/To go and sell our goods and wine/Each from his trade at ease/ To earn, without dues of oath or mastery/Hey ho!, no oath or mastery' (ibid.).

of master now became more like a royal concession and a tax arrangement. A new hierarchical stratum was created, that of the *agrégés*, who enjoyed the same privileges as masters except that of having apprentices. Even women and foreigners could join the new system.

This apparent liberalization was accompanied by an increasingly tight control over the journeymen, and above all over day-labourers. They were forbidden to establish confraternities. In September 1781, letters patent compelled them to enrol on registers kept by the masters. They now needed written dispensation to leave their employer, and the use of the personal *livret* (workbook) was extended to all these previously unorganized workers. Lenoir, the lieutenant-general of police in Paris, decided to arrest all who lacked papers or official employment. He deployed nocturnal squads to round up any 'workers without shops or certificates'. Deprived of the possibility of moving, choosing, or changing their minds, workers were now 'no better off than the slaves of Algiers or the blacks who are used for work on sugar and indigo on the islands' was the verdict of the journeymen printers.[20]

This conscription did not proceed without resistance. Mercier noted with regret that:

> There has been visible insubordination among the people for several years now, and especially in the trades. Apprentices and lads want to display their independence; they lack respect for the masters, they form corporations [associations]: this contempt for the old rules is contrary to order . . . Formerly, when I went into a print works, the lads raised their hats. Today they just look at you and snicker, and you have scarcely crossed the threshold when you hear them speaking of you in a coarser way than if you were their mate. All the printers will tell you that the workers lay down the law to them, and provoke one another to infringe any restraint of obedience. The workers transform the print shop into a real smoke den, and delay as they please the printing of any text scheduled for a particular occasion.[21]

20 Kaplan, *La fin des corporations*, p. 317.
21 Mercier, *Tableau de Paris*, pp. 368–9.

From snickering to rioting would be only a short step.

The attention of the police bore also on that part of the urban population who were often termed *bas peuple*. This comprised 'the army of useless servants employed simply for show, the mass of the most dangerous corruption that could enter a city in which the countless and ever increasing disorders that arise from it threaten to bring sooner or later an almost inevitable disaster'.[22]

Also found here were

> those known as *gens de peine*, who are almost all foreigners. The Savoyards are crossing-sweepers, polishers and sawyers; the Auvergnats are almost all water-carriers; the Limousins are builders; the Lyonnais are generally locksmiths and chair-carriers; the Normans are stone-cutters, pavers and pedlars; the Gascons, wigmakers or carabineers; the Lorrains are itinerant cobblers known as *carreleurs* or *recarreleurs*.[23]

All these immigrants, whose number has been estimated at two-thirds of the Paris population, had to request a passport in their region of origin in order to avoid being arrested en route as vagabonds and sent to the beggars' colonies, a possible stepping stone to the galleys.

Finally, there were those women and men who were destitute, with no other shelter but the street: beggars, stray children, prostitutes, the unemployed. The litany of their wretched existence covers many pages of the Paris police archives, of which Arlette Farge has made an exemplary study:

> 2 September 1770. Ten in the evening. Posted at the Saint-Jean cemetery and doing the rounds on the rue des Arcis, arrested on the corner of the rue Vieille [and] place aux Veaux a woman soliciting passers-by who gave her name as Françoise Biquier, wife of Alexander, clock-maker, and her age as 28, native of Namur,

22 Ibid., p. 95.
23 Ibid., p. 276.

herself a gold polisher by trade, dwelling place Saint Michel, and took her to the Saint Martin station.

3 September 1770. Eleven in the morning. Jacques Mézières, age ten and a half, native of Paris, living rue Sainte Marguerite, faubourg Saint-German, at the potter's shop, arrested rue Neuve Notre Dame, found asking for alms during the last week by order of his mother to obtain bread.

3 September 1770. Seven in the evening. Gilles Fouchet, age fifteen, native of Yvetot in Normandy, in Paris for the last three days sleeping at the Lion d'Or in a street whose name he doesn't know. He was asking people to buy brushes and a saddle, and 32 liards were found in his pocket. Sent to the Petit Châtelet prison.[24]

Arrests were not always that simple:

Report of 2 May 1785, at six in the evening from the Paris guard at the Vaugirard post. Florentin, sergeant of the guard at Vaugirard, having been called by monsieur Dupont, wine-seller, regarding a number of individuals who were drinking at his establishment and had caused damage, breaking earthenware jars and unwilling to pay for these or even the wine they had drunk, we proceeded there and most of those involved had escaped with the exception of Durant, a stone-cutter, who was arrested along with Hurlot, also a cutter. When we set off, some sixty other stone-cutters ran behind us and attacked us to free the two arrested men, I ordered bayonets fitted and they, seeing that they could not approach any closer, took up stones and cobbles from the street and threw them at us, a certain Gateblie, a member of my squad, was struck in the legs, in the belly kidneys and in the face, and is dangerously wounded. The Vaugirard guard came out to help us, we were able to arrest the two mentioned above and also another, but informed that there was a further ambush I sent for two

24 Arlette Farge, *Vivre dans la rue au XVIIIe siècle*, Paris: Gallimard, 1979, p. 23.

> sections of infantry and the cavalry brigade from the Contrescarpe station as reinforcements and to take them to prison, following which we closed down the bars.[25]

Two infantry sections and a cavalry brigade, to take three stone-cutters to prison. This affair – just one of many riots that plagued the last years of the Ancien Régime – is exemplary: the watch in the cities or the mounted constabulary in the countryside were often overpowered by an angry crowd. When things got rough they had to call in the army, and from the first days of the Revolution it became clear that this force was far from reliable.

'Intellectuals'

In this rapid review of the very diverse elements that made up the Third Estate, I have not yet mentioned the best known, among whom we find almost all those who went on to play an important personal role in the Revolution: the group that today would be called liberal professionals and intellectuals. Lawyers were very prominent among them – they included Barnave, Danton, Desmoulins, Robespierre, Barère, Hérault de Séchelles, Vergniaud and Barbaroux – but also magistrates, notaries and medics such as Dr Guillotin, professor of anatomy at the university of Paris, who would be brought before the courts for having published the *Pétition des six corps*, in which he demanded an equal number of members of the Third Estate in the Estates-General to that of the two privileged orders combined. In the sphere of education, the expulsion of the Jesuits in 1764 had left a vacuum that would be filled by laymen or by those with only minor orders, such as Fouché or Billaud-Varenne, who both taught at the great school of the Oratorians at Juilly.

The most vocal and strident, those who often attracted the attention of the censorship and police, were journalists ('*nouvellistes*'), publicists and writers. They included Tallien, a legal clerk with

25 Ibid., p. 156.

journalistic ambitions, who founded a democratic newspaper in Marseille before 'going up' to Paris to become one of the leading figures of the Montagne; Brissot, the thirteenth child of a master-renderer in Chartres, sent to the Bastille in his youth for debts, perhaps a police spy, a pamphleteer for any cause, who became editor of *Le Patriote français* and leader of the Girondins (known accordingly as *brissotins*).[26] The future leading players even included successful writers: Jean-Baptiste Louvet, who opposed Robespierre in the Convention, was the author of *Les Amours du chevalier de Faublas*, a bestseller of the time. Choderlos de Laclos, having abandoned the military and written *Les Liaisons dangereuses*, became a commissioner at the war ministry and clandestine head of the Orleanist party at the Jacobins club. Mercier, a future deputy to the Convention, also enjoyed success with a futuristic novel, *L'An 2440*, although it led him to seek exile in Neuchâtel in order to avoid prison.

This intelligentsia were clearly very au fait with the modern ideas that they helped to disseminate. But what were these ideas? There was certainly a common foundation, as they had all read the works of the Enlightenment generation, just before their time.[27] But beyond this? What was there in common between Physiocrats such as Malesherbes or Samuel Dupont de Nemours, friends of Turgot and champions of economic liberalism, and Mably, the theorist of citizenship and natural law? The diversity of philosophical ideas and political propositions was such that to read about the 'cultural' or 'intellectual' origins of the Revolution can make your head spin.[28] You emerge amazed at such erudition, but with scarcely any clearer notions than before. Besides, with the acceleration of revolutionary time, ideas evolved at such a pace that a detailed depiction of the landscape of *origins* may well be a pointless exercise. And we should

---

26 On Brissot's younger days, see Robert Darnton, *The Literary Underground of the Old Regime*, Cambridge, MA: Harvard University Press, 1982, pp. 41–70.

27 Montesquieu had died in 1755, Helvétius in 1771, Rousseau and Voltaire in 1778, D'Alembert in 1783 and Diderot in 1784.

28 Daniel Mornet, *Les Origines intellectuelles de la Révolution française*, Paris: Armand Colin, 1933; Roger Chartier, *The Cultural Origins of the French Revolution*, Durham, NC: Duke University Press, 1991.

not forget what the young Marx wrote in *The Holy Family*: 'Ideas can never lead beyond an old world order but only beyond the ideas of the old world order. Ideas cannot carry out anything at all. In order to carry out ideas men are needed who can exert practical force.'[29]

Three phenomena need to be mentioned in this connection. The first concerns the 'discovery' of Herculaneum and Pompeii. The excavations were begun in 1738, and Charles de Brosses, who would later be president of the Burgundy Parlement, had already visited the site when he wrote his *Lettres d'Italie* for his friends in 1739–40. Yet it was not until shortly before the Revolution that the results of the excavations became generally known in France, through the publication of engravings.[30] The study of antiquity had certainly always been an essential part of the humanities, and both the Sorbonne and Port-Royal considered Cicero and Titus Livius indispensable for any learning worthy of the name. But this learning scarcely spread beyond the world of schools, universities and *belles-lettres*. Neither Colbert, nor Cardinal Fleury, prime minister under Louis XV, nor controller-general Turgot, would ever have thought of citing the ancients in their texts: antiquity was not a political subject. The discovery of Roman frescoes suddenly brought a change of tone. These Romans, who had previously been no more than characters in books, now appeared endowed with faces, clothing, houses, children and pets. There were even women among them, and beautiful ones at that. Ancient Rome erupted into the modern city. Its heroes, its writers, its ruins, would constitute throughout the revolutionary period the great storehouse from which political actors drew their references, refined their insults and polished their threats – far more so than Greece, whose share was most commonly reduced to the invocation of Aristides the Just or the legendary character Lycurgus, reputed author of Sparta's constitution.

---

29 Karl Marx, *The Holy Family*, in *Marx-Engels Collected Works*, vol. 3, London: Lawrence & Wishart, 1975, p. 119.

30 The seven volumes of *Antiquités d'Herculanum, ou les plus belles peintures antiques et les marbres, bronzes, meubles, trouvés dans les excavations d'Herculanum* were published in Paris in 1780. For a bibliography of this period, see Georges Vallet's preface to *La Peinture de Pompéi*, Paris: Hazan, 1993.

At more or less the same time, the severity of neoclassicism came to be combined with a very different sensibility (not a word used at that time): hearts swelled, tears flowed, nature was an endless source of emotion and touching effusions. *La Nouvelle Héloïse* did far more for Rousseau's fame than *The Social Contract*. Cincinnatus and Cato on the one hand, *Paul et Virginie* on the other: these were the heroes of the day. Diderot, a great admirer of Greuze's sugary young girls, was able nonetheless to acknowledge the beginnings of David's work with his 'Belisarius' at the Salon of 1781: 'This young man has soul; his figures are noble and natural; he draws, he knows how to cast drapery and make fine folds.' The national costume that this 'young man' would design in 1793 was a compromise between the black coat of the Parisian bourgeois and the dress of the inhabitants of Pompeii.

The second remark concerns the influence of the American Revolution. This owed much to the character of Benjamin Franklin, the first United States ambassador to France in 1776, then from 1779 to 1785. By his prestige as both scientist and founding father of the American union, by the simplicity of his life in a rural house in Passy, he became one of the most popular figures in 1780s Paris, welcomed in both aristocratic and philosophical salons – especially that of Mme Helvétius, whom he hoped to marry. And from 1785 to 1789, his successor at the United States embassy would be the prestigious Thomas Jefferson, chief author of the federal constitution.

Franklin had the constitutions of the American states translated and widely distributed in Paris. The publication of the Declaration of Independence was not authorized but circulated none the less, translated by the duc de la Rochefoucauld at Franklin's request. The tone is given by the preamble:

> We hold these truths to be self-evident, that all men are created equal, that they are endowed by their Creator with certain inalienable Rights, that among these are Life, Liberty and the pursuit of Happiness. That to secure these rights, Governments are instituted among Men, deriving their just power from the consent of the governed. That whenever any Form of Government becomes

> destructive of these ends, it is the Right of the People to alter or to abolish it, and to institute new Government, laying its foundation on such principles and organizing its powers in such form, as to them shall seem most likely to effect their Safety and Happiness.

The text dates from 1776, thirteen years before the French Declaration of the Rights of Man and of the Citizen, which reproduced this text almost word for word – thirteen years in which several more or less tolerated editions were distributed throughout France.

In 1784, the Académie des Jeux floraux of Toulouse set for the subject of a prize essay 'The grandeur and importance of the revolution that has just been carried out in northern America'. In 1786, Condorcet published under a pseudonym a text in response to another essay subject, proposed by Abbé Raynal of the Lyon Académie: 'Has the discovery of America been useful or harmful to the human race? If benefits have resulted from it, how may these be preserved and increased? If it has produced ills, how may these be remedied?' Condorcet's short work, dedicated to Lafayette, was entitled 'On the influence of the American revolution on Europe': 'The spectacle of the equality that reigns in the United States, and which assures its peace and prosperity, can also be useful to Europe. We no longer believe here, in truth, that nature has divided the human race into three or four orders, like the class of Solipeds, and that one of these orders is also condemned to work much and eat little.' And again: 'Liberty of the press is established in America, and we see with good reason the right to speak and to hear truths that one believes useful as one of the most sacred rights of humanity.'[31] The example of Condorcet – among many others – whose role would be so important between 1789 and 1793, shows the tremendous influence of America on the principles of the revolution in France.

The final remark concerns intellectual and political life in the provinces before the Revolution. The network of popular societies across the country, thanks to which the revolutionary *journées* in

31 Jean-Antoine-Nicolas de Caritat Condorcet, *Selected Writings*, London: Macmillan, 1976, pp. 79–81.

Paris were relayed (and sometimes anticipated), was not built up from nothing. Over the last twenty years of the Ancien Régime, academies, scientific societies, reading rooms, public lectures and public libraries proliferated throughout France. Provincial universities attracted students who sometimes came from far afield: the law faculty in Reims had Danton, Brissot, Roland and Saint-Just among its alumni. Prizes awarded by provincial academies had echoes far beyond their own city: Rousseau became famous when he obtained the prize of the Dijon academy for his *Discours sur l'origine et les fondements de l'inégalité parmi les hommes.*

We need not imagine a direct filiation between a particular reading society and the branch of the Jacobins created in the same town some years later. Nor embrace Augustin Cochin's thesis that 'societies of thought' lay at the origin of a revolution of elites.[32] But these meeting places were fertile soil, where ideas were exchanged, readings shared, connections formed – among the lettered classes of the towns, to be sure, but theirs would be no minor role during the Revolution. The political fever of the provinces would thus form a decisive counterpoint to the Paris revolution.

The privileged orders

How many nobles and churchmen were there in France on the eve of the Revolution? In *What Is the Third Estate?*, Sieyès calculates them rather tendentiously to arrive at a total of 81,400 'ecclesiastical heads' and 110,000 nobles. Modern estimates yield higher figures: for Soboul, 120,000 and 350,000 respectively,[33] making up close to 1.6 per cent of the French population.

The nobility did not form a class, nor even a genuine order: it was a set of disparate castes, often mutually hostile. There was the *noblesse d'épée* of ancient lineage, and the *noblesse de robe* whose members, as

32 Furet, *Interpreting the French Revolution*, p. 164ff.

33 Albert Soboul, *The French Revolution, 1787–1799: From the Storming of the Bastille to the Coming of Napoleon*, London: Unwin Hyman, 1989.

Sieyès puts it, 'acquired noble status by way of a door that, for mysterious reasons, they have decided to close behind them'.[34] But above all, there was a deep divide between the Court and the provinces.

The court aristocracy numbered some 4,000 families, 'presented' at court after a meticulous examination of their titles of nobility. They lived at Versailles and in their *hôtels* in the faubourg Saint-Germain, went hunting with the king and shared in 'the 33,000,000 livres annually expended on the households of the king and the princes, the 28,000,000 of pensions entered in serried rows in the Red Book, the 46,000,000 of pay of the 12,000 officers in the army, who alone absorbed more than half the military budget, and, lastly, all of the millions spent on the numerous sinecures, such as the offices of provincial governors.'[35]

But despite this largesse the great lords were heavily in debt: the court ceremonial, clothing, carriages, livery, receptions, everything required for 'show', cost very dear:

> Biron, duc de Lauzun, a notorious Don Juan, had squandered 100,000 écus at the age of twenty-one, besides contracting debts of 2,000,000. The comte de Clermont, a prince of the blood, abbot of Saint-Germain-des-Près, who had an income of 360,000 livres, managed to ruin himself twice over. The prince de Rohan-Guémenée went bankrupt for some thirty million, the greater part of which was paid by a grant from Louis XVI. The king's brothers, the comtes of Provence and Artois, owed over ten million by the time they reached the age of twenty-five.[36]

There was a total contrast between the great pomp of the court and the life of most provincial *hobereaux* (squires).[37] Granted, they were

---

34 Sièyes, *Political Writings*, p. 105. [The *noblesse de robe* were recent creations, essentially awarded for services in the state administration. – Translator]

35 Mathiez, *The French Revolution*, p. 5.

36 Ibid., p. 6.

37 'The people, who often have a word that goes straight to the idea, have given this petty gentleman the name of the smallest bird of prey, naming him the *hobereau* [hobby falcon]' (Tocqueville).

more or less exempt from taxation, as was the whole nobility. If they owned lands, they received rent from farmers or sharecroppers; but otherwise their main resource came from the levying of seigniorial dues, which had been fixed long ago and throughout the eighteenth century declined in real terms with the depreciation of the currency. One route for their sons was the army, but this could be barred by an edict of 1781 that reserved entrance to the officer schools to those who could boast an undiluted noble heritage. All that was left for these provincial nobles was to extract from the peasants their due and then some. A kind of feudal reaction took place in the countryside, where ancient charges that had fallen into disuse were revived and existing ones demanded with the utmost severity.

The Catholic Church remained a power in the land, although its moral and intellectual influence was declining. 'The Jews, the Protestants, the deists, the Jansenists, no less guilty in the eyes of the Molinists,[38] the *riennistes* ['nothingists'], thus live as they please; nowhere does anyone question them over religion. That is an old argument definitively closed', wrote Mercier.[39] The clergy were as divided as the nobility, despite the existence of an assembly that met every five years to safeguard the interests of their order. It was this assembly that set the amount of the 'free gift', the Church's only contribution to the country's finances. Its amount was derisory: a few million livres, which the clergy got back, moreover, in the king's payment for the costs of state borrowing – the 'Hôtel de Ville' bonds guaranteed by the Paris municipality, the interest on which went to the clergy. On the other hand, the Church received one of the three most important taxes of the Ancien Régime (along with the royal *taille* and seigniorial dues), the *dîme* or tithe. This was paid in kind, on all land including that of the nobility. In October 1789, the Constituent Assembly's finance committee assessed the total amount of the tithe as 123 million livres. Lavoisier's estimate was that the

---

38 ['Molinists', after the Jesuit Luis Molina (1536–1600), a theological doctrine whose followers stressed human freedom and were accused of moral laxity; '*riennistes*', those who pejoratively believed in nothing. – Translator]

39 Mercier, *Tableau de Paris*, p. 123.

dîme on wheat alone brought in 70 million.[40] It is true that the clergy kept the population registers, conducted the greater part of teaching – even if the expulsion of the Jesuits had reduced this role – and were responsible for the functioning of many hospitals.

The Church was the leading landowner in the kingdom. In Paris, monastic foundations and their holdings occupied a quarter of the city surface, and the Church profited from the rise in rents throughout the second half of the century. Its rural properties were also considerable, especially in the north of the country, bringing in 130 million a year, according to Necker.

These millions were by no means equally divided among the 'ecclesiastical heads'. It was the bishops, abbots, canons and high clergy who received the lion's share. These were recruited almost exclusively from the aristocracy: in 1789, the 139 French bishops were all nobles. Many lived at court, with a lifestyle as brilliant as that of the great lords. They could hold leading positions in politics: in 1787, at a critical moment, it was the archbishop of Toulouse, Loménie de Brienne, who became controller-general of the kingdom in place of Calonne. For Tocqueville,

> the Church was itself the leading political power and the most loathed even though it was not the most oppressive. For it had come to join the political sphere without being called to do so either by vocation or nature. It often sanctified failings in politics which it condemned in other spheres, surrounded them with a sacred inviolability and seemed to want to immortalize them as it did itself. In the first place by attacking the Church, the writers were sure to strike a chord with the passions of the masses.[41]

The 50,000 or so parish priests and vicars were kept well away from the prestigious prelates of the court. They were almost all commoners, and often lived in material conditions closer to those of their flock: their regular monthly emolument, levied from the parish *dîme*,

40 Jaurès, *Histoire socialiste*, vol. 1, p. 89.
41 Tocqueville, *The Ancien Régime*, p. 152.

was 700 livres, whereas a bishop received between three and four hundred thousand livres per year. The village priest, besides his religious duties, had a social and political role that was by no means unambiguous. He was charged with making known and explaining royal edicts from the pulpit to a largely illiterate congregation, but he might also defend the ideas of freedom and justice to which his own wretched condition clearly made him sensitive. Many of these priests were elected to the lists of the Third Estate.

They were not alone in dissociating themselves from the order to which they belonged. Among the privileged, we find famous individuals who took the side of the Third Estate at the start of the Revolution. The comte de Mirabeau, the marquis de Condorcet, the marquis de Lafayette, the abbé Grégoire, or Michel Lepeletier marquis de Saint-Fargeau, all these have streets, squares and schools named after them in France today. However long or short the road they travelled with the people, they are honoured for this courageous transgression.

CHAPTER 2

Towards the Estates-General

Impending bankruptcy, the rebellion of the Parlements, provincial disturbances, elections

The idea of the Estates-General was then in everyone's mind, only it was impossible to see where it would lead. For the mass of people, the object was to make good a deficit that the lowliest banker today would take it upon himself to eliminate. So violent a remedy, applied to so trivial a problem, demonstrated that we had entered unknown regions politically.

– Chateaubriand, *Memoirs*

Imminent insolvency

As the 1780s went on, despite tensions and conflicts, things might have carried on as before for a long time, if the Treasury had not been empty and France facing imminent insolvency.

This was not the first time. Back in 1770, at the end of Louis XV's reign, the state funds were exhausted in the wake of the disastrous Seven Years' War. At that time, however, chancellor Maupeou, the last great minister of the Bourbon monarchy, had taken on as controller-general the cantankerous abbé Terray, and together they put through measures that still seem extraordinary, however blasé we are today about such matters: increased taxes, massive reduction of interest rates on the national debt, cutting of pensions paid by the state, forced loans, sale of new offices – a package that Terray's enemies called bankruptcy, but that made it possible to stabilize the situation for a while.

This episode came against a background of chronic financial stagnation that had two major causes. First of all, there was no forward planning, for the country did not have a budget. It was accepted that the king should spend as he saw fit, and that receipts were subsequently adjusted to this. Since the different accounts overlapped from one year to the next, the controller-general himself never knew exactly how things stood, except at the moment when the funds ran out. The second reason had to do with aberrations in the tax system. The richest people – the senior clergy and high nobility – were practically untaxed. Exempt from the *taille*, they were in principle subject to the *vingtième* and the *capitation*, but these taxes were badly allocated and badly collected.[1] The yield from indirect taxes was better, since their collection had been entrusted to the farmers-general, but here again the imposition was far from standardized: with the *gabelle*, for example, the price of a pound of salt varied from half a sou to thirteen sous depending on the region, which encouraged the activity of smugglers whom the *gabelous* hunted down to send to the galleys.

It was possible to maintain the state finances, one way or another, so long as there was no war. But at the end of the Ancien Régime, funds had been mopped up by the two billion livres or so spent on participation in the War of American Independence. During the fifteen years of Louis XVI's reign the debt tripled, reaching 4½ billion livres in 1789, while interest had risen to 300 million livres per year, out of total receipts that were less than 500 million.

---

1 [The *taille* was the most important direct tax of the Ancien Régime, though its application varied between the different provinces. The *capitation* was a poll tax, and the *vingtième* (twentieth) a direct tax on property. – Translator]

Necker, Calonne and the 'territorial subvention'

For five years, from 1776 to 1781, the finances of France were directed by a Genevan banker, Jacques Necker. His reputation in Paris was due to his success as a speculator and to the philosophical salon held by his wife on the rue Michel-le-Comte, in the sumptuous Hôtel d'Halwyll built by Ledoux. Necker was seen as a financial genius, and an enlightened one. In reality, his main asset was his ability to inspire confidence for the loans that he raised. In February 1781 he had his *Compte rendu au roi* published, a remarkable double coup: on the one hand, he gave an account of finances that were in slight surplus, thanks to his wise management;[2] on the other, he won genuine popularity by denouncing abuses of all kinds, from the royal kitchens to forests, prisons, the postal service and the *gabelle*, and by revealing the names of the beneficiaries of royal pensions. It mattered little that the accounts were completely fabricated. The text, published by the Imprimerie Royale, was a bestseller: seventeen successive editions were sold, a total of some 40,000 copies.[3] But Necker's vanity led to his losing everything. He asked to supervise the expenditure of the ministers of war and the navy, and demanded to be admitted to the Conseil d'En-haut,[4] which was impossible for a foreigner. Maurepas, who presided over the Conseil, pressed the king to demand Necker's resignation in May 1781. Yet this was good timing for Necker, as voices were being raised to denounce the false balance sheet of the *Compte rendu*.

After a two-year interval, the post of controller-general was entrusted in 1783 to Charles Alexandre de Calonne, who had previously been *intendant* of Lille. He began by following Necker's

---

2 'The actual state of the finances is such that, despite the deficit of 1776 [on top of the previous deficits], despite the immense expenses of the war, and despite the interest on the loans taken out to support it, the ordinary revenues of Your Majesty at this moment exceed Your Majesty's ordinary expenses by 10 million and 200 thousand livres' (*Archives de la Révolution française*, Oxford: Maxwell, n.d., pp. 12–13).

3 Chartier, *The Cultural Origins of the French Revolution*, p. 180.

4 [The Council of State, the body of the king's highest advisers, comprising no more than six ministers, had been known since Louis XIV's time as the Conseil d'En-haut, as it met on the first floor of the Versailles palace, close to the royal chamber. – Translator]

lead and disguising the disaster. New loans were used to continue the payments on state bonds (*rentes*), to ensure the credit of the Caisse d'Escompte[5] and undertake major works such as the construction of the naval port of Cherbourg. Calonne maintained that the deficit would be paid off by 1797, but he must have been well aware that this was an impossible target. In August 1786, therefore, he submitted to the king a 'plan for the improvement of finances' that relied on a real financial revolution: the establishment of a 'territorial subvention', a tax on land that would be applied to all properties – noble, ecclesiastical or common – in proportion to their income. In parallel with this, trade in grain would be made free and internal customs duties suppressed. Finally, the plan envisaged the creation of municipal and provincial assemblies, elected on a property qualification and charged among other things with collecting the territorial subvention.

It was clear that the Parlements would refuse to register such a rupture with the existing system.[6] So Calonne convened in February 1787 an assembly of notables, whose 144 members were prelates, great lords, parliamentarians and representatives of the provincial assemblies. It was a strange idea indeed to ask an assembly of the privileged to approve a plan reducing their privileges. Sure enough the assembly prevaricated, asked for details of the accounts, demanded compensation – in short, the whole business was a failure. Calonne also had powerful enemies, and was correctly accused of speculating in his own interest; when Vergennes died, the minister for foreign affairs and his main supporter, his position became untenable and he was dismissed on 8 April 1787.

---

5 [Following the collapse of John Law's Banque Royale in 1720, France did not have a central bank, but the Caisse d'Escompte (discount counter), established in 1767, performed some of the functions of such a bank, purchasing commercial paper and government securities and having a monopoly on coinage. – Translator]

6 There were fourteen Parlements in France at this time, the Paris one being the oldest and most influential. The parliamentarians bought their office for a high price, and bequeathed it to their heirs. Their role was chiefly a judicial one, but also political as they had the power to refuse to register royal edicts and decrees.

The Parlements rebel

At this point, events gathered pace: 'From 1787, the kingdom of France [was] a society without a state', writes Furet.[7] Loménie de Brienne, who succeeded Calonne after the campaign against him, could do nothing but take over the same projects. The notables maintained their opposition, and Brienne dismissed them on 25 May 1787. But since the country was on the verge of defaulting on its payments, he had now to force the Parlements to register the indispensable loans.

Under the double influence of Locke and Montesquieu, the Parlements viewed themselves as 'intermediary bodies' between the people and the king, guarantors of the contract made between the king and the nation. Their remonstrations provide an interesting sample of the democratic thought of that time. The basic laws, declared the Parlement of Rouen in 1771, were 'the expression of the general will'. The law, the Parlement of Toulouse maintained in 1763, was based on 'the free consent of the nation'. In 1768, the Parlement of Rennes proclaimed that 'man is born free, men are originally equal, and these are truths that there is no need to prove', while it was 'one of the first conditions of society that particular wills must always bend to the general will'.[8] In 1787–88, the popularity of the Parlements was at its height, and they did not hesitate to defy royal authority.

On 16 July 1787, the Paris Parlement called for a meeting of the Estates-General, which alone, it claimed, had the power to raise new taxes. On 6 August, the king was obliged to hold a *lit de justice*[9] in order to obtain the registration of an edict establishing a tax on newspapers and posters, but the next day the Parlement annulled the registration, deeming it illegal. The crowd acclaimed the parliamentarians as they came out of the palace. The king then exiled the

---

7 Furet, *Interpreting the French Revolution*, p. 24.

8 See on these points Alfred Cobban, *A History of Modern France*, London: Penguin, 1990, vol. 1: 1715–1799, p. 130.

9 This was a session of the Parlement held in the presence of the king. His presence reduced the Parlement to an advisory role, and decisions were taken by royal authority, whatever the Parlement's reluctance.

Parlement to Troyes, but the agitation spread to the provinces where other Parlements declared their solidarity with Paris. The whole *noblesse de robe* was in revolt. Brienne was obliged to concede: the new tax was withdrawn, the territorial subvention was buried, and the Parlement returned to Paris in a festive atmosphere, amid celebratory fireworks.

Bankruptcy, however, was imminent, and Brienne had to return to the Parlement to have a new loan of over 400 million livres accepted. In return, he granted the convocation of the Estates-General for 1792. On 19 November, during a dramatic session that was transformed at the last minute into a *lit de justice*, the king demanded registration of the loan. His cousin, the duc d'Orléans, rose to tell Louis XVI that the procedure was illegal, to which the king replied in *Louis-quatorzien* style: 'It is legal, because I wish it.' The next day, the duke was exiled to Villers-Cotterêts. The war continued. On 4 January 1788, the Parlement condemned the instrument of *lettres de cachet*,[10] going on to present remonstrations to the king against the illegal registration of 19 November. On 3 May, it recalled the 'fundamental laws of the kingdom': only the Estates-General had the power to vote taxation, the Parlements must have the right of control over new laws, and *lettres de cachet* must be abolished.

That was too much, even for the easy-going Louis XVI. He had two parliamentarians arrested in the Palais de Justice itself, Goilard de Montsabert and Duval d'Esprémesnil, and on 8 May 1788 decreed the application of six edicts that Lamoignon, his minister of justice, had prepared to put an end to the Parlement's opposition. Royal acts would now be registered by a plenary court whose members were appointed by the king. The Parlements saw their judicial role cut back in favour of forty-seven 'grand bailiwicks'. Many special courts were suppressed. Lamoignon's edicts thus removed from the Parlements the best part of their financial, judicial and legislative power.

---

10 [These 'letters of the signet' were orders direct from the king and countersigned by one minister, but they particularly came to mean orders of arbitrary imprisonment. In the eighteenth century it was not uncommon for wealthy families to purchase a *lettre de cachet* in order to dispose of inconvenient relatives; the marquis de Sade was imprisoned under such a *lettre*. – Translator]

But this move came too late. Agitation spread in both town and country, extending from the Parlements to enlightened fractions of the privileged orders. Not of course without ambiguity: their concern was both to defend their freedoms with the inspiration of new ideas, *and* to maintain threatened traditions. Chateaubriand recalled: 'Forced registrations, *lits de justice* and imposed exile, in making the magistrates popular, drove them to demand freedoms of which they were not at heart sincere partisans. They called for the Estates-General, not daring to admit that they desired legislative and political power for themselves.'[11]

Disturbances in Grenoble and Vizille

It was in the Parlement cities that open rebellion broke out in the spring and summer of 1789. On 9 May, a big demonstration was held in the streets of Rennes, attracting nobles, parliamentarians and students. The following day, the *intendant* Bertrand de Molleville and the commander of the royal forces, the comte de Thiard, 'gentleman of the court, erotic poet, a gentle and frivolous soul',[12] came close to being hacked to pieces. The confrontation between demonstrators and a hesitant army continued throughout the month of May. In Pau, where people feared the suppression of the provincial Estates of Béarn, the hill folk led by the local nobility imprisoned the *intendant* and reinstalled the Parlement in the Palais de Justice. But it was in the Dauphiné that the disturbances acquired national significance. In Grenoble, a considerable number of people – advocates, *procureurs*,[13] clerks and public scribes – made a living from the Parlement. Despite being closed down by the Lamoignon edicts, this Parlement continued to meet. On 7 June, the duc de

11 François-René de Chateaubriand, *Memoirs of Chateaubriand: From his Birth in 1768, Till His Return to France in 1800*, Whitefish, MT: Kessinger, 2010, p. 190. (Translation modified)

12 Ibid.

13 [The *procureur* was a state official at a variety of levels, essentially the legal representative of a local or national administration. – Translator]

Clermont-Tonnerre, lieutenant-general of the province, called on its members to go into rural exile. Egged on by the judicial auxiliaries, protestors invaded the streets and occupied the city gates. Some climbed up on the rooftops and hurled tiles at the soldiers of the Royal-Marine. Women seized church bells to sound the tocsin, unharnessed vehicles to block the roads and protected the parliamentarians who had gathered in the *hôtel* of their president.[14] The governor's mansion was pillaged, and Clermont-Tonnerre narrowly escaped a beating. At the end of the day, the rioters, now masters of the city, joyfully reinstated the parliamentarians in their palace. This *journée des tuiles*[15] led to an event on a quite different scale: on 21 July, at the initiative of Mounier and Barnave, two advocates who would soon become famous, a total of 490 representatives of the Dauphiné – nobles, ecclesiastics, and 276 deputies from the municipalities around Grenoble – met at the château de Vizille. This assembly in which the Third Estate was a majority demanded for the Dauphiné a meeting of the provincial Estates with double representation for the Third, and for the kingdom as a whole an Estates-General to be summoned where voting would be not by order but by head. 'The three orders of the Dauphiné will never divide their cause from that of the other provinces and, in sustaining their particular rights, they will not abandon those of the nation.' The assembly further called for no more taxes to be paid before the Estates-General was convened.

This had a tremendous echo throughout the kingdom. Faced with a revolt in which the Third Estate was joined by a part of the privileged orders, capitulation became inevitable. On 8 August, Brienne announced that the Estates-General would be convened for 1 May 1789. After using up the last available monies – the funds of the *invalides* (veterans), subscriptions for hospitals and the victims of hailstorms – he was obliged to suspend state payments. On 24 August he resigned, and Louis XVI recalled the man who appeared the only

---

14 Martine Lapied, 'Une absence de révolution pour les femmes?', in Michel Biard, ed., *La Révolution française, une histoire toujours vivante*, Paris: Tallandier, 2010.

15 The event gave rise to the expression '*faire une conduite de Grenoble*', i.e. chase someone out with hisses and boos.

possible saviour, Necker whom he had dismissed seven years previously. Finally, as Mirabeau put it, Necker was king of France.

The recall of Necker

The last moments of the Ancien Régime, the eight months between the recall of Necker and the opening of the Estates-General at Versailles, were anything but a calm before the storm. Political struggles over the manner of voting in the Estates-General were accompanied noisily offstage by popular reactions to an economic crisis and a crisis of provisions that came to a head at precisely this time.

Necker was appointed director-general of finance and minister of state, which enabled him to attend the Conseil d'En-haut despite being a foreigner. He did what he did best, bring in funds: thanks to various advances, he was able to resume the kingdom's payments. He recalled the Parlements. In Paris, on 23 September 1788, the 'fathers of the nation' made a triumphant return, saluted by cannon and fireworks. But this popular celebration was short-lived: on the 25th, the Parlement decreed that the Estates-General would be convened 'following the form observed in 1614' under the regency of Marie de Médicis – which meant that the delegates would deliberate in separate orders, and that voting would be by order and not by head. That would mean keeping the Third Estate in its place, that is, nowhere.

This was a fatal decision: the last chance for reform had not been grasped. Indignation was as strong as enthusiasm had been shortly before: those whom the Third Estate had thought were its champions cared only for their own privileges. A great public debate was launched in hundreds of pamphlets. As Arthur Young noted: 'The business going forward in the pamphlet shops of Paris is incredible. I went to the Palais-Royal to see what new things were published, and to procure a catalogue of all. Every hour produces something new. Thirteen came out today, sixteen yesterday, and ninety-two last week.' Discussions were held in clubs, in cafés, and under the arcades of the Palais-Royal, which belonged to the duc d'Orléans:

> But the coffee-houses in the Palais-Royal present yet more singular and astonishing spectacles; they are not only crowded within, but other expectant crowds are at the doors and windows, listening *à gorge déployée* to certain orators, who from chairs or table harangue each his little audience: the eagerness with which they are heard, and the thunder of applause they receive for every sentiment of more than common hardiness or violence against the present government, cannot easily be imagined.[16]

The question was to get the Estates-General to adopt the rules laid down at Vizille: doubling the number of delegates for the Third Estate, and voting by head. In the Paris *hôtels*, far from the tumult of the streets and cafés, leading bourgeois and representatives of the privileged orders met together to form what was called the 'patriotic party' or 'national party' – the word *nation*, little used until then, suddenly acquired a revolutionary resonance. This was also, significantly, the moment when the expression 'Ancien Régime' appeared.

These meetings, held at the homes of Adrien Duport and Lafayette, and at the United States embassy under Thomas Jefferson, were attended by great lords – including the duc d'Aiguillon and duc de La Rochefoucauld, men of the law such as Hérault de Séchelles and Lepeletier de Saint-Fargeau, and financiers such as Clavière, as well as Sieyès, the Lameth brothers, Talleyrand, Condorcet and Mirabeau. The aim, for many of them, was an English-style constitutional monarchy, and several who aspired to this goal would later be found in the club des Feuillants[17] alongside the Moderates[18] of the Constituent Assembly.

---

16 *Arthur Young's Travels in France*, pp. 153–4.

17 See below, p. 133.

18 [The term 'Moderate' was first used politically in 1789; after the Declaration of Rights was voted in, its opponents sought to 'moderate' its principles. *Modérés* came subsequently to mean the followers of Lafayette who sought a constitutional monarchy, then of the 'triumvirate' (see below, p. 91), and in 1793 was used of Danton and his supporters. – Translator]

EXCURSUS: MIRABEAU AND SIEYÈS

It was then that these two characters came to the fore, each of whom would play leading roles in the events that followed, in the same camp but not in the same style. Mirabeau was forty years old in 1789. He was notorious for his scandalous life, his internments in the fort de Vincennes, his pornographic writings and his pamphlet *Des lettres de cachet et des prisons d'État*. But suddenly, galvanized by the general commotion and furious at having been rejected by the order of the nobility in Provence, he turned into an orator, with an eloquence that owed nothing to Quintilian's rules and aroused wild enthusiasm wherever he spoke. In January 1789, he pronounced before the Estates of Provence, convened along traditional lines, a *Discours sur la représentation illégale de la Nation provençale dans les États actuels, et sur la nécessité de convoquer une Assemblée générale des trois ordres*. Following this speech, flower-sellers embraced the speaker and bankers acclaimed him. A little later, 'When he was elected, a splendid procession of three hundred carriages accompanied him from Marseille to Aix, and these rich carriages of the haute bourgeoisie were draped with garlands of flowers that the people had woven.'[19]

Nowadays, when everything provides an occasion for speeches that no one listens to, it is rather hard to imagine such a passionate reception. On the eve of the Revolution, however, speech-making was a new political instrument. The king of France never gave speeches, and neither did his ministers. Eloquence was the business of lawmen and above all of the Church – funeral orations, homilies of various kinds, great sermons that sometimes touched on political topics – but those who ran the business of the state never spoke in public. And besides, what public would they have spoken to? But suddenly, in the twilight of the Ancien Régime, political eloquence sprang up and immediately reached a zenith. Mirabeau was the first of the great revolutionary orators whose speeches, printed in hundreds of thousands of copies,

---

19 Jaurès, *Histoire socialiste*, p. 125.

were heard right across the country. With them, speech became a political act – a phenomenon that, to my knowledge, has never been repeated since the Revolution, at least in France.[20]

Abbé Sieyès was as drab as Mirabeau was flamboyant. Steered unwillingly into the priesthood, in 1788 he was grand vicar of the bishop of Chartres. He found public speaking hard, but his pamphlet *What Is the Third Estate?*, published in January 1789, was an immediate success: 30,000 copies were sold in the first few weeks, and four editions followed one another – with only the fourth bearing the author's name. Public readings of it were given in cafés. Thinking no doubt of Diogenes and his lantern, Mirabeau wrote to Sieyès: 'So there is a man in France.' Sieyès himself confidently maintained that his book had been 'the theoretical manual by which the great developments of our Revolution were effected, and the only guide of our loyal representatives'.[21]

'Theoretical manual' is scarcely saying too much. Sieyès saw further and faster than others. The duplication of the Third Estate's representation, and voting by head, were from his point of view highly insufficient demands:

> I have emphasized that the deputies of the clergy and the nobility have nothing in common with the national representation, that no alliance is possible between the three orders in the Estates-General, and that, not being able to vote in *common*, they cannot vote either by *order* or by *head* . . . How can the people not be panic-stricken at the sight of two privileged bodies, and perhaps part of a third, seeming to be disposed in the guise of the Estates-General to determine its future and subject it to a fate as immutable as it would be unhappy? . . . It is certain that the deputies of the clergy and the nobility are not the representatives of the Nation. They are, therefore, incompetent to vote on its behalf.[22]

---

20 Parliamentary eloquence in the early years of the Third Republic never reached the same level, or the same relationship to action. It seems far more dated than the words of Danton or Saint-Just.

21 In *Opinions publiques du citoyen Sieyès*, year VIII, p. 17. Cited by Albert Mathiez, *Le Directoire*, Paris: Armand Colin, 1934, p. 6.

22 Sieyès, *Political Writings*, pp. 148, 150.

Sieyès, whose programme would be carried out to the letter during the Estates-General, went through the Revolution in silence ('the mole of the Revolution', Robespierre called him) but acquired great influence again under the Directory. If Mirabeau was fully and joyously a man of the eighteenth century, Sieyès, for his part, belonged already to the nineteenth – not because he lived until 1836, but because his thoughts in action inspired, sometimes unbeknown to themselves, the doctrinaires, the liberals and the constitutionalists of the Restoration and the July monarchy.

Food crisis, peasant riots, economic crisis, unemployment

The unrest stoked by the patriotic party spread to the whole country. The Paris Parlement was forced to revoke its September edict and agree to the doubling of representation for the Third Estate, but it would not give way on voting by order, which was clearly the essential point. Necker, always careful to 'seem much and do little', as Michelet put it, did however wrest from the king concessions that were spelled out by the royal decree of 24 January 1789, and changed the composition and mode of convocation of the Estates-General. 'The inhabitants of the towns would no longer be represented by oligarchic municipalities, but by electors of their own choosing who would nominate the deputies, in concert with electors chosen by the inhabitants of the countryside, who would for the first time have a vote. Parish priests would sit in person, in the assemblies of their order, and would be in a majority there.'[23] These innovations, without ceding on voting by order, did however pave the way for the victory of the Third Estate.

This political tussle took place in a context of serious economic crisis. The views of historians on the French economy before the Revolution seem at first to show strange contradictions. For Jaurès, 'the Revolution did not arise from a background of misery', while Mathiez is even more explicit: 'And so the Revolution was not to

23 Mathiez, *Le Directoire*, p. 6.

break out in an exhausted country, but, on the contrary, in a flourishing land on a rising tide of progress. Poverty may sometimes lead to riots, but it cannot bring about great social upheavals.'[24] Michelet, however, addressing himself to 'sensitive men who weep over the evils of the Revolution', wrote: 'Come and see, I beseech you, this people lying in the dust, like poor Job, amid their false friends, their patrons, their influential protectors – the clergy and royalty.'[25] Many contemporary testimonies are in the same vein:

> The 10th [June]. The want of bread is terrible: accounts arrive every moment from the provinces of riots and disturbances, and calling in the military, to preserve the peace of the markets. The prices reported are the same as I found at Abbeville. 5f. a pound for white bread, and 3½ to 4f. for the common sort, eaten by the poor: these rates are beyond their faculties, and occasion great misery.[26]

Ernest Labrousse did not mince his words: 'The Revolution did indeed appear in certain respects a revolution of poverty, as Michelet had presented it, and contrary to the thesis of Jaurès taken up by Mathiez.'[27]

These contradictory opinions relate to different moments in time. Over the relatively long run, it is generally accepted that the second half of the eighteenth century in France was a period of economic growth, as we say today, and of improvement in living standards – although unequally distributed, as we have seen. 'By comparing different periods, moreover, it is easy to convince oneself that in no period since the Revolution has public prosperity improved more rapidly than it did in the twenty years prior to the Revolution.'[28] But in the years 1786–89 this tendency went into

24 Mathiez, *The French Revolution*, p. 12.

25 Jules Michelet, *Histoire de la Révolution Française*, Paris: Robert Laffont, 1999, vol. 1, p. 86.

26 *Arthur Young's Travels in France*, p. 154.

27 Ernest Labrousse, *La crise de l'économie française à la fin de l'Ancien Régime et au début de la Révolution*, Paris: Presses Universitaires de France, 1944, p. xlii.

28 Tocqueville, *The Ancien Régime*, p. 155.

reverse, due to the combination of a series of measures and events whose deleterious effects would come to a head, by fatal chance, in the summer of 1789.

In 1787, as we have seen, Calonne had suppressed all regulation of the grain trade. Farmers, previously obliged to take grain to the market, were now permitted to sell it directly. Movement by land and sea became free, including exports, with the idea that better prices would thereby be obtained for the producers. But the harvest of 1788 was catastrophic, because of a drought followed by hail. Barns were empty, which triggered a general rise in prices that peaked in summer 1789, the lean time before the harvest. At that point, bread, the popular staple, cost up to double its customary price.

In April 1789, after putting a stop to exports of grain, Necker finally authorized a census of stocks and a requisition, but few *intendants* complied with these measures. The people, seeing carts loaded with grain and flour on the roads every day, began to exercise a '*taxation populaire*': helping themselves and paying (or not) the price deemed fair. As the *syndic* (mayor) of Avoise, in the Pays de la Loire, wrote: 'It is impossible to find within half a league's radius a man prepared to drive a cartload of wheat. The populace is so enraged that men would kill for a bushel. No decent people dare leave home.' Riots flared up in succession from top to bottom of the kingdom. 'In the future department of the Nord, which was not the most distressed area: a riot in Cambrai on 13 March, in Hondschoote on the 22nd, in Hazebrouck and Valenciennes on the 30th, in Bergues on 6 April, in Dunkirk on the 11th, Lille on the 29th, Douai on the 30th.'[29] In the south-east, riots broke out on 14 March at Manosque, with stones being thrown at the bishop, on the 17th in Toulon where the arsenal workers had not been paid for three months, at Aix on the 24th, then at Barjols, Pertuis and Saint-Maximin.[30]

At the same time, the effects of the free-trade treaty signed with England in September 1786 began to make themselves felt. The

29 Georges Lefebvre, *The Great Fear*, Princeton: Princeton University Press, 1982, p. 125.

30 Andress, *The French Revolution and the People*, p. 96.

French had hoped for an increase in wine exports, but the most notable outcome was a textiles crisis. The country's main industry suddenly experienced the competition of British manufactures with more advanced mechanization than in France, where the great bulk of work was still done by hand and at home. In 1785 there were 5,672 cotton weavers in Abbeville and Amiens, reduced by 1789 to no more than 2,000; it is estimated that a total of 36,000 individuals lost their livelihood.[31] There was little desire to follow the English example. The drapers of Caen, in their book of grievances, were frankly hostile: 'As the machines will considerably prejudice the poor people and reduce weaving to nothing, we demand their suppression. This suppression is all the more just in that the weaving with these instruments is very bad and the materials produced are all defective and of poor quality.'[32] In the south, the silk harvest of 1787 was bad, and Lyon in 1789 counted some 30,000 unemployed. According to some estimates, unemployment in the silk industry reached a level of 50 per cent.[33]

The Réveillon affair in Paris: electoral system, the books of grievances

In Paris, where bread cost four and a half sous per pound up from three sous a few months earlier, anger was reinforced by a feeling of humiliation on the part of working people who would be unable to vote, as this required an income on which at least six livres was paid in tax. In the faubourg Saint-Antoine, it was said that Réveillon, a rich manufacturer of wallpaper, proposed a reduction in workers' wages in order to lower prices and stimulate the economy. This Réveillon was not a bad employer and there is no certainty that he actually did make this suggestion, but it was unfortunately echoed by a certain Henriot, who possessed saltpetre works in the faubourg. On

---

31 Ibid., p. 14.

32 Jaurès, *Histoire socialiste*, p. 140.

33 Cobban, *A History of Modern France*, p. 140.

the night of 26 April, gatherings formed in the faubourg Saint-Marcel, where news had arrived that Réveillon and Henriot had spoken ill of the workers. A procession set out towards the right bank, carrying effigies of the two villains to be burned on the place de Grève. On the following day, the crowd, now swelled by workers from the faubourg Saint-Antoine and dockers from the Seine river port, sacked Réveillon's house, which was poorly protected by a small contingent of *gardes-françaises*. The cavalry and infantry were promptly called in, opening fire first of all with blanks, then with live bullets. At the end of the day, twelve dead were counted on the soldiers' side, and more than 300 on the side of the rioters.[34]

Despite these dramatic developments, the electoral campaign opened in a general atmosphere of hope. '*La France profonde*' had changed a great deal since Brienne's creation of the provincial and district assemblies, and above all of the municipalities for villages and small towns. The *syndic*, no longer appointed by the *intendant* but elected by the taxpayers, decided the business of the commune along with the municipal council, and in particular the allocation and utilization of tax: an apprenticeship in public affairs whose effects would not be long in making themselves felt.

The electoral system was different for each of the three orders. The geographical framework was the *baillage* (bailiwick) or *sénéchaussée* (seneschalsy) – the 373 judicial constituencies of the Ancien Régime. For the privileged orders, the electoral assembly met in the capital of the *baillage* to appoint its delegates to the Estates-General. The assembly of the nobility was made up of all those 'possessing a fief', and that of the clergy of all ecclesiastics, including parish priests; the lower clergy took advantage of its majority position to remove from its deputation most of the court prelates. For the Third Estate, voting was indirect, the primary electors being all men over twenty-five who were inscribed on the tax rolls. In the towns, these electors voted by corporation or by district, appointing one or two deputies per

---

34 Michelet was the first, if I am not mistaken, to see the Réveillon affair as a police provocation, an opportunity for the Court to concentrate troops around Paris (*Histoire de la Révolution Française*, p. 100). Although his arguments are indirect and not very convincing, they have been adopted by many historians in his wake.

hundred voters. These deputies formed a town assembly, which sent delegates to the *baillage* assembly that in turn elected deputies to the Estates-General. In the countryside, the electoral system was more or less the same, with parish assemblies instead of town ones.

At the end of this process, a total of 1,139 deputies attended the Estates-General. The nobility's deputation counted 270 members, of whom only a few were court nobles, with a good number, around a third, supporting liberal ideas. In the clergy's deputation parish priests were a large majority (200 out of 291), and they would end up aligning themselves with the Third Estate. The latter, for its part, sent a delegation of 578 members to Versailles, chiefly lawyers of one kind or another (over 400), including advocates and holders of minor office in the legal and administrative system of the provinces. The rest were businessmen, bankers and industrialists. Agriculture was represented by some fifty large landed proprietors. The deputation of the Third Estate did not include either artisans or peasants, and so the majority of the kingdom's population went unrepresented: it was far from 'this union of different classes, this great appearance of the people in its formidable unity' that Michelet speaks of.[35] We should instead listen to Tocqueville: 'It is strange to see the odd state of security in which those who occupied the middle and upper levels of the social edifice lived on the eve of the Revolution, and to hear them cleverly discussing among themselves the virtues, gentleness, devotion, and innocent pleasures of the people, when 1793 was already opening the ground beneath their feet; the spectacle is at once absurd and terrifying.'[36]

The 60,000 *cahiers de doléances* (books of grievances), compiled at each level of the various assemblies and subsequently merged at the *baillage* level, form an immense treasure trove that defies any attempt at overall study. Let us once more quote Tocqueville to close this chapter:

> I have carefully read the registers of grievances drawn up by the three orders before their meeting in 1789. I underline the three

35 Ibid., p. 98.

36 Tocqueville, *The Ancien Régime and the French Revolution*, p. 123.

orders – the nobility, the clergy and the Third Estate. In one place a change of law is requested, in another a change of practice and I take note of these. Thus I continued my reading to the very end of this immense work. When I came to gather all the individual wishes, with a sense of terror I realized that their demands were for *the wholesale and systematic abolition of all the laws and all the current practices* in the country. Straightaway I saw that the issue here was one of the most extensive and dangerous revolutions ever observed in the world.[37]

37 Ibid., p. 145. My emphasis.

CHAPTER 3

May to September 1789

The Estates-General, the Constituent Assembly at Versailles – the Tennis Court oath, the storming of the Bastille, the Great Fear, the night of 4 August, the Declaration of Rights

With all these advantages, Necker did not succeed in making a quiet reform out of a revolutionary movement. The great sickness was not to be healed with attar of roses.

– Karl Marx, 'The Camphausen Ministry'

Even for those most reticent towards the idea of rupture in history, the summer of 1789 certainly does appear as the moment when everything collapsed, from legalism into illegality, from strict formalism into street improvisation. In short – to repeat the words of a celebrated reply that in all likelihood was never actually pronounced – from revolt to revolution.

The opening of the Estates-General

The Estates-General initially followed the model of 1614, which clearly established the Third Estate in its place, the lowest one. Already during the presentation to the king, the deputies of the clergy and nobility were received with respect while the Third Estate was herded through the royal chamber en masse and at the double. On 4 May 1789, the deputies, the king and the queen crossed Versailles in procession along with the whole court, from the church of Notre-Dame to that of Saint-Louis, to hear a Mass of the Holy Spirit celebrated by monseigneur de la Fare, the bishop of Nancy. Next morning, in the first issue of *États Généraux*, a newspaper founded by Mirabeau, Parisians could read how, on this occasion, 'Every commonplace was included, from the baptism of Clovis to the sickness of Louis [XV] the Beloved at Metz, and from declarations about luxury to calumny against philosophy.'

The Estates-General opened on 5 May in the Salle des Menus-Plaisirs, which could hold up to 1,200 people, with galleries for a further 2,000 or more – indeed, the large number of spectators made no secret of their feelings throughout the sessions, a habit that would persist as a characteristic feature of successive revolutionary assemblies.[1]

First of all the Assembly heard a speech from the king, which began with 'an awkward grumbling, timid and shifty, on the spirit of innovation' (Michelet), and ended with a warning:

> Minds are agitated; but an assembly of the nation's representatives will certainly listen only to counsels of wisdom and prudence. You will have judged for yourselves, gentlemen, how these have been ignored on several recent occasions; but the ruling spirit of your deliberations will respond to the true feelings of a generous nation, whose love for its kings has always been its distinctive trait; I shall refuse any other memory.[2]

---

1 Arthur Young was scandalized: 'The spectators in the galleries are allowed to interfere in the debates by clapping their hands, and other noisy expressions of approbation: this is grossly indecent: it is also dangerous; for, if they are permitted to express approbation, they are, by parity of reason, allowed expressions of dissent; and they may hiss as well as clap; which it is said, they have sometimes done: – this would be, to overrule the debate and influence the deliberations' (*Arthur Young's Travels in France*, p. 165).

2 P. J. B. Buchez and P. C. Roux, *Histoire parlementaire de la Révolution française*, Paris: Paulin, 1834, vol. 1, p. 355.

The speech that followed, that of Barentin, the Garde des Sceaux,[3] was delivered in such a low voice that no one heard it. But what everyone was awaiting was Necker's speech, and the disappointment this caused matched the expectations aroused. Mirabeau, in the second issue of his paper (6 May), complained of 'insufferable longueurs, countless repetitions, pompously uttered trivialities, unintelligible remarks; not a single principle, not one unchallengeable assertion, not one statesmanlike resource, not even a major financial measure, no plan of recovery despite what had been announced.' The following day, newspapers were banned from reporting the sessions of the Estates. Mirabeau did not waver, and three days later launched his *Lettres du comte de Mirabeau à ses commettants*, the first issue of which proclaimed: 'Twenty-five million voices demand freedom of the press; the nation and the king unanimously demand the cooperation of all enlightened minds. And then we are faced with a ministerial veto; after tricking us by an illusory and treacherous tolerance, a so-called popular ministry dares blatantly to put a seal on our thoughts!' On 8 May, the meeting of Paris electors of the Third Estate likewise protested against the newspaper ban, which 'violates the freedom of the press that the whole of France demands': this was the first public demonstration of the Paris electors, who would soon move to the front of the stage.[4]

The very day after the opening session, battle was joined on the principle of voting by head. The three orders each met in a separate hall, with the Third Estate in the Salle des Menus-Plaisirs. The nobility decided by a large majority (188 votes to 47) to constitute itself as a separate order. The clergy did the same, but by a much smaller majority (133 votes to 114). This already indicated a rift between the privileged orders, which would steadily widen until it brought about the victory of the Third Estate – or rather of the Commons, as it was called with increasing frequency, a term that 'the Court and the great

3 [The Garde des Sceaux, literally 'keeper of the seals', remains a title of the French minister of justice today. – Translator]

4 These were the 407 second-level electors, those who chose the deputies. They continued to meet after the electoral process was concluded, first of all in the Salle du Musée, rue Dauphine, then at the Hôtel de Ville.

lords reject with a species of apprehension, as if it implied a design that was hard to fathom', Arthur Young noted.[5]

That same evening, the members of the Commons met together province by province to discuss a collective action. The Bretons, around Lanjuinais and Le Chapelier, were the most determined.[6] The decision was taken to invite the two other orders to meet with the Third Estate to verify together the powers of all the deputies. While awaiting this, the Commons rejected forming a chamber of their own: they would have neither office, nor president, nor clerical staff.

For nearly a month, the Commons sent emissaries to the privileged orders in hopes of an agreement, but it was no use. If the clergy were hesitant, the greater part of the nobility were unwilling even to listen. Mirabeau harangued them forcefully in the session of 18 May, replying to Malouet who advised conciliation: 'Let them do it, gentlemen; they will give you a Constitution, regulate the state, settle the finances, and they will solemnly bring you an extract from their records to serve henceforth as a national code. No, gentlemen, one cannot compromise with such pride, without soon becoming a slave!'[7]

The Third Estate proclaims itself the National Assembly – the Tennis Court oath

Enough was enough. On 10 June, Sieyès proposed an address to the privileged orders that ended as follows:

> Given the necessity for the representatives of the nation to commence their activity without further delay, the deputies of the

5 *Arthur Young's Travels in France*, p. 151.

6 They soon adopted the custom of meeting at a café on the avenue de Saint-Cloud; when the Assembly was transferred to Paris, the Breton club became the Société des Amis de la Constitution and met at the Couvent des Jacobins.

7 *Archives parlementaires de 1787 à 1860. Recueil complet des débats législatifs et politiques des chambres françaises, 1re série: de 1787 à 1799*, Paris: Paul Dupont, vol. 8, p. 42. (Henceforth abbreviated to A. P.)

> Commons once again beseech you, gentlemen, as indeed their duty prescribes, issuing both individually and collectively a final appeal for you to come to the hall of the Estates in order to assist and cooperate in submitting together with them to a common verification of powers. We are charged at the same time to advise you that the general roll-call of all the *baillages* convoked will take place in an hour; that following this, verification will begin and those not appearing will be taken as being in default.[8]

The assembly of the Third Estate immediately got organized and set up offices; on 12 June it proceeded to the verification of powers of the deputies of the three orders. The following day, three priests from Poitou responded when their names were called, and sixteen others – including abbé Grégoire, parish priest of Embermesnil in the *baillage* of Nancy – joined them in the next two days: the rift was beginning to widen.

At the beginning of the year, Sieyès had written in *What is the Third Estate?*: 'The Third Estate, it is said, cannot form the Estates-General all by itself. Very well! So much the better! It will form a *National Assembly*.'[9] In the session of 17 June, after different formulations had been discussed, it was voted by 490 to 90 that 'the only appropriate title is that of National Assembly'. The same day, the Assembly declared that all existing taxes were illegal but that it would grant them provisional legality 'until the day of the first separation of this Assembly, from whatever cause it may ensue'; this was an appeal to a tax strike if the Assembly were dissolved. Two days later, following very lively debates, a majority of the clergy (149 votes to 137) adopted the principle of meeting together with the Commons.

Faced with this dismantling of the system, Louis XVI could not remain passive. In the evening of 19 June he decided to revoke the decisions of the Third Estate in a solemn session, after the fashion of

8 Reprint of *Le Moniteur*, Paris: Plon, 1858, vol. 1, p. 55.

9 Sieyès, *Political Writings*, pp. 147–8.

the *lit de justice*. Meanwhile, the hall in which the sessions were held would be closed for repairs.

On the morning of 20 June, the deputies found the doors shut and guarded by soldiers. Rabaut Saint-Étienne, a Protestant pastor and deputy for Nîmes, relates what followed:

> They [the deputies] asked one another what power had the right to suspend the deliberations of the representatives of the nation . . . Finally [Bailly, president of the Assembly] gathered the deputies in the *jeu de paume* [royal tennis] court of Versailles, which has become eternally famous for the courageous resistance of the first representatives of the French nation . . . The people besieged the gate and showered their representatives with blessings. Soldiers disobeyed their orders to come and guard the entrance of this new sanctuary of liberty.[10]

A voice was then raised, that of Mounier, who proposed 'that all members of this assembly should immediately take a solemn oath never to separate but to gather wherever circumstances required until the Constitution of the kingdom was established and set on solid foundations'. All those present swore and signed, except for one.[11]

The deputies of the Third Estate were aware of the threat hanging over them, as Swiss and German regiments were massed around Versailles. The most active of their number met to decide on the mode of resistance. Abbé Grégoire recalled:

> The previous evening [22 June] twelve or fifteen of us deputies met at the Breton club, so called because the Bretons had been its founders. Informed of what the Court was planning for the following day, each article was discussed by all and all gave their opinion on the course to take. The first resolution was that of remaining in the hall [of sessions] despite the king's prohibition. It was agreed

10 Rabaut de Saint-Étienne, *Précis d'histoire de la Révolution française* [1807], 1819 reprint, pp. 56–7. Cited in Mathiez, *Les Grandes Journées de la Constituante*, Paris: Les Éditions de la Passion, 1989, p. 10.

11 Martin-Dauch, deputy for Castelnaudary.

> that before the opening of the session we would circulate among the groups of our colleagues, explaining to them what was going to happen before their eyes and how it was to be opposed.[12]

On the morning of the 23rd, the day of the royal session, the hall was surrounded by soldiers. The nearby streets were blocked off to prevent the mass of people who had arrived from witnessing the expected confrontation. The main doors opened to let the privileged orders enter, while the Commons waited in the rain for the back door to be opened for them. In the hall, the clergy and nobles were seated on the sides as on 5 May, and the Commons massed in the centre. The absence of Necker was noted: he did not want to jeopardize what was left of his popularity. The king arrived around eleven o'clock, surrounded by the princes of the blood, dukes and peers, and by captains of the guard. He started off reading in person, before having it read by a secretary, the lengthy and uncompromising speech prepared for him: 'The king wishes the old distinction between the three orders of the state to be preserved in its entirety, as being fundamentally bound to the Constitution of his kingdom . . . As a consequence, the king has declared null and void the deliberations taken by the deputies of the order of the Third Estate on the 17th of this month, as well as any that may follow, being illegal and unconstitutional.' And Louis XVI ended with a clear threat:

> If, by a fatality far from my mind, you abandon me in such a fine undertaking, I shall act alone for the good of my peoples; I shall alone consider myself their true representative . . . I order you, gentlemen, to separate immediately, and to attend tomorrow morning in the rooms respectively assigned to your orders to resume your sittings. I accordingly command the grand master of ceremonies to have the halls prepared.[13]

---

12 *Mémoires de Grégoire, ancien évêque de Blois*, Paris: Ambroise Dupont, 1837, vol. 1, p. 380. Cited in Mathiez, *Les Grandes Journées*.

13 A. P., vol. 8, pp. 143–7.

The king left, followed by the nobility and part of the clergy. The members of the National Assembly, along with several parish priests, stayed in their seats. It was Mirabeau who spoke: 'What is this insulting dictatorship? The display of arms, the violation of the national temple, to command you to be happy? Who has given you this command? Your mandatory. Who gives you these imperious laws? Your mandatory, who should receive them from you, from us, gentlemen, who are wrapped in a political and inviolable priesthood.'

The marquis de Dreux-Brézé, grand master of ceremonies, then approached the president (Bailly) and said: 'Gentlemen, you have heard the king's intentions.' And Mirabeau improvised the response that did more for his fame than all the rest of his life. There are several versions of it, including that which he published himself in his *Treizième lettre à ses commettants*:

> Yes, sir, we have heard the intentions that have been suggested to the king, and you who can by no means be his organ in the Estates-General, you who have neither place here, nor vote, nor right to speak, it is not for you to remind us of his words; if you have been instructed to expel us from here, you must ask for orders to use force, as only the power of the bayonet can drive us from our seats.

After a moment's silence, Camus spoke, followed by Barnave, both advocating firmness. Then it was the turn of Sieyès, whose speech, greeted with applause, ended with the words: 'Is there a power on earth who can take away your power of representing your constituents?' 'Gentlemen,' he added as he left the rostrum, '*you are today what you were yesterday!*'[14] In a vote taken by deputies rising in their seats, the Assembly 'unanimously declares that it will persist in its previous decisions'.

---

14 Ibid., p. 147.

Meeting of the three orders; the Assembly becomes Constituent

This attempt at a royal coup d'état ended downright lamely. The use of force – the only possible next step – was highly risky, for two reasons. Firstly, when the royal session was announced, all the Paris banks closed their counters. Stocks on the Bourse went into free fall. The Caisse d'Escompte sent envoys to Versailles to explain to the king the dangers of the situation. In a state verging on bankruptcy, finance was no longer available. Also, and most important, the disintegration was now affecting the army. At the end of June, the ambassador of Saxony wrote to his minister:

> On Thursday [25 June] the soldiers of the regiment of *gardes-françaises* left their barracks and scattered across Paris, bands of them going into all public places and shouting: *Vive le Roi, vive le Tiers!*[15] Fearing a general revolt, no one dared to stop them. On Friday they disarmed several patrols of Swiss Guards that they encountered . . . I have just learned that the king can no longer rely on his own bodyguards . . . The loyalty of the foreign regiments is also becoming suspect. The bourgeois are seducing them, and the Swiss of Salis-Samade camped at Issy and Vaugirard have assured their hosts than if they were ordered to march they would disable the mechanisms of their muskets.[16]

From then on, the king and the recalcitrant section of the privileged orders had no option but to retreat. On 24 June, '151 ecclesiastics

---

15 The *gardes-françaises* regiment had around 4,000 men and was responsible for guarding the royal palaces together with the Swiss Guards. Many of them came from Paris and had ties to the population. 'The French Guards, residents in Paris, and mostly married, had seen the depot in which the children of the soldiers were educated, free of expense, shortly before suppressed by M. du Châtelet, their hard-hearted colonel. The only change made in the military institutions, was made against them' (Jules Michelet, *Histoire de la Révolution Française*, p. 128).

16 Dispatch from Salmour, minister plenipotentiary of Saxony, 28 June 1789, in Flammermont, *Rapport sur les correspondances des agents diplomatiques étrangers en France avant la Révolution, Nouvelles archives des missions*, vol. 8, p. 231. Cited in Mathiez, *Les Grandes Journées*, p. 20.

who formed the majority, with the archbishops of Vienne and Bordeaux at their head along with the bishops of Coutances, Chartres and Rodez, advanced into the centre of the hall of sessions which resounded with applause and universal acclamation.'[17] The following day, a delegation of forty-seven members of the nobility, led by the comte de Clermont-Tonnerre and including the duc d'Orléans, the duc d'Aiguillon, the comte de Crillon, the comte de Montmorency and the duc de La Rochefoucauld, followed their example: 'We bring you the tribute of our zeal and our sentiments, and we have come to work with you on the great task of public regeneration.'[18]

On the 27th, the king gave in. He wrote to the minority of the clergy and the majority of the nobility to invite them to join in the National Assembly, which on 9 July took the name of Constituent Assembly.

The dismissal of Necker; preparations for insurrection

After the union of the three orders, the pace of events quickened. When Versailles learned of the king's retreat, there was huge rejoicing: 'The assembly, uniting with the people, all hurried to the château. *Vive le Roi* might have been heard at Marly; the king and queen appeared in the balcony, and were received with the loudest shouts of applause.'[19] But the king felt humiliated and, pressed it seems by the queen and by his brother the comte d'Artois, prepared his revenge by assembling around Paris and Versailles a force of 20,000 men, largely made up of German and Swiss troops.

In Paris, the wildest rumours circulated as the concentration of troops became evident: the Assembly would be dissolved, the members of the Third Estate imprisoned or killed, the gun batteries installed on top of Montmartre would bombard the city, which would then be delivered to looters and marauders. 'It is impossible to

---

17 *Le Moniteur*, vol. 1, p. 96.

18 Ibid., p. 98.

19 *Arthur Young's Travels in France*, p. 183.

depict', wrote one pamphlet from this time (*Lettre au comte d'Artois*), 'the shiver that the capital experienced at the single phrase: "the king has quashed everything". I felt a fire burning beneath my feet; only a sign was needed and civil war would break out.'[20] On 30 June it was learned at the café du Foy, the heart of the agitation in Palais-Royal, that eleven soldiers of the *gardes-françaises* had been imprisoned in the Abbaye, accused of belonging to a secret society within the regiment. A bunch of young people headed for the Abbaye, in Saint-Germain-des-Prés. This small group expanded en route, joined first of all by some workers armed with iron bars, then by a multitude of passers-by: by the time they reached the prison, they numbered almost 4,000 men. The first gate was quickly demolished with the aid of mallets, iron bars and axes, followed by the inner gates. By eight o'clock the prisoners were free. When the Assembly learned of the event, it sent a deputation to the king led by the archbishop of Paris. Finally, the soldiers returned to the Abbaye on the 4th and were released and pardoned the next day.

On 8 July, in the Assembly, Mirabeau attacked the king's advisers whom he held responsible for the military build-up: 'Thirty-five thousand men are already posted between Paris and Versailles. Twenty thousand more are expected. Artillery trains will follow. Placements have been designated for gun batteries . . . The preparations for war, in a word, are plain to see and fill all hearts with indignation.'[21] He ended by tabling a motion that demanded the withdrawal of these troops, voted through the next day.

On 10 July, the electors of Paris (those who elected the deputies) gathered in the Saint-Jean hall of the Hôtel de Ville, joining with the former municipality to constitute 'a real and active assembly of the Paris Commons'. In permanent contact with the Assembly, they laid the foundations of a Parisian guard to maintain order and protect property.

The following day, the king, having decided to escalate matters, dismissed Necker and ordered him to leave the kingdom immediately. In his place he appointed the baron de Breteuil, with the old

---

20 Quoted in Buchez and Roux, *Histoire parlementaire*, vol. 1, p. 343.

21 A. P., vol. 8, p. 208.

duc de Broglie as minister of war – both names well chosen to excite popular fury. Towards midday on Sunday 12 July the news reached Paris and triggered a tremendous movement that went well beyond the popular classes. The dealers on the Bourse met and decided to shut up shop as a sign of protest. In the Palais-Royal, Camille Desmoulins came out of the café de Foy and climbed on a table, brandishing a pistol and calling out: 'To arms, let's wear a cockade!' He pulled a leaf off a lime tree and put it in his hat, followed by the crowd around him.[22] It was decided that gaming and entertainment venues would be closed as a sign of mourning. One group took wax busts of Necker and the duc d'Orléans from a shop, put black crepe around them and formed a procession that would swell to several thousand men. Armed with sticks, axes and pistols, they crossed Paris by way of rue de Richelieu, the boulevards, rue Saint-Martin and rue Saint-Honoré until at place Vendôme they clashed violently with a detachment of dragoons. At the customs barriers the people set fire to the new tollbooths of the Ferme-Générale, the object of general detestation.

In the afternoon, as the unrest continued to grow, the baron de Besenval, a familiar of the queen and commander of the Paris troops, disposed a regiment of Swiss Guards and two regiments of German cavalry in battle order on the place Louis XV (now place de la Concorde). The concentration coincided with the time when the Sunday crowds were approaching the Tuileries via the Champs-Élysées gardens. Insults and stones were hurled at the horsemen of the Royal-Allemand regiment. Their colonel, the prince de Lambesc, ordered his riders into the Tuileries and brutally repelled the crowd, who responded by lobbing stones, bottles and chairs. Shots were fired. Finally, seeing that some people were engaged in blocking the swing bridge that divided the Tuileries from the square, the prince deemed it prudent to leave the gardens. But the whole of Paris reverberated with accounts of these brutalities: how the Germans had ridden their horses at women, old men and children.

---

22 This is reported by several sources, even if Desmoulins undoubtedly exaggerated his own role.

When night fell, the city was lit up by lanterns placed in windows. Detachments of soldiers of the watch, armed civilians, *gardes-françaises*, passed one another in the streets. Musket shots were fired, and the tocsin was heard from time to time. The tollbooths continued to burn. At the Hôtel de Ville, occupied by the crowd, the electors were obliged to open up the weapons stores of the city guards. They decided to set up a permanent committee that would sit day and night.

The whole day of the 13th was spent looking for weapons. Armouries were plundered, and ironworkers forged thousands of pikes. The people clamoured for muskets to Flesselles, the provost of merchants,[23] who played for time and finally refused. But the *gardes-françaises*, ordered to leave Paris for Saint-Denis, refused to obey and joined the people, who thereby gained decisive reinforcements: 3,000 men with their arms, cannon, and some of their officers.

The storming of the Bastille

On the morning of 14 July, the cry 'To the Invalides!' was heard outside the Hôtel de Ville. Éthis de Corny, the city *procureur*, set out at the head of a procession in that direction. The ambassador of Saxony recalls:

> The Hôtel des Invalides, in full view of the troops camped on the Champ-de-Mars, was taken by seven or eight thousand unarmed townsmen who emerged furiously from three adjacent streets, and hurled themselves into a ditch twelve feet wide and eight feet deep, which they rapidly crossed by standing on each other's shoulders. Arriving pell-mell on the esplanade, before the veterans knew what was happening, they seized twelve pieces of cannon and a mortar. They then presented the governor with an order from the city to hand over all weapons, and no longer seeing any way to defend his building, the governor opened its doors. They seized 40,000 muskets and a powder magazine.

23 This function was comparable to that of mayor of Paris.

> After witnessing this incredibly speedy operation, I crossed to the adjacent camp, where the spectacle of sad, dull and defeated troops, who had spent two weeks shut up in quite a narrow space, struck me as different from that of the enterprising and courageous men I had just left.[24]

At the same time, deputations from the districts and the electors arrived at the Bastille and urged the governor, De Launay, to hand over the fortress's arms and withdraw the cannon that were threatening the faubourg Saint-Antoine. The discussions dragged on as the people massed around the fortress, and finally, after the garrison had fired on the representatives, the assault began. What followed has been repeatedly described: the first drawbridge taken, the crowd in the courtyard under fire from the towers, the artisans from the faubourg reinforced by the *gardes-françaises* bringing up their cannon to break down the gates, and at last, around five in the afternoon, the surrender of the Swiss Guards and the veterans of the garrison. The battle cost a hundred lives on the side of the attackers and a single death on the other side. De Launay, who was (wrongly) held responsible for the order to fire on the negotiators, and Flesselles, who was (rightly) condemned for having deceived the people about the arms stores, were killed on the place de Grève, and their heads paraded on pikes.

To wage a street battle and retake Paris, Louis XVI would have needed an army such as he did not have. And Paris was not the only cause for alarm: news arriving from far and wide indicated that the whole country was rising up. The king accordingly had to retreat. On 15 July, he came to the Assembly and announced that he had ordered the troops to leave both Paris and Versailles. The next day, after a new representation on the part of the Assembly, he reinstated Necker and the ministers who had been sacked along with him. In Paris, the archbishop had a *Te Deum* celebrated in Notre-Dame. Bailly was appointed mayor of the city, and Lafayette commander of the force that would soon become the National Guard. On 17 July, the king

---

24 Dispatch from Salmour, minister of Saxony, 14 July 1789. Cited in Mathiez, *Les Grandes Journées*, p. 238.

agreed to come to Paris. His presence on the balcony of the Hôtel de Ville, where Bailly handed him the new tricolour cockade, sealed the victory of the Paris insurrection. The king, after fixing the cockade to his hat, said only: 'You may always count on my love.'

The storming of the Bastille is the most famous event in the French Revolution, and has moreover become its symbol throughout the world. But this glory rather distorts its historical significance. It was neither a moment of miracle, nor a conclusion, nor a culminating point of the 'good' revolution before the start of the 'bad', that of 1793 and the Terror; the storming of the Bastille was one shining point on the trajectory of the Paris insurrection, which continued its upward curve on 10 August 1792 and 31 May–2 June 1793, before falling tragically back again after Thermidor, with the hunger riots of Prairial in year III.

The municipal revolution

In three or four days, news of the capture of the Bastille spread across the country and gave a lively impulse to the movements that had been bubbling almost everywhere for several weeks with greater or lesser vigour. During the second half of July, an exceptional fortnight, it was the very scaffolding of the monarchy that collapsed: the centralized administration, the Parlements, the municipalities or 'city bodies', the collection of taxes, even the army – everything disintegrated with amazing speed.

In the provincial capitals, the majority of the *intendants* – representatives of central government – abandoned their posts. Everywhere the storm blew away the 'city bodies', whose members owed their power to heredity, the purchase of office or direct appointment by the royal authority. They were everywhere replaced by permanent committees, which were in fact new municipalities. These were either composed of the electors who had appointed the deputies to the Estates-General, or were themselves elected by general assemblies of citizens. This municipal revolution, a decisive step in the Revolution as a whole, was largely though not invariably peaceful. On 21 July, Arthur Young on his way through Strasbourg witnessed the sacking of the Hôtel de Ville:

> Passing through the square of the *hôtel de ville*, the mob were breaking the windows with stones, notwithstanding an officer and a detachment of horse was in the square . . . Perceiving that the troops would not attack them, except in words and menaces, they grew more violent, and furiously attempted to beat the door in pieces with iron crows; placing ladders to the windows. In about a quarter of an hour, which gave time for the assembled magistrates to escape by a back door, they burst all open, and entered like a torrent with a universal shout of the spectators.[25]

The first act of the new municipalities was to establish urban militias to maintain order and ensure respect for property. It was the shortage and high price of bread that fuelled the rebellions rumbling everywhere; urban populations were demanding the abolition of duties and taxation on wheat and bread.

> In Poissy there was a riot against a man suspected of hoarding. In Saint-Germain-en-Laye, a miller by the name of Sauvage had his head cut off. In Pointoise an insurrection for grain was stopped by the presence of a regiment returning from Paris. In Le Havre, when the inhabitants learned that 400 hussars had been embarked at Honfleur to reinforce the city garrison, they attacked the naval arsenal, broke down the doors, pointed cannon at the jetty and forced the ships carrying the hussars to turn back.[26]

In Paris, on 20 July, each of the sixty districts sent two representatives to the Hôtel de Ville to form the new municipality: advocates (the largest group), notaries, businessmen, doctors, rentiers, two bankers, a few nobles . . . There was also a baker and a builder, but these were

---

25 *Arthur Young's Travels in France*, p. 208.

26 Quoted in Buchez and Roux, *Histoire parlementaire*, vol. 1, p. 421.

entrepreneurs rather than workers.[27] At the first session, Bailly was elected mayor of the city and Lafayette commander-in-chief of the National Guard.

Difficulties soon arose. When Foulon, who had been appointed controller-general on 12 July, was arrested along with his son-in-law Berthier, all the efforts of the Hôtel de Ville to have them taken to the Abbaye prison and tried according to due process were in vain. The crowd hanged Foulon from a lamppost and cut off his head, which was paraded through Paris at the end of a pike. Berthier, arrested in Compiègne and brought into Paris through the porte Saint-Martin, was preceded by posters bearing the slogans: 'He stole from the king and from France – He devoured the people's subsistence – He was the slave of the rich and the tyrant of the poor – He drank the blood of widows and orphans.' On reaching the Maubuée fountain, close to the Saint-Merry church, he was shown Foulon's head, the mouth stuffed with hay. Questioned at the Hôtel de Ville, taken to the Abbaye on Bailly's orders but swallowed up by the crowd on the way, Berthier was cut down by a sabre in the rue de la Vannerie. The fear inspired by these events hastened the first wave of emigration, which began as early as 17 July with the departure of the comte d'Artois, the king's brother, along with the Condés, Contis and Polignacs, the duc de Broglie, the prince de Lambesc and other grandees.

The Great Fear

Throughout this period, the countryside was in the grip of the Great Fear – which had actually begun at the beginning of July. There was first of all the fear of an aristocrats' and foreigners' plot. 'It is imagined,' so a noble deputy explained to the marquise de Créquy, 'that the princes cannot see themselves exiled from a kingdom that is their

---

27 This list contains few who would later play any significant role. These include Quatremère de Quincy and Moreau de Saint-Méry, who, despite representing the slave-owning colonists of Saint-Domingue, was named vice-president of the new municipality, as well as Brissot, who represented the district of Les Filles-Saint-Thomas.

homeland and their inheritance without meditating projects of revenge, to which we may suppose them capable of sacrificing all they have. They are believed capable of bringing in foreign troops, caballing with the nobility to exterminate Paris and everything connected with the Estates-General.'[28] We thus see the emergence, in July 1789, of the suspicion of collusion between aristocracy and foreign powers that would have such consequences in the future.[29]

This fear of a plot was combined with another, already well rooted in the peasant imaginary: the fear of brigands, partly aroused by the mass of itinerants on all the country's roads – beggars, drifters in search of employment, seasonal migrants in the harvest season, not to mention the 'professional' itinerants such as pedlars, bear-trainers, tinkers and silverers. 'These wanderers might go further if hunger pressed them. When their numbers grew, they began to gather in groups, and emboldened in this way, slipped into brigandage. A farmer from Aumale wrote on 30 July: "We do not go to bed unafraid, we are much troubled by the night-time beggars, not to mention those who come in the daytime in great numbers." '[30]

Georges Lefebvre has described in detail the spread of the Great Fear from 20 July on. Radiating out from six centres that had already been in revolt since the start of the month – Franche-Comté, Champagne, Beauvaisis, Maine, and around Nantes and Ruffec – it struck almost the whole of France, with the exception of Brittany, Alsace and Languedoc.[31] But after a week or so, it became clear that there

---

28 Lefebvre, *The Great Fear*, p. 62.

29 For Timothy Tackett ('La Grande Peur et le complot aristocratique sous la Révolution française', *AHRF* no. 335, Jan–Mar 2004, pp. 1–17), the fear of such a plot was strongest in Paris and the surrounding region. Elsewhere his explanation is rather post hoc: 'It was after the event that a certain number of individuals came to suspect the nobility of having triggered the panic' (p. 9).

30 Lefevbre, *The Great Fear*, p. 17.

31 A sample of this meticulous description: 'The panic passed through Bonnétable moving northwards and crossed the Perche via Bellême, Mortagne, Moulins-La-Marche and Laigle. By the 23rd, it was well installed in Évreux. Mostly it moved westwards. On the 22nd, it began to move towards the Sarthe: it appeared in Mamers and Ballon about nine in the evening and at some time later in the day in Le Mans. During the night of 22nd–23rd, a messenger carried it from the latter town to La Flèche and at the same time the current crossed the Bas-Maine from the Sarthe to the Mayenne; the entire area was affected – Lassay,

were no brigands around at all. On 27 July, the third number of *Révolutions de Paris* reported:

> It is said that several thousand armed brigands coming from the Montmorency plains are causing considerable damage, cutting the green wheat, pillaging people's houses, even murdering anyone who opposes their designs. Women and children who fled the bloodshed arrive in tears from these places: orders are already given and the civic militia hasten to these places, along with cannon; after a forced march they finally arrive; there is general alarm, and the tocsin can be heard in every parish. And then, who would believe it? There are no enemies and no brigands, and it is hard to know how the alarm could have started.

But if the Great Fear was based on chimera, it prepared people's minds – and weapons – for a movement that was highly serious. Impoverished peasants, taking advantage of the general disorder, made for the châteaux and aggressively demanded the old archival documents in which feudal rights were laid down, which they then tossed on bonfires. If a lord refused to hand over his parchments, they set fire to his château.

The nobles (and those commoners who had acquired land in the course of the century) felt threatened and, seeing the disorganization of the public forces, took the defence of their properties into their own hands. Having a majority in the new municipalities, as befitted their privileges, they organized the repulsion of this fourth estate that was rising from the depths of the countryside. In the Mâconnais, in what was one of the greatest peasant rebellions of the century, more than seventy châteaux were burned down. The backlash was violent. On 29 July, near the château de Cormatin, a band of peasants lost twenty men in battle, and sixty more were taken prisoner. Near Cluny, another band lost a hundred men, and 170 were captured. In Mâcon, an improvised tribunal had twenty-six rioters hanged.

Mayenne, Laval and, by the end of the day, Château-Gontier' (ibid., p. 173).

The night of 4 August

The Assembly was frightened by this insurrection in the countryside, where more than eight out of ten of the population lived. Its first reaction was a call for repression. On 3 August, with Le Chapelier in the chair, Salomon, a deputy for the Orléans *baillage*, proposed a decree that began with the following statement: 'It appears from letters from every province that properties are prey to the most reprehensible brigandage; châteaux are being burned everywhere, monasteries destroyed, farms abandoned to pillage. Taxes and seigniorial dues are all destroyed, the laws without force, the magistrates without authority; justice is now no more than a phantom that is uselessly sought in the courts.' One member (whose name is not given) proposed a decree expressing 'that it is necessary to hasten to remedy the present ills, that France will be in the greatest disorder, that it is *a war of the poor against the rich*', before enjoining bailiffs, seneschals and provosts to pursue 'all those who attack the liberty and property of any individual'.[32]

But the enlightened fraction of the nobility realized that the moment had come to make concessions. The session of 4 August, prepared for at the Breton club, opened in the evening with Le Chapelier presiding,[33] and a declaration by the vicomte de Noailles, Lafayette's brother-in-law (nicknamed, as a younger son with no lands, Jean sans Terres[34]). Noailles proposed a series of measures that amounted to a real upheaval: that tax should be paid in future 'by all persons in the kingdom in proportion to their income'; that 'all feudal rights should be redeemable by communities'; and that 'seigniorial corvées, mortmains and other personal servitudes should be abolished without compensation'. The feudal system was thereby divided in two: that bearing on individuals would be suppressed, and that bearing on properties would be redeemable.

The duc d'Aiguillon, the largest fortune in France after the king and

32 A. P., vol. 8, pp. 336–7. My emphasis.

33 Ibid., pp. 343-50.

34 ['Jean sans Terres' was the French appellation of England's King John, 'John Lackland'. – Translator]

one of the first nobles to join with the Third Estate in May, then took the floor to support these proposals, starting by justifying the insurrection: 'The people are seeking at last to shake off a yoke that has weighed on them for centuries, and, it must be admitted, this insurrection, despite being blameworthy (as is every violent aggression), can find its excuse in the vexations of which they are victim.' He went on to emphasize the necessity of redemption: 'These [seigniorial] rights are property. Equity prohibits demanding that any property be relinquished without granting a fair indemnity to its owner.' It was then the turn of an obscure Breton deputy, Leguen de Kerangal:

> Bring us these titles that outrage humanity itself, requiring men to be tethered to a plough like draft animals. Bring us these titles that oblige men to spend nights beating ponds to prevent the frogs from troubling the sleep of their pleasure-loving lords. Which of us, gentlemen, in this century of enlightenment, would not make an expiatory bonfire of these wretched parchments?

The idea of redemption reassured the deputies. They understood that the sacrifice would be more symbolic than real, and in a rush of enthusiasm that doubtless was not altogether insincere, they resolved to destroy the most visible foundations of the Ancien Régime. All the privileges of the orders would be abolished: the franchises of provinces and towns, seigniorial rights – hunting, *garenne*, *colombier*,[35] seigniorial justice, etc. The clergy would renounce the tithe, the bourgeois the purchase of offices. This grandiose abjuration took the whole night.

These sacrifices were clearly intended to restore order in the provinces.[36] But a week later, when the moment came to give legal shape

35 [*Garenne* was the right to capture small game, especially rabbits, on common land, which had been steadily whittled away by noble enclosures. The right to keep a dovecote (*colombier*) had been likewise restricted to the nobility, whose pigeons were also entitled to feed with impunity on peasant crops. – Translator]

36 Mirabeau, in no. 26 of *Le Courrier de Provence* (10 August): 'Eighteen articles drafted and decreed with such haste have the object of restoring in the kingdom the authority of the laws, giving the people a deposit on their happiness and moderating their discontent by a prompt enjoyment of the first benefits of liberty.'

to what had been proclaimed in the heady night of 4 August, the Assembly sought to narrow its scope, despite the first sentence of the text adopted: 'The National Assembly destroys the feudal system in its entirety.'[37]

In Paris, news of the session of 4 August was greeted with general enthusiasm: 'The intoxication of joy spread into every heart; people congratulated one another . . . Fraternity, sweet fraternity, reigned on all sides', wrote Loustalot in no. 3 of *Les Révolutions de Paris*. At the same moment, however, a newcomer to journalism was searching in vain for a printer who would produce his article, which stated: 'Let us beware; they are seeking to lull us to sleep, to deceive us. The truth is that the faction of aristocrats has always dominated the National Assembly, and the deputies of the people have always blindly followed the directions it has given them.' This man's name was Jean-Paul Marat, and this article, written on 6 August, would appear in the 21 September issue of his new paper, *L'Ami du peuple*.

The peasants also rejoiced to see the disappearance of tithe and seigniorial burdens. Soon, however, they perceived that their demands had been ignored, since the final decrees stipulated the payment of rent until redemption was completed. The visits of bailiffs showed them that nothing had changed: they had to go on paying *champarts*, *terrages*, *cens*, *lods*, and even the feudalized tithes.[38] And not only did the obligation of redemption maintain the feudal yoke on all poor peasants, the conditions of this redemption were impractical even for those who possessed certain resources: all tenants of the same fief were declared jointly responsible for payment of the sum due to the lord.[39] Trouble flared up again. In many places, the peasants came together and collectively refused to pay taxes and dues. On 2 September, the king sent the archbishops and bishops of the kingdom a letter of distress:

37 A. P., vol. 8, pp. 397–8.

38 [Nobles drew *champart* or *terrage* as a share of peasant crops, most generally one-eighth. The *cens* was a form of feudal rent, and *lods* was charged on transfer or inheritance of land. – Translator] The feudalized tithes, which could be drawn by secular landowners, had not been suppressed on 4 August, as distinct from ecclesiastical tithes.

39 Mathiez, *The French Revolution*, p. 56.

> You know the disturbances that are ravaging my kingdom. You know how in many provinces, brigands and disloyal people are rife, and that not content with abandoning themselves to every excess, they have succeeded in inflaming the minds of the inhabitants of the countryside . . . Exhort all my subjects accordingly to await in peace the success of these patriotic measures, dissuade and prevent them from disturbing their course with insurrections apt to discourage men of goodwill. Let the people trust in my protection and my love; if the whole world abandon them, I shall watch over them.[40]

A single chamber; the right of royal veto

Concurrently, the Assembly had begun debating the Declaration of Rights and the Constitution. The patriotic party divided for the first time on the very principle of such a declaration, with the Moderates deeming it pointless and dangerous.[41] Under pressure from Barnave, the principle was adopted, but by a small majority of 140 votes. The Declaration itself – voted on 26 August – was the preamble to the Constitution, on which debate was far more impassioned. There were two crucial points at issue: should there be one chamber or two, and should the king be granted the right of veto?

The rapporteurs of the constitution committee, Mounier and Lally-Tollendal, advocated a system on the English model: two chambers, one elected by the people and the other hereditary, like the House of Lords. They proposed giving the king an absolute right of veto over the decisions of the two chambers. The monarchists, as they were now called, had the support of Necker and Archbishop

---

40 Document from the Bibliothèque historique de la ville de Paris (BHVP), classification mark 136159.

41 Malouet's line of argument against the principle of the Declaration was a subtle one: 'There is no natural right that has not been modified by positive law. Now, if you have both the principle and the exception, where is the law? If you do not indicate any restrictions, why present men in all their plenitude with rights that they can only exert within just limits?' (A. P., vol. 8, pp. 322–3).

Champion de Cicé, the Garde des Sceaux. Under their influence the king refused to sign the decrees adopted by the Assembly after 4 August, and published a message that criticized these point by point. Finally, on 10 September, after a highly chaotic session, the question was clearly posed by Camus: 'Shall there be one chamber or two?' On a roll call, the single chamber was adopted by 490 votes to 89, with 122 votes being 'missing or not expressed'.[42] The provincial nobility, who knew they had no chance of sitting in an upper chamber, had voted with the Third Estate.

There remained the question of the veto, which Sieyès had called a '*lettre de cachet* launched against the general will'. Barnave had been in negotiations with Necker: the Assembly would grant the king a suspending veto for two legislatures (i.e. four years) in exchange for his signing the decrees of 4 August. This was a fool's bargain: once the veto was passed, the king prevaricated and still did not sign. Against a background of increasing agitation in Paris, the monarchist party asked the king to move the government and Assembly to Compiègne, so as to shelter them from pressure from the Palais-Royal. The king declined, but decided to concentrate troops once again around Versailles, including the Flanders regiment that would soon become notorious.

The Declaration of Rights

The 1789 Declaration of Rights was not written in the silence of a study or the seclusion of an office. In the Assembly's final session on 26 August, amendments of every kind were made against a hubbub of individual conversation, and even the published proceedings convey a rare sense of disorder. This is why the Declaration was incomplete, its seventeen articles omitting such important points as the right to education, the right of petition, the right of association . . . It was drafted at a troubled moment when the link between the Moderates and the advanced party in the Assembly was not yet

42 A. P., vol. 8, pp. 487–9.

broken, which explains the caution and contradictions of a text which has to be read as a snapshot, the reflection of a moment, and not as a coherent whole to be engraved in stone. It was agreed, in any case, that it would be reviewed and completed once the Constitution was finalized.

Much has been written about its sources, which were many: the Declaration of Independence and the constitutions of the American states, as we have seen, the remonstrations of the Parlements, Montesquieu's *Spirit of the Laws*. But this Declaration is above all imbued with the doctrine of natural right, as indicated by its preamble: 'The representatives of the French People . . . have resolved to set forth in a solemn Declaration the natural, unalienable and sacred rights of man . . .' Article 2 lays down that 'The aim of every political association is the preservation of the natural and imprescriptible rights of man. These rights are Liberty, Property, Safety and Resistance to Oppression.' And in defining liberty, article 4 indicates that 'the exercise of the natural rights of every man has no bounds other than those that ensure to the other members of society the enjoyment of these same rights.'

Florence Gauthier has shown that there is a contradiction in the Declaration between the natural right to liberty and the natural right to property. While the right to property is seen as natural and hence inalienable, the production and distribution of the most important means of subsistence (especially grain) are entrusted to those whose aim is to enrich themselves, with no possible control. From this point, the liberty of the poor becomes an empty word, as they can no longer secure their own existence. Three years later, Robespierre would say: 'All that is indispensable to preserve life is the common property of the whole society; it is only the surplus that is an individual quality to be left to the work of merchants.' In the meantime, 'in the Declaration of Natural Rights of 1789, the universal property of liberty stands in contradiction with the private property of material goods.'[43]

Yet the significance of this Declaration was immense: it signalled the

---

43 Florence Gauthier, *Triomphe et mort du droit naturel en Révolution*, Paris: Presses Universitaires de France, 1992, p. 48.

end of the Ancien Régime. To write that 'the principle of all sovereignty lies essentially in the Nation', that 'the law is the expression of the general will', and that 'all citizens are equally admissible to all public dignities, positions and employments', was to tear down the whole edifice of kingship by divine right. These sentences that sound self-evident today – even if their true consequences are not always drawn out – were the death-knell of the old order, and they set out the programme of the Revolution. This is the reason why the revolutionaries always clung to the 'rock of the rights of man', and why Chaumette would term the Declaration the 'French people's Sinaï'.[44]

EXCURSUS: WAS THE FRENCH REVOLUTION A BOURGEOIS REVOLUTION?

This question has divided historians quite passionately. Champions of the 'bourgeois revolution' position are particularly found among 'Marxists'. Jaurès first of all, who took up the theses developed by the German Social-Democrats and wrote in the opening lines of his introduction: 'The French Revolution realized the two essential conditions for socialism: democracy and capitalism. But at bottom it represented the political advent of the bourgeois class.'[45] In his wake, historians working in the orbit of the French Communist Party and backed up by their colleagues in the Soviet Union did much for the thesis of the bourgeois revolution, which fitted neatly with the teachings of barracks Marxism, or 'proletarian science': the bourgeoisie, a rising class during the Revolution, destroyed feudalism and established capitalism; it was a progressive element inasmuch as it gave rise to the proletariat, destined to construct a classless society and carry out the great revolution of October 1917.[46]

44 *Journal de la Montagne*, 6–7 September 1793.

45 Jaurès, *Histoire socialiste*, vol. 1, p. 61.

46 The thesis of a 'bourgeois revolution' also finds support from François Furet and his disciples; here it is put to a different use, as a revolution of the elites, erasing the people from the history of the Revolution.

Besides the fact that Marx wrote nothing that might relate to such a schema – notes on the French Revolution are few and far between in his work, and sometimes contradictory – this reading is highly debatable, for at least three reasons. The first is that it was not 'the bourgeoisie' that destroyed feudalism; Louis XIV dealt the decisive blows. On this point, we can agree with Tocqueville and Furet: the night of 4 August simply swept away the debris of an already moribund feudalism. Secondly, by making the bourgeoisie the driving force of the Revolution, its progressive element, 'Marxist' historians are led to an untenable dilemma: in their struggle against the bourgeoisie, the revolutionary peasants and sans-culottes were working against the grain of history as they opposed the establishment of capitalism, an indispensable stage in the Stalinist pattern.[47] The people were thus objectively reactionary in their struggle for survival – like the Ukrainian peasants of the 1920s.[48]

The third reason is semantic, but not merely. During the Revolution the words 'bourgeois' and 'bourgeoisie' are highly uncommon in speeches, debates and newspapers. I have sought for them in Robespierre, in Brissot, in Loustalot, in Marat and in Hébert: I have found 'the rich', 'hoarders', 'aristocrats', 'plotters', 'monopolists', 'rogues', 'rentiers', but scarcely a single 'bourgeois'.[49] This rarity of the word, to my mind, means something very clear, expressing the absence of the thing. *The bourgeoisie did not exist as a class.* There were certainly rich and poor, haves and have-nots, but this does not amount to a bourgeoisie and a proletariat. Was the Revolution bourgeois or not? That is a question I refuse to ask, as it basically has no meaning.

---

47 See on these points the Introduction to the new edition of Mathiez's *La Réaction thermidorienne*, by Yannick Bosc and Florence Gauthier (Paris: La Fabrique, 2010); and Florence Gauthier, 'Critique du concept de "révolution bourgeoise"', *Raison Présente*, no. 123, 1997, pp. 57–72 (online at *révolution-française.net*).

48 'Our peasants thought only of arresting the advances of capitalism; they wanted to keep to their old routine . . . These men were turned towards the past. In their state of mind, there was undoubtedly more conservatism and routine than innovative ardour' (Lefebvre, 'La révolution française et les paysans', p. 349).

49 To be fair, I did not conduct a systematic computerized search. It is true that the word appears here and there, but not with the meaning it has today. It certainly features in the *Histoire parlementaire* of Buchez and Roux, but in their own commentary – written in the 1830s – rather than in the contemporary reports they published.

CHAPTER 4

October 1789 to July 1790

The Constituent Assembly in Paris – The journées of 5 and 6 October, the clubs, administrative reorganization, the Fête de la Fédération

Such a phenomenon in the history of the world will never be forgotten; as it discovered in the depth of human nature a possibility of moral progress that no man of politics had previously suspected.

– Kant, *The Conflict of the Faculties*

Financial crisis, provisions crisis

In early autumn 1789, while the Assembly was legislating nonstop and conflicts were coming to light within the Third Estate itself, what was already called a 'crisis' – a word with a great future – was raging throughout the country.

Necker had been forced to admit defeat in his great plan to borrow 30 million livres: three weeks after its launch, only two million had been subscribed. In Paris, the emigration of the aristocracy had led to massive unemployment in luxury industries and trades. Two hundred thousand passports had been applied for since July, and many domestic servants swelled the charity workshops of the École Militaire and Montmartre. Tailors, wig-makers and shoemakers demonstrated on 18 August, and bakers' boys almost every day. Not only did bread cost over three sous a pound, it was increasingly scarce:[1] 'Today the horrors of dearth are felt once more, the bakeries are under siege, the people are short of bread; and it is after the richest harvest that we are on the verge of dying of hunger. Can there be any doubt that we are surrounded by traitors seeking to consummate our ruin?' wrote Marat in the second issue of *L'Ami du peuple* (16 September). On 2 October he went further: 'What is the remedy? Sweep from the Hôtel de Ville all suspect men, royal pensioners, prosecutors, advocates, academicians, advisers to the Châtelet, court clerks of the judiciary and Parlement, financiers, speculators and stock-exchange sharks, with the Bureau at their head.'

The journées of 5 and 6 October: women bring the king to Paris

An economic crisis and a crisis of supplies, against a background of political crisis: the conditions were ripe for an explosion. As often happens, it was a minor incident that served as a spark. On 1 October, a grand dinner was held at Versailles in the hall of the Opéra: the royal bodyguards invited the officers of the Flanders regiment to celebrate their arrival. The king and the queen, carrying the dauphin in her arms, came to greet the guests who, warmed up by wine and music, welcomed them with tremendous cheers. A little later, in the evening's exaltation, a number of officers tore off the tricolour cockade and replaced it with a white one – or a black one, the colour of the queen. The banquet turned into a counter-revolutionary demonstration.

On 3 October reports of it reached Paris, already at boiling point, in Gorsas's *Courrier*. 'On Sunday 4th, circular letters, troop movements, commotions at the Palais-Royal and the shortage of bread

1 The 1789 harvest had been good, but threshing took a great deal of time, so that supplies were not assured until late in the autumn.

that aggravates everything, all excited the liveliest ferment . . . On Monday morning, a throng of women went to the Hôtel de Ville and routed the guard there . . ., taking possession of the cannon of La Basoche and heading for Versailles.'[2]

This decisive *journée* of 5 October seems still more unexpected than the capture of the Bastille, as it was now women of the people, poor and anonymous, who made a loud and effective appearance on the revolutionary stage. In the morning, groups of angry women gathered in Paris, around the Halles and in the faubourg Saint-Antoine. They then converged outside the Hôtel de Ville, where they screamed for bread. Not getting an answer, they overwhelmed the guard, forced the doors and entered the building, making off with pikes, muskets, and four cannon. Then, taking one of the heroes of the Bastille, Stanislas Maillard, as their captain, they formed a procession and set off for Versailles.[3] Towards five o'clock in the afternoon, there was a crowd of six or seven thousand women outside the palace railings, joined by workers and *gardes-françaises* whom they met along the way.

The women sent a delegation to the Assembly, with Maillard as their spokesperson: 'We have come to Versailles to ask for bread, and at the same time to have the royal guards who insulted the patriotic cockade punished.'[4] A national cockade was then presented to Maillard on behalf of the royal guards. He showed it to the women, and everyone shouted: 'Long live the king, long live the guard!' The Assembly sent Mounier, its president, to see the king, accompanied by some twenty deputies, and to request 'the pure and simple acceptance of the Declaration of Rights, and the full force of the executive power to provide the capital with the grain and flour that it needs'. Louis XVI met with his council, rejected the suggestion of the monarchists that he should flee to Rouen, and at ten in the evening he at last validated the August decrees and the Declaration of Rights.

2 Mirabeau, in *Le Courrier de Provence*, 5–6 October 1789.

3 Maillard, a strange bailiff's clerk still dressed in black, was prominent in three episodes of the Revolution: the storming of the Bastille, the *journée* of 5 October, and the September massacres of 1792.

4 A. P., vol. 9, pp. 346–7.

Around midnight, Lafayette arrived in Versailles with 15,000 men of the Paris National Guard. The night passed quietly, but on the morning of the 6th a slogan began to circulate among the crowd: 'The king to Paris!' A group entered the palace by a poorly guarded gate, breaking into the Marble Court. A guard fired, a man fell, the crowd flung themselves on the royal guards and killed two of them, carrying off their heads on pikes. The crowd invaded the royal apartments, almost reaching the queen's bedroom. Lafayette managed with difficulty to clear the palace with the help of the National Guard. The king showed himself with the general on the balcony, followed by the queen with her children. At first she was booed, but Lafayette prevailed on her to return, kissed her hand, and the crowd decided to applaud, though shouting '*À Paris!*' During this time, at Mirabeau's suggestion, the Assembly decided that 'the king and the National Assembly are inseparable during the present session.'[5]

Around one o'clock in the afternoon, a tremendous procession left Versailles to the sound of cannon fire. At its head marched the National Guard, with loafs of bread skewered on their bayonets, followed by carts with sacks of flour decorated with leaves, then the *gardes soldés*[6] (the new name for the *gardes-françaises*) surrounding the royal bodyguards, who needed protecting. Behind them, the Flanders regiment and the Swiss Guard preceded the king in his carriage, with Lafayette prancing alongside. Finally a hundred or so members of the Assembly, and the immense crowd in which women carried poplar branches already tinged with autumnal yellow. 'All of it gay, sad, violent, joyous and gloomy at the same time,' wrote Michelet.

The procession, which was welcomed on the Champ-de-Mars by Bailly, reached the Hôtel de Ville at eight in the evening, and at ten o'clock the king and his family arrived in their new home, the Tuileries palace.

5 Ibid., p. 349.

6 [The name indicating that they were paid, whereas the National Guard were volunteers. – Translator]

The Constituent Assembly in the Salle du Manège

The October *journées* close the heroic phase of 1789. The period that followed is often described, following Michelet, as that of 'French unanimity', or 'the happy year'[7] – which clearly highlights by contrast the abomination of the following phase, in which the revolution 'got out of hand'. In actual fact, if there was an idyllic fraternity – and at times, in certain places, this is undeniable – it was not the dominant note. From October 1789 to the end of the Constituent Assembly (you could even say until the fall of the monarchy), the possessing classes and their representatives who controlled both the Assembly and the Commune de Paris did their utmost to keep the 'low people' at arm's length, knowing they were capable of ungovernable reactions. They organized the repression of the people's outbursts of anger and manoeuvred to retract the concessions obtained under pressure, so that this period was in fact *a long phase of ebbing of the Revolution*.

The great winner of 5 and 6 October was Lafayette, who made the most of these *journées* he had not foreseen and had followed only unwillingly. Drawing closer to the royal couple, he persuaded them that the riot had been fomented by the duc d'Orléans, whom he managed to get sent to England on a 'diplomatic mission'. Mirabeau, his other rival, persisted in his own manoeuvrings: he wanted to become a minister, but the Assembly was nervous of him and decided not to choose ministers from its own ranks. Mirabeau plotted unsuccessfully with the comte de Provence, and in 1790 ended up on the king's payroll; the king settled his enormous debts and gave him 6,000 livres a month. He remained popular, but his venality, which was all but publicly known, prevented him from having any real influence. 'What can we expect,' wrote Marat in *L'Ami du peuple* on 10 August 1790, 'from a man without principles, manners or honour? Now he has become the inspiration of scurvy wretches and ministerial hopefuls, the inspiration of plotters and conspirators.'

Lafayette, who seems to have won the trust of Louis XVI, tried to

---

7 A chapter title in François Furet and Denis Richet, *The French Revolution,* London: Weidenfeld and Nicholson, 1970.

make him accept the idea of a constitutional monarchy, and the king, in a note sent on 15 April 1790, wrote in his own hand: 'I promise M. de Lafayette my entire confidence in all matters which may concern the establishment of the Constitution, my legitimate authority as specified in the memorandum, and the return of public tranquillity.'[8] Lafayette had become the 'palace mayor', writes Mathiez, repeating a phrase of Marat's.[9]

The losers of October were the Moderates and monarchists: their project of an English-style constitution had been rejected, and they were terrified by the popular movement. Already on 8 October, their leader Mounier resigned the presidency of the Assembly for reasons of health and left Paris for his native Dauphiné, emigrating to Savoy shortly after.[10] In the days that followed, close to 200 representatives of the people asked for a passport to emigrate or else took refuge in their home province, so fearful were they of taking their seats in Paris.[11] The Assembly actually hesitated to follow the king. It did not leave Versailles until 19 October, settling first of all in a hall in the Archevêché, then in the Salle du Manège, alongside the Tuileries gardens next to the Terrasse des Feuillants. Tiers were hastily constructed for the deputies and platforms for the public, who constantly intervened in the debates of the successive revolutionary assemblies, making their loud, unruly voices heard at the heart of the representative system.

In the Salle du Manège, the deputies arranged themselves as they had done at Versailles, but instead of speaking of the 'Palais-Royal side' and the 'queen's side', the terms now used were 'left' and 'right' in relation to the presidential dais. This was the time

8 Cited by Mathiez, *The French Revolution*, p. 70.

9 [In the Merovingian period, the *maire du palais* was the head of the royal household, with a power that eventually led to Charles Martel becoming the French sovereign. – Translator]

10 On 26 October he would send the Assembly a long justification, 'It indeed is a duty to brave every danger in the service of the country, but there must be no more useful means, and one must still have a hope of success', A. P., vol. 9, p. 570.

11 In Paris, the offices of the Hôtel de Ville were besieged by people demanding passports. This second emigration, following that of the princes in July, was numerically significant: one report counted 60,000 émigrés in Switzerland alone.

and the place that these words first acquired their political meaning. There were no parties in the modern sense of the term, but rather tendencies and personalities. From right to left were the *noirs* (the aristocrats, black being as we have seen the colour of the queen); the monarchists, or what was left of them; the partisans of a constitutional monarchy, soon dubbed the Fayettists; the left around the triumvirate of Barnave, Duport and Alexandre de Lameth; and finally a tiny far left (a term not used at the time) comprised of Buzot, Grégoire, Pétion and his friend Robespierre, the deputy for Arras.

The clubs: Jacobins and Cordeliers

These tendencies had their meeting places in Paris, along with organized clubs and the papers that supported them. The ideas of the aristocrats, who met on rue Royale at the Salon Français, were aired in *Les Actes des Apôtres*, to which Rivarol anonymously contributed, and in *L'Ami du roi*, whose animating spirit was the talented polemicist abbé Royou. The constitutionalists attended the Société de 89, founded by Sieyès, which held its meetings in luxurious premises at the Palais-Royal. The high entrance fee made this a club restricted to high society. Grand dinners were held there, attended by everyone who mattered among the 'moderate' revolutionaries – Lafayette and Bailly, Mirabeau and Condorcet, as well as financiers such as Clavière and farmer-general Lavoisier. The left side, for its part, met in two clubs whose names have retained their evocative power down to our own day: the Jacobins and the Cordeliers.

When the Constituent Assembly met in Paris, it was followed by the Breton club, which had set the pace in Versailles:

> Premises were needed that were close to the sessions of the legislature, which had just been established in the Manège des Tuileries; the prior of the Jacobin convent on the rue Saint-Honoré was prepared to lend its library, and this is what was used. Le Chapelier was its first president, and myself the secretary; the members were

all deputies, and only matters relating to the Constituent Assembly were discussed.[12]

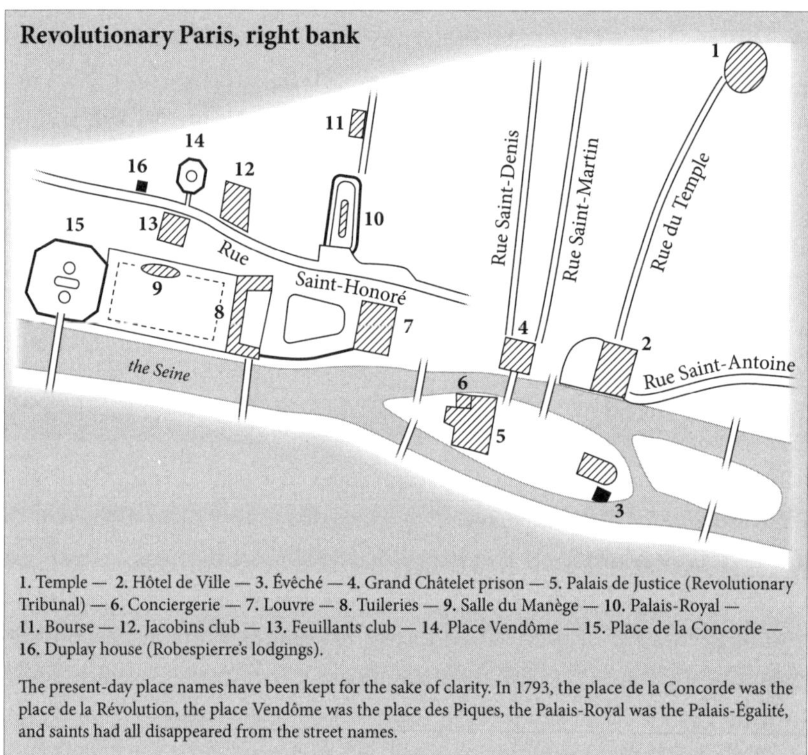

Revolutionary Paris, right bank

1. Temple — 2. Hôtel de Ville — 3. Évêché — 4. Grand Châtelet prison — 5. Palais de Justice (Revolutionary Tribunal) — 6. Conciergerie — 7. Louvre — 8. Tuileries — 9. Salle du Manège — 10. Palais-Royal — 11. Bourse — 12. Jacobins club — 13. Feuillants club — 14. Place Vendôme — 15. Place de la Concorde — 16. Duplay house (Robespierre's lodgings).

The present-day place names have been kept for the sake of clarity. In 1793, the place de la Concorde was the place de la Révolution, the place Vendôme was the place des Piques, the Palais-Royal was the Palais-Égalité, and saints had all disappeared from the street names.

The Breton club then became the Société des Amis de la Constitution. Though the name 'Jacobins' was given them in mockery, 'They revelled in it, and the name was extended to all societies of the same kind established in the provinces.'[13] The admission fee was fairly high (twelve livres), and the annual subscription twenty-four livres.[14] Article 1 of its rules, drafted by Barnave, spelled out the

12 Dubois-Crancé, *Analyse de la Révolution française*, cited in Aulard, *La Société des Jacobins*, Paris: Jouaust et Noblet et Quentin, 1889, vol. 1, 'Introduction', p. xviii. The library later became too small, and from May 1791 the club held its sessions in the convent chapel.

13 Mounier, *De l'influence attribuée aux philosophes*, p. 118, cited by Aulard, *La Société des Jacobins*, vol. 1, p. xxiii. The club officially became the Société des Jacobins in September 1792, with the proclamation of the Republic.

14 A deputy in the Constituent Assembly was paid eighteen livres per day.

objectives of the society, which met every day at six o'clock except when the Assembly had an evening session: '1) to discuss in advance questions to be decided in the National Assembly; 2) to work for the establishment and strengthening of the Constitution; 3) to correspond with other societies of the same kind that may be formed in the kingdom.'

The club rapidly expanded beyond deputies alone. It was sufficient to be nominated by five existing members, and by the end of 1790 there were over a thousand. On the whole, this co-option tended to recruit individuals who were well-off and educated. It was not until October 1791 that the club opened its doors to the public, and from then onwards the meetings at the Jacobins marked the rhythm of revolutionary life in Paris.

What distinguished the Jacobins from other clubs, and gradually gave them such power, was their spread throughout the country by way of affiliated groups. As Alexandre de Lameth recalled: 'Round about December 1789, many leading inhabitants of the provinces, visiting Paris, were presented at the society and manifested the desire to establish one similar in the principal towns of France.'[15] By August 1790, according to Aulard, there were 152 affiliated societies, and in year II over a thousand.[16] Relations between the Paris club and its offshoots were close, *in both directions*. Abbé Grégoire recalled:

> By prior agreement, one of us would take a suitable opportunity to raise his question in a session of the National Assembly. He was certain to be applauded by a very small number and booed by the majority; no matter, he asked for the question to be referred to a committee, where opponents hoped to bury it. The Jacobins would take it up in their circular invitations or their papers, it was

---

15 A. de Lameth, *Histoire de l'Assemblée constituante*, vol. 1, p. 422, note 4. Cited by Aulard, *La Société des Jacobins*, vol. 1, p. xix.

16 To give an idea of the spread of affiliated societies even in small towns, the following appear under the letter 'B': Bar-le-Duc, Barjac, Bayonne, Beaune, Beauvais, Bédarieux, Bergerac, Bergues, Besançon, Béthune, Béziers, Blois, Bolbec, Bordeaux, Boulogne, Bourbonne, Bourg, Bourges, Brest, Brignoles, Brioude, Brive, Buxy.

> discussed by four or five hundred affiliated societies, and three weeks later addresses poured into the Assembly asking for a decree on a matter that had initially been rejected, but which the Assembly then accepted by a large majority, since public opinion had been matured by discussion.[17]

The society and its branches operated as a system for spreading revolutionary ideas across the country. Nothing is more absurd than the idea of 'Jacobinism' as an authoritarian and meddlesome Paris dictatorship. That is an interpretation handed down by Thermidor, as lasting as hatred of the Revolution.[18]

The Cordeliers were altogether different. The club appeared in June 1790 under the name of the Société des Amis des Droits de l'Homme et du Citoyen. For a year, its meetings were held in the Cordeliers convent on rue de l'École-de-Médecine, but in May 1791 the municipality – now owning the building, which had become national property – had the premises closed. After a month of itinerancy the club settled in the Salle du Musée on rue Dauphine, where it would meet for the rest of its existence.[19] Its aim, more modest and more practical than that of the Jacobins, was to 'denounce to the tribunal of public opinion the abuses of the various powers and any kind of infringement on the rights of man'.[20] As protectors of the oppressed and redressers of abuses of power, the Cordeliers had as their emblem the 'eye of surveillance', wide open on the failings of the elected representatives. 'They made accusations, undertook inquiries, visited oppressed patriots in the prisons and found defenders for them, and addressed public opinion by way of posters. In

---

17 *Mémoires de Grégoire*, vol. 1, p. 387.

18 See Florence Gauthier, 'Centralisme "jacobin", vraiment?', in *Utopie Critique*, 2005, no. 32, pp. 75–86, also available at *revolution-francaise.net*. On the same website, see Yannick Bosc and Marc Belissa, 'L'essence du jacobinisme: un universalisme blanc, masculin et catholique?'

19 The Musée de Paris was a literary and scientific academy, with premises for lectures and meetings.

20 Albert Mathiez, *Le Club des Cordeliers pendant la crise de Varennes et le massacre du Champ-de-Mars*, Paris: Champion, 1910, p. 6.

short, they were a group of action and struggle.'[21] The membership fee was minimal (one livre four sous per year, i.e. two sous per month), and the club accepted members of any condition, including passive citizens.[22] Women could also attend the sessions and take part in discussions. Its members included lawyers such as Danton and Desmoulins, journalists such as Fréron, Robert and Chaumette, printers such as Momoro and Brune, but also many tradespeople, both retailers and wholesalers – the butcher Legendre, the brewer Santerre, the café-owner Berger . . .

The great strength of the Cordeliers was their links to the fraternal societies, local clubs in the Paris *quartiers* that began to mushroom in winter 1790. The first and most famous, known simply as the Société Fraternelle, was founded in February of that year by Claude Dansard, a boarding-house keeper who invited every evening, to a small room in the Jacobins, 'artisans, fruit and vegetable sellers from the quarter, along with their wives and children, and read to them, by the light of a candle that he carried in his pocket, the decrees of the Constituent Assembly which he went on to explain'.[23] Soon there were popular societies in every Parisian neighbourhood, whose founders were often members of the Cordeliers: the fraternal society of the Friends of the Rights of Man and Enemies of Despotism, inspired by Santerre, which met in the Montreuil section; the fraternal society of the Enfants-Rouges section, which met at the Minimes on place Royale, freely accepting all citizens male and female without distinction, even children over the age of twelve; the fraternal society of Les Halles, founded by the engraver François Sergent, which met on rue Mondétour; the society of Sainte-Geneviève on place Maubert; the society of Indigent Friends of the Constitution, on rue Jacob . . . Their activities were coordinated by a central committee chaired by François Robert, a journalist on the *Mercure National*.[24] It was in these societies, constantly encouraged by Marat and all the democrats, that

---

21 Ibid., p. 7.

22 On the distinction between active and passive citizens, see below, p. 105.

23 Mathiez, *Le Club des Cordeliers*, p. 14.

24 The *Mercure National* had been founded by Robert's wife, Louise de Kéralio, who also led the Société Fraternelle de l'Un et l'Autre Sexe.

the people of Paris, the people who would soon be called the sans-culottes, acquired their political education.

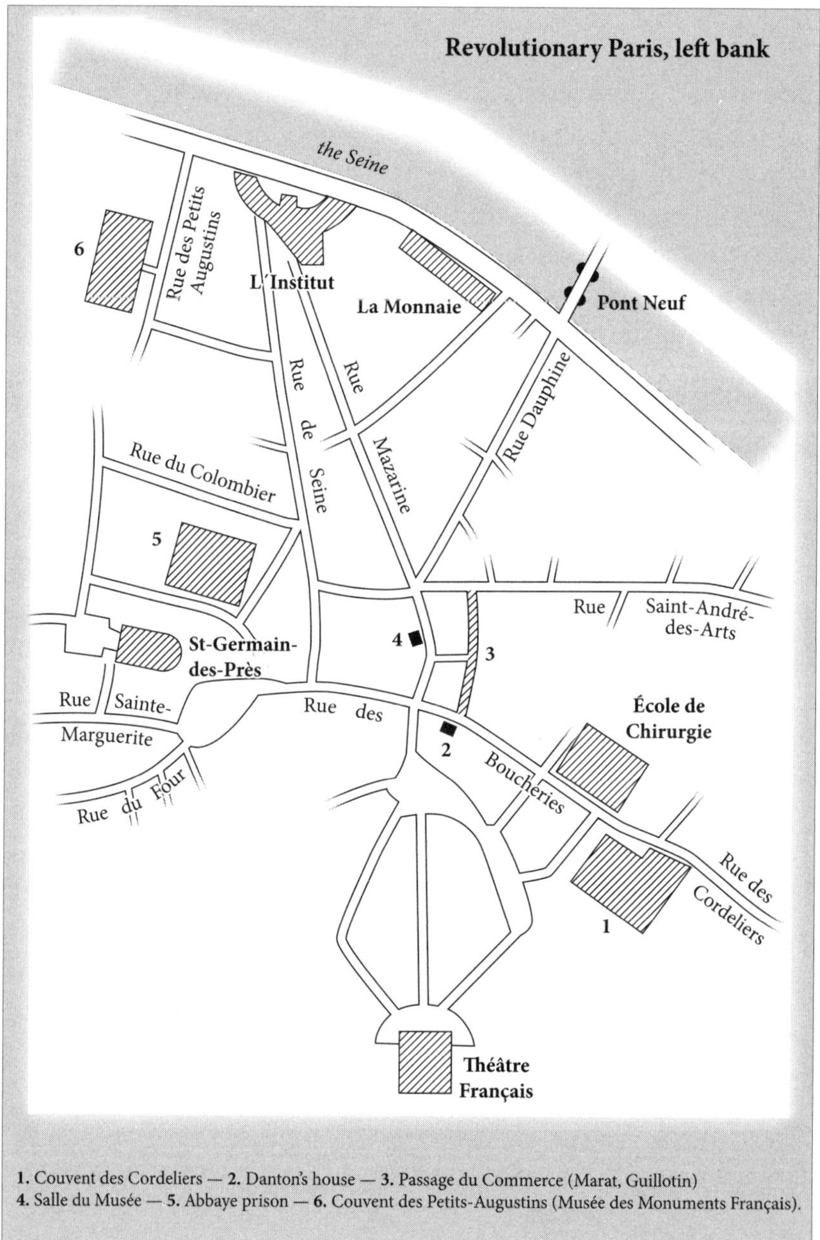

1. Couvent des Cordeliers — **2.** Danton's house — **3.** Passage du Commerce (Marat, Guillotin) **4.** Salle du Musée — **5.** Abbaye prison — **6.** Couvent des Petits-Augustins (Musée des Monuments Français).

Newspapers

This efflorescence went hand in hand with the extraordinary development of a 'democratic' press (the great word of the time). Clearly there was nothing comparable to the newspaper kiosks of today; news-sheets were distributed by subscription – at a fairly high price: thirty-six livres per year, for example, for *Le Patriote français* – but they were also cried in the streets and posted on walls, despite repeated prohibitions by the Commune. Public readings of them were given, they were consulted in cafés; as the sole source of information, the press played a role that is hard to imagine today.

The moderate papers (in the present-day sense: at that time 'Moderate' meant counter-revolutionary) were so numerous that it is impossible to mention them all. *La Chronique de Paris* was an austere periodical whose main contributor was Condorcet. *Le Courrier*,[25] launched in July 1789 by Gorsas – a future member of the Convention, sitting with the Girondins – championed advanced ideas while deploring disorder, and took a republican position after Varennes. *Les Révolutions de Paris*, a weekly founded by Louis Prudhomme who was also a printer, had the young and brilliant Élysée Loustalot as its sole writer until his premature death. 'Ready to sacrifice even his reputation to the public good, he demonstrated to the end a perseverance and style that served as a model to us all', Camille Desmoulins said of him in his funeral oration, delivered before the Jacobins.[26] After Loustalot, Sylvain Maréchal, Fabre d'Églantine, Sonthonax and Chaumette are believed to have contributed to *Les Révolutions de Paris*.[27] The weekly moved steadily to the left, taking a stand for democracy and for equality – not only of rights but also of wealth – and against 'the idols', namely Lafayette, the Lameth brothers and Barnave. According to Desmoulins, the paper had up to

25 The title of the *Courrier* changed several times. It was initially the *Courrier de Versailles à Paris et de Paris à Versailles*; eventually it became the *Courrier des 83 départements*.

26 Gilles Feyel, 'Le journalisme au temps de la Révolution', *AHRF*, no. 333, July–September 2003, p. 33.

27 Fernand Mitton, *La Presse française sous la Révolution, le Consulat, l'Empire*, Paris: Guy Le Prat, 1945, vol. 2, p. 85.

200,000 readers: while the number of copies distributed was lower than this, each was read by several people.

Le Patriote français, founded by Brissot in July 1789, was a daily containing chronicles in the form of letters written by Condorcet, Pétion, Grégoire, Manuel, Clavière and other notable figures, including Roland and his wife. Its print run is estimated at 10,000 copies, and it was distributed throughout France, especially in the regions that would subsequently be *girondines* (Lyon, Bordeaux, Bouches-du-Rhône). Under the Constituent Assembly the paper was against despotism, defended the name of 'citizen' and the renaming of streets that evoked royalty; it became discreetly republican from the end of 1790. On the colonial question, it took the position of the Société des Amis des Noirs (of which Brissot had been one of the founders), demanding an improvement in the condition of slaves rather than the abolition of slavery.

We should also mention the *Bouche de fer*, the organ of the Cercle Social – a Masonic institution – edited by Bonneville and abbé Fauchet; the door of the Cercle had a box (an 'iron mouth') for receiving letters, notes and messages from passers-by, which the paper published; and the *Annales patriotiques*, founded in October 1789 by Mercier and Carra, which proved so popular that Carra was elected to the Convention by seven departments.[28]

The section of the press most committed to the Revolution was dominated by three illustrious figures, each of them the founder, director and sole writer of his paper: Desmoulins, Marat, and Hébert – and each detesting the others.

Les Révolutions de France et de Brabant, launched by Desmoulins in November 1789, was read throughout the country despite a rather irregular rhythm of publication.[29] It cost ten sous, with a three-

---

28 For a deeper study, see C. Bellanter, J. Godechot, P. Guiral and F. Terron, *Histoire générale de la presse française*, Paris: Presses Universitaires de France, 1969, vol. 1.

29 From no. 73 on, 'Brabant' disappeared from the title, as a result of the disastrous course of the Belgian revolution. [The Duchy of Brabant, finally conquered by the Revolutionary armies in 1794, comprised the greater part of the southern Netherlands not already under French rule. – Translator]

month subscription at six livres. In a letter to his father, Desmoulins spoke of 3,000 subscribers, and in another letter: 'Judge for yourself the success of my paper. I have 100 subscribers in Marseille alone, and 140 in Dunkirk. If I had foreseen such numbers, I would not have made the deal with my publishers for 2,000 écus a year.'[30] Each issue carried three sections: France, Brabant ('and other countries sporting the cockade'), and Variétés (book reviews, theatre, etc.). The paper violently attacked the monarchy and was very early in declaring itself republican. It was Desmoulins who, after Varennes, took the Cordeliers' petition for the deposition of the king to the Paris municipality. The 86th and final issue appeared in July 1791, at the time of the massacre on the Champ-de-Mars (see below, p. 130), when Desmoulins was forced into hiding by the repression.

Marat launched the first issue of *L'Ami du peuple* in September 1789, and published over a thousand issues under different titles until his death in 1793, despite several interruptions due to warrants for his arrest – in October 1789, in January 1790 when he had to take refuge in England for three months, and in July 1791 after the Champ-de-Mars. He often had to move premises, though he worked for the most part in the Cordeliers district. He also changed printer several times, even becoming his own printer when required. The print run, estimated at 2,000 copies, was not among the highest, but its influence was great: *L'Ami du peuple* was read in groups by sans-culottes, many of whom were illiterate. Each issue was eight or twelve pages in small format, composed around a single long article – what would today be called an editorial – which was sometimes continued from one issue to the next. The paper published letters, as part of a dialogue between Marat and his readers. For example, the builders of the former Sainte-Geneviève church (now the Panthéon) wrote to him: 'Dear prophet, true defender of the class of the destitute, allow us workers to reveal to you all the embezzlements and turpitudes that our master builders are plotting.'[31]

The title of *Le Père Duchesne* refers to a fairground character, a

---

30 Mitton, *La Presse française sous la Révolution*, p. 100.

31 Cited in Michel Vovelle, *Marat, écrits*, Paris: Messidor, 1988, p. 22.

kind of Guignol symbolizing the man of the people – several plays, books and pamphlets had used the name, and Hébert would face a number of counterfeits. His paper, the first issue of which was dated January 1791,[32] appeared four times a *décade*.[33] It had eight pages and sold for two sous, with a summary designed to be cried in the street. The prose was fairly rough and ready – which was never the case with Marat – but written with intensity, verve and humour. Politically, *Le Père Duchesne* attacked both abbé Maury and Lafayette, both Mirabeau and Bailly, and demanded the Republic after Varennes. 'In singular fashion, *Le Père Duchesne* enjoyed success in the highest social classes as well as in the lower depths . . . It was bought ostentatiously and perused with simulated joy to give the impression of civic virtue, to "sans-cullotize" oneself, as Hébert put it.'[34]

Martial law

For its part, the Paris municipality or Commune – that is, the Council of Three Hundred (electors) that had imposed itself after 14 July – organized its authority by appointing from among its number a city council: sixty administrators divided into eight departments,[35] forming a veritable executive that would soon have much to attend to.

Indeed, after a few days of relative calm in Paris, agitation began brewing once more in October 1789. The question of subsistence, bread above all, became acute – free trade in grain had led to an artificial shortage, and sentinels had to be placed outside bakers' shops. A riot broke out at the Halle aux Farines, where women looted the sacks of flour, and rumours spread that the flour was polluted. An

32 Hébert had already published, from August 1790, various part-works bearing the name *Le Père Duchesne*.

33 [The ten-day period that replaced the week in the revolutionary calendar. – Translator]

34 Mitton, *La Presse française sous la Révolution*, p. 98.

35 These were: supplies, police, public works, hospitals, education, land, taxes, and National Guard.

incendiary article appeared in *L'Ami du peuple*, 'When will we have bread?', which focused the Commune's attention on Marat. On 21 October, a baker by the name of François, accused – no doubt falsely – of being a hoarder, was seized from the police committee by the crowd and hanged from a lamppost.[36] His head was cut off, stuck on the end of a pike and paraded through Paris.

News of this led the Commune to send a delegation to the Assembly and request 'a law against gatherings to be decreed right away', otherwise 'the Paris Commune and National Guard will be unable to contain the gatherings that are daily becoming more alarming'.[37] In the course of discussions, Barnave, Buzot and Pétion abdicated responsibility: 'It would be dangerous', said Pétion, 'for the people to believe we can exercise a surveillance that lies beyond our remit.'

Only two voices were raised against the principle of martial law. Robespierre protested:

> Those who have followed the Revolution foresaw the point you are at now; they foresaw that terrible situations would require you to demand violent measures, with the aim of destroying at one stroke both yourselves and liberty. The demand is for bread and soldiers, in other words: the people have gathered wanting bread; give us soldiers to immolate the people. You have been told that the soldiers refuse to march . . . Indeed! Can they attack an unhappy people whose misfortune they share?[38]

And Mirabeau added: 'Everything is silence, everything has to be silenced, everything must give way faced by a hungry people; what use would martial law be, if the people gather and shout "There is no bread at the bakery!" What monster would answer this with gunshots?'[39]

---

36 François's shop was on rue du Marché-Palu, close to the seat of the Assembly at the Archevêché, and the crowd, discovering there bread destined for the deputies, believed he was keeping it back to boost the price. On this affair, see Riho Hayakawa, 'L'assassinat du boulanger Denis François', *AHRF* no. 333, July–Sept 2003, pp. 1–19.

37 A. P., vol. 9, p. 472.

38 Ibid., p. 474.

39 Ibid., p. 475.

But they were ignored. The constitution committee of the Assembly seized the opportunity and immediately met to draft the decree of martial law.

The recourse to military force would be announced 'by displaying a red flag[40] at the main window of the Hôtel de Ville and carrying it through every street . . . At the simple signal of this flag, all gatherings, armed or otherwise, become criminal and shall be dispersed by force' (Article 3). After three summonses, the soldiers could open fire. Persons arrested could expect a year in prison if they were unarmed, three years if they were armed, and the death sentence if they were 'convicted of having committed violence. The leaders and instigators of this sedition will be likewise condemned to death.'[41] This martial law was immediately given royal assent.

The following day,

> a dreadful and lugubrious ceremony spread terror in the city at the decrees of the previous day . . . The officials of the Hôtel de Ville, dressed in ceremonial costume, progressed on horseback, each escorted by a sergeant and four city guards. Before them marched a body of infantry in two lines that each occupied one side of the street. When this procession reached the places appointed, it halted and stood to attention. The drums rolled, the trumpets sounded, and the official read aloud the law passed the day before. Everywhere that it passed, this ceremony left a deep feeling of anger and terror.[42]

At the same time, the man who had hanged François and been sentenced to death was executed.

Loustalot, in *Les Révolutions de Paris*, was one of the few to voice a criticism: 'They assure us in vain that this law will give citizens tranquillity and liberty for the work of the National Assembly, and prevent bloody sacrifices. It exists simply to deprive us of popular insurrection,

---

40 It was only after the *journées* of June 1832 that the red flag ceased to be a sign of repression and passed to the side of insurrection.

41 Ibid., p. 476.

42 Buchez and Roux, *Histoire parlementaire*, vol. 3, p. 209.

a frightful and disastrous resource, but the only one that has saved us until now.' On 10 November, in *L'Ami du peuple*, Marat also attacked the Paris municipality that had demanded this law: 'Fools! Do you think that a piece of red cloth will protect you from the effects of popular indignation? Do you think that a few devoted satellites will defend you from the just fury of your fellow citizens?'

The decree on martial law – to which Bailly, the mayor of Paris and president of the city council, was a major contributor – was an event of prime importance in the course of the Revolution. This law would be used to repress many popular movements in Paris and across the country. But right away, it acted as the spark for a conflict that was already latent between the Commune and the sixty districts. On 23 October, a certain Martin put a motion to the assembly of the Saint-Martin-des-Champs district: 'Considering the inconveniences that could result from the imposition of martial law, [the Assembly] decrees that this martial law will not be imposed, and that the present decree be communicated to the fifty-nine [other] districts so that they can agree this object.' At which another member proposed an amendment: that until the law was withdrawn, the citizens of the district would abstain from wearing uniform. The district president proposed sending envoys 'to inquire of the representatives of the Commune what motives impelled them to ask, on two occasions, for martial law, and summon them to approach the National Assembly to beg it to revoke this law'.[43]

The next day several districts passed similar motions, and on 25 October the presidents of forty districts met in order to form a 'correspondence bureau', a kind of central committee charged with coordinating their actions. On 11 November the Cordeliers district, presided by Danton, took up the defence of Marat, who had been threatened with arrest, and made its representatives swear an oath to the effect that their mandate became imperative. This was the start of a series of district initiatives towards genuine democracy, via the creation of systems of liaison between them and against the Commune

43 Buchez and Roux, *Histoire parlementaire*, vol. 3, p. 219. Citizen Martin was arrested by the Commune's investigation committee on 25 October.

– like the assembly in the Archevêché that from spring 1790 onwards developed its own plan of communal government. This muffled movement grew when the Commune decided, in May 1790, to suppress the sixty districts and replace them by forty-eight sections (or subdivisions) of the Commune. The centre of gravity of the Paris *quartiers* was shifted slightly, but the unrest continued. It would come to a head on the night of 9–10 August 1792, when the Commune of the possessor class and notables was expelled and the insurrectional Commune arising from the sections, from communal democracy, took its place in the Hôtel de Ville.

The electoral system: active and passive citizens

The activity of the Constituent Assembly was not confined to issuing decrees for the maintenance of order. During the latter months of 1789 and the two years that followed, it undertook a tremendous constitutional and legislative work, elements of which, such as the division of the country into departments, are still with us today. Politically speaking, the Constituent members, many of whom belonged to – or represented – the possessor class, and who were committed to the idea of a constitutional monarchy, conducted their work with two distinct but coherent goals: to limit the executive powers of the monarchy, and to keep the people well away from major decisions and the distribution of wealth.

Louis XVI was now no longer 'king of France' but 'king of the French', 'by the grace of God and the Constitution of the state'. The state paid him a civil list, the administration of which was entrusted to an official. The ministers, whom he chose, were tightly controlled by the legislature: each of them had to account monthly for the use of his ministry's funds, and their decisions only became effective once their management had been approved by the Assembly. The king could neither sign treaties nor declare war without the Assembly's consent.[44] There remained the right of suspensive veto, but this was

44 This measure was taken at the time of a new threat of war, in May 1790. Spain,

itself limited, not applying to constitutional laws but only to regular ones, apart from tax legislation and decisions that challenged ministers. This primacy of the legislative and active distrust of the executive would be further reinforced during the Legislative Assembly, and especially by the Convention, before Thermidor, and it was only under the Directory that this great revolutionary principle would be reversed, and for a long time.

As for the people, the Assembly sought to curtail the expression of their discontent, particularly its electoral expression. But this would mean violating the Declaration of Rights: how could they deprive men 'equal in rights' of an equal right to vote? How to get around Article VI, according to which 'The law is the expression of the general will. All citizens have the right to contribute to its formation, personally or through their representatives.' It was Sieyès who proposed the necessary contrivance: there would be two categories of free and equal men, 'active citizens', 'the true stakeholders of the great social undertaking', those who paid tax to a minimum equivalent to three days' pay, and 'passive citizens', 'labouring machines' who owned no property and were excluded from the electoral system.

On 22 October 1789 the Assembly debated the 'criteria of eligibility':[45] to be a Frenchman, aged twenty-five or above, living for at least a year in the constituency of the primary assembly, not a domestic servant, neither bankrupt nor insolvent, and above all paying a direct tax of the local value of three days' wages.

This article was attacked by Grégoire, who feared an 'aristocracy of the rich', by Duport ('This article gives credence to wealth, which is nothing in the order of nature. It is contrary to the Declaration of Rights'), and by Robespierre:

---

which had entered into conflict with England in a remote territory of North America, asked the help of France under a 'family pact'. In a kind of prefiguration of the events of 1792, the left denounced a counter-revolutionary plot while the right wing – Mirabeau, Lafayette – exalted patriotic fibre. After vigorous popular agitation, the Assembly declared that the king could *propose* peace or war, but it was up to the Assembly to make the decision.

45 At this time, 'eligibility' meant the right to take part in the primary assemblies that appointed the *electors*; it was these who chose the deputies.

> If the person who pays a contribution equivalent to no more than a day's wage has fewer rights than the one who pays the value of three days, the person who pays ten days has more rights than the one whose tax is worth only three; from now on the person with a hundred thousand livres in *rentes* has a hundred times more rights than the one who has only an income of a thousand livres. [Yet] it follows from all your decrees that every citizen has the right to cooperate in legislation, and hence to be elector or eligible, without distinction of fortune.[46]

In the end, the electoral system was fixed by the law of 22 December 1789: active citizens (somewhat over four million, against around three million poor or passive citizens), meeting in primary assemblies in the capital of the canton, would elect the municipalities and appoint the electors on the basis of one for a hundred active citizens. Being an elector required a tax liability equal to the local value of ten days' wages. The electors would meet in the local capital and select the judges, the members of the departmental assemblies, and above all the deputies to the National Assembly (which would then be the Legislative Assembly). To be elected a deputy, it was necessary to own land and pay a tax equal to the value of a silver *marc*, or 50 livres.[47]

Having learned from experience, the Assembly also decreed that the electoral assemblies would no longer have the right to meet once the elections were over. The municipal law marked a regression in relation to the regime established after the municipal revolution of July: general assemblies of the inhabitants were forbidden. Only active citizens had the right to meet, once a year, to appoint the mayor and the municipality. Thus all municipal powers – including local taxes, and maintenance of order with the possibility of declaring martial law – were concentrated in the hands of a minority of possessors elected by a propertied suffrage. Finally, the Assembly decided

46 A. P., vol. 9, p. 479.

47 In August 1791, after the king's flight to Varennes, the Constituent Assembly withdrew the obligation of the silver *marc*. But elections to the Legislative Assembly were by then almost over, and had been conducted on the former basis.

that only active citizens had the right to enrol in the National Guard: they wanted a people both mute and disarmed.

The democratic press were unanimously against these laws. Loustalot: 'Already the pure aristocracy of the rich has been shamelessly established. Indeed, who knows if it is not already a crime to say that *the Nation is sovereign*' (*Révolutions de Paris*, no. 21); Desmoulins: 'To realize the full absurdity of this decree, suffice it to observe that Jean-Jacques Rousseau, Corneille and Mably would not have been eligible' (*Révolutions de France et de Brabant*, no. 3); Marat: 'A representation that has become proportionate to direct taxation will place the realm in the hands of the rich; and the fate of the poor, always subject, always subjugated and always oppressed, can never be improved by peaceful means . . . Besides, laws only hold sway so long as people are willing to submit to them' (*L'Ami du peuple*, no. 52; the threat is scarcely concealed).[48]

But the Constituent Assembly did not have to deal with the protests of these malcontents. It was faced with two great questions that needed tackling: the financial crisis and the administrative reorganization of the country.

Clerical property placed at the nation's disposal; the civil constitution of the clergy

Necker's last expedient – a new loan, the compulsory 'patriotic contribution' – had led to nothing, the state treasury was empty, the Caisse d'Escompte faced a shortfall of 30 million livres. It was at this point that Talleyrand, the bishop of Autun, made a remarkable proposal – to put the properties of the clergy at the disposition of the nation:

48 In April 1791, Robespierre would write one of his finest speeches, demanding that the qualification of the silver *marc* and the whole system of property qualification be abolished. Owing to systematic obstruction, this speech was never delivered in the Assembly, but it was printed and discussed in the popular societies. See Maximilien Robespierre, *Virtue and Terror*, London: Verso, 2007, pp. 5–19.

> No matter how sacred the nature of a property held under the law might be, the law can only maintain what its founders have granted. We all know that the portion of these properties that is needed for the subsistence of its beneficiaries is all that belongs to them; the rest is the property of the churches and the poor. If the nation assures this subsistence, the property of the beneficiaries is in no way attacked . . . There are 80,000 ecclesiastics in France, whose subsistence has to be assured, including 40,000 parish priests . . . who need at least 1,200 livres [per year] apiece, not including lodging.[49]

In the days that followed, this idea received strong support from Mirabeau, who proposed a decree in the following sober terms: 'It is declared that all goods of the clergy are the property of the nation, save in so far as the decency of religious practice and the subsistence of those ministering to the altars be provided for in an acceptable manner.'[50] Abbé Maury, one of the heavyweights on the right wing, eloquently asserted his opposition: 'In this crisis of runaway impiety we may confidently remind the legislative body that religion is the only solid foundation of the law . . . France is not yet reduced to the deplorable extremity of being able to avoid bankruptcy only by confiscation.'[51] In the end, on 2 November 1789 Mirabeau's motion was adopted by a fair majority of 568 votes to 346.

To implement this measure, on 19 December a Caisse de l'Extraordinaire was established, financed by the sale of ecclesiastical property (to which would later be added the funds from the sale of crown property, and above all property confiscated from émigrés, the whole ensemble being rebranded as 'national property'). To start with, 400 million livres' worth of properties were put on sale, with *assignats* issued in parallel for an equal sum. At that initial point, the *assignat* was not a unit of currency so much as a treasury bond bearing interest at 5 per cent and secured on the goods of the clergy. As

49 A. P., vol. 9, pp. 398–404.
50 Ibid., p. 415.
51 Ibid., p. 424.

these goods were sold, a corresponding quantity of *assignats* would be destroyed, which would end up in principle extinguishing the debt of the state. Unfortunately, however, that is not what happened. The transformation of the *assignat* into paper money, its steady devaluation, its hopeless competition with hard currency, and the establishment of a forced exchange rage – all these difficulties would weigh heavily on the future course of events.

By nationalizing the property of the clergy, the whole structure of the Church was turned upside down; it had to be reorganized. There was not yet any question of the separation of Church and state, still less of de-Christianization. The members of the Constituent Assembly, even if followers of Voltaire, were respectful of Catholicism, which remained the de facto dominant religion and the only one subsidized by the state. But as teaching and hospitals were in the hands of the Church, it was necessary to close down some religious establishments, otherwise the incomes from the properties sold would be spent on their operation. On 13 February 1790, the monastic orders were abolished, and soon afterward another law relieved the church of the management of its properties.

On 12 July 1790, the civil constitution of the clergy spelled out the new organization.[52] The number of dioceses was reduced from 130 to eighty-three, to coincide with the departments. Bishops, like other magistrates, would be selected by the departmental council, and priests by the electors of their district. Their investiture would no longer come from the pope, but from their superior in the hierarchy. Like all public officials, these employees of the state were required to swear loyalty to the constitution ('The appointee shall take a solemn oath, in the presence of the municipal officers, the people and the clergy, to watch over the faithful of the diocese, to be loyal to the nation, to the law and to the king, and to maintain with all his power the Constitution decreed by the National Assembly and accepted by the king.')

In an unexpected manner, it was this oath of loyalty to the Constitution that would compromise the whole arrangement. The bishops,

52 A. P., vol. 17, pp. 55–60.

traditionally Gallican, and even the king who had signed the civil constitution without demur, believed that the pope would accept the new system. But Pius VI, pressed by the émigrés and the Catholic powers, ended up rejecting it categorically in March 1791, condemning the Declaration of Rights as heretical into the bargain. From this point on, the oath became a serious matter of division among the French clergy: out of 160 bishops, only seven agreed to take the oath. Among the lower clergy who had previously been favourable to the Revolution, around a half accepted, but there were many retractions after the pope announced that he would suspend all priests who did not withdraw their oaths. This gave rise to a serious religious schism, which would be of great benefit to the counter-revolution.

Administrative reorganization, the departments

The administrative and judicial reorganization carried out from November 1789 to January 1790 aroused less opposition. The Assembly voted to divide the country into 83 *départements*, whose boundaries, following Mirabeau's idea, were – and remain – drawn, not with a ruler like many North American states, but following borders inspired by physical geography and the pattern of the former provinces. The electoral assembly of each department was to elect a council of thirty-six members, who appointed a directorate of eight members responsible for the departmental administration – without a representative or any control from the central power. The department was divided into cantons, and the canton into communes. This was a system of property-based decentralization, which gave great autonomy of management to the possessor class. 'It is no longer possible to doubt,' wrote Loustalot in December 1789, 'that the will of the twelve hundred [of the Assembly] is simply the will of the municipalities, that is, of the rich families, and does not uphold the will of the communes.'

The reform of the judiciary abolished all existing jurisdictions, in particular the Parlements (invited to 'remain on leave'), establishing a hierarchy of courts that followed the new administrative divisions:

a justice of the peace for each canton, elected for two years from among all those 'eligible' on the basis of a tax liability of ten days' wages, a district court, and in the departmental capital a criminal court for penal matters that operated with a dual popular jury, one for investigation (charged with determining whether prosecution should take place) and the other for judgement. The jurors would be drawn by lot, and professional judges appointed by the electoral assemblies, choosing from those with legal qualifications. Measures were taken to protect the accused: court appearance within twenty-four hours of arrest, suppression of the 'question' (torture), compulsory presence of an advocate, public trials, penalties that were equal for all.

This set of reforms, no matter how 'bourgeois' in terms of property qualification, was striking in its scope. The Assembly, a disparate set of landowners, rentiers, nobles, advocates and priests, managed to construct a coherent system on the ruins of the Ancien Régime, one that was both decentralized and unified, democratic in appearance and aristocratic/anti-popular in reality. And despite all the modifications made since, it is still in the spirit of the Constituent Assembly that we are living two centuries later.

Economic liberalism

In order to understand how close this Assembly was to what is today called 'liberalism',[53] the most telling aspect is its economic policy, bent above all on liberalizing trade and finance. Trade in grain had already been deregulated in August 1789, but from September the price of wheat could be set with no legal limit, which benefited the large producers but made it difficult to supply the poor peasants and the towns, especially as prices were rising steadily. Free movement of goods throughout the territory was established step by step by

53 This word only appeared some thirty years later, under the Restoration. 'Liberals' such as Benjamin Constant were then champions of economic freedom, but also of political freedom, in particular that of the press.

suppressing the *gabelle*, internal duties, and the tolls at city gates, but here again, the expected reduction in prices did not take place. The Bourse operated freely, and large-scale trade was favoured by the removal of the trading companies' or city monopolies, such as that of the Compagnie des Indes for trade beyond the Cape of Good Hope, or the privilege of Marseille for trade with the Levant, etc. The power of businessmen in the Assembly, however, managed to maintain the so-called 'exclusive' system: the colonies (essentially Saint-Domingue, the world's leading producer of sugar) were still allowed to trade only with the metropolis.

The rapid rise in the price of wheat, the slow progress – and even regression – with regard to feudal rights,[54] the reactionary attitude of lords who called in all arrears and generated hundreds of lawsuits in the villages, the impossibility for the great majority of peasants to acquire the lands confiscated from the Church – this sum of disappointments and frustrations led to a new upsurge of violence in the countryside in the early months of 1790. In February, Grégoire, as rapporteur of the committee on feudalism, reported that insurrection was spreading. Thirty-seven châteaux had been burned in Brittany. In January the town of Sarlat had been invaded by peasants who had opened the prison, freed their companions inside, and put the lord in jail instead. In the Bourbonnais, Charolais and Nivernais, rebel peasants demanded the fixing of grain prices and an 'agrarian law' (the division of lands). 'Brigands' invaded the town of Decize. At Saint-Étienne de Forez the people killed a hoarder and appointed a new municipality, which it forced to reduce the price of bread.[55]

By 2 June, the Assembly was downright panic-stricken at the 'disorders' in the countryside, particularly in the Limousin and the

---

54 The Assembly made redemption almost impossible for the peasants, by making each feudal charge redeemable only as an indivisible sum. On top of this, on 15 March 1790 it passed a law that made it compulsory to redeem rights that the lord could prove he had held for more than thirty years. 'If peasants rebelling in August 1789 had forced a lord to renounce certain of his rights, or had burned his titles, now he needed only produce proof of possession for thirty years for these rights to be re-established' (P. Sagnac, *La législation civile de la Révolution française*, Paris: Hachette, 1898, pp. 105–6).

55 On this new '*jacquerie*', see Pëtr Kropotkin, *The Great French Revolution* [1909], theanarchistlibrary.org, chapter 16.

region of Tulle. 'How can it possibly be a crime' – demanded the Tulle deputies – 'to open fire, without having read the proclamation of martial law, on people caught *in flagrante delicto*, gathered in a crowd of seven or eight hundred, piercing the dykes and causeways of ponds, pillaging châteaux, etc.?' The repressive law now voted was preceded by a preamble that says much about the fears of the people's representatives:

> The National Assembly, informed of and deeply afflicted by the excesses that have been committed by gangs of brigands and thieves in the departments of Cher, Nièvre and Allier, and that have spread to that of Corrèze, excesses that attack the public tranquillity as well as properties and possessions, the safety and boundaries of houses and inheritances, that sow terror everywhere and would quickly lead, if they were not repressed, to the calamity of famine . . .

The final decree stipulated that: 'All those who excite the people of town and country to action and violence against properties, possessions, and boundaries of patrimonies, the life and safety of citizens, the collection of taxes, and the free sale and circulation of goods, are hereby declared enemies of the Constitution, of the work of the National Assembly, of Nature and of the King.'[56]

Martial law would be proclaimed against them, with tens of deaths and hundreds imprisoned. In Lyon, the tension between a militia recruited by the possessor class and the National Guard led to a riot in which the arsenal was raided and arms distributed to the population. The city's elite was forced to give in; it dissolved its militia and agreed to make a large number of plebeians into active citizens.

56 *Le Moniteur*, vol. 4, p. 539.

The foreign plot

Among the causes of these popular rebellions was one particular fear: that of a counter-revolutionary plot in the royal entourage, a foreign invasion, a vengeful return of the émigrés. This fear was not unfounded. In Turin, the comte d'Artois was organizing an uprising in the south of France. At Montauban in May 1790, and at Nîmes in June, there were confrontations between royalist Catholics and Protestant patriots. In August, 20,000 National Guards holed up in the château of Jalès, in the Ardèche, with the cross as their flag and the white cockade on their hats. The leaders of this movement launched a manifesto, proclaiming that they would not lay down their weapons before having 're-established the king in his glory, the clergy in its possessions, the nobility in its honours, the Parlements in their former functions'. The encampment at Jalès would not be forcibly dissolved until February 1791.

Such was the background noise of this period, sometimes described as a time of calm and reconciliation – and indeed experienced in this way by many contemporaries, despite the warnings given by Marat:

> When I hear Parisians singing their victories, when I see them regarding the enemies of the revolution as a defeated party, floored and disabled, when I see them prostrate themselves before the National Assembly and worship every one of its decrees, swearing to uphold them to the death and blessing Providence for the great work of the Constitution, it is like hearing a man at death's door, peacefully congratulating himself on his good health.[57]

The Fête de la Fédération

The crucial event, inflated to mythic levels to celebrate that rediscovered unanimity, was the Fête de la Fédération, a great festival

---

57 *L'Ami du peuple*, 8 July 1790. Marat had just returned from England, where he had fled after an arrest warrant was issued against him.

organized for the first anniversary of the storming of the Bastille. It had been preceded by a series of local federations between patriotic National Guards, in the Dauphiné, in Brittany, in Alsace and in the Nord: mutual assistance and fraternal friendship were sworn. For example, a letter sent from Saint-Omer on 1 June noted that

> Detachments of National Guard from Boulogne, Calais, Ardres and Andrecies passed through here yesterday on their way to Arras in order to form a federal pact of all the National Guard of the Pas-de-Calais department, and from there on to Lille, to a general federation of all those of the Belgian provinces. They were given a very fine meal, attended by every corps, at which the officers of the Provence regiment mingled fraternally with their soldiers and their drummers.[58]

The Assembly decided to profit from this movement while at the same time controlling it. The symbolic value that the moment has preserved to this day is due in large measure to the account of it given by Michelet: 'Fraternity overcame every obstacle, all the federations came to bind together, a union tending to unity. No more federations, they are not needed, only one is needed, that of France. It appears transfigured in the light of July.'[59]

Michelet describes the work on the Champ-de-Mars to create the hill on which the altar of the *patrie* would be erected: 'The whole population took part. It was an amazing spectacle. By day and by night, men of all classes and ages, even children, everybody, citizens, soldiers, priests, monks, actors, sisters of mercy, fine ladies, market women, all wielded an axe, rolled a barrow or pulled a cart.'[60] He relates the day of the Fête with its 'bold and stubborn gaiety' despite driving rain, the 160,000 people packed on the tiers of the Champ-de-Mars, the 50,000 armed men showing off their paces in the great amphitheatre, Lafayette on his white horse, Talleyrand officiating in

58 *Le Moniteur*, vol. 4, p. 550.

59 Michelet, *Histoire de la Révolution française* [1847], Paris: Robert Laffont, 1999, vol. 1, p. 324.

60 Ibid., p. 335.

the midst of two hundred priests wearing the tricolour sash, the 1,200 musicians. Suddenly 'a silence fell: the fire of forty cannon made the ground shake. At this clap of thunder all rose and raised their hands to the sky . . . O king, o people! Wait . . . the sky was listening, the sun deliberately broke through the cloud . . . Be sure to keep your oaths!'[61]

In the days that followed, a section of the press echoed the upbeat mood. Brissot, in *Le Patriote français* of 17 July: 'This people that blessed the revolution, that shook our hands as we went,[62] encouraged us with their cries . . . One could read the pleasure felt by brothers on seeing their brothers, slaves casting off their fetters.' Or again, the same day, in *Les Annales patriotiques*: '80,000 armed men, representing more than 3 million, formed for themselves and for their representatives a fearsome alliance, eternal, invincible, and worthy at last of the great sentiments of human reason.' But there were others who were not fooled – always the same ones, in fact. Loustalot, who faithfully followed the feelings of the people:

> A king who braves the heaviest rain when hunting, but on account of the rain will not walk beside the law-making and arms-bearing representatives of the nation, who does not take the trouble to go from his throne to the altar to give his people, who allow him 25 million livres, the satisfaction of seeing him take an oath there . . . The conquerors of the Bastille are ignored, and not a word, not the least homage in memory of those who, on such a day, perished beneath the walls of that dreadful fortress.[63]

And Marat, on 16 July, in *L'Ami du peuple*:

> Immediately after the universal oath comes a great *Te Deum* to thank the Supreme Being for all the benefits that have been showered on France since the Revolution. It is scarcely surprising that

61 Ibid., p. 339.

62 Brissot was a member of the Commune, for the district of Les Filles-Saint-Thomas.

63 *Les Révolutions de Paris*, no. 53, 17 July 1790.

> the city administration, Bailly and all the rogues that handle major affairs, dream only of prosperity and happiness; they are swimming in opulence . . . Do they think to impose, by means of this false image of public felicity, on men who have constantly before their eyes the hordes of the destitute and the multitude of citizens reduced to beggary by the revolution? Do they flatter themselves that their scandalous wastefulness will be pardoned if they speak of public happiness?

The status of actors and Jews

The Constituent Assembly, united in this celebration of fraternity, was by no means so on the subject of those excluded from the status of citizen: in France, actors and Jews; in the colonies, freemen of colour and slaves (see 'Excursus', p. 138).

On 23 December 1789, Clermont-Tonnerre had argued that 'profession and religion can never be grounds for ineligibility'.[64] He proposed a vote on the notion that 'no active citizen combining the conditions of eligibility required by the law will be kept off the list of the eligible, or excluded from public functions, by reason of the profession he practises or the religion he professes.'[65] On the subject of actors, abbé Maury spoke rather weakly against the decree: 'Morality is the first law; the theatrical profession fundamentally violates this law, by removing a son from paternal authority.' On Jews he was far more incisive:

> The Jews have gone through seventeen centuries without mixing with other nations. They have never done anything but trade in money; they have been the plague of agricultural provinces; none of them has been able to ennoble his hands by guiding the plough . . . In Alsace they have 12 million livres of mortgages on

64 It should be remembered that 'eligibility' meant the right to vote in the primary assemblies, that is, the status of active citizen.

65 A. P., vol. 10, pp. 754–8. The excluded professions also included that of executioner, on which there scarcely seems to have been any discussion.

> lands. In a month they will own half that province; in ten years they will have conquered it entirely, it will be no more than a Jewish colony. The people have a hatred for the Jews that this expansion will be sure to bring to bursting point. For their sake, we need not deliberate this point.

To which Robespierre replied:

> How can [the Jews] be blamed for the persecutions that different peoples have inflicted on them? . . . They are furthermore charged with vices, prejudices, sectarian spirit and self-interest. But what can we ascribe these to, except our own injustice? Having debarred them from all honours, even the right to public esteem, we have left them no other goal than that of financial speculation. Let us restore them to happiness, to the *patrie*, to virtue, by restoring to them the dignity of men and of citizens.

On 24 December, the Assembly passed Clermont-Tonnerre's decree 'without intending to prejudge anything relating to the Jews, on whose state the National Assembly will pronounce at a later date'. The Jews of the Midi obtained civil rights on 28 January 1790, and those of Alsace after the end of the Constituent Assembly, in December 1791.

CHAPTER 5

July 1790 to September 1791

The Nancy massacre, the flight to Varennes, the massacre on the Champ-de-Mars, repression

The account of Louis XVI's arrest at Varennes arrived this morning via M. le duc de Choiseul, peer of France. The narrowness of mind at the time, the moral pettiness of those people, a fine contrast with the natural spirit of Drouet in arresting the king. It is certainly attention to a thousand little things that shrank Louis XVI's poor mind still more.

– Stendhal, *Journal*

Revolt and repression in Nancy

The soldiers' revolt in Nancy, the most serious and bloody incident of the year 1790, broke out only a month after the great festival of fraternity. Discontent had been brewing in the army; the officers, all aristocrats, were annoyed at seeing their men on good terms with the population, attending local assemblies, organizing committees and fraternizing with the National Guard, for whom these nobles had scant consideration. But times had changed, and patriotic soldiers were beginning to demand justice from their officers, who were responsible for paying them but kept a veil of secrecy over the accounts. Instances of embezzlement soon came to light, but instead of the anticipated restitution a shower of punishments rained down. Revolts broke out in several garrisons – Lille, Strasbourg, the Toulon arsenal and Marseille. But the most dramatic of these took place in Nancy, in August 1790, in the region commanded by the marquis de Bouillé, cousin and friend of Lafayette.[1]

There were three regiments here, two French (the king's regiment and that of the Mestre-de-Camp) and one Swiss, the Châteauvieux's regiment made up of men from Geneva and the Vaud. It was remembered for playing a major role in July 1789, when its troops, stationed on the Champ-de-Mars, had said they would not fire on the people. Seeing their French friends demand accounts from their officers, they thought to do the same. But the Swiss patricians, who were by law supreme judges over their men, had the two soldiers who came to bring them the demand arrested and publicly whipped. Outraged, the patriotic soldiers and Nancy National Guards went to find the two Swiss soldiers, marched them through the streets in a lap of honour, and forced the officers to pay each of them 100 *louis d'or* by way of indemnity. At the same time, the two French regiments sent an eight-man delegation to the National Assembly, requesting a clarification of the accounts.

Lafayette opted for the big stick. He had the eight delegates arrested, and urged the Assembly to pass a decree enjoining the soldiers to recognize their error and express their repentance. At the same time, he sent Bouillé an order to repress the mutiny by force. Bouillé appointed a certain Malseigne to check the accounts, a man better known as a fencer than a calculator. No sooner had this swashbuckler arrived than he went to the quarters of the Swiss and provoked them, then ran off to seek refuge with the Lunéville carabineers, shouting that there had been an attempt on his life – the carabineers quickly handed him over to their friends in Nancy.

---

1 The region was already tense, as Austrian forces were active across the border, crushing the revolution in Brabant.

Bouillé had the pretext he needed. Assembling the garrison and a part of the Metz National Guard, he advanced towards Nancy. On 31 August he was at the city gates and imposed conditions: Malseigne was to be released, and the regiments to come out and each hand over four of their comrades – a terrible condition for the Swiss, who could only expect the worst. The two French regiments submitted and left the city, but Châteauvieux refused to surrender. Reinforced by a section of the National Guard and the people of Nancy, it occupied the Stainville gate, the only one that was fortified. Bouillé's hussars attacked, took the gate and occupied the town under heavy fire from the windows. By evening, however, order was restored and hundreds of corpses lay in the streets. This was followed by the 'legal' repression: twenty-one Swiss soldiers were hanged, and one broken on the wheel. Fifty prisoners from Châteauvieux's regiment were sent to Brest and on to the galleys.[2] The political clubs in Nancy were closed, and Bouillé imposed martial law throughout the region.

The king and the Assembly were unanimous in their congratulations to Bouillé, and the Paris National Guard held a funeral ceremony on the Champ-de-Mars in honour of the victors killed in the battle. But the people of Paris showed their anger on 2 and 3 September, to cries of 'Down with the ministers!'[3] Loustalot wrote an article that was to be his last word, as he died suddenly a short while after:

> We dare to accuse M. de Bouillé, we denounce him to the French people, not just for his criminal offence against the nation but for his crime against humanity . . . You ordered bloodshed without being forced to so do; you were moved neither by the tears of the unhappy inhabitants of city distraught at the impending siege, nor by the humble supplications of repentant soldiers who came and laid down their arms at your feet. Tiger! You needed blood to assuage your aristocratic rage, and you bathed with delight in the blood of patriots.[4]

---

2 They would be released and rehabilitated by the Legislative Assembly.

3 This was aimed particularly at Necker and above all Montmorin, held responsible for the repression.

4 *Les Révolutions de Paris*, no. 53.

In the wake of the Nancy affair, the popularity of Lafayette, who was rightly held to bear the main responsibility for it, steadily declined among the people, as did that of the king, the ministers, and the Assembly that had approved the crackdown.

The flight of the king and his arrest at Varennes

In our own day, when 'politics' no longer arouses so much passion, it is hard to imagine what went on in people's minds when each day brought fresh rumours and surprises. It is particularly difficult to understand the depth and the ramification of *fears* among the people: fear of an émigré plot, fear of the machinations of aristocrats and priests, fear of foreign intervention and, recurrent since summer 1789, fear lest the king run away. Counter-revolutionary historians have portrayed these fears as the expression of a paranoia orchestrated by journalists, with Marat at their head, no matter that all these fears turned out to be well-founded in due course, particularly that of an attempted escape on the part of the king.

During summer and autumn 1789, the king's entourage had pressed Louis to flee on several occasions, but he had always refused. In spring 1791, two new factors led him to change his mind. First of all, the death of Mirabeau on 2 April; since becoming a paid adviser to the king, Mirabeau had exerted what influence he still had to persuade Louis to accept the Constitution. The Lameth brothers offered to replace him and the king accepted their services, but he hated and distrusted them, with the result that Mirabeau's death left Louis under the thumb of Marie-Antoinette, who saw escape abroad as the only solution. The second factor was the pope's rejection of the civil constitution of the clergy. Having accepted this himself, Louis XVI found himself in a delicate situation, particularly as far as his personal religious practice was concerned. On 17 April 1791, for example, he took communion in his private chapel from the hands of cardinal de Montmorency, who like almost all the high prelates had refused to take the oath. The National Guard who were in attendance made this known. The following day, Easter Saturday, Louis expressed his intention to go to Saint-Cloud. A great crowd, convinced that the king was seeking to avoid an Easter ceremony celebrated by a constitutional priest, and fearing that this departure would be simply the prelude to another, lengthier journey, blocked the road out of the Tuileries. Lafayette ordered the National Guard to clear a passage, but the guards refused to obey their general-in-chief. The crowd attacked the gentlemen-in-waiting and bodyguards, and the royal family were ultimately forced to return to the palace on foot, amid a hail of insults. After this, what remained of the royal court in the Tuileries was dismantled: nobles and bishops were forbidden to stay there, and the royal couple were now surrounded only by a revolutionary guard and domestic servants.

Louis justly felt himself to be a prisoner, and it was then that he accepted the plan drawn up by Axel von Fersen, a Swedish nobleman on intimate terms with the queen. The royal family would make for the Montmédy fortress in Lorraine, held by Bouillé's troops, and close to Belgium that was now occupied by the Austrian army. This departure would mark the beginning of an intervention by the European powers led by Emperor Leopold of Austria, Marie-Antoinette's brother.[5]

What followed has become part of the popular imaginary of the Revolution. On the night of 20 June, the king and the queen, together with their two children, the children's governess and Madame Élisabeth, the king's sister, secretly left the Tuileries and boarded a hired carriage – the only part of the plan that went without a hitch – which exited from Paris through the Saint-Martin barrier (now place Stalingrad) and took the road for Meaux. At a country rendezvous the heavy *berline* that Fersen had had specially constructed was waiting, and Fersen himself acted as coachman at the start of the

---

5 Prussia and Austria met together at Reichenbach in July 1790, under English mediation. Breteuil, who acted in exile as Louis XVI's foreign minister, sought a coalition with these two powers, along with Spain, Russia, Sweden, the pope and the Catholic Swiss cantons. But Leopold played for time, refusing Louis the 15 million he had requested, and decided that if he did send troops, it would only be when the king and queen had left Paris and published a manifesto rejecting the constitution.

journey. Very soon, however, things ceased to go according to plan.[6] Bouillé's hussars, who were supposed to await the fugitives after Châlons and escort them to Montmédy, did not turn up. Nor were they at Sainte-Menehould, where the horses were changed under the eye of the postmaster, a certain Drouet. At eleven in the evening the carriage reached Varennes, where neither the hussars nor the expected change of horses were to be seen. Drouet arrived shortly after, having recognized the king, he later said, from a fifty-livre *assignat* that bore his portrait. The tocsin was sounded, the bridge over the Aire was blocked, the town's patriots were woken and the National Guard alerted. The royal family spent the night in the home of a grocer named Sauce, the commune *procureur*, and in the early morning they started back to Paris.

All these episodes have been related and illustrated a hundred times over. But how to explain that the small town of Varennes dared to prevent the king from continuing his journey to the frontier? What moved these people to take the enormous risk of a confrontation with Bouillé's hussars – a risk they took knowingly, as the Nancy affair was fresh in every mind? Timothy Tackett has provided some elements of an answer.[7] Like thousands of small French towns, Varennes had formed a citizens' militia in summer 1789: two companies, each with its uniform – the *chasseurs* in green, the *grenadiers* in blue – its flags, and its officers (the inn-keeper, the lawyer's son), elected by their men. And in March 1791 a local branch of the Amis de la Constitution had been founded, affiliated to the Jacobins club in Paris. They had recently removed the parish priest from his office after he refused to take the constitutional oath. Whenever an emergency arose, all the small towns and villages of the region, similarly organized, sent reinforcements of every kind. Thus 'the small, undistinctive town of Varennes', Tackett writes, 'was far better prepared – institutionally, militarily, and psychologically – to meet the crisis of June 21 than any of the conspirators of

6 For a detailed and vivid description of the flight to Varennes, see Mona Ozouf, *Varennes, la mort de la royauté*, Paris: Gallimard, 2005.

7 Timothy Tackett, *When the King Took Flight*, Cambridge: Harvard University Press, 2004.

the king's flight might have imagined.'[8] More generally, the failure of all the aristocratic intrigues and plots was undoubtedly due to the failure to grasp the transformations that had taken place in popular mentality and organization.

On the return journey, envoys from the Assembly[9] who had come from Paris took up position in the royal carriage, initially accompanied by 6,000 National Guard from the nearby towns. But 'as they made their way west, country people converged from every direction: men, women, and children, often whole villages arriving en masse, in carts or on foot, carrying every conceivable weapon.'[10] In the Paris faubourgs, the crowd that had initially been just curious turned aggressive. The deputies thought it too dangerous to follow the direct route and decided to skirt round the city: the carriage reached the Tuileries via the Roule gate and the Champs-Élysées. 'On the place Louis XV the statue's eyes had been covered, so that the humiliating symbol would represent to Louis XVI the blindness of the monarchy. The heavy German carriage rolled slowly like a hearse, its blinds half down; it looked like the monarchy's funeral procession.'[11]

Anger in Paris; the king on trial?

In Paris, amazement rapidly gave way to anger. The lengthy 'Declaration from the king addressed to all the French upon his leaving Paris', which Louis XVI had left behind on his departure, was read out in the National Assembly, then posted in the streets; in it he wrote that he had accepted the laws and decisions of the Assembly only under duress: 'What remains for the king, other than the vain simulacrum of monarchy? . . . Would you wish the anarchy and despotism of the clubs to replace the monarchical government under

8 Ibid., p. 16.

9 These were Pétion, Barnave and La Tour-Maubourg. Michelet claims it was then that Barnave fell under the spell of the queen. Whatever the reason, this marked the beginning of his sharp turn to the right.

10 Tackett, *When the King Took Flight*, p. 79.

11 Michelet, *Histoire de la Révolution française*, vol. 1, p. 507.

which the nation has prospered for 1,400 years?' After listing all the vexations he had suffered, Louis concluded: 'Given all these reasons, and the impossibility in which the king finds himself of acting for the good and preventing the harm that is being committed, is it surprising that the king should seek to regain his freedom and place himself in safety along with his family?'[12]

The king's perjury and false oath were clear enough. In no. 61 of Hébert's *Père Duchesne*, a dialogue expressed the feeling of the people:

> 'How are you, Père Duchesne, my good friend,' the great lout says to me.
>
> 'Good friend you say, you bleeding coward, friends, are we, after what you've just done? You clapped-out hypocrite! Putting me and everyone else in the shit. I knew well enough you were a blockhead, but I didn't realize you were the biggest scoundrel and most abominable of men!'
>
> 'Cheeky rogue,' the drunkard replies, 'remember that you're speaking to your king.'
>
> 'My king, are you! Not anymore! You're just a cowardly deserter; a king must be the father of the people and not their executioner. A nation that has come into its rights won't be fool enough to take back a capon like you. You, king? You're not even a citizen, and you'll be fortunate enough if, for wanting to slaughter millions of men, you don't end up with your head on the block.'

Within a matter of hours, portraits, busts, signs, coats of arms, all the symbols of monarchy disappeared from the city. But the movement was not confined to hostility towards the monarchy; the idea of a republic, limited until that point to small circles of intellectuals, suddenly burst into broad daylight. As early as 21 June, the Cordeliers club addressed a petition to the Assembly that was read by Desmoulins:

> It no longer exists, this pretence of a convention between a people and its king. Louis has abdicated the throne; now Louis means

12 A. P., vol. 27, pp. 378–83.

> nothing to us, unless he becomes our enemy. Here we are then at the same point as we were when the Bastille was taken: free and without a king. It remains to be seen whether it is advantageous to appoint another . . . We beseech you, in the name of the *patrie*, either to declare right away that France is no longer a monarchy, but rather a republic; or, at least, to wait for all the departments, all the primary assemblies, to express their desire on this important question, before thinking of plunging the finest realm in the world into the chains and trammels of monarchy for a second time.[13]

This petition, posted on Paris walls the next day, received the enthusiastic approval of fraternal societies in Paris and of many societies in the provinces.

On 23 June, the celebration of Fête-Dieu (Corpus Christi) around Saint-Germain-l'Auxerrois spontaneously turned into a popular rally to celebrate the news of the king's arrest. Religious music was replaced by patriotic songs, including the new '*Ça ira!*' Finally, the National Guard, who took part in the parade along with the deputies, asked to follow these to the National Assembly and swear an oath to the Constitution. And in the evening thousands of Parisians, grouped by *quartiers* or fraternal societies, flocked to the Salle du Manège to take the oath themselves. For two hours they filed past to the sound of music played by an improvised orchestra that took up position in the benches left empty on the right side: 'Marching through the hall, six abreast, were butchers and colliers and fishwives, bakers with loaves of bread on the end of pikes, and stocky porters [from the Halles] with their large round hats . . .'; 'in one door and out another, joining in the songs and raising their hands to shout "I so swear!" as they passed in front of the Assembly's president.'[14]

The next day, 24 June, a great crowd gathered on place Vendôme to bring the Assembly a petition 'of 30,000 citizens' drafted by the Cordeliers. Lafayette had positioned a detachment of National Guard in the square, complete with cannon. The demonstrators appointed

13 Mathiez, *Le Club des Cordeliers*, p. 47.

14 Tackett, *When the King Took Flight*, pp. 107, 106.

seven delegates to take the petition to the Assembly. Beauharnais, who was in the chair, put it aside. It was only read the next day by a secretary, in a manner designed not to be heard.

Over the days that followed, the Cordeliers and fraternal societies kept up their pressure, organizing public debates and sending petition after petition that violently attacked Bailly, Lafayette, the liberticidal laws recently passed by the Assembly and the property-based electoral system: 'If you do not set the date for universal sanction of the law by the absolute totality of citizens, if you do not end the cruel demarcation you have drawn with your decree of the silver *marc*, if you do not get rid of these different degrees of eligibility that so blatantly violate your Declaration of the rights of man, then the *patrie* is in danger.'[15]

The Assembly was all the more terrified in that Paris workers were causing trouble independently: there were strikes by typographers, carpenters, blacksmiths . . . Every day in July, the National Guard were required in the faubourgs to quell these movements.

And this was not the only reason for concern. It was widely believed that the king's attempted flight was a portent of war with the European powers. In *L'Ami du roi*, abbé Royou, a royalist pamphleteer, wrote on 28 June: 'We are no longer for our neighbours simply an object of pity for our misfortunes, we have become for them a veritable plague; we have become born enemies of all authorities that had up to now been regarded as legitimate; and it is we ourselves who have summoned up all the powers of the earth and forced them to ally against us.' The Assembly had the frontiers closed, mobilized National Guards in the north and east, and decreed the raising of 100,000 volunteers. Representatives of the people went off to inspect fortresses and arsenals.

These fears, moreover, were not unfounded. On 6 July, the Habsburg emperor had written to all the European sovereigns asking them to join him 'in reclaiming the liberty and honour of the most Christian king and his family, and setting limits to the dangerous extremities of the French Revolution'. But this coalition did not

15 Ibid., p. 31.

happen, and the emperor was reduced, together with the Prussian king Friedrich-Wilhelm, to issuing the very cautious Pillnitz declaration on 27 August. The two sovereigns declared themselves ready to intervene, but only if the other powers joined in as well. This declaration was clearly only a matter of form, but it had a great resonance in French public opinion.

Besides the agitation in France and the foreign threat, there was a third reason that motivated the Assembly to keep Louis XVI on the throne; after months of work, it was putting the final touches to the Constitution, and did not want to see the result of its efforts compromised. The representatives agreed on urgent temporary measures to keep the government functioning without the king. They abolished the royal assent to decrees, so that those awaiting this had immediate force of law. They entrusted executive power to the ministers in place and the committees of the Assembly. But this unity would not hold: the right wing wanted the king to be rapidly restored to his duties.

To appease the furious indignation aroused by his flight – and even more by the letter he left behind – it was quickly put about, on Bailly's initiative, that the king had really been abducted, and so was not guilty of any crime. Already, on 21 June, Beauharnais had opened the session from the presidential chair with the words: 'I have a very sad piece of news to announce. M. Bailly just came to my home to tell me that the king and members of his family were taken away tonight by enemies of the public good.' The deputies that followed him all spoke in similar terms, until a certain Gouvion, the officer responsible for the guard at the Tuileries, struck a different note, referring to 'activity that indicated, on the part of the queen, the project of leaving along with the dauphin and Madame Royale'. The word 'abduction' then gave way to that of 'departure', without that of 'flight' yet being spoken.[16]

Rejecting this convenient excuse, the left side of the Assembly held that the king should be prosecuted; but even the Jacobins were divided. Robespierre violently accused 'the near totality of my colleagues, members of the Assembly', of being 'counter-revolutionaries: some

16 *Le Moniteur*, vol. 8, pp. 715–9.

through ignorance, others through fear, some through resentment and injured pride, but others because they are corrupt'.[17] The majority of the club, however, led by Charles Lameth, Barnave and Sieyès, preferred to deal with the crisis by a policy of reconciliation.

The Assembly charged seven of its committees with presenting a report on the Varennes events, which was adopted on 15 July after a lengthy discussion on the inviolability of the king. Grégoire spoke in favour of prosecution ('The highest public official deserts his post and equips himself with a false passport, . . . he breaks his word, and leaves the French people a declaration contrary to the principles of our liberty . . .'), whereas Barnave argued for moderation, mentioning the threat of civil war. Finally it was decided that the king would not go on trial, but that his powers would remain suspended until the Constitution was completed. He would only recover them if he accepted this, including its final modifications. In the contrary case he would be deposed.[18]

The massacre on the Champ-de-Mars; the 'tricolour terror'

When they saw that the National Assembly committees were determined to absolve the king, the Cordeliers resorted to threats. In an *Appel à la Nation* written by Chaumette on 12 July, they invited the electoral assemblies to appoint a 'national directory', a new government not envisaged in the Constitution.[19] They were seconded in this by the fraternal societies; that which met at the Jacobins launched an address to the French people on 13 July, urging them to 'reclaim the exercise of sovereign power'. *Les Révolutions de Paris* clearly threatened deputies with lynching: 'Remember well that Launay [the governor of the Bastille whose head was paraded on a pike] had committed no other crime than that of supporting *your* Louis XVI in

17 *Les Révolutions de France et de Brabant*, no. 82; Tackett, *When the King Took Flight*, p. 136.

18 A. P., vol. 28, p. 311ff.

19 Mathiez, *Le Club des Cordeliers*, p. 108. The following quotations are all from this book unless explicitly stated.

the face of public opinion . . . We have only too much reason to fear that the present senate seeks to perpetuate its dominion; if it resists, there are cases when *insurrection is the holiest of duties.*'[20] On 16 July, Hébert entitled his article 'Great anger of Père Duchesne against the traitors of the National Assembly who want to hand back the crown to Gilles Capet, the former king of France'.

The Assembly decided to stand up to the petitioners, whom it now regarded as nothing but trouble-makers. It called on the backing of large bodies of troops, and asked Lafayette and Bailly to show the greatest firmness. On the evening of 15 July, the Cordeliers who had been rebuffed in the Assembly proceeded en masse to the Jacobins, enjoining the club's members to support their decision no longer to recognize Louis XVI as king, unless the departments when consulted decided otherwise. A great tumult ensued, which marked the beginning of a split in the Jacobins club; almost all the deputies present left the room, vowing never to return.

The day of the 16th was spent in preparing a giant petition for signature on the altar of the *patrie*, with or without the Jacobins.[21] The planned procession was to assemble on the place de la Bastille and cross Paris to reach the Champ-de-Mars. But on the morning of Sunday 17 July, Lafayette had the square occupied by the National Guard. The procession could not take place, and the demonstrators, an estimated 20,000 people, reached the Champ-de-Mars in scattered groups, calm and without arms.[22] Copies of the petition were distributed at different points on the wide expanse and were signed by a large number, from all strata of the Paris population, including

---

20 *Les Révolutions de Paris*, no. 105, certainly written by Chaumette.

21 These withdrew their signatures at the last minute, so that the final version was actually written on the spot by François Robert, a long-time republican, on his knee. It demanded 'in the name of the whole of France that this decree [absolving the king] be revoked, taking into consideration that the crime of Louis XVI is proven, that the king has abdicated; accepting his abdication, and convening a new constituent body to proceed to a judgement of the guilty party and above all to the replacement and organization of a new executive power'.

22 Before the arrival of the demonstrators, local inhabitants had noticed two individuals hidden beneath the altar. Accused of seeking to place a bomb, they were lynched by the crowd and decapitated. The incident would be used as a pretext for the proclamation of martial law.

those unable to write their name. An estimated 6,000 signatures had been collected by the time things began to deteriorate.

Around three o'clock, a few stones were thrown at Lafayette's aides-de-camp on their way to the École Militaire. Lafayette used this pretext to move his troops towards the Champ-de-Mars, where he set up two cannon. During this time, under pressure from the Assembly, Bailly proclaimed martial law. At six o'clock the Paris municipal council set out from the Hôtel de Ville towards the Champ-de-Mars, escorted by infantry and cavalry detachments. At their head, the red flag was carried by the colonel of the city guards. In the rue Saint-Dominique, Lafayette took up position beside the flag.

Around the altar of the *patrie*, the organizers of the demonstration calmed the crowd, saying that they would disperse at the first summons. But no such summons was given:[23] instead, a pistol shot gave the signal for a massacre. The National Guard responded to stones with a hail of bullets. The demonstrators fled, some towards the river where the cavalry was waiting for them, others towards the plaine de Grenelle were they were met by musket fire.

Bailly estimated the dead at around a dozen. Marat for his part asserted that 400 corpses had been thrown into the Seine. Chaumette, in *Les Révolutions de Paris*, gave the number at around fifty. In the evening, the Cordeliers found the doors of their premises closed when they arrived for a meeting. Two cannon prevented them from entering. The repression had begun.

On the following day, 18 July, Bailly and the city council gave their version of events to the Assembly:

> This part of the glacis [on the side of the Gros Caillou] and the part on the same side that extends towards the river were full of rebels who insulted the National Guard, threw stones, and even fired shots from muskets and pistols. The National Guard used the power given by Article 7 [of the martial law decree]: it deployed

23 Bailly subsequently recognized this, in the Assembly (see below) and at his trial before the revolutionary tribunal. He would also be criticized for not having marched at the head of the armed force as the law specified.

> force because the most criminal violence had made a summons impossible; and it was here that the most of the firing occurred.[24]

Charles Lameth, presiding, congratulated the mayor and praised the National Guard. A decree on sedition – with retroactive effect – was voted that very morning: its second article provided that 'Any person who, in a gathering or riot, is heard to issue a cry of provocation to murder, will be punished with three years in chains if the murder was not committed, and as an accomplice to murder if it was.' Over the following days, the investigation committee and the Paris departmental council collaborated on raids and arrests, particularly among the editors and printers of *Le Père Duchesne*, *L'Orateur du peuple* and *L'Ami du peuple*. On 9 August, the public prosecutor demanded a series of arrests, particularly those of Desmoulins, Santerre, Robert, Momoro, Danton, Fabre d'Églantine and others . . . What Mathiez called the 'tricolour terror' would last until the general amnesty of 14 September.

The split in the Jacobins club

The dead of the Champ-de-Mars were not the only victims of that day. What also died was such understanding as still remained between the possessor classes and the poor, between those who had come to power on the shoulders of the people and those who had no hesitation in shooting them down. In the months and years that followed, the memory of the 'July dead' would continue to haunt those who would soon call themselves sans-culottes.

A further direct consequence of this *journée* was to finalize the split in the Jacobins. All members of the club who were deputies decided to leave it permanently, except for just four: Robespierre, Pétion, Anthoine and Coroller. For their part, Duport, Barnave and Alexandre Lameth, in a sharp turn to the right, established with their supporters the Club des Feuillants, with premises in a disused convent

24 A. P., vol. 28, pp. 398–401.

close by.[25] There would be violent clashes between the two clubs, particularly in the provinces, where the Jacobins still had the majority of local societies.

The triumvirate pressed the king to sign the Constitution, duly amended after his return[26] – which he did on 14 September, before the Assembly. On the same occasion he proposed a general amnesty, and the prison gates were opened for political prisoners of every stripe.

Liberticidal laws

In its final months, the Constituent Assembly passed a series of laws with the combined effect of strictly limiting the right of the people to associate and express themselves: a law on the right of petition and bill-posting, a law on assemblies of citizens of the same occupation, a law on popular societies. All three were the work of the same rapporteur, Le Chapelier, who had moved a long way to the right since the time that he was one of the pillars of the Breton club. In practice, these laws were a complement to martial law.

On 9 May 1791, in his report on the right of petition and bill-posting, Le Chapelier stated first of all that the right of petition was 'the right of each active citizen to present his wishes to the legislative body, to the king and to the administrators on matters of legislation regarding public order and administration . . . The right of petition is a right that the citizen may and consequently must exercise individually.'[27] From this he concluded that 'no body, no administration and no society may exercise the non-transferable right of petition; a petition may not be drawn up

25 On what is now rue de Castiglione, on the corner with rue de Rivoli.

26 Abbé Grégoire: 'There then came the revisers of the Constitution, who made it that much worse' (*Mémoires de Grégoire*, p. 408). The civil constitution of the clergy was no longer inscribed in the Constitution, and became an ordinary law. And though the silver *marc* was no longer required to be elected a deputy, the property conditions for being an elector were increased. These measures came too late to be applied in the election of the Legislative Assembly.

27 A. P., vol. 25, p. 678ff.

under a collective name, and only those who sign their petition may be considered as petitioners.' On the principle of limiting this right to active citizens:

> No one may join [a political association] if they are nothing within it, or if they attack society instead of serving it, if they do not contribute to its expenses, if this failure to contribute comes from a failure to work and apply themselves . . . It should be said to those who, almost always by their own fault, are tormented by poverty: use your limbs usefully, take up work, plough this fertile soil, and you will receive the title of citizen.

On the right to put up posters: 'The streets and public places are common property; they do not belong to anyone, they belong to all . . . It is not in the streets that education is acquired; it is in peaceable societies where people discuss without arguing, where they gain enlightenment without passion or partisan spirit; it is in books, and finally in laws dictated by sound philosophy.'

This report was strongly criticized by Pétion, as well as Grégoire, who retorted: 'I attack the proposal presented to you as unjust, impolitic, contradictory and contrary to the natural rights of man.' Robespierre, too, objected: 'Should not the right of petition be particularly assured to non-active citizens? The more unfortunate a man is, the more needs he has, the more such prayers are necessary to him. And you would refuse to accept petitions presented to you by the poorest class of citizens?' Despite this opposition, the Le Chapelier law was passed without amendment.

On the subject of 'assemblies of citizens of the same occupation', Le Chapelier's project, presented on 14 June 1791, was a direct consequence of the abolition of corporations. A previous law, whose rapporteur was the baron d'Allarde, a deputy of the nobility for Saint-Pierre-le-Moûtier, had been passed on 16 February, with an Article 8 that spelled out: 'Every person shall be free to conduct any business or exercise any occupation, art or trade that they deem suitable, after being provided with a patent and having paid the price', signifying the disappearance of the corporation system – the legal status of which had in any case been unclear since summer 1789.[28] But once corporations were abolished, workers sought to strengthen their own organizations the better to stand up to their employers against a background of economic crisis and unemployment. In certain respects – mutual aid, assistance for elderly and infirm members – the associations now established or reinforced were close to the old fraternities or guilds that had undertaken since the Middle Ages what is today called social protection. The Club Typographique et Philanthropique, founded in July 1790, organized the Paris typographers and proceeded according to the principles born of the Revolution: each print-works elected two delegates and these in turn elected the club's bureau, which had no compunction about calling a strike to obtain satisfaction over wages. The Union Fraternelle des Ouvriers en l'Art de la Charpente, established in April 1791, represented carpenters from across Paris. It held its meetings in the same premises on rue Dauphine as the Cordeliers club, and was affiliated to the central committee that this club, as we have seen, set up to coordinate the activity of fraternal societies.[29] It was the threat presented by clubs and unions such as these that lay behind the Le Chapelier law.

His report was skilfully couched, presenting the new workers' associations as revivals of the former corporations, 'an infringement of the constitutional principles that abolished the corporations, one which entails great danger for public order.'[30] We must return, he said, 'to the principle of free agreements between individuals to settle each man's working day'. As for popular social policy and the distribution of assistance, these too 'tend to revive the corporations, requiring the frequent meeting of individuals of the same occupation, the appointment of *syndics* and other officers, the establishment of regulations; thus it is that privileges, masteries and the like are reborn.' The law prohibiting workers' associations was passed

28 A. P., vol. 23, p. 218.

29 See on these points: William H. Sewell, Jr, *Work and Revolution in France: the Language of Labor from the Old Regime to 1848*, Cambridge: Cambridge University Press, 1980, pp. 92–100.

30 A. P., vol. 27, p. 210ff.

immediately, with no objections, even from the left. Perhaps the habitual champions of the popular cause were unwilling to appear as defenders of corporations, one of the symbols of the old order.

The day before the Assembly was due to adjourn, on 28 September 1791, Le Chapelier presented a report 'on popular societies'. He began by praising 'these societies that were formed out of enthusiasm for liberty', but went on to note that they 'had soon departed from their purpose and acquired a kind of political existence that they should not have'.[31]

This report was one long harangue against agitators: 'Everyone wants the Revolution to come to an end. The time of destruction has passed, there are no further abuses to remedy or prejudices to combat . . . Those who seek to slander or denigrate the established authorities, to take over certain societies and make them take an active role in public administration, must be regarded as our most fearsome enemies.' The grounds for this decree give a good idea of its intention: 'The National Assembly, considering that no society, club or citizens' association may have a political existence in any form whatsoever, or exercise any influence or inspection over the acts of the established authorities . . .'

In his report, Le Chapelier explicitly targeted the Société des Amis de la Constitution – the Jacobins – and in particular the correspondence between its provincial branches: 'The societies that were founded to teach and support the maxims [of the Constitution] are simply meetings, clubs of friends who are no more the sentinels of the Constitution than all other citizens.'

In his reply, Robespierre argued:

> [The report] has contrived to speak the language of liberty and of the Constitution in order to destroy these and hide personal views and particular resentments . . . It is from within these societies that a large number of those who now occupy our seats have emerged (*applause from the far left and the galleries*) . . . When I see the extraordinary means that they [the right side] are employing to

31 A. P., vol. 31, p. 617ff.

> kill the public spirit by resurrecting old prejudices, frivolities and idolatries, I do not believe that the Revolution is at an end. Far from condemning the spirit of intoxication that inspires those who surround me, I see only the spirit of vertigo that propagates the enslavement of nations and the despotism of tyrants.

The Le Chapelier bill was passed without amendments.

EXCURSUS: THE COLONIAL QUESTION IN THE CONSTITUENT ASSEMBLY

When this topic is discussed, which is not often, it is presented as a kind of appendix, despite its being patently obvious that the colonial question was a key neuralgic point, the detonator of unusually violent confrontations between the left and the slave-owning planters supported by the Moderates, with Barnave as their leader. The matter was important for two reasons: it spotlighted the participation of slaves and free men of colour in a common humanity, and involved a substantial economic interest. Saint-Domingue, the most important colony, was at this time the leading sugar producer in the world, not counting its cotton, tobacco, indigo, cocoa and rum. All this agriculture was based on slave labour, provided entirely by the slave trade. Purchased in Africa and shipped out in horrendous conditions, the slaves were rapidly worn out by work; their lifespan on the island was scarcely more than ten years, after which they were replaced by new captives.[32] With such a labour force at their disposal, the planters had little incentive to invest in equipment or even draught animals. But towards the end of the century the picture began to change. Slaves could only be obtained by penetrating deeper into the African continent, which made the business more expensive. It was

---

32 For a good explanation, see Florence Gauthier, 'La Révolution française et le problème colonial, 1787–1804. État des connaissances et perspectives de recherche', in M. Lapied and C. Peyrard (eds), *La Révolution française au carrefour des recherches*, Aix-en-Provence: Publications de l'Université de Provence, 2003, pp. 101–11.

then projected to replace the African trade by raising slaves in the colonies themselves, and to economize on labour with the help of machines and animals. In France, the Société des Amis des Noirs, founded in 1788 by the Swiss banker Clavière – with such major figures as Brissot, Sieyès, Mirabeau, Condorcet and Lafayette among its members – supported this development. Often wrongly presented as abolitionist,[33] the Society supported ending the slave trade and easing the conditions of slavery in the colonies. The benefits of this would be twofold: on the one hand an improvement in yield, 'because with the black population increasing of itself in the islands, the result would be more labour, more new land brought into cultivation, and less mortality, as it has been shown that blacks born in the islands are more hard-working, more placid, better acclimatized and consequently less prone to disease than are African blacks.'[34] On the other hand, the possibility of exploiting local labour in Africa itself: 'Would it not be more just and worthwhile to leave in Africa the men that divine providence has placed there, and teach them to cultivate a land whose riches they would bring forth?'[35]

But slaves were not the only problematic human beings in Saint-Domingue in the late eighteenth century: there were also the Creoles, free descendants of white colonists and African women. These *free people of colour* – often described in deprecating terms as 'mulattos' or 'half-breeds' – found themselves increasingly discriminated against by the colour prejudice that appeared at that time: 'The system of segregation went as far as residential quarters: fleeing the white-dominated towns, free people of colour tended to concentrate in particular zones of the colony. A note of racial background was

---

33 See for example Brissot's article in *Le Patriote français* on 24 August 1789: 'Not only does the Société des Amis des Noirs by no means demand the abolition of slavery at this time, it would be dismayed were this to be proposed.'

34 'Adresse pour l'abolition de la traite des Noirs', February 1790, cited by Gauthier, 'La Révolution française et le problème colonial', p. 105.

35 A. Bonnemain, *Régénération des colonies, ou moyens de restituer graduellement aux hommes leur état politique et d'assurer la prospérité des nations*, Imprimerie du Cercle Social, 1792, p. 43. Cited by Marcel Dorigny, 'La Société des amis des Noirs et les projets de colonisation en Afrique', in *Révolution aux colonies*, Paris: Publications des Annales historiques de la Révolution française, 1993, p. 84.

included in their official papers, stating the degree of mixed blood and accompanied by occupational prohibitions and exclusion from white society.'[36]

In the wake of disturbances in the colonies, this question was the subject of a long and tumultuous debate in the Assembly, occupying nearly ten days in May 1791. In the name of the committees on the Constitution, the colonies, the navy, and agriculture and trade, Delattre presented on 7 May a draft of a constitutional decree whose first article spelled out that 'the legislative body shall make no law on the status of persons except on the express and formal demand of the colonial assemblies',[37] which amounted to leaving the fate of both slaves and free people of colour – the focus of the greater part of the debate – to the colonists. The committees proposed the formation of a general colonial committee: each colonial assembly would appoint commissioners, who would meet on the island of Saint-Martin.

Grégoire spoke as follows: 'I see here only the means to a more cunning oppression, a way of perpetuating the oppression of a class of men who are free by nature and by law,[38] and an attempt to reduce them to slavery by delivering them to the domination of others.' Moreau de Saint-Méry, the main spokesman for the slave-owning planters, threatened secession:

> You must either renounce your wealth and your trade, or declare frankly that the Declaration of Rights does not apply to the colonies . . . If you want the Declaration of Rights, then as far as we are concerned there will be no more colonies . . . If this is the case, I draw the necessary conclusion and I ask, by way of amendment, the deputies of the colonies to withdraw from this Assembly.

---

36 Gauthier, 'La Révolution française et le problème colonial', p. 107.

37 A. P., vol. 25. All the following quotations are taken from vols 25 and 36 of this work.

38 According to Colbert's Code Noir, freedmen (and also free people of colour) had 'the same rights, privileges and immunities as are enjoyed by persons who were born free'.

Pétion exhorted the Assembly not to cave in: 'Will you sacrifice the existing laws and the tranquillity of the colonies to the pretensions of a few colonists? Do you believe that if there are two classes of men fully conscious of their rights, the ones condemned to slavery and the others entitled to oppress, tranquillity can last very long?' After very heated exchanges, the debate was adjourned.

Discussions resumed on 11 May. The left demanded a vote on the previous question, thus sending the decree back to the committees. Grégoire proposed that 'the Assembly [should enjoin] the commissioners charged with restoring order in the islands to do everything in their power to ensure that men of colour enjoy all the rights of active citizens'.[39] Barnave's reply emphasized the dangers of English competition and the need for caution; best to settle matters case by case. 'By pronouncing on the political status of people of colour, you run the risk of losing the colonies.'

On 13 May, after a further heated discussion on the question as to which 'persons' were affected by the first article of Delattre's draft, Moreau de Saint-Méry proposed a modification that removed any ambiguity: 'The National Assembly decrees, as a constitutional article, that no law on the state *of slaves* in the American colonies shall be made . . .'[40]

At that point Robespierre stood up:

> The moment you pronounce, in one of your decrees, the word *slave*, you will be pronouncing your own dishonour and the overthrow of your constitution . . . [T]he supreme interest of the nation and of the colonies themselves is that you conserve your liberty and do not overturn the foundations of that liberty with your own hands. Faugh! Perish your colonies, if you are keeping them at that price. Yes, if you had either to lose your colonies, or to lose your happiness, your glory, your liberty, I would repeat: perish your colonies.[41]

---

39 A. P., vol. 25, p. 743.

40 A. P., vol. 26, p. 48.

41 Robespierre, *Virtue and Terror*, pp. 20–1; A. P., vol. 26, p. 60.

In the end, the Assembly decided to replace the word 'slave' by the word 'unfree' – which amounted to the same thing – and passed the decree that made slavery constitutional. The debate thus ended with a victory for the colonial party.[42]

The end of the Constituent Assembly

At almost the same moment, and in a quite surprising way, the Constituent Assembly did unanimously adopt a courageous measure, renouncing their own re-election to a future Legislative Assembly. This decision was carried on 13 May 1791 thanks to a single speech by one man, Robespierre, whose ascending star was confirmed even though he was still regularly in a minority, not to say a lone voice, in the positions he took. 'Can you imagine,' he said, 'what imposing authority could accrue to your Constitution by the sacrifice, pronounced by you, of the greatest honours to which your fellow citizens could call you? . . . We have neither the right nor the presumption to think that a nation of 25 million people, free and enlightened, is reduced to the inability to find 720 defenders as worthy as ourselves.'[43]

The Constituent Assembly ceased to exist on 30 September 1791. Most representatives doubtless thought that they no longer needed to fear a royal reaction, that the people were calm, that the Revolution had come to an end, in short, that they had done their work well. Some were of a different opinion: 'This National Assembly that was

---

42 On 15 May, Reubell proposed an amendment: 'The National Assembly decrees that the legislative body shall never debate the political status of people of colour who are not born of a free father and mother without the preliminary desire of the colonies expressed freely and spontaneously', and that 'people of colour born of a free father and mother shall be admitted to all future parochial and colonial assemblies if they otherwise meet the requisite conditions' (A. P., vol. 26, p. 90). This amendment was opposed by the colonial party. Robespierre refused to vote for it unless the words 'born of a free father and mother' were withdrawn, since: 'All free men of colour must enjoy all the rights that belong to them.' The Reubell amendment was finally adopted unchanged.

43 A. P., vol. 26, pp. 111, 123.

previously such a good woman, so prudent and honest, has become a shameless hussy, a prostitute sold to the highest bidder. Ambition, avarice and tricks have turned her head, and the wretch has ended up so vile that the day on which she clears off to hell will be a day of joy for all good citizens.'[44]

44 Hébert, in *Le Père Duchesne*, no. 81, late September 1791.

CHAPTER 6

October 1791 to June 1792

The Legislative Assembly moves towards war, the duel between Brissot and Robespierre, the first defeats

> The French Revolution saw the invention of a pretext for war unknown until then, that of rescuing peoples from the yoke of their governments, supposedly illegitimate and tyrannical. This pretext was used to bring death to men, some of whom lived quietly under institutions softened by time and custom, and others who had enjoyed for many centuries all the benefits of liberty.
>
> – Benjamin Constant, *On the Spirit of Conquest*

Composition and tendencies of the Legislative Assembly

The 745 deputies who assembled on 1 October 1791 to form the Legislative Assembly were new men – we recall that the members of the Constituent Assembly had declared themselves ineligible for this first legislature. The electoral assemblies had elected deputies above all from those candidates possessing landed property of some kind, and subject to a tax of at least a silver *marc*. They were young, more than half being under the age of thirty. The majority were men of the law, chiefly advocates, and almost all had exercised some function or other in the municipal or departmental assemblies.[1] Michelet met an old man who

> in September 1791 had come from Bordeaux to Paris in a public coach that was bringing the Girondins. There were the likes of Vergniaud, Guadet, Gensonné, Ducos, Fonfrède, etc., the famous pleiad that would personify the spirit of the new Assembly . . . They were men full of energy and talent, admirably young and extraordinarily energetic, with an unbounded devotion to ideas. Yet despite this, he soon noticed that they were very ignorant, strangely inexperienced and fickle; they were talkers and controversialists, dominated by the habits of the bar, which reduced their invention and initiative.[2]

Indeed, inexperience and fickleness would be the hallmark of the Legislative Assembly, as we shall see.

There were no parties in the new Assembly, any more than there had been in the Constituent, but rather political affinities grouped around prominent individuals. More than a third of the deputies (264) would enrol in the Club des Feuillants. These Moderates, that is, constitutional monarchists, were divided into two groups or two clienteles: on the one hand, the 'Lamethists' around the triumvirate Barnave-Duport-Lameth, increasingly tied to the court; on the other, the 'Fayettists', who followed the general on the white horse. The 'left' was made up of 136 deputies who joined the Jacobins club. Between the two, the largest group numerically was the undecided mass of 'independents' (345 deputies).

---

1 To take two departments at random: in the Indre-et-Loire the eight deputies were the mayor of Tours, the *procureur syndic* of the Chinon district, a member of the departmental directory, two departmental administrators, a judge at the Chinon court, a businessman, and the commander of the Tours National Guard. The nine deputies for the Tarn were a judge on the Albi court, a commissioner with the Castres court, a member of the directorate of the Lavaur district, two members of the departmental directorate, the *procureur* of the Puylaurens commune, a 'man of the law', and another man on whom no details were given (after Auguste Kuscinski, *Les Députés à l'Assemblée législative de 1791*, Paris: Société d'histoire de la Révolution française, 1790).

2 Michelet, *Histoire de la Révolution française*, vol. 1, p. 614.

In Paris, the Moderates had won the election, which took place in two stages with a property qualification and a very high rate of abstention. Danton had been defeated, and Brissot prevailed only with difficulty. But thanks to the divisions of the Feuillants, the Jacobins triumphed in the November municipal election: Pétion was elected mayor of Paris against Lafayette, and Danton became the deputy *procureur* of the Commune.

Popular movements

The Legislative Assembly would have its work cut out standing up to both popular movements and the counter-revolutionary movements that broke out across the country.

In the towns, discontent was caused once again by a crisis of provisions. The 1791 harvest had been good, but torrential rain in autumn gave rise to floods, endangering the supply of flour. Prices shot up, all the more so as the *assignat* was losing value against 'real' money: in the autumn it still stood at 85 per cent of its nominal value, but steadily fell to reach 60 per cent by the spring of 1792.[3] On top of this, sugar and coffee became scarce and costly after the outbreak of the great slave rebellion in Saint-Domingue. Sugared *café au lait*, however, had become one of the staples of the popular diet. In the faubourgs, bowls of it were served to washerwomen and ironers to enable them to carry on to the end of the day.[4] Disturbances erupted in Paris around grocers' shops, where crowds forced traders to lower their prices by threatening to help themselves. In January 1792 the Jacobins club decided to dispense with sugar. In Louvet's words: 'Who among us could find anything sweet in an enjoyment that he knows is denied to the largest and most precious part of the people?'[5] In the enthusiasm of this session, it was decided also to do without coffee.

---

3 Andress, *The French Revolution and the People*, p. 172.

4 Roger Dupuy, *La Garde nationale, 1789–1792*, Paris: Gallimard, 2010, p. 155.

5 Aulard, *La Société des Jacobins*, vol. 3, p. 351.

By November 1791, the rise in the price of wheat led to major disturbances in the rural north. On the Aisne and the Oise, groups of peasants and artisans stopped and pillaged barges loaded with grain. In the markets, thousands of peasants, often led by the village mayors, imposed a *taxation populaire*: payment for goods – wheat, but also eggs, butter, wood and coal – at a price they deemed fair. In Étampes, the mayor, Simonneau, was shot dead while preparing to impose martial law to prevent this *taxation*. In the Assembly, the Feuillants made him a martyr to the law, and even the Jacobins sent his son a letter of condolence, evoking 'the heroic virtue of the author of your days'.[6]

The peasants had another reason for anger, and a deeper one. They saw ever more clearly that the feudal regime was still well and truly alive, and that the latest measures taken by the Constituent Assembly made the redemption of seigniorial rights impossible: 'These former lords, their agents and their present tenants, gang up with the nonjuring priests and fanatics of all kinds, and crush the revolutionary zeal of the cultivators, who are simple and ignorant, by making them fear a return of the old order of things,' so the free citizens of the commune of Lourmarin wrote to the Assembly on 15 December.[7] This anger was unleashed in the centre and south of the country: in the villages of the Lot, Tarn, Cantal and Dordogne, the peasants, often supported – a remarkable fact – by the National Guard, pillaged and set on fire the châteaux of émigrés, demanding the complete abolition of the seigniorial regime – but it was only the Convention under the Montagne that would finally carry this out.

Counter-revolutionary insurrections

At the same time as these popular uprisings, there was wide counter-revolutionary agitation: whether flocks of the faithful defending refractory priests, or openly royalist movements led from afar by the émigrés.

---

6 Ibid., p. 431. Robespierre did not sign this letter.

7 Cited in Jaurès, *Histoire socialiste*, vol. 2, p. 28.

The Assembly learned in October that in Montpellier 'an insurrection broke out, which lasted the whole night', following the opening of a chapel by a nonjuring priest. In the Vendée, departmental commissioners reported that 'the fanatical priests, excited by the hope of counter-revolution, are agitating the people in all directions'. In the Haute-Loire, 'the constitutional priests are persecuted, murdered and put to flight, and the courts are powerless'.

Royalist revolts broke out in the Midi, 'on the still burning embers of the old religious wars' (Michelet). In the Lozère, a notary by the name of Charrier, a former deputy to the Constituent Assembly whom the comte d'Artois had appointed to the command of the region, openly organized counter-revolutionary militias and even established an artillery section. Claude Allier, the prior of Chambonnaz, boasted of being able to raise an army of more than 50,000 men, led by priests under the white flag and supported by Sardinia and Spain. In Chambéry, which still belonged to the kingdom of Piedmont-Sardinia at this time and a major émigré centre, Bussy, an artillery captain, formed a royalist legion that he marched in broad daylight. In Perpignan, royalist militias prepared to open the frontier to the Spanish armies. In Arles and Aigues-Mortes, where the counter-revolutionaries initially had the upper hand, it took a major expedition on the part of Marseille volunteers to overcome the entrenched royalists.[8] On 16 October in Avignon, the papal city that had recently been reunited with France, the counter-revolution 'had the population murder at the foot of the altar a Frenchman, Lescuyer, head of the French party against the papists . . . But when the revolutionary party prevailed, it avenged Lescuyer the same night by massacring some sixty individuals, cutting their throats in the Palais des Papes and flinging their bodies to the bottom of the Tour de la Glacière.'[9]

8 See on these points Kropotkin, *The Great French Revolution*, op. cit., chapter 31.

9 A. P., vol. 34, pp. 310–6.

Measures against émigrés and refractory priests

Faced with the threat of chaos, the Legislative Assembly, the majority of which still clung to the monarchy like a life raft, did not dare to take frontal measures. To end the pillage and burning of châteaux, it decided on 9 February 1792 that the goods of émigrés would be sequestrated. Despite its concern to calm peasant unrest, it rejected in February Couthon's bill to suppress without indemnity all feudal rights that could not be clearly justified – in June, it merely abolished charges on property transfer.

Against the émigrés, the Assembly followed Brissot in distinguishing between the leaders and those that followed them, who 'will say to you, correctly: what right have you to punish us? Are there two different weights and measures for a free people? You respect the titles and assets of our leaders and you crush their subaltern accomplices!'[10] On 31 October, the Assembly decided that Louis-Stanislas-Xavier, the king's brother, would have his rights of regency removed if he did not return to France within two months.

Against the refractory priests, on 29 November 1791 the Assembly voted a decree cancelling the stipends of any who refused to take a new oath, and authorizing local administrations to evict them from their dwellings in case of disturbance to public order. But Louis XVI, though accepting the decree concerning his brother, vetoed the measures against the émigrés and refractory priests. The situation was blocked.

A popular movement for war?

How, against this background of unrest, did the executive and Assembly come to unleash a war against the main powers of the continent? How was this country, which in May 1790 had issued a veritable declaration of peace to the world in the name of the Constituent Assembly, taken towards war?

---

10 Michelet, *Histoire de la Révolution française*, vol. 1, p. 621.

The man in the street and the ordinary deputy, hearing incessant talk of imminent invasion in the Assembly and in the papers, might well believe that Austria and Prussia were preparing to attack France, which would have justified a preventive riposte. But in the case of the ministers, who received reports from their ambassadors, or Brissot and his friends who also had access to genuine information, it is highly unlikely that the noise of boots across the border could really have disquieted them. They knew that the Pillnitz declaration, signed in August by Emperor Leopold and the Prussian king Friedrich-Wilhelm, did not amount to anything, as the two sovereigns, we have seen, only declared themselves prepared to intervene if the other powers joined them. And the king of Sweden and Empress Catherine of Russia, while forceful enough in words, had no intention of proceeding to action, being rather more preoccupied with Poland and Turkey. On 4 November, Fersen wrote to the king of Sweden: 'Everything confirms me in the view that the Viennese cabinet intends to do nothing.'[11] These dispositions were perfectly well known to those who led the war party in France. As for the danger represented by the émigrés in Coblenz, even if they took every opportunity to play it up, they could hardly have taken it seriously.

The king and queen were well aware of the indecision and paralysis of Austria. Their secret correspondence – that of Louis with Breteuil, that of Marie-Antoinette with Fersen and Mercy-Argenteau, the Austrian ambassador – was full of recriminations. They wanted the powers to assemble an armed congress at the frontier that would put pressure on France to change the Constitution, but at no time did such a congress look likely.

Was there a popular movement in favour of war? Patriotic gifts were certainly made 'for the costs of war', but these were isolated acts that were publicized for the good of the cause. What could have motivated such a movement? Sophie Wahnich emphasizes the sense of honour: 'It was a matter of bearing "the glory of the French name" and defending the honour of the Revolution against enemies who

11 *Le Comte de Fersen et la Cour de France*, Paris, 1878, vol. 1, p. 213. Cited in Jaurès, *Histoire socialiste*, vol. 2, p. 71.

refused to recognize and respect the revolutionary nation.'[12] For Jaurès, by contrast, it was 'the weakening and discouragement of the democrats and revolutionaries' that explains the movement towards war: 'The people were now silent, and no other goad than that of wars abroad could have roused them from their torpor. And so it was not, as many historians have repeated, the overflowing enthusiasm of liberty that kindled the war; this arose on the contrary from a faltering of the Revolution.'[13]

A sense of honour in the face of insult; war to combat discouragement – both are possible. But if indeed there was a popular movement for war, it was above all the result of a propaganda campaign, to use an anachronistic expression. This campaign was waged by groups that were opposed to one another but had one point in common: they looked to war to resolve their domestic difficulties and permit them to get rid of their enemies in France itself. It would not be the last time that a war, or a colonial expedition, would be launched purely for reasons of domestic politics.

The war party and the opposition

In a strange paradox, the court and the 'left' found themselves here on the same side.

On the left, the war party was led by Brissot, a figure who became so important at this point that the term 'Brissotins' was used to denote the group around him (they would only be called 'Girondins' later on, under the Convention). We may well ask why individuals such as Vergniaud, Isnard or Buzot, who were far superior to the mediocre Brissot, agreed to accept him as their leader. One possible explanation is that he was the only Parisian in the group. It is hard to imagine today how out of place these provincials felt in revolutionary Paris, and what prestige someone at home in the place, the editor of a major newspaper, could have in their eyes.

12 Sophie Wahnich, *La Longue Patience du peuple*, Paris: Payot, 2008, p. 70.

13 Jaurès, *Histoire socialiste*, p. 84.

The Brissotins wanted war, and pinned all their hopes on it: this diversion would mean an end to the popular movements that were racking the country, as well as revealing the traitors (the Court, the ministers) who would be put down. It would be an easy war, as peoples labouring under the yoke of tyrants would come with open arms to meet the soldiers of liberty. Such themes and variations on the advantages of war recur constantly in the speeches and newspapers of the time. Little by little, the idea that 'the people want war' was established as self-evident fact.

The Court – and above all the queen – could turn the bellicose stance of the Brissotins to their own purposes. For a long time they had seen foreign intervention as their only hope. On the one hand, the Court pretended to follow the advice of Lameth, Duport and Barnave, who stood for strict respect of the Constitution and were fiercely opposed to war, as for them it risked upsetting the balance, either towards the democratic party or towards the aristocratic one, and they wanted neither one thing nor the other. At the same time, however, through its emissaries abroad and secret letters, the Court was inciting Austria to armed intervention. As Louis wrote to Breteuil, 'the physical and moral state of France renders her incapable of sustaining even half a campaign', and defeat would enable the restoration of the monarchy to its former splendour.

The duel between Brissot and Robespierre

The opening shot in this campaign for war was fired by Brissot in the Assembly on 20 October 1791, in a long, confused speech, full of contradictions, in which he notably declared:

> Need I remind you of all the outrages committed against your representatives, or simply against French citizens? Need I remind you of the protection openly afforded to the French rebels in the Netherlands . . . ? We respect your peace and your Constitution; respect ours in return; stop sheltering these malcontents, stop associating yourselves with their sanguinary projects. Or, if you prefer

> to the friendship of a great nation your relations with a few brigands, then expect vengeance; the vengeance of a people is slow, but it strikes surely.[14]

The official report states that applause 'accompanied M. Brissot back to his seat, and the uproar continued for several minutes'.

On 29 November it was Isnard's turn, a far better speaker than Brissot:

> Let us say to Europe that we respect all the constitutions of the different empires, but that if the cabinets of foreign courts seek to unleash a war of the kings against France, then we shall unleash against them *a war of peoples against kings*. Let us say to them than ten million Frenchmen, fired with the flame of liberty, armed with sword, reason, and eloquence, could, if they are roused, change the face of the world and make every tyrant tremble on his throne.[15]

In the face of this massive movement, opposition to war was scarcely visible. It was non-existent in the Assembly, where the far left had no presence. In the Jacobins club, it was confined for a long time to Robespierre alone. He was certainly listened to with respect, but not to the point of taking the whole club with him. On 12 December: 'To whom would you entrust the conduct of this war? To the agents of the executive power. So you will abandon the security of the realm to those who want to destroy you. It follows from this that the thing we should fear most is war.' And on 2 January 1792, about the real enemy: 'Do we have them, any enemies within? No, you don't know of any, you know only about Koblenz. Did you not tell us that the seat of evil is in Koblenz? So it is not in Paris? So there is no connection between Koblenz and another place that is not far from here?'[16]

In the same great speech from Robespierre: 'The honour of the French name, you say. Heavens above! . . . The honour that you seek

---

14 A. P., vol. 34, pp. 313–7.

15 A. P., vol. 35, p. 442.

16 Robespierre, *Virtue and Terror*, p. 31.

to revive is the friend and support of despotism; it is the honour of the heroes of the aristocracy, of all the tyrants, it is the honour of crime.' And on the crusade for liberty:

> The most extravagant idea that can arise in the mind of a politician is the belief that a people need only make an armed incursion into the territory of a foreign people, to make it adopt its laws and its constitution. No one likes armed missionaries; and the first counsel given by nature and prudence is to repel them as enemies.[17]

The duel over the war between Robespierre on the one side, and Brissot and his friends on the other, continued for several months, in the Jacobins club and in the press. This cleavage was not simply conjunctural, it was profound, foreshadowing the confrontation between Montagnards and Girondins in the Convention. But that point had not yet been reached. Even at the Jacobins, and with the help of Desmoulins, Marat and Billaud-Varenne, Robespierre did not manage to stem the tide. On 15 February 1792, the club's correspondence committee sent the following letter to its affiliated societies:

> The salvation of our country depends on a forthright measure, which is war. We need this to consolidate the Constitution and strengthen our national existence; we need war to stamp our Revolution with the imposing character that befits the movements of a great people . . . The nation ardently desires it, it burns to see the moment approach when the soldiers of liberty will measure themselves against the satellites of despotism, when this great trial of peoples and kings will be decided by the outcome of battle.[18]

---

17 Robespierre, op. cit ., p. 31, and *Pour le bonheur et pour la liberté*, pp. 122–50. All other quotations from Robespierre are taken from his *Œuvres complètes*, Éditions du Centenaire de la Société des études robespierristes [1912–1967], reprinted Enghien-les-Bains: Éditions du Miraval (11 vols), 2007, vol. 8.

18 Aulard, *La Société des Jacobins*, vol. 3, pp. 376–81.

The declaration of war

The champions of war – and Louis XVI himself – appointed as minister of war in December 1791 the comte de Narbonne, lover of Madame de Staël and supposedly an illegitimate son of Louis XV. For him, war was a means of restoring the power of the Crown. He was opposed in the government by de Lessart, the minister of foreign affairs, who was an ally of the followers of Lameth in the peace camp. de Lessart managed to get Emperor Leopold to lean on the elector of Trier to disperse the concentration of émigrés on his territory. The elector complied, as Leopold informed the Assembly in a note in early January 1792. This put paid to one justification for war, but Brissot pointed out that the emperor had not disavowed the Pillnitz declaration, and had indicated in his note that any attack on the elector would constitute a *casus belli*.

On 25 January, Hérault de Séchelles proposed a decree that was a kind of ultimatum. Its Article 2 invited the king 'to ask the emperor whether he intends to live in peace and on good terms with the French nation, whether he renounces any treaty or convention directed against the sovereignty, independence and security of the Nation', and further, in Article 3, 'to declare to the emperor that unless he renders to the Nation before 1 March full and complete satisfaction on the points listed above, his silence, or any evasive or dilatory response, will be regarded as a declaration of war'.

De Lessart, opposed to this bellicose pressure, prevailed upon the king to dismiss Narbonne. But the furious Brissotins accused him of treason and dragged him before the high court for having negotiated with 'a cowardice and weakness unworthy of a free people'. Louis XVI took fright, abandoned de Lessart to his fate and replaced the Feuillant administration with a Brissotin one: Clavière at the finance ministry, Roland at the interior ministry, Grave and then Servan at the ministry of war. Foreign affairs were entrusted to Dumouriez, whose previous career had been typical of a certain kind of eighteenth-century adventurer. He was the strong man of this government. Immediately on his appointment, he proceeded to the Jacobins, donned a red bonnet and uttered these fighting words: 'If diplomatic efforts fail, I shall lay down my political pen and take my rank in the army, either to triumph or to die free along with my brothers.' Robespierre did not want this speech to be printed: 'It is out of respect for the rights of the people, who alone are great and respectable in my eyes, and before whom all the baubles of ministerial power vanish, that I recall the society to its principles.'[19]

Emperor Leopold died on 1 March. His successor, Franz II, a 'devotee of Machiavelli' (Michelet), was a militarist by temperament, and replied to the French notes curtly and negatively. Finally, on 20 April 1792, Louis XVI entered the Assembly accompanied by the ministers and the twenty-four commissioners. He asked Dumouriez to read the report made to the council of ministers two days earlier, which concluded that 'ever since the time of its regeneration, the French nation has been provoked by the Viennese court and its agents', and that Franz's non-response to French demands was 'formally equivalent to a declaration of war'. At the end of the report, the king said ('his voice faltering somewhat'):

> You have just heard, gentlemen, the result of the negotiations that I have pursued with the court of Vienna . . . All citizens prefer war to seeing the dignity of the French people continue to be affronted and its national security threatened. According to the terms of the Constitution, I have come before you formally to propose war against the king of Hungary and Bohemia.[20]

The army, the first defeats

The war had been willed and unleashed by the Court and the Brissotins, who each expected from it quite opposite results. But by one of the habitual ruses of history, events turned out equally badly for both. Nothing happened as it was supposed to, everything conspired against them and drove them to catastrophe.

---

19 Aulard, *La Société des Jacobins*, vol. 3, p. 439.

20 A. P., vol. 42, pp. 196–9. Franz had not yet been elected Holy Roman Emperor.

The republican army had the advantage of numbers. France was at this time, in terms of population, the largest European country outside of Russia. More than a million men could be raised from the National Guard alone (made up of active citizens, we recall).[21] There were already some 100,000 volunteers on the frontiers, the recruiting of whom had begun in June 1791 after Varennes. Their battalions had kept the names of their departments of origin, which had provided their equipment. There was no general conscription: each battalion opened its own register for volunteers, many of whom were politicized young townsmen. They elected their officers,[22] attended the clubs and met with patriots in the towns where they were posted. The volunteer battalions (the 'blues') were not integrated with the troops of the line (the 'whites') who had made up the old royal army.[23]

This division of the army into two parts, each of which had scant esteem for the other, was a handicap, but not the worst. The command had been disrupted by the emigration of more than half the officers. These gaps had been filled with difficulty by non-commissioned officers and by men who had exercised a position in the National Guard. The officers distrusted their troops, and vice versa. The three generals appointed by Louis XVI in November 1791, moreover, were no great strategists: Rochambeau, hero of the war of American independence, was old and sceptical; Luckner was a Bavarian who had become a marshal of France at the age of seventy, with no other quality to recommend him except his friendship with Lafayette, who dominated the high command but remained a politician beneath his uniform.

Opposite the 150,000 men of this ill-trained and poorly commanded force, there were just 35,000 Austrians – the Prussians were still getting ready. Dumouriez, the de facto head of the government, had ordered an offensive, but right from the first engagements

21 In actual fact, many volunteers were recruited among passive citizens not in the National Guard.

22 According to Article 8 of the decree of 21 June 1791, 'All individuals making up the company [i.e. fifty men] will appoint their officers and non-commissioned officers; the battalion's general staff will be appointed by the whole battalion' (A. P., vol. 37, p. 294).

23 On these points, see Dupuy, *La Garde nationale*, chapter 5.

the uncertainty of command led to a series of reverses, the most fateful of which took place outside Lille on 28 April, when a column supposed to proceed to Belgium and take Tournai retreated upon sight of the enemy. The two cavalry regiments at its head disbanded and fell back to Lille, passing the corps of retreating volunteers who massacred Dillon on their way, an officer whom they accused – probably unfairly – of treason.

The generals denied all responsibility for these defeats, blaming the lack of discipline of their troops. When they met at Valenciennes on 18 May, they sent the ministers a note explaining that the offensive was impossible, hostilities had to be ended and an immediate peace concluded.

The Brissotins had every reason to be crestfallen, all the more so as Robespierre struck an 'I told you so' pose (at the Jacobins, on 1 May: 'No! I do not trust the generals one whit, and, with certain honourable exceptions, I say that almost all of them pine for the old order of things . . .').[24] Marat, for his part, lampooned them in *L'Ami du peuple* on 6 May: 'We had been assured that the very cannonballs would retreat in the face of the Rights of Man.'

The trial of strength, dismissal of the ministry, Lafayette's threats

The Court openly supported the generals' *fronde*, while the Brissotins now sought confrontation. On 27 May, the Assembly voted for the deportation of refractory priests who had refused the oath and were provoking disturbances.[25] On 29 May, it decided to dismiss the king's guard – 1,200 horse and 600 foot – composed of aristocrats who openly rejoiced at the military setbacks. The Assembly had the head of the guard, the duc de Cossé-Brissac, brought before the high court.

On 4 June the minister of war, Servan, proposed the formation of a National Guard encampment outside Paris: 'Why do you not ask

24 *Le Défenseur de la Constitution*, no. 1.

25 Article 3 of the decree provided that: 'When twenty active citizens of a canton meet to demand the deportation of a nonjuring ecclesiastic, the departmental directorate is required to pronounce deportation' (A. P., vol. 44, p. 169).

each of the cantons in the kingdom for five National Guards, uniformed and armed, to assemble in Paris on 14 July? This method would give you a mass of 20,000 men . . . This army would camp close to the capital so as to provide part of the guard for both the Assembly and the king.'[26] This measure, opposed in the Jacobins by Robespierre ('The army that we would not fear would be composed of all those soldiers dismissed with yellow cartridges for deeds of patriotism'),[27] was passed on 8 June.

The king vetoed the decrees on refractory priests, on the dissolution of his guard, and on the camp of 20,000 men, which he saw as a weapon in the hands of the Jacobins. On 10 June, Roland advised him to sign, in a letter that most historians attribute to his wife: 'The conduct of the priests . . . has led to a wise law against these troublemakers. Let Your Majesty give it his sanction: public tranquillity demands this, and it is needed for the salvation of the priests.' The text went on to mention 'the extreme disquiet that the conduct of your guard had aroused, and that was encouraged by the testimonies of satisfaction that Your Majesty had given it by a proclamation truly impolitic in the circumstances'. And finally: 'Any further delay, and the people will sadly perceive its king as the friend and accomplice of the conspirators.'[28]

The king's response to this abrupt demand was to dismiss the Girondin ministry on 13 June. The replacements he appointed were members of the Feuillants, with Dumouriez at the ministry of war. The Assembly voted that the dismissed ministers had the regrets of the nation, and when Dumouriez came to read a pessimistic report on the military situation he was received with boos. In the same session it was decided to establish a twelve-man parliamentary commission, to investigate the conduct of the ministers and to check on Dumouriez's allegations. Feeling threatened, the latter sought to persuade the king to calm the situation by signing the decrees, but

26 Ibid., p. 550.

27 Session of 7 June 1792. Aulard, *La Société des Jacobins*, vol. 3, p. 669. [The 'yellow cartridge' was symbolically handed to a soldier dishonourably discharged from the army. – Translator]

28 Cited in Jaurès, *Histoire socialiste*, vol. 2, pp. 503–5.

Louis would not hear of it. He accepted the resignation of Dumouriez, who left to join the army of the North.

The confrontation between the Brissotins and the Court turned into a trial of strength. It was at this point that Lafayette sent the king a letter from his camp at Maubeuge, which was read by a secretary at the session of 18 June. It consisted above all of a violent attack on the Jacobins:

> Can you conceal from yourself that one faction, and, not to beat about the bush, the Jacobite [*sic*] faction, is the cause of all this disorder? Their very actions accuse them: organized as a realm of their own in their metropolis and its affiliations, blindly directed by certain ambitious leaders, this sect forms a distinct corporation within the French people, whose powers it usurps, subjugating their representatives and their mandataries.

There followed a denunciation of Dumouriez, 'a worthy product of his club . . ., all of whose calculations are false, his promises vain, his information deceptive or frivolous, his counsels perfidious or contradictory'.

What Lafayette was recommending was a counter-revolutionary coup d'état, as Vergniaud remarked: 'When a simple citizen addresses a petition to you, you have to hear it. When a general of the army wants to give you advice, he can only do so by way of the ministry. If this were otherwise, there would be an end to freedom, as I am not afraid to tell you.' And Guadet: 'M. de Lafayette is not unaware that when Cromwell used similar language, liberty was lost in England.'[29] But the Brissotins, still indecisive, did not dare to make a formal accusation against the factious general. They merely refused to forward his letter to the departments.

Brissot, however, in the next day's *Patriote français*, roundly attacked Lafayette: 'This is the most violent blow that has been struck against liberty, and all the more dangerous in being struck by a general who boasts of having an army of his own . . .' He was thus of

29 For the session of 18 June, A. P., vol. 45, p. 338ff.

one mind with Robespierre, who wrote in no. 7 of his paper, *Le Défenseur de la constitution*: 'Has the time already come when army chiefs can interpose their influence or their authority in our public affairs? . . . Have we already lost our freedom, or is it rather you who have lost your reason?'[30] A kind of truce set in between Brissot and Robespierre, as they faced the common enemy.

30 Robespierre, *Œuvres complètes*, vol. 4, pp. 195–6.

CHAPTER 7

June to August 1792

The journée of 20 June, the Brunswick Manifesto, the taking of the Tuileries, the end of the monarchy, the September massacres

> For too long you have ruled above my head,
> You in the dark cloud, God of Time!
> Too wild and fearful around me,
> Whatever I look at wavers and breaks.
>
> – Friedrich Hölderlin, 'The Spirit of the Age'

The journée of 20 June

The head of the army plotting sedition, the Court speaking a double language, an indecisive majority in the Assembly: the situation was clearly favourable to any counter-revolutionary movement. But with the Revolution still in its ascendant phase, when such a stalemate appeared, it was the people who went into action.

They had already made themselves loudly heard on 15 April, even before the declaration of war, at an immense festival celebrating Châteauvieux's Swiss Guards – the victims of Nancy, and the forty soldiers who had just been freed from the galleys. A procession from the faubourg Saint-Antoine crossed the whole of Paris to the

Champ-de-Mars. 'The table of the Declaration of Rights was positioned there, and around it they placed all the signs, emblems and flags that had decorated the march,' with banners displaying the names of the eighty-three departments, along with the keys and flag of the Bastille . . . 'These joyous dances,' wrote Michelet, 'had something of the ardour of the festivals of antiquity, with slaves intoxicated by their new freedom.'[1]

On 19 June, Cambon, a deputy for the Hérault, read from the Assembly rostrum an address from the Marseille patriots which can be seen as heralding what would happen just a few hours later: 'Legislators, the liberty of France is in danger; the men of the Midi have risen to defend it. The people's day of anger has arrived. This people, who so long have been massacred or enchained, are tired of parrying blows, and ready in their turn to deal them.'[2]

At dawn on the following day, two armed columns left the faubourg Saint-Antoine and the faubourg Saint-Marceau, converged close to the Pont-Neuf and approached the Assembly that was starting its session. The president read out a letter from Santerre, the brewer of Saint-Antoine, who commanded the faubourg's battalion:

> The inhabitants of the faubourg Saint-Antoine are today celebrating the anniversary of the Tennis Court oath. They wish to pay their respects to the National Assembly. Since their intentions have been slandered, today they request admittance to the bar to refute their cowardly detractors and prove that they are friends of liberty and the men of 14 July.[3]

Vergniaud and Guadet had the letter welcomed, but the Assembly hesitated, and only after a stormy discussion was the admission of

---

1 Michelet, *Histoire de la Révolution française*, vol. 1, p. 693. On the fêting of the Swiss Guards, see Wahnich, *La Longue Patience du peuple*, pp. 223–6.

2 A. P., vol. 45, p. 397. Under the Legislative Assembly, Joseph Cambon evolved from Brissotist positions towards the Montagne. He became a specialist in financial questions, later under the Convention becoming a quasi-minister in this field, with a position of exceptional independence.

3 On the session of 20 June, see A. P., vol. 45, pp. 413–20.

armed petitioners agreed. The people poured into the Salle du Manège, and for several hours, close to 10,000 men 'armed some with pikes, others with knives, twibills, axes and sticks . . . a number of women bearing sabres, marched through the hall dancing to the tune of the song "*Ça ira*", and shouting: "*Vivent les sans-culottes! Vivent les patriotes! À bas le veto!*"'[4]

Emerging from the Assembly, the petitioners forced the gates of the Tuileries and reached the Œil-de-Bœuf room where the king was. A famous scene ensued: Louis XVI wedged into a window seat for two hours, the red bonnet on his head, drinking the nation's health but refusing to give in, repeating that he was loyal to the Constitution. At last Pétion arrived with a delegation from the Assembly, and had the palace calmly evacuated.

A defeat, therefore, from which the royalists profited. The Paris department, run by the Feuillants, decreed the removal of Pétion, the Commune's mayor, and Manuel, the Commune *procureur*, for doing nothing to stop the riot. The minister of justice announced an inquiry into the outrage of 20 June. Addresses flooded in from the provinces calling for vengeance 'against the wretches who violated the safe haven of the hereditary representative of the Nation and insulted his inviolable and sacred person'.[5]

On 28 June, Lafayette, deserting his post in front of the enemy, arrived at the Assembly to deliver what was a formal notice: 'I beg the National Assembly to order that the instigators of the crimes and violence committed on 20 June in the Tuileries be prosecuted and punished as criminals for *lèse-nation*, and to destroy a sect [the Jacobins] that infringes sovereignty and tyrannizes citizens, and whose public debates leave no room for doubt about the atrocity of the plans of those who lead it.'[6] His speech was mostly applauded, and a motion proposed by Guadet, indicting him for having left his post without ministerial authorization, was rejected by 339 votes to 234. But Lafayette did not confine his hopes to the Assembly: he also

4 *Le Moniteur*, vol. 12, p. 718.

5 Address from the citizens of Le Havre, A. P., vol. 45, p. 644.

6 A. P., vol. 45, p. 533.

planned to win over the bourgeois battalions of the Paris National Guard, which he was to review the next day together with the king. Being warned of this, Pétion called off the review, and Lafayette returned to his troops without having been able to try anything.

'La patrie en danger'

In one of those sudden accelerations of revolutionary time, this counter-revolutionary situation led in less than six weeks to the insurrection that would bring down the monarchy.

The Prussian army, under the command of the duke of Brunswick, was now massed on the frontier. The king of Prussia was in Coblenz with 50,000 men, backed by the army of the princes under the orders of Condé. Lafayette had scarcely returned to his post when the news of Luckner's retreat came through. After a timid offensive towards Courtrai he had pulled back to Lille, on the pretext that the Belgians had not come out en masse and thrown themselves into the arms of the republican soldiers. It was clear that the war would rapidly move onto French territory, and no less clear that the greatest danger came from the defeatism of the king and the generals.

At the same moment there was royalist agitation in the provinces. The marquis de la Rouerie attempted to bring together in the west those nobles who had not emigrated; in the southern Ardèche, colonel de Saillans holed up with a force of several thousand in the château de Bannes; in the departments of Côtes-du-Nord, Finistère and Loire-Inférieure, insurrections broke out to prevent the departure of refractory priests. A general uprising was expected to follow the first successes of the enemy kings on the frontiers.

Despite the gravity of the situation, the Girondins remained hesitant. Their newspapers and spokesmen constantly named Louis XVI as the main obstacle to national defence. On 3 July, Vergniaud thundered:

> It is in the name of the king that the French princes have sought to move all the courts of Europe against the Nation; it is to avenge

> the dignity of the king that the treaty of Pillnitz has been concluded, and a monstrous alliance formed between the courts of Vienna and Berlin; it is to defend the king that former companies of the royal bodyguard have gathered in Germany under the flags of rebellion; it is to come to the aid of the king that the émigrés solicit and obtain employment in the Austrian armies, and prepare to tear the breast of their *patrie*.[7]

The logical conclusion of such a charge-sheet could only be to demand the king's immediate deposition. But no: Vergniaud was content to propose a message to the king from the Assembly, asking him to speedily refute these terrible accusations. The Girondins were afraid, in fact, that the king's deposition would unleash an uncontrollable popular movement. Brissot and his friends still hoped that Louis XVI would finally bow to pressure, and summon them back to government.

On 9 July, during an interminable speech, Brissot demanded an immediate proclamation of *la patrie en danger*, and a declaration that the ministers now in office did not enjoy the confidence of the Assembly.[8] The next day, the Garde des Sceaux, Dejoly, came to the Assembly and announced that, no longer able to do what was needed, the six ministers had handed the king their collective resignation.

On 11 July, at the proposal of Hérault de Séchelles, the Assembly officially proclaimed *la patrie en danger*. The same evening, Robespierre said at the Jacobins: 'Before this declaration, we knew that a conspiring general was at the head of our armies; we knew that a corrupt court was ceaselessly machinating against our liberty and our Constitution . . . The nation knew these dangers very well, but it seemed paralysed on the edge of the abyss, and the National Assembly has now sought to rouse it from this lethargy.'[9]

As there was no sign of this arousal, a few days later Robespierre demanded the dismissal of both the king and the Assembly: 'Has the

7 A. P., vol. 46, pp. 78–83.

8 Ibid., pp. 261–73.

9 Robespierre, *Œuvres complètes*, vol. 8, p. 391.

head of the executive power been faithful to the nation? Then he must be maintained. Has he betrayed it? Then he must be dismissed. The National Assembly is unwilling to pronounce this dismissal, and if the king is deemed to be guilty, then the Assembly itself is complicit in his offences.'[10] Robespierre proposed the calling of a National Convention, this time elected by universal suffrage:

> Let us therefore expiate this crime of *lèse-nation* and *lèse-humanité* by effacing such injurious distinctions, which measure the virtues and rights of a man by the amount he is taxed . . . Only by this action will you revive the patriotism and energy of the people; multiply our country's resources to infinity; destroy the influence of aristocracy and intrigue; and prepare a genuine national convention, the only legitimate and complete one that France will ever have seen.[11]

The Paris fédérés, advance signs of insurrection, the Brunswick Manifesto

The king had vetoed the encampment of 20,000 *fédérés*, but the Assembly found a way round. Those who were already en route – and there were many of them, especially coming from the Midi – would receive five sous for every league they travelled between their home department and Paris, as well as accommodation when they arrived in the capital. The largest contingent came from Marseille. On their departure, the mayor of Marseille, old Mouraille, harangued them: 'Go and make the tyrant blanch on the throne he no longer deserves! Go and tell him that the sovereign people are here to sanction the decrees he struck down with his monstrous veto!'[12] The battalion took twenty-seven days to reach Paris, spreading as it went the words

10 Ibid., p. 413.

11 Ibid., p. 415.

12 Albert Mathiez, *Le 10 août* [1931], republished Paris: Les Éditions de la Passion, 1989, p. 49.

of the 'Marseillaise'[13] and everywhere transmitting the patriotic passion that inspired it.

After the festival of 14 July 1792, most of the *fédérés* set out for the camp prepared for them at Soissons, but a good thousand or so remained in Paris, especially the most resolute patriots. The Jacobins found lodgings for them, collected money, invited them in and offered meals, so that the club became something of a headquarters for the Revolution.

On 18 July, the *fédérés* presented a petition to the Assembly calling for the deposition of the king: 'Do with the executive power what the salvation of the state, and the very Constitution, demand if ever the nation were betrayed by the executive power.' On several occasions it seemed as if insurrection would imminently break out, but Pétion and the Girondin Commune succeeded in forestalling this – particularly on 5 August, when the Marseille *fédérés* led by Chaumette and Momoro had established themselves in the Cordeliers convent, in the Théâtre-Français section on the left bank.[14] They acted as guards for this section after the minister of justice launched a prosecution against the Cordeliers for signing a resounding declaration against the status of passive citizens.[15]

At the end of July, the Paris sections had established a central correspondence bureau that met every day in the Hôtel de Ville. Information was exchanged, but there were no debates. In the first days of August a very different body came together: a meeting of the

---

13 [The song that became the French national anthem was actually composed in Strasbourg by Rouget de Lisle, at the commission of the city's mayor, and originally entitled 'Chant de guerre pour l'Armée du Rhin'. But as the people of Paris learned it from the Marseille *fédérés* it became universally known as the 'La Marseillaise'. – Translator]

14 The name of this section, centred on what is now the Odéon intersection, came from the fact that the Comédie-Française had long had its theatre on the rue des Fossés-Saint-Germain (now rue de l'Ancienne Comédie).

15 'The [active] citizens who up till now exclusively composed the section of Théâtre-Français, declaring loud and clear their repugnance towards their former privilege, call to their side all who have a domicile of any kind in this section, promising to share with them the exercise of the portion of sovereignty that belongs to the section and to regard them as brothers. Signed: Danton, president, Chaumette, vice-president, Momoro, secretary' (*Mémoires de Chaumette sur la Révolution du 10 août 1792*. Introduction and notes by F. A. Aulard, Paris: Société d'histoire de la Révolution française, 1893, p. 42).

section commissioners, a kind of central directorate whose role in the impending action would be crucial.[16]

From this point on, events accelerated. On 23 July, the section of La Fontaine-de-Grenelle proposed the deposition of Louis XVI. On 31 July, the Mauconseil section declared that it no longer recognized the dethroned king. On 2 August, the Gravilliers section declared that if the Assembly could not save the *patrie*, the people would rise to save it themselves. 'More than 3,000 citizens gathered on the Champ-de-Mars had signed a petition to the same effect, attaching to it a demand for the formal accusation of Lafayette and the dismissal of the army general staff. The petition was borne by a very large procession, preceded by a red bonnet on the end of a pike with the words: "Depose the king".'[17] On 3 August, forty-seven of the forty-eight sections signed the deposition petition, which Pétion presented to the Assembly in their name.

It was amid this tension that news reached Paris of the Brunswick Manifesto – written by an émigré and signed on 27 July – in which the commander in chief of the Austrian and Prussian armies proclaimed:

> If the Tuileries palace is breached or insulted, if the slightest violence or outrage is done to Their Majesties, the king, the queen and the royal family, if their safety, their preservation and their liberty are not immediately guaranteed, they [the Austrian emperor and the king of Prussia] will take an exemplary and unforgettable revenge, delivering the city of Paris to military invasion and total destruction, and the rebels guilty of the attack to the punishments they deserve.

This text, which was widely distributed, only increased popular fury. On 9 August, the sections of Gravilliers, Montreuil, Quinze-Vingt, Innocents, Gobelins and Tuileries proclaimed that 'at midnight, the

16 See Ernest Mellié, *Les Sections de Paris pendant la Révolution française*, Paris: Société d'histoire de la Révolution française, 1898.

17 *Mémoires de Chaumette*, p. 47.

sovereign [people] will rise up to reconquer their rights.'[18] During the night, twenty-eight of the forty-eight sections sent commissioners to the Hôtel de Ville with unlimited powers. The commissioner of the Fontaine-de-Grenelle section explained: 'The people made their way in a crowd to the Hôtel de Ville, and invited the commissioners to take over the Commune administration on a provisional basis. Having established themselves as representatives of the Commune, they [the commissioners] abolished the municipality, dismissed the commander-general [Mandat] and elected Santerre, whose nomination was confirmed by shouts of joy on the part of the people.'[19] It was in this strange and magnificent fashion that the *insurrectional Commune* was born on the night of 9–10 August, ready to play a leading role from now on vis-à-vis the Assembly.

The 10th of August, the taking of the Tuileries

As distinct from the two great revolutionary moments of 1789 – 14 July and 5–6 October – when the spontaneous surge of the people carried all before it, the insurrection of 10 August 1792 was carefully prepared and led by the Paris sections. They received decisive support, as we have seen, from the *fédérés*: those from Marseille, linked to the section of Théâtre-Français, and those from Brest with the faubourg Saint-Marceau section, which took the name of Finistère in their honour. 'At the sound of the tocsin ringing out in the clear night, first from the bell-towers of the Théâtre-Français section and gradually extending to the centre and east of the city, the National Guard unhurriedly took up their arms and made for the assembly point. The streets of the faubourg Antoine were lit up. A general mobilization was called.'[20]

18 Mellié, *Les Sections de Paris*, p. 117.

19 Ibid., p. 118.

20 Mathiez, *Le 10 août*, pp. 89, 96. Regarding the controversial role of Danton in the run-up to the insurrection, we have a first-hand document: 'Danton came to bed, he did not seem in any hurry. Midnight approached. People came several times to fetch him. Finally, he left for the Commune. The tocsin of the Cordeliers rang out, it rang for a long time!

The left bank sections concentrated their forces around the barracks of the Marseillais. Under the command of Alexandre, a leading figure from the faubourg Saint-Marceau, they came down the rue Dauphine to the Pont-Neuf, where an artillery battery blocked the way. Manuel, *procureur* of the legal Commune, had the cannon withdrawn, and around six o'clock in the morning the column reached the Carrousel.[21]

The right bank sections gathered around the Enfants-Trouvés battalion, in the faubourg Saint-Antoine. Santerre divided these forces into three columns: one would proceed along the river, protecting the flank from a possible attack by the royalist battalions on the Île Saint-Louis, in Saint-Étienne-du-Mont and Les-Thermes-du-Julien; another went along the boulevards to secure the sections of Petits-Pères and Filles-de-Saint-Thomas; and in the centre, the bulk of the troops marched in a straight line down the rues Saint-Antoine and Saint-Honoré.

At the palace, the defence forces were made up of gentlemen of the Court, detachments of the National Guard from sections loyal to the king, gendarmes on foot and on horse, and above all three battalions of Swiss Guards: a total of between two and three thousand men who took up position with their cannon on two sides of the palace, in the courtyards and in the Tuileries gardens.

After Mandat had left for the Hôtel de Ville,[22] Rœderer, the chief *procureur* of the Paris department, managed to convince the king to seek sanctuary at the Assembly. Between two lines of Swiss Guards,

---

Alone, bathed in tears, on my knees in front of the window, hidden in my handkerchief, I listened to the sound of that fatal bell.' And further on, in the words of Mme Robert (Louise de Kéralio): 'But that Danton, the supposed rallying point, who stayed in his bed, if my husband dies I shall be the woman who stabs him!' (Lucile Desmoulins, *Journal*, text established and presented by Philippe Lejeune, Paris: Éditions des Cendres, 1995, pp. 154–5).

21 In those days the Carrousel was not the dusty steppe it has since become, but a whole popular quarter wedged between the Louvre and the Tuileries (see Eric Hazan, *The Invention of Paris*, London: Verso, 2010, p. 26ff).

22 He was sent by what remained of the legal Commune, but did not return. Accused by the section commissioners of having given a written order to fire on the people 'from the flank and behind' if the Tuileries were attacked, he was killed on the steps of the Hôtel de Ville.

the king and queen, surrounded by ministers and members of the department, crossed the Tuileries gardens and made their entrance into the hall of the Manège. 'Gentlemen,' said the king, 'I come here to prevent a great crime. I shall always believe myself and my family to be safe amid the representatives of the nation.' To which Vergniaud, who was presiding, replied: 'The National Assembly is aware of all its duties, and sees one of the dearest of these to be the maintenance of all established authorities', which amounted to a commitment to maintaining the monarchy. When the triumph of the insurrection began to seem increasingly inevitable, this commitment was watered down until it turned into its opposite.

During this time, the Marseillais and the faubourg Saint-Marceau, who had occupied the place du Carrousel, began to fraternize with the National Guard, particularly the gunners positioned in the courtyards. These first of all removed the ammunition from their guns, then turned them against the palace, leaving it with no artillery except on the garden side. Resistance was becoming problematic, and the National Guard, who had already begun to defect, withdrew almost entirely. The gendarmes were scattered in external positions where they could hardly be useful. All that remained for the defence of the palace were seven or eight hundred Swiss Guards, 200 gentlemen, and a few dozen grenadiers of the National Guard. At nine in the morning, the order was given to abandon the courtyards and retreat into the palace.

The insurgents entered the courtyards and managed to penetrate the building by the main door, which had not been well secured. Slipping along the walls, they started to fraternize with the Swiss Guards, promising to treat them as brothers if they went over to the side of the nation. Many of the Swiss responded to these advances at once, throwing cartridges from the top of the staircase to the people occupying the courtyard and vestibule, to show that these were only powder. But suddenly a shot rang out, no doubt fired by one of the gentlemen positioned in the Louvre gallery. This was the signal for a general volley of gunfire. The Swiss Guards fired down on the courtyard from the first floor, and from the top of the staircase into the vestibule. The insurgents were caught off guard by what seemed to them to be a betrayal. Captain Durler, the commander of the Swiss Guards, came out at their head and raked the courtyard of the Carrousel. The dead and wounded lay scattered on the ground and the insurgents panicked, some of them falling back to the Hôtel de Ville.

But the Marseillais and the faubourg Saint-Marceau stood their ground. The Marseille gunners stopped the Swiss advance and forced them to retreat into the palace. Reinforcements arrived from the faubourg Saint-Antoine, with cannon that backed up the fire of the Marseillais:

> Sprayed with bullets, choked by smoke, overwhelmed by the ever-growing number of their attackers, the Swiss found it hard to stand their ground in the courtyards. Around eleven o'clock, the *maréchal de camp* d'Hervilly, hatless and unarmed, ran out amid gunshots shouting for them to cease fire at the king's request, and withdraw into the National Assembly . . . The retreat across the Tuileries gardens was deadly, under a hail of bullets. The disarmed Swiss, between one and two hundred, were taken into an outbuilding of the Feuillants convent to protect them from the rage of the crowd.[23]

In these two hours of battle, the Paris insurgents and the *fédérés* had nearly a thousand of their number killed or wounded. The losses among the besieged were certainly greater still, but no inquiry was launched to establish them precisely.

EXCURSUS: THE PARISIAN SANS-CULOTTES

In our day there is an image behind this word: a man wearing a short jacket with metal buttons (the Carmagnole), and cloth trousers instead of the silk breeches and stockings of the aristocrats. On his head is a red woollen bonnet, the headgear of freed slaves in Rome.

23 Mathiez, *Le 10 août*, pp. 117–8.

He is armed with a pike, the popular weapon par excellence. But beyond this iconography, who were the sans-culottes?

> A sans-culotte, you rogues, is a man who always goes on foot, who has neither millions nor a château, no valets to serve him, but dwells simply with his wife and children, if he has any, on the fourth or fifth floor . . . In the evening he attends his section, not powdered, perfumed and booted in the hope of being noticed by every woman citizen on the benches, but to support good motions with all his might and demolish those that come from the abominable faction of men of condition.[24]

Sans-culottes worked for their living, and more precisely, with their hands. It was they, wrote Hébert in *Le Père Duchesne* in September 1793, 'who make the fabrics in which we are clothed, who work the metals and manufacture the weapons that serve to defend the Republic'. Many of them received a wage, but they also included plenty of small employers, as well as artisans in solitary workshops. The majority of sans-culottes thus belonged to the artisan class, even if the number of wage-earners in the manufactories scattered across Paris has perhaps been underestimated.[25] We must also count the many poverty-stricken patriots in the faubourgs Saint-Antoine and Saint-Marceau, which may explain the political activism of those *quartiers*.

The sans-culottes clearly detested the aristocrats, but by this term they included not only the former nobles but also the upper layers of the former Third Estate. 'On 21 May 1793, a popular orator from the Section du Mail stated that "aristocrats are the rich, wealthy merchants, monopolists, middlemen, bankers, trading clerks, quibbling lawyers and citizens who own anything".'[26]

---

24 Archives nationales, F[7] 4775 (48), Vingternier file, 23 April 1793. Quoted in Haim Burstin, *L'Invention du sans-culotte*, Paris: Odile Jacob, 2005, p. 57. The 'men of condition', often denounced by Marat, were an object of popular execration.

25 This point is stressed by those historians who see the sans-culottes as a kind of pre-proletariat. See for example Daniel Guérin, *La lutte de classes sous la Première République*, Paris: Gallimard, 1946.

26 Albert Soboul, *The Parisian Sans-Culottes and the French Revolution*, Oxford: Oxford University Press, 1964, p. 22. We have not yet reached year II, and Soboul's great

The demands of the sans-culottes focused on three distinct issues: the price of provisions, equality of consumption, and democracy in the sections.

On provisions, there was a wide gulf between them and the assemblies – not just the Legislative but also the Convention – in which the majority supported the ideas of the Physiocrats: free trade, particularly in grain, had been brought into being by the Revolution. The sans-culottes, for their part, believed that the rise in prices and the constant devaluation of the *assignats* made it essential to fix the prices of staple foods and household supplies, if they were to be able to feed and clothe themselves. Popular movements for wage increases were far rarer than those that pressed for a price cap on subsistence goods, by force if need be.

This demand was coupled with a quest for equality in all areas of life. The rich should live no better than the poor, their surplus should be taken away, they should be compelled to share. Money should not enable them to eat better. The general council of the insurrectional Commune decided that there would henceforth be only one kind of bread, 'equality bread'. Since 'Wealth and poverty must disappear in a world based on equality', it was announced: 'In future the rich will not have their bread made from wheaten flour whilst the poor have theirs made from bran.'[27]

In their sections the sans-culottes applied a principle of radical democracy. On 25 August 1792, the assembly of the section of Marché-des-Innocents proposed that 'public officials can be recalled by their electors, whose decisions they are obliged to implement'. On the same day, the assembly of Bonne-Nouvelle reminded its delegates of 'the imprescriptible right which they [the sections] possess to deprive them of their authority'.[28] For the Convention elections, several sections decided that electors would vote aloud and in the presence of the public.[29] During the crisis of spring 1793

work *Les Sans-culottes parisiens en l'an II* will be drawn on below.

27 Ibid., p. 57.

28 Ibid., p. 113.

29 The electors: once again, those who had been elected by the primary assemblies, and would go on to choose the deputies.

the sans-culottes imposed voting by acclamation, or by standing up, as the only way of displaying popular unanimity. It was around this time too that *fraternization* appeared, sealing the unity of sans-culottes across the sections. 'On 21 April 1793, a large deputation from the general assembly of the Section des Lombards visited the general assembly in the Section du Contrat-Social. Its speaker denounced "the intrigues, anarchy, and endless disturbances produced by the royalist party of Dumouriez, and the bitter divisions which result in the assemblies".' The two sections swore a solemn oath 'to live and correspond with one another fraternally in a close and affectionate union, and to crush the aristocratic monster under their feet'.[30]

Soboul has been criticized for having made the sans-culotte into 'an ideal type, a kind of abstraction constructed as a function of the political context from which he emerged'.[31] It is true that the notion is fairly elastic, sometimes conjuring up by metonymy the world of popular Paris, sometimes the crowds of the great revolutionary *journées*, sometimes again the militants who dominated the life of the sections. But the often violent confrontations with the assemblies and established authorities were not the work of a stereotyped ideal: they show the very real presence of this being of flesh and blood, the Parisian sans-culotte.

The Assembly and the insurrectional Commune

Once the outcome of the battle was decided, the session of 10 August in the Assembly was long, agitated and confused.[32] The president of the insurrectional Commune, Huguenin, who the previous day had been simply a customs clerk, addressed the deputies in an imperious and almost brutal tone:

---

30 Soboul, *The Parisian Sans-Culottes*, p. 153.

31 Burstin, *L'Invention du sans-culotte*, p. 76.

32 A. P., vol. 47, pp. 634–92.

> It is the new magistrates of the people who present themselves at your bar . . . The people have charged us with declaring to you that they invest you anew with their trust, but it has charged us at the same time with declaring to you that they can only recognize, as sole judge of the extraordinary measures to which necessity and resistance to oppression have brought them, the French people, your sovereign and ours, gathered together in their primary assemblies.[33]

– which clearly meant the end of the Legislative Assembly. Guadet, presiding, replied in vague terms, urging the petitioners to restore calm to the city.

In the same sitting, however, Vergniaud proposed that the head of the executive power should be 'provisionally suspended', and the French people invited to elect a National Convention on the basis of universal suffrage. The king and his family would be placed in safety at the Luxembourg palace. Six ministers would be provisionally appointed by the Assembly, by individual election. They could only be drawn from its ranks. In theory, therefore, the monarchy would remain; indeed, Vergniaud had already persuaded the Assembly to appoint a 'tutor for the Prince Royal'.[34]

The measures taken over the following weeks reflected the confrontation between the Assembly and Gironde on the one hand, and the Commune and the majority of the Jacobins club on the other. On 11 August, Robespierre was elected to the Commune by his section, that of place Vendôme.[35]

A number of decisions would tip the balance towards the Brissotin side, starting with a non-decision: there was no proclamation to depose the king or found a republic. But the idea of a tutor for

33 Ibid., p. 641.

34 [This was the dauphin Louis-Charles, seven years old at this time. – Translator]

35 We should remember that, on the night of 9–10 August, only twenty-eight sections had sent a commissioner to the Hôtel de Ville. So there had to be elections in the twenty remaining sections to complete the insurrectional Commune. Place Vendôme was then the heart of a popular quarter, and the section subsequently renamed itself the Piques (Pikes) section.

the dauphin was very vigorously opposed. Anthoine, for example, at the Jacobins on 13 August: 'What, you are launching an attack on the monarchy, you have pulled down the statues of kings and now here is a decree for the education of a Prince Royal! But what use have we for this Prince Royal?'[36] In the same speech, Anthoine demanded the condemnation of Lafayette and the sacking of the general staff, which the Assembly refused to do until Lafayette went over to the enemy on the 19th.

The ministers it appointed to replace those resigning were the three Brissotins dismissed by the king in June: Roland at interior, Servan at war, and Clavière at finance. To them were added Monge at the navy, Lebrun at foreign affairs and, as a token to the people, Danton was elected minister of justice by 222 out of 284 votes.

Universal (male) suffrage was decided at the same session of 10 August. On a report by Jean Debry, the Assembly voted without debate that all citizens over twenty-five would be electors. This spelled the end of the property qualification and the distinction between active and passive citizens, but Robespierre demanded more: the direct election of deputies by the primary assemblies, instead of a two-tier system. Since 1789, in fact, the primary assemblies had functioned on a democratic basis, and it was not uncommon for women to be able to vote in them. Robespierre was not supported, leading him to write: 'The useless and dangerous intermediary of the electoral bodies ought to have been suppressed, and the people enabled to choose their representatives themselves. The Assembly has followed routine rather than principles.'[37] And Marat echoed: 'On hearing the manner decreed for the election of deputies to the Convention, I exclaimed aloud. I saw this simply as an artificial means for filling the supreme council of the nation with corrupt men, conferring the choice of the people's representatives on the electoral bodies.'[38]

---

36 Aulard, *La Société des Jacobins*, vol. 4, p. 197.

37 *Le Défenseur de la Constitution*, no. 12 [and last: Robespierre subsequently changed the title of his paper to *Lettres à mes commettants*], *Œuvres complètes*, vol. 4, p. 358.

38 *L'Ami du peuple*, 15 September 1792. By this date, Marat had been elected to the Convention as a deputy for Paris.

On the other hand, the Commune succeeded in getting rid of the Paris department, 'a name that has become odious in Paris' (Robespierre). On 21 August, the general council of the Commune requested the Assembly to jettison it, 'considering that, in order to assure public safety and liberty, it needs all the powers delegated to it by the people at the moment when they were forced to take back the exercise of their rights.'[39]

Marat unreservedly supported the Commune against the Assembly. He wrote in *L'Ami du peuple*, 13 August: 'Oh you, worthy commissioners of the Paris sections, true representatives of the people, beware of the traps laid for you by the faithless deputies, beware of their seductions . . . Do not leave the helm of public authority placed in your hands until the National Convention has freed us of the despot and his unworthy breed.'

On 11 August, the king and his family were brought to the Luxembourg, but the Commune had them removed from this royal residence to the Temple, where Louis was now no more than a prisoner. In parallel with this, the Assembly decided that all its decrees that had been vetoed would immediately come into force, in particular that on the deportation of refractory priests. A decree signed on 26 August gave them two weeks to leave France; once this deadline had passed, they would be deported to Guyana.

The king in the Temple

Even if the *fédérés* from the south played a major role in it, the *journée* of 10 August took place in Paris. It was urgent for the country as a whole, still attached to the monarchical Constitution, to understand and accept what had happened. It was also necessary to prevent the army being misled by the words of its factious generals.

On 12 August, the Commune had the authors and printers of

39 The text presented by the Commune was drafted by Robespierre, *Œuvres complètes*, vol. 8, p. 440. There would indeed be a new departmental administration, but its role was reduced to that of a 'commission of contributions'.

'anti-civic', royalist and Feuillant newspapers arrested.[40] Heading a deputation from the Commune, Léonard Bourdon, the president of the Gravilliers section, came to the Assembly to say: 'The incendiary papers are no longer polluting either the capital or the departments. Their presses and their stocks of type will now be used to serve the Revolution.'[41]

The Assembly, for its part, published papers that had been found in the home of Laporte, in charge of the civil list, which revealed the king's treasonable collusion with foreign powers. These were widely distributed and dealt a severe blow to monarchist sentiment.[42]

Since the Tuileries had been taken, however, petitions were pouring in to the Assembly from peasants complaining of lawsuits against them and difficulties in redeeming seigniorial rights. The Assembly decided to suspend all prosecutions based on former feudal rights. On 16 August, following a petition from a citizen in Laon, it decreed on Chabot's proposal 'that all feudal and seigniorial rights of all kinds are suppressed without indemnity, unless they were the price of the original granting of the tenement'.[43] At the time that this great decree was promulgated, citizens began to gather for the coming formation of primary assemblies. 'There were thus echo chambers on all sides that irresistibly propagated the laws of emancipation.'[44]

Meanwhile Lafayette, the other great loser of 10 August, called on his army to march on Paris to restore the Constitution and put the king back on his throne. At one point he managed to win over the municipality of Sedan and the department of Ardennes, and jailed the commissioners sent by the Assembly, but the volunteers very

---

40 The chief of these were *L'Ami du Roi*, *La Gazette universelle*, *L'Indicateur*, *Le Mercure de France*, *Le Journal de la cour et de la ville* and *La Feuille du jour*.

41 A. P., vol. 48, p. 69.

42 These were not yet the contents of the 'iron cabinet', but the documents seized were highly compromising: among other things, orders from the king to pay the stipends of his bodyguards who had gone over to Coblenz, and letters from émigrés full of joy at the French defeats.

43 A. P., vol. 48, p. 291. The conditions of the proof (of concession) were to be sent to the committee on feudalism.

44 Jaurès, *Histoire socialiste*, vol. 2, p. 644. At the end of this volume, Jaurès has some remarkable pages on the suppression of seigniorial rights in August 1792.

soon refused to obey him and he was forced to flee to the enemy along with his general staff. The Assembly only voted the indictment against him at the moment when he crossed the frontier. Dumouriez was appointed to the army of the East, and Kellermann replaced Luckner in the North.

The people demand revenge for the 'ambush' of 10 August

What most excited the people after 10 August was the question of how those responsible for the Tuileries massacre, which everyone saw as a deliberate ambush, would be punished. The popular voice called for vengeance against the Swiss Guards and the general staffs of the gendarmerie and National Guard.[45]

The Commune issued an appeal for calm ('Sovereign people, suspend your vengeance. A justice that had gone to sleep is today resuming all its rights. All those guilty will perish on the scaffold'),[46] but the same evening the administrators of police at the Hôtel de Ville handed a note to Santerre: 'We have learned of intentions to enter the prisons of Paris in order *to abduct all the prisoners and render summary justice*. We request you to promptly extend your surveillance over the prisons of the Châtelet, the Conciergerie and the Force.'[47]

Thus the disaster that would unfold in September was already foreshadowed. Clear measures would have been needed to avoid it, but the Assembly, worried about legality and unwilling to give in to the Commune, hesitated and dithered. On 14 August it referred the investigation and judgement of the crimes of 10 August to the regular courts. The next day, the Commune sent a delegation to the Assembly. Robespierre spoke in its name:

---

45 Danton had great difficulty on 11 August in getting the Swiss Guards who had taken refuge on the premises of the Assembly to leave, finally conducting them in person to the Abbaye.

46 *Procès-verbaux de la Commune de Paris (10 août 1792–1er juin 1793)* [extracts taken from a manuscript in the Archives Nationales by Maurice Tourneux], Paris: Société d'histoire de la Révolution française, 1894, p. 10.

47 Cited by Mathiez, *La Révolution française*, vol. 2, p. 10. My emphasis.

> Since the 10th, the just vengeance of the people has remained unsatisfied. I do not know what invincible obstacles seem to stand in the way . . . The people are resting but not asleep. They want the punishment of the guilty, and rightly so. We pray you to rid us of the established authorities, in whom we have no confidence at all; we wish the culprits to be judged by commissioners taken from each section, in sovereign fashion and as a last resort.[48]

In the end the Assembly gave in. On 17 August it decided to establish an extraordinary tribunal composed of juries and judges elected by the sections. Robespierre, appointed president by virtue of being top of the list, refused the post: 'I could not be the judge of those whose adversary I have been, forced to remember that besides being enemies of the *patrie*, they were also my own.'[49]

These debates exacerbated the conflict between the Commune and the Assembly, which moved onto the offensive on 30 August. Roland declared that he could not answer for the provisioning of Paris, as the Commune had disrupted the existing system by abolishing the committee on subsistence goods. Attacks multiplied against 'these men who, without a legal mission, have placed themselves at the head of the Commune of Paris and illegitimately exercise there, in the name of the people, functions that the people have not delegated to them'.[50] Finally a decree was passed ordering the immediate replacement of the entire Commune. Robespierre, legalistic as he often was, asked the Commune to demand a new investiture from the people, but for once he was not supported.

> M. Robespierre, in an eloquent speech in which he exposed all the treacherous manoeuvres that have been used to lower the general council in the public esteem, ended by requesting the council to hand back to the people the powers it had received from them. The Commune *procureur* [Manuel], while applauding the

48 Robespierre, *Œuvres complètes*, vol. 8, pp. 436–7.

49 A reason that seems perfectly respectable, though hatred of Robespierre is so strong that many historians (even Jaurès) have seen this as a Machiavellian manoeuvre.

50 Henry-Larivière, in the Assembly (A. P., vol. 49, p. 142).

principles of the previous speaker, reminded the council of the oath it had taken to remain at its post to the death, and to only abandon this when the *patrie* was no longer in danger. He concluded that the council should continue to fulfil its functions. Resolved.[51]

The capture of Longwy, the threat to Verdun; Danton launches the levée en masse

Meanwhile, the war in Lorraine was turning into a catastrophe. On 15 August it was learned that Thionville was under siege, and on the 20th it was the turn of Longwy, which surrendered on the 23rd. This news reached Paris on the 25th. At the time of the attack the local commander, Lavergne, was nowhere to be found; his cowardice, if not treason, was flagrant. The Assembly decreed the death penalty for any citizen who spoke of surrender anywhere that was under siege. On 1 September, news arrived that Verdun, the last fortified point between the enemy and Paris, was besieged by the duke of Brunswick. The garrison commander, lieutenant-colonel Beaurepaire, sent a letter to the Assembly vowing to die rather than surrender, which was noble of him but scarcely reassuring.[52]

Almost at the same time, it was learned that the royalists in the Vendée had risen up against recruitment. Setting out from Châtillon-sur-Sèvre, they had seized Bressuire, a republican town in the midst of the royalist *bocage*. The patriots had a very hard job repelling them, and the battle left more than 200 dead.

After the fall of Longwy, the ministers met to listen to Kersaint, one of the deputies dispatched to see the armies, who predicted

51 *Procès-verbaux de la Commune*, p. 76. The Assembly finally backed down, deciding that instead of two commissioners each section could appoint six to the general council, but that the commissioners acting since 10 August would remain council members. 'The revolutionary Commune was, as it were, enveloped in a broader legal Commune' (Jaurès).

52 A. P., vol. 49, p. 192. Beaurepaire was as good as his word. When the municipal council called on him to capitulate, he shot himself in the head during their session. Some believed he had been assassinated, to facilitate surrender.

that Brunswick would be in Paris within two weeks. The Girondin ministers panicked. Roland declared that the government should leave for Tours or Blois, taking the treasury and the king with it. Clavière and Servan supported him, but Danton stood firm: 'I have brought my seventy-year-old mother to Paris. I have brought my two children, who arrived yesterday. Before the Prussians enter Paris I would wish my family to perish with me, and that 20,000 torches should turn Paris into a heap of cinders in an instant. Roland, be careful in talking of flight, be afraid, lest the people are listening!'[53]

During these days when alarming news was coming thick and fast, it was Danton who found the words and took the measures that were needed. On 28 August he spoke before the Assembly:

> The anxieties that are being spread with regard to our situation are much exaggerated, for we still have armies ready to pursue the enemy and fall on him if he advances inward . . . It was only through a great upheaval that we destroyed despotism in the capital; it is only through a national upheaval that we shall be able to repel the despots . . . Up to now you have seen only the simulated war of Lafayette; today we must wage a far more frightful war, the war of the Nation against the despots. It is time to tell the people that the people en masse must hurl themselves against their foes.[54]

In the same speech, he proposed that the Assembly should authorize house searches 'to distribute to the defenders of the *patrie* the weapons that indolent or ill-disposed citizens may be hiding', and appoint commissioners 'from its ranks, to go along with those of the executive power to encourage the citizens, in the name of the *patrie*, to march to its defence'.

These raids began on 30 August and went on for two days: all the houses in Paris were searched, and some 3,000 suspects led off to prison.

On 2 September, Danton launched the first *levée en masse*:

53 Mathiez, *La Révolution française*, vol. 2, pp. 16–17.

54 André Fribourg (ed.), *Discours de Danton*, Paris: Hachette, 1910, pp. 48–9.

> Everywhere there is stirring and commotion, a burning wish to fight, an uprising in France from one end of the realm to the other. One part of the people will head for the frontiers; another will dig trenches; and a third will defend our town centres with pikes . . . We demand that within forty leagues of the point where battle is waged, those citizens who have weapons shall march against the enemy; those who remain are to arm themselves with pikes. We demand that anyone who refuses to serve in person or to hand over his weapons shall be punished with death . . . We demand that couriers be sent to all departments to advise them of the decrees that you have issued. The ringing of tocsins will resound throughout France. This is not a signal of alarm, but a signal to charge against the enemies of the *patrie*. In order to conquer, gentlemen, we need boldness, more boldness, and boldness again, and France will be saved.[55]

A very famous speech, and a just foundation for Danton's historic glory, whatever he might be criticized for later on.

The same day, the delegates of the Commune came to the Assembly to read a proclamation: 'Citizens, march out forthwith under your flags; let us gather on the Champ-de-Mars; let an army of 60,000 men be formed this instant. Let us expire under the blows of the enemy, or exterminate him under our own.'[56]

The September massacres

Inside the tense city, however, different rumblings were being heard: how could citizens depart for the frontier while Paris was teeming with traitors, while suspects were plotting in the prisons, preparing to escape with help from abroad and to massacre patriots . . . Since the justice of the 17 August tribunal was so slow and tentative, it was up to the people to render justice themselves. Such were the explosive

55 Ibid., pp. 52–4.
56 *Procès-verbaux de la Commune*, pp. 77–8.

fears that spread on the news that Verdun was under siege. The Quinze-Vingt section demanded the imprisonment of the wives and children of émigrés and the punishment of conspirators, before any citizens left for the army. Faubourg-Poissonière called for all priests and imprisoned suspects to be put to death before the volunteers departed. Its decree was approved by the sections of Luxembourg, Louvre, and Fontaine-Montmorency.[57]

On the morning of 2 September, the Commune decreed that 'the alarm gun will be fired immediately, the tocsin and the call to arms sounded'. This tocsin – and we can barely imagine the collective fear unleashed by this sinister tolling from every bell tower in Paris – marked the start of the September massacres.[58]

These began in the afternoon of the 2nd, when refractory priests being taken to the Abbaye prison were massacred en route by their guards, *fédérés* from Marseille and Brittany. Next came the turn of refractory priests held in the Carmelite convent, and later on, at nightfall, of the prisoners in the Abbaye, where priests were held together with Swiss and royal guards. That night the killers repaired to the Conciergerie, the Châtelet and the prison of La Force on the rue Pavée. In the morning of the 3rd they continued their deadly work at the seminary of Saint-Firmin, near Saint-Nicolas-du-Chardonnet, and, not far from there, at the Bernardins, where condemned prisoners waited to be sent to the galleys. In the afternoon it was the turn of the Bicêtre prison, and finally on the 4th, that of the Salpêtrière.

The killing happened differently in different places. In the Abbaye an improvised tribunal was set up, under Stanislas Maillard.[59] With

---

57 Ibid., p. 83, and Mathiez, *La Révolution française*, vol. 2, p. 25.

58 Happily (for us), there is an exemplary book on this subject, whose critique of the sources, meticulous research and absence of any moral consideration have greatly clarified it: Pierre Caron, *Les Massacres de septembre*, Paris: Maison du livre français, 1935. In his introduction, Caron explains that almost all the documents on the massacres (the prison records in particular) were burned in the Hôtel de Ville fire of 1871. His study is based on historical work dating from before the fire, and on what remains of contemporary documents. All these sources are evaluated with exceptional care and discernment.

59 We have twice already come across this strange bailiff's clerk, always dressed in black: at the taking of the Bastille, when he was one of the heroes, and during the *journées* of October 1789, when he was the guide and spokesman of the women at Versailles.

the prison register before him, he questioned the prisoners and delivered the verdicts together with his assessors. At the Force, Pétion relates that on the morning of the 3rd, 'the men who judged and those who executed behaved as confidently as if the law had summoned them to fulfil these functions'. There was nothing of this kind, however, in the prisons affected by massacres over the following days – the Conciergerie, the Châtelet, Bicêtre and the Salpêtrière. Here the slaughter was carried out by smallish squads working with pikes, sabres and cudgels – in silence, according to Pétion's testimony.[60]

How many died in these massacres? Caron establishes that, in the last days of August, the Paris prisons contained 2,600 individuals – which puts paid to the eight or ten thousand dead cited by such classic historians as Thiers or Mignet. Of this number, rather less than half were killed: between 1,090 and 1,395.[61] What is most striking is that almost all of the victims – in every prison save for the Abbaye and the Carmes – were 'non-political'; they had nothing to do with the events of 10 August, yet bore the brunt in far greater numbers (between 737 and 1,003 according to Caron). It has often been claimed that these were 'common law' prisoners, but can the thirty or so minors killed in a Bicêtre reformatory – a bad lot, no doubt, aged between twelve and seventeen – or the thirty-five young and not so young women, perhaps of 'ill repute', massacred in the Salpêtrière, be classified in this way?

Who were the killers? We get an idea of this from the minutes of the trial of the *septembriseurs* held in year IV, at the peak of the Thermidor reaction. The majority were artisans, small businessmen and shopkeepers, along with a few *fédérés*, soldiers and gendarmes. However, Caron emphasizes, these were actually 'the social categories that public opinion in year IV considered to have supplied the killers'.[62] What is certain is that they were not 'the dregs of the people',

---

60 According to Caron, the drunken clamour, the evisceration of the princesse de Lamballe, and the glass of blood drunk by Mlle de Sombreuil to save her father are among the myths put about by the Girondins. The princesse de Lamballe was beheaded and her head paraded on a pike, which is quite enough.

61 Caron, *Les Massacres de septembre*, p. 101.

62 Ibid., p. 109. Besides, the majority of defendants in these trials were acquitted.

as was often heard at the time, particularly from the Girondin side.

The established authorities reacted feebly to news of the first massacres. Santerre held (not without reason, to be sure) that the obedience of the National Guard could not be relied on. The Assembly, on Basire's proposal, sent commissioners to the Abbaye. One of these, Dusaulx, reported on his return: 'The deputies whom you sent to calm the people arrived with much difficulty at the gates of the Abbaye. There we tried to make ourselves heard. One of us stood on a chair, but scarcely had he spoken a few words than his voice was drowned by tumultuous cries.'[63]

Danton, the minister of justice, seems to have been unmoved by the prisoners' fate. There remained the Commune and its supervisory committee. On the morning of the 3rd, it appointed commissioners 'to proceed to the Palais-Bourbon, protect the Swiss Guards who are held there and defend their lives by every possible means'.[64] The same evening, 'the general council, greatly alarmed and distraught by the harshness employed against the prisoners, appointed commissioners to calm the excitement and bring back to due principles those who may have strayed from these.' Tallien reported: 'The council of the Commune sent a deputy [to the Abbaye] to stop the disaster. The Commune *procureur* was the first to arrive, and used every means that his zeal and his humanity suggested to him. He was unable to prevail and saw several victims fall at his feet. He found himself in danger and had to be escorted out.'[65] And on the 4th: 'The council, deeply afflicted by the news still coming in from the Abbaye, is sending two commissioners there to restore order.'[66] These commissioners were no more heeded than the others. 'The failure was fatal,' writes Caron, but the intention was clear.

Marat recalls his eagerness to protect 'the innocent' from harm:

> I happened to be at the surveillance committee when it was announced that the people had seized from the hands of the

---

63 A. P., vol. 49, p. 219.

64 *Procès-verbaux de la Commune*, p. 83.

65 *Le Moniteur*, vol. 13, p. 603.

66 *Procès-verbaux de la Commune*, p 88.

> guards and put to death several refractory priests being sent to the Force [Marat's mistake, it was the Abbaye] by the committee, and that the people were threatening to proceed to the prisons. On this news, Panis and I cried out, as if by common inspiration: 'Save the poor debtors, those imprisoned for brawling, and the petty criminals',[67]

which implies that the others might as well be massacred, nothing much could be done about it.[68]

This terrible episode has given rise to reams of commentary, from September 1792 through to today, identifying it as the start of the fatal 'slippage' of the Revolution into bloodthirstiness. Taking an altogether different line, Timothy Tackett has made a study of the rumours circulating in Paris at that time, basing himself above all on correspondence exchanged between the revolutionaries at the precise time of the massacres.[69] His first conclusion is that the great majority of them accepted and even applauded the actions. For example, the Montagnard deputy Dubreuil-Chambardel: 'This whole scoundrel race of non-jurors is getting what it deserves for all its misdeeds. We have reason to think that the realm will soon be purged of all such monsters.'

As for the rumours, widespread in the 'upper' strata of society as well as among the people, Tackett distinguishes two kinds. The first sprang from fear of the prisons and their inmates. The prisons, located inside the city, were not yet the bunkers they would become. The fear of counter-revolutionary prisoners swarming out to take

---

67 *Journal de la République française*, no. 12 (6 October 1792). This was the new title of Marat's paper after his election to the Convention.

68 Marat and the surveillance committee have been much criticized for the circular sent on 3 September to the provinces (and countersigned by Danton): 'The Commune of Paris hastens to inform its brothers in the departments that some of the ferocious conspirators held in its prisons have been put to death by the people', going on to hope that 'the whole nation . . . will shortly adopt this necessary measure of public safety'. For Mathiez, it was 'a superfluous circular. Those in the provinces had no need for Paris to offer them an example. In some cases they had preceded it' (*La Révolution française*, vol. 2, p. 30).

69 Timothy Tackett, 'Rumor and Revolution: The Case of the September Massacres', in *French History and Civilization*, vol. 4, January 2011, pp. 53–64, h-France.net/rude/rudevoliv/tackett. The following quotations are taken from this remarkable work.

revenge on the patriots was compounded by the word that they had managed to get hold of weapons. It was also said that the prisons were full of 'brigands' who would back up the aristocrats: 'We fear' – wrote a bourgeois by the name of Guittard – 'that brigands will set fire to Paris.'

The other family of rumours was fuelled by the fear of a conspiracy mounted by the aristocrats. As old as the Revolution itself, this grew under the Legislative Assembly, spread by Brissot and his friends, reaching a peak with the first military defeats. Lafayette's defection to the enemy could only pour oil on the fire:

> Stories spread rapidly that 400 nobles, escaped from the Tuileries on August 10, were now hiding out underground and waiting to strike; that the seminarians of Saint-Sulpice were secretly manufacturing daggers and paying the surviving Swiss Guards to use them; that huge caches of weapons were concealed beneath the Pantheon and under the Palais-Royal in preparation for a counter-revolutionary coup; that armed men were threatening to attack the Jacobins; that evildoers had placed pieces of glass in the city's flour supply.[70]

The anxiety and uncertainty, Tackett concludes, were so strong and so pervasive throughout society, that a consensus could come about on these rumours, and 'a large body of Parisians sympathized with the idea that "one must kill the devil before he kills us".'[71]

---

70 Tackett, 'Rumor and revolution', p. 63.

71 *Journal de Nicolas-Célestin Guittard de Floriban, bourgeois de Paris sous la Révolution, 1791–1796*, cited by Tackett, 'Rumor and Revolution', p. 64.

CHAPTER 8

September 1792 to January 1793

The opening of the Convention – Valmy, the proclamation of the Republic, the clash between Gironde and Montagne, the trial and execution of the king

They were alone in the hall. Danton had before him a glass and a dust-covered bottle of wine, reminiscent of Luther's beer mug; in front of Marat, a cup of coffee; and in front of Robespierre, just papers.

– Victor Hugo, *Ninety-Three*

Responsibility for the massacres – Marat

In the days and weeks that followed the massacres, the Girondins sought to pin the responsibility on their political opponents: the massacres were not the action of the people of Paris, but perpetrated by a small number of 'hired brigands'. Under whose direction? That of a few 'tyrants' who sought to climb to power over the corpses of their enemies. These tyrants were to be found in the Commune of Paris and its surveillance committee, and among the leaders of the Montagne – Robespierre, Danton, and above all Marat.

There is a common opinion, maintained by many historians

(including Jaurès, who could not find words harsh enough for this 'theorist of systematic murder'[1]), that Marat had called for the massacre and bore sole responsibility for it. This view is based on an article in *L'Ami du peuple* on 19 August, in which Marat wrote: 'The final option, which is the safest and most wise, is to proceed armed to the Abbaye, seize the traitors, particularly the Swiss officers and their accomplices, and put them to the sword.' Between 19 August and 2 September, however, Marat published nothing (for the good reason that his paper did not appear in this interval), and it is hard to see people suddenly rushing to the prisons on the basis of an article two weeks old. One might just as well maintain that the staunchly Girondin Gorsas justified and supported the massacres, when he wrote in *Le Courrier des 83 départements* on 3 September: 'Let them perish! The furious people, knowing that the prisons are full of conspirators, are meting out a terrible but necessary justice . . . for we cannot disguise from ourselves the fact that we are in open war with the enemies of our liberty.'

The Montagnards defended themselves vigorously against this accusation. Thus Marat, in *Le Journal de la République française* on 14 October: 'Too commonly, slander . . . is the chosen weapon of public rogues, and it has sped from the platform of the Assembly and the offices of Roland to all points of the realm, painting the Commune of Paris as a horde of cannibals on the grounds of *the disastrous events of 2 and 3 September*' (my emphasis). Robespierre defended the Commune in similar terms:

> Could the magistrates have stopped the people? For it was a popular movement, not the partial sedition of a few wretches paid to murder their fellows . . . I have heard people coolly tell me that the municipality should have proclaimed martial law. Martial law on 2 September! Martial law, as the enemy approaches! Martial law, after 10 August! Martial law for the accomplices of the dethroned tyrant against the people![2]

---

1 Jaurès, *Histoire socialiste*, vol. 3, p. 140.

2 At the Convention on 5 November, in his speech in reply to Louvet (see below,

But the Montagnards did not wish for an extended debate on a subject they found troubling. Even the Société des Jacobins, in a circular of 30 November to its affiliated societies, struck a note of caution: 'Let us draw a religious veil over all these events, leaving their judgement to posterity alone.'[3]

The elections to the Convention

As it spread across the departments, the news of the September massacres coincided with the elections to the Convention. The electoral assemblies started meeting on 2 September (for the second level of the elections). In the provinces, the Girondin candidates were the best placed. They had dominated the platform in the Legislative Assembly, and the Girondin press, by far the most widely read outside of Paris, campaigned against the 'brigands' responsible for the massacres. On 10 September, Brissot's *Le Patriote français* proclaimed victory: 'Today we can begin to cherish the highest hopes for the new assembly, following the good choices made in the departments.' The provinces did indeed elect a large number of Girondins, including Brissot, Condorcet, Carra, Louvet and Gorsas.

Paris, on the other hand, voted for the party of the Commune. Not one of the Girondin candidates, criticized for their softness towards the king and their hostility to the Commune, was elected. Robespierre came top of the list, followed by Marat, Collot d'Herbois, Billaud-Varenne, Danton, Desmoulins, Panis, Sergent, David . . .

It is impossible to enumerate precisely how the Convention was divided between Girondins and Montagnards, as neither of these formed a compact bloc that could be represented by a diagram. The Gironde and the Montagne were groups centred around core leaders, around which there moved fluctuating majorities recruited from the Plaine, the great mass of those whose allegiance was sometimes to one of the opposing tendencies and sometimes to the other.

---

p. 208), A. P., vol. 52, p. 162.

3 Caron, *Les Massacres de septembre*, pp. 168–70.

EXCURSUS: DID THE CONVENTION REPRESENT THE PEOPLE?

The Convention was the first of the revolutionary assemblies to be elected on universal (male) suffrage. But was it representative (leaving aside the theoretical aspect of the representation of the people)?

Looking just at the electoral system, the answer is unhesitatingly negative. The two-level ballot did not encourage participation (it seems people did not flood to the primary assemblies). Ultimately it favoured the selection of the new notables who were officials of the Revolution: judges, administrators of departments, districts and communes, *procureurs*, officers of the National Guard, etc., as well as more traditional notables such as doctors and notaries, landowners and large farmers. Given that the great majority of the French people at this time were peasants or artisans, we have to accept that the Convention was not a representative assembly in terms of composition.[4]

In terms of operation, however, the position was quite different. I do not mean the speeches and debates, which remained parliamentary exercises, even if their tone, their intensity and their consequences were of a quite different order than those of today. I mean rather the intervention of the people in the sessions of the Convention.

First of all, there were ordinary people in the galleries who were not shy about making their opinion known. It is true that the size and layout of the Salle du Manège – as later, that of the Salle des Machines – prevented any large numbers from being admitted. In *L'Ami du peuple* on 15 September 1792, Marat warned:

> Beware of holding the National Convention in the pestilent air of the Manège des Tuileries. Prepare premises for it that are large enough to hold three thousand citizens in galleries that are quite

---

4 As for wage-earners, a quite small category at this time, there were only two: a cabinet-maker from Saint-Étienne and a wool-carder from the Marne.

> open and absolutely free from guards, in such a way that the deputies are constantly under the eyes of the people and have no other safeguard but their civic spirit and their virtue.

Of course, this advice was not implemented. But just as important as the direct pressure of the people was the way each session of the Convention began with several hours set aside for the reading of letters and hearing of delegations that were a direct emanation from the people. True, these were often simple revolutionary acts of faith, delegates from far-flung communes bringing their gifts to the Nation, asserting their support for their representatives or congratulating them on this or that measure. But they could also involve criticisms or proposals, which sometimes had immediate effects. On many occasions, as we shall see, the Convention listened to them and followed them on matters as important as the renewal of administrations, de-Christianization, or the setting of price caps (known as '*le maximum*'). In this respect, the Convention certainly was the first and only French national assembly in which the people were able to make their voice directly heard.

Valmy

With the *journées* of 20 and 25 September 1792, events speeded up: first Valmy, then the opening of the Convention, where momentous decisions were taken right from the start.

Valmy, first of all, as it is impossible to relate everything at the same time. Late in September, Kellermann, a veteran of the Seven Years' War, was commanding the army of the Centre, in Lorraine. To the south, the army of the Rhine was led by Biron, then Custine. Dumouriez headed the army of the North, part of which was around Sedan and the rest facing Belgium – which Dumouriez dreamed of conquering – from Maubeuge to Dunkirk. Opposite them, the Austro-Prussian army was commanded by the duke of Brunswick, whom Michelet describes as 'a man of prodigious education, and all the more hesitant and sceptical as a result. Whoever knows much, doubts much.' Brunswick would have preferred to methodically besiege the French strongholds in the East and then take up his winter quarters, but the émigrés would not stay still and even the king of Prussia was growing impatient.

Brunswick therefore moved to the attack on 12 September, north of the Argonne in the forest of La Croix-aux-Bois. Dumouriez had got peasants to block the gorges of the Argonne leading from Lorraine into Champagne (the 'French Thermopylae', as he said, 'but we shall be more fortunate than Leonidas'). But the route via La Croix-aux-Bois was left unguarded. Dumouriez risked being cut off, but Brunswick was slow and indecisive, which enabled the French to retreat at night in the rain. Servan, minister of war, had given the order to retire to Châlons and hold a line on the Marne. Dumouriez disobeyed and retreated south towards Sainte-Menehould, which was daring, as it left the road to Paris wide open. The Prussians, however, had forgotten the lightning manoeuvres of the great Frederick: they took up position on the hills facing the French army, in a paradoxical situation in which they were on the Paris side whilst Kellermann, occupying a kind of forward promontory marked by the Valmy windmill, was on the far side. King Friedrich-Wilhelm gave the order to attack. The Prussians 'assumed that the French who, for the most part, had never heard cannon fire, would be amazed by this novel concert of sixty guns. But sixty French guns responded, and for the whole day this army, made up in part by National Guard, withstood a harder test than any battle: immobility under fire.'[5] At eleven in the morning, the Prussian infantry advanced in three columns through the valley separating them from the French, and prepared to attack. It was at this moment that Kellermann, in a famous gesture, brandished his hat on the point of his sword and cried: '*Vive la Nation!*' The entire army followed suit, and their shout 'filled the whole valley: it was like a shout of joy, but astonishingly prolonged; it lasted no less than a quarter of an hour, for whenever it subsided it started up again with still greater force, making the earth

5 Michelet, *Histoire de la Révolution*, vol. 1, p. 892.

tremble: *"Vive la Nation"*.'[6] The Prussian infantry halted. Brunswick dared not order the assault and had them return to their positions. A torrential rain began to fall, and that evening the two armies bivouacked where they were.

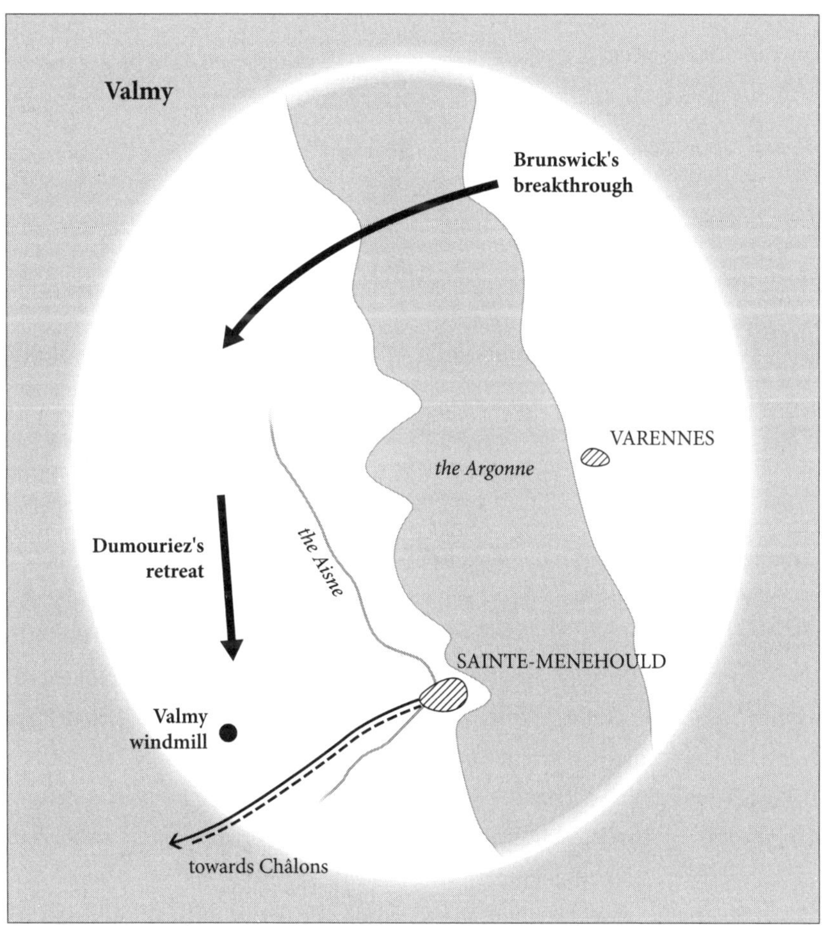

Valmy – a victory won by shouting. Strategically it meant very little, as the Prussian army remained intact and the road to Paris open. Symbolically, however, it was a tremendous event, and the Austro-Prussians understood that this army they so despised would not be so easily defeated. They retreated in good order in the rain, unimpeded by Dumouriez, eager as he was to resume his plans against Belgium.

---

6 Ibid., p. 893.

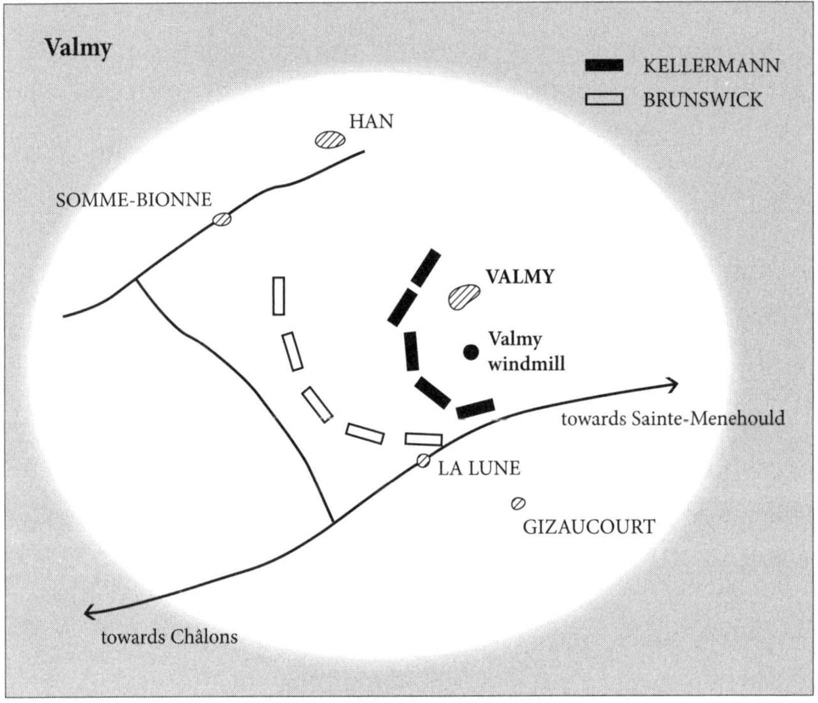

The opposition of Gironde and Montagne

The news of the Valmy victory reached Paris on 21 September, the day after the opening of the Convention in the Salle du Manège.[7] But right from the election of its bureau, the Girondins benefited from their majority position: Pétion was elected president almost unanimously,[8] and the secretaries were all from the same side – Condorcet, Brissot, Rabaut Saint-Étienne, Vergniaud and Lasource, together with Camus, a former Feuillant.

The antagonism between the Gironde and the Montagne was not based on social background. There was rather a geographical

7 Work was not yet finished in the Salle des Machines, the Tuileries theatre transformed by Soufflot, where Sophie Arnould had triumphed in Rameau's *Castor et Pollux*. The Convention did not move there until 10 May 1793.

8 Marat, in the final number of *L'Ami du peuple* (21 September): 'Pétion is a good man, an honest man, I am sure; he would cut a marvellous figure as a justice of the peace, an arbitrator, a municipal treasurer or a college bursar; but he has eyes that see nothing, ears that hear nothing, and a head that reflects on nothing.'

difference between them. The great figures of the Montagne, if not all Parisian, were at least Paris deputies, whereas the heroes of the Gironde (except for Brissot) came from the south.[9] And the south was (and is still today) traditionally and culturally more jealous of its identity, more hostile to Parisian domination, than the rest of the country. The Protestant pastor Lasource, deputy for the Tarn, was among the Girondins who best expressed the sentiments of the group towards Paris:

> I fear the despotism of Paris, and I do not want those who there command the opinions of men whom they lead astray to dominate the National Convention and all of France . . . Paris must be reduced to an eighty-third share of influence, the same as the other departments. I shall never consent to its tyrannizing the Republic, as sought by certain intriguers against whom I shall be the first to rise up, because I shall never remain silent before any species of tyrant.[10]

But the conflict was deeper still, with two opposing conceptions of the society to be created. The Girondins saw property as a basic natural right, and believed that the state had no business interfering in the free play of supply and demand. The Montagnards, while also upholding respect for property, defined this in a different way, subordinating it to the right to existence. There were discordant voices even among them. Thus Momoro, an influential member of the Cordeliers and a friend of Danton, who was sent as commissioner to the Eure department to recruit volunteers, distributed a declaration of rights there which affirmed that '1) the nation recognizes industrial properties, guaranteeing their inviolability; 2) the nation equally assures to citizens the guarantee and inviolability of what are mistakenly called landed properties, *until such time as it will have promulgated laws on this subject.*'[11] In Lyon, a justice of the

---

9 Though we should not forget that the Midi elected several of the most resolute Montagnards: Moïse Bayle, Baille, Granet, Gasparin, Rovère.

10 In the Convention on 25 September 1792, A. P., vol. 52, p. 130.

11 My emphasis. Momoro retracted in May 1793. In his *Opinion sur la fixation du*

peace named Lange proposed the creation of a subscription system by which consumers would collectively purchase the whole of the harvest from proprietors and merchants on fixed terms. A farming company, controlled by the state, would store the harvest in 30,000 granaries, and set the price of bread which would be the same for the whole of France.[12] Proposals of this kind scared the Girondins, who saw in them the hand of 'those who wish to level everything – property, well-being, the price of commodities . . ., who want even to level talent, knowledge and virtue, as they have none of these things themselves!'[13]

Even the functioning of the two 'parties' was sufficiently different to be seen as symbolic. The Girondin leadership met in salons such as those of Madame Roland at her husband's ministry or of Madame Dodun, the mistress of Vergniaud, on the place Vendôme. The Montagnards, for their part, made it a point of honour to deliberate only in public, at the Jacobins club.

The proclamation of the Republic and the Gironde's attack on the 'triumvirs' (Danton, Robespierre, Marat)

Following the verification of mandates, the Convention began its proceedings on 21 September. In its opening session, major decisions were taken in an atmosphere of reconciliation. The only intervention that betrayed the underlying tension was that of Couthon: 'I have heard talk, not without horror, of the establishment of a triumvirate, a dictatorship, a protectorate: these rumours are surely a means of disturbance dreamed up by enemies of the Revolution.'[14]

Danton, in a skilful speech, began by announcing his resignation as minister of justice: 'I received [these functions] to the sound of the

---

maximum du prix des grains, he denied the cultivator the ownership of those products of the soil 'destined for the provisioning of society'.

12 On Lange (or L'Ange), see Jaurès, *Histoire socialiste*, vol. 3, pp. 415–31.

13 Brissot, in 'Appel à tous les républicains de France', cited by Jaurès, *Histoire socialiste*, vol. 3, p. 68.

14 A. P., vol. 52, p. 70.

cannon with which the citizens of the capital were demolishing despotism . . . but now that the union of our armies is accomplished, and the political union of the people's representatives effected, I am no more than a mandatory of the people and will confine myself to that honourable function, and proceed to speak in that capacity.' He continued: 'The empty phantoms of dictatorship, the extravagant idea of a triumvirate, all these absurdities invented to frighten the people, will disappear, since nothing will be constitutional that is not accepted by the people.' He demanded 'laws as pitiless against those who would attack them as the people were in overthrowing tyranny.' On the other hand, to reassure the possessor classes, he proposed to decree that 'all landed, individual and industrial property shall be held in perpetuity and placed under the safeguard of the entire French people.'[15] These proposals were well designed to disarm his critics – one of the supposed triumvirs denouncing the idea of a triumvirate, one of the supposed 'disrupters' (*désorganisateurs*) defending property.

In the discussion that ensued, Collot d'Herbois asked to speak on a motion of order: 'You have just made a wise decision [on the collection of taxes]; but there is a great, salutary and indispensable one that you cannot postpone until tomorrow, that you cannot postpone to this evening, that you cannot delay a single moment without being disloyal to the wish of the nation: that is, the abolition of the monarchy.' Grégoire supported him: 'We have to destroy the word "king", which is still a talisman with a magic power able to stupefy many men.'

'The president sought to put the proposal to the vote, but the members of the assembly all rose spontaneously to their feet and, by unanimous acclamation, protested their hatred for a form of government that had caused so much harm to the *patrie*.'[16] The next day, on Billaud-Varenne's proposal, the Convention decided that, starting from the day before, all public acts would be dated from year I of the Republic, and that the state seal 'would bear as

15 *Discours de Danton*, pp. 55–6.

16 A. P., vol. 52, p. 73.

motif a woman leaning with one hand on a fasces and holding in the other a lance topped by the bonnet of liberty, with the motto: *La République française.*'

This fine unanimity would not last. As early as 22 September, discord broke out when a delegation from Orléans arrived to complain of the city administrators. Billaud-Varenne: 'I favour the re-election of all the administrators [not just those of Orléans]. As for the courts, I believe it is not enough to re-elect their members, they should be swept away. The courts have been nothing more than pillars of tyranny.' There were shouts of 'anarchy'. Lasource: 'Nothing is worse than this mania for destruction without having any replacement to hand.' But it was finally decreed that 'the administrative, municipal and judicial bodies, the justices of the peace, the bailiffs, shall be renewed in their entirety, apart from those worthy of the *patrie*, who may be re-elected.'[17]

At this point, Tallien proposed that 'any citizen may be elected judge without needing to be enrolled on the list of men of the law'. Despite violent protests from the right side of the hall, the Convention decided that 'judges may be chosen from among all citizens without distinction'.[18] This was a defeat for the Girondins, and the end of the truce.

The counter-attack was not long in coming. On 24 September, Buzot came to the platform to demand that the Convention be surrounded by a guard recruited in the departments, with a view to ensuring the safety of the deputies. Tallien, Collot d'Herbois and Billaud-Varenne denounced this sign of distrust towards Paris, but to no avail; the Convention decided to establish for its protection a public force drawn from the eighty-three departments.[19]

The memorable session of the next day, 25 September, was long

---

17 Ibid., p. 84.

18 Ibid., p. 87.

19 Ibid., pp. 124–8. The following day, when the session opened, Maure ('What need have we of a formidable apparatus in the midst of the citizens of Paris who opposed tyranny with invincible courage?') and Merlin de Thionville ('I put the motion that no project for an armed force to secure the Convention be presented') sought in vain to have the decree rescinded.

and stormy. The Gironde had prepared a general attack on the 'triumvirs', the three most feared and hated leaders of the Montagne: Danton, Robespierre and Marat.

After Lasource had launched an anathema against 'the men who have constantly incited daggers against those members of the Legislative Assembly who most firmly defended the cause of liberty', Rebecqui, deputy for the Bouches-du-Rhône, made a short and strange intervention: 'The party that has been denounced to you, whose intention is to establish a dictatorship, is the party of Robespierre; that was common knowledge in Marseille, as my colleague, M. Barbaroux, will testify, and it is to combat it that we were sent here.'[20]

Danton's reaction to this was, characteristically, an attempt at pacification ('a synthesis', as we would say today). His proposal was in two parts: first of all, 'it is incontestable that a vigorous law is needed against those who seek to destroy public liberty. Well, let us pass this law, let us pass a law that lays down the death penalty for anyone who speaks out in favour of dictatorship or a triumvirate'; secondly, he demanded that the death penalty be also applied 'against anyone who seeks to destroy the unity of France'. At the end of this speech, aimed equally at both dictatorship and what would soon be called federalism, his appeal for unity brought loud applause: 'The Austrians will tremble to learn of this sacred harmony, and at this point, I swear to you, our enemies are dead.'[21]

After Robespierre had supported Danton's proposal, Barbaroux returned to the debate on dictatorship:

> We don't want a dictatorship! Why then oppose a decree by the Convention that citizens from all the departments should gather for its safety and that of Paris? . . . Marseille has sent 800 men drawn from the most patriotic and independent citizens. Their fathers have given them each two pistols, a sword, a musket and an *assignat* of 500 livres. They are accompanied by 200 cavalry, armed

20 A. P., vol. 52, p. 131.

21 Ibid.

and equipped at their own cost . . . Hasten then to pass this decree, confirming the principle that the Convention belongs not only to Paris but to the whole of France.[22]

The discussion descended to invective when Marat came to the platform. Angry murmurs, cries of 'Down with the speaker' arose from all sides. Marat: 'Do I have in this assembly so many personal enemies, then?' – 'All of us!' Marat let the storm pass and continued: 'I have a large number of enemies in this assembly; I call on them to behave with decorum and not oppose with vain shouts, boos or threats a man who is devoted to the *patrie* and to their own safety.' He admitted having several times proposed the appointment of a dictator, but 'in all fairness I must declare that my colleagues, Robespierre, Danton and all the rest have always disapproved of the idea either of a tribunal, or of a triumvirate, or of a dictatorship. If anyone is guilty of having thrown ideas of this kind to the public, it is I! I call down on my head the vengeance of the Nation: but before unleashing opprobrium or the sword, listen to me!' Marat's courage impressed the assembly and he was able to go on. 'When the established authorities were doing nothing but murder patriots in the name of the law, do you call it a crime for me to have called for the avenging axe of the people to fall on the heads of traitors?'[23] The remarkable boldness, sincerity and eloquence of this speech subdued the Convention, and when Vergniaud called Marat a 'man dripping all over with slander, bile and blood', he was interrupted by murmurs.

Toward the end of the session, as invective and accusation flew in all directions, suddenly Couthon spoke up: 'I ask that we speak of the Revolution and not of individuals. I ask the Convention to decree the unity of the Republic.' After a lengthy debate on the best possible formulation, the Convention opted for the famous phrase: 'The French Republic is one and indivisible.'[24]

---

22 Ibid., p. 135.
23 Ibid., p. 139.
24 Ibid., pp. 142–3.

The fédérés in Paris – the Girondins leave the Jacobins club

Despite no official decision, the Girondin departments sent contingents of *fédérés* to Paris. Those from Marseille, as announced by Barbaroux, arrived on 19 October. Marat went to see them in their barracks, showed concern for their arrangements and invited three from each company to dine with him. By mid-November, the 15,000 or so *fédérés* now in Paris were thoroughly beguiled by the Parisians. Many would leave for the front, while the others formed the Société des Fédérés des 83 Départements, a kind of club inspired by the Jacobins.[25] The Girondin manoeuvre had misfired.

On 29 October, Roland presented an interminable report on the situation in Paris, in which he attacked the Commune as an institution 'precipitated by the revolutionary movement, carried away by its zeal, mistaken in its aims, [which] has seized all powers and not always exercised them justly'.[26] Robespierre asked to speak against the printing of this speech.[27] In the stormy discussion that ensued, he lamented that no one dared accuse him to his face. Louvet then advanced to the platform: 'I present myself against you, Robespierre, and demand the right to accuse you.'[28] His speech was one of the most vicious and dangerous attacks that Robespierre had yet been forced to hear: a long and rhetorically effective speech, punctuated by a rapid volley of accusations: of having persecuted and demeaned the national representation, 'of having continually presented yourself as an object of idolatry, of having accepted its being said in your presence that you are the only virtuous man in France', of having tyrannized the electoral assembly of Paris, and of 'clearly marching towards supreme power, which is proved both by the facts I have indicated, and by your whole conduct, which will speak louder to

25 Mathiez, *La Révolution française*, pp. 118–19.

26 A. P., vol. 53, p. 38.

27 A vote by the assembly to have a speech printed was a sign of approval, compounded by sending it to the departments.

28 Jean-Baptiste Louvet, author of *Les Amours du chevalier de Faublas*, was one of the most talented Girondin deputies.

accuse you than I can.'[29] The assembly decided to have the speech printed, and deferred Robespierre's reply to 5 November.

In this response, not only did Robespierre ridicule Louvet's accusations, he took the opportunity to justify revolutionary illegality:

> What idea have we formed, then, of the recent revolution? Did the fall of the throne seem so easy before its success? Was it just a matter of a surprise attack on the Tuileries? Was it not necessary to annihilate the party of tyrants throughout France? . . . Citizens, did you want a revolution without revolution? What is this spirit of persecution that wants to revise, so to speak, the actions that broke our chains? Who can mark after the event the precise point at which the swell of popular insurrection is to break? If this were the price, what people would ever be able to shake off the yoke of despotism?[30]

This was the context in which the Girondins abandoned the Jacobins club. Brissot had been summoned to explain himself on the subject of an article in *Le Patriote français* (23 September) in which he had slandered the Paris deputation and the Commune, denouncing the presence of a 'disruptive party' in the Convention. He did not show up. Expelled from the club on 10 October, he replied with a pamphlet inviting his supporters to follow him, and the provincial societies to break their ties with the rue Saint-Honoré.[31] The Montagnards now had a free hand in the Jacobins club.

Provisions crisis and peasant insurrections

Of the many failures of the Girondin ministry under Roland, the most serious was certainly in economic policy, and above all the

29 A. P., vol. 53, p. 170 (as appendix to the session of 29 October). For Mathiez, Robespierre was being 'conspiratorial'. I would rather see it as a great polemical speech.

30 Robespierre, *Pour le bonheur et pour la liberté*, pp. 163–4.

31 The Marseille and Bordeaux clubs followed Brissot; a few others threatened to secede but did not.

question of provisions. A serious crisis broke out in autumn 1792, despite the harvest being good: as Beffroy put it, *procureur* of Laon and deputy to the Convention: 'It is in the midst of abundance that the people are threatened with famine.'[32] An artificial famine, whose causes were clear – not least to Saint-Just, in his speech on provisions of 29 November: 'Everything is converted into money, the fruits of the soil are hoarded or hidden; in all the state I see nothing but poverty, pride and paper.'[33] The *assignat* was steadily falling, producers were little inclined to exchange their grain for paper, and traders covered themselves against the depreciation of that paper by raising their prices. The massive purchases for the army and the prohibition, in the name of equality, of putting rye in the bread, also contributed to the scarcity and expense of a product vital to the majority of the population. There were certainly grass-roots movements to have wages raised in line with the cost of bread, but without the right to organize, the workers had no power to press their demands. And, to quote Saint-Just again: 'It is said that the pay of artisans rises with the price of foodstuffs; but if the artisan has no work, who will pay for his idleness?'[34]

Le Père Duchesne (no. 199, December 1792) railed against Roland:

> Twenty cooks loaded with the finest delicacies cry out: 'Make way, make way, these are the entrées of the virtuous Roland'; others, 'the hors-d'oeuvres of the virtuous Roland'; others again, 'the roasts of the virtuous Roland'. – 'What do you want?' says the virtuous Roland's valet to the deputation. – 'We want to speak to the virtuous Roland.' – 'He's not to be seen at the moment.' – 'Tell him that he must always be available for the magistrates of the people.'

Jacques Roux, spokesman for the Gravilliers section, accused the Convention of covering up for speculators and hoarders, and denounced 'senatorial despotism'. Varlet, a postal clerk, set up a

---

32 A. P., vol. 53, p. 438.

33 Saint-Just, *Œuvres complètes* (ed. Michel Abensour), Paris: Gallimard, 2004, p. 490.

34 Ibid.

mobile platform outside the Assembly from which he harangued the crowd, accusing members of the Convention on all sides of forming an oligarchy and confiscating the sovereignty of the people.

At Lyon, where 30,000 silk-workers were unemployed, other Enragés stirred up the crowds: Dodieu, who proposed a special tribunal to punish hoarders, and Hidins, who presented the Lyon Commune with a project that included the abolition of trade in grain, the creation of a national board for subsistence goods, the nationalization of mills and the regulation of baking. Priests also joined the movement: Dolivier, the parish priest of Mauchamp, had already defended the peasants arrested for the killing of Simonneau, the mayor of Étampes who had opposed the fixing of prices; Petitjean, parish priest of Épineuil in the Cher, preached that 'goods will be common, there will be only one cellar and one barn, from which each will take whatever they need.'[35]

On 19 November, a deputation from the electoral body of the Seine-et-Oise, led by a certain Goujon, came to the bar of the Convention with an unusual proposal:

> Citizens, the first principle we put before you is this: free trading in grain is incompatible with our republic. What is our republic made up of? A small number of capitalists and a large number of the poor. Who trades in grain? The small number of capitalists. Why do they do so? To grow rich. How can they grow rich? By increasing the price of grain when they sell it to the consumer . . . The second truth: we must act so that there is grain, and that the invariable price of this grain is always proportionate to the daily wage . . . Decree that all grain shall be sold by weight. Set a maximum price. Make it for this year 9 livres a quintal, an average price that is equally good for the producer and the consumer.[36]

In response to this, Grégoire, who was chairing the session, read out a letter from Roland: 'Perhaps the only thing that the Assembly can permit itself on the question of staples is to pronounce that it must

35 Albert Mathiez, *La Vie chère et le mouvement social sous la Terreur* [1927], Paris: Payot, 1973, vol. 1, p. 88.

36 A. P., vol. 53, p. 475.

do nothing, that it suppresses all restrictions and declares the most total freedom in the circulation of commodities.' The Convention decided not to have the dangerous petition printed, lest it 'spread terror among owners of property'.

This vote was soon followed by a peasant insurrection that spread rapidly to the whole of the Beauce. Bands led by the local authorities fixed food prices; on 21 November at Nogent-le-Rotrou, on the 23rd at Vendôme, they did so while dancing around liberty trees to the cry of '*Vive la Nation!* Wheat will come down.' Early in December, 10,000 peasants marched on Tours:

> The three commissioners sent by the Convention to the Eure-et-Loir, Birotteau, Maure and Lecointe-Puyraveau, proceeded on 29 November to the great market at Courville. They were surrounded by 6,000 armed men who threatened to throw them into the river or hang them. To save their lives, they were forced to approve not only the fixing of the wheat price, but also the prices of barley, candles, beef, cloth, shoes and iron.[37]

The Convention decided to send troops under the command of a general, and repression was unleashed throughout the Beauce.

Robespierre made a final effort in his speech on provisions of 2 December, in which he spelled out his conception of property: 'The first social law is therefore the one that guarantees all members of society the means to live; all the others are subordinate to that one; property was only instituted and guaranteed to consolidate it . . . Everything essential to conserve life is property common to the whole of society. Only the surplus can be individual property and left subject to the enterprise of merchants.'[38] But to no avail. On 8 December, all regulation was abolished and it was decreed that 'the fullest freedom shall continue to prevail in trade in grains, flours and pulses throughout the territory of the Republic'.[39] This was a victory

37 A. Mathiez, *La Vie chère*, pp. 101–2.

38 Robespierre, *Virtue and Terror*, p. 51.

39 A. P., vol. 54, p. 687.

for Roland, but hatred of the Gironde now spread among the people of both town and country.

The trial, judgement and execution of the king

With the accusation and trial of the king, violence and confrontation rose a further notch. The Montagnards wanted the tyrant punished. The Girondins could not frontally oppose this without giving succour to the accusation of royalism, but they put up a series of obstacles designed to avoid, delay or divert what would seem the inevitable outcome of any trial: the execution of the king.[40] It is not that they were inclined to 'royalism' in any shape or form; everything shows the Girondins to have been sincerely republican. To say that they worked against that outcome for the simple reason that the Montagnards were working for it, and they did not want their opponents to have this satisfaction, is not sufficient. Perhaps Jaurès's insight was closer to the mark:

> Sometimes, therefore, in rapid and secret melancholies, the tragic mystery of their own destiny led them to sense the tragic mystery of the king's destiny. Their thoughts encountered, on the threshold of annihilation, the monarchy abolished and the king under threat. And like shadows that touch at the edges, the fate of the Gironde seemed contiguous with the fate of the king. Were the Girondins sure that in striking, they would not be striking themselves?[41]

The legislation committee, tasked on 16 October with proposing the procedure to be followed, worked slowly. It was only on 7 November that Jean-Baptiste Mailhe, a lawyer from Toulouse, presented his report. He began by discarding the argument of the inviolability of the king as inscribed in the 1791 Constitution: 'Citizens, the nation has spoken; the nation has chosen you to be the organ of its sovereign

40 Danton: 'If he is tried, he is dead.'

41 Jaurès, *Histoire socialiste*, vol. 5, pp. 21–2.

wishes; here royal inviolability is as if it had never existed.' He went on to show that only the Convention – and not a regular court, or one set up for the occasion – could judge the king, as only it represented the nation.

In the discussion on this report, Saint-Just spoke on 13 November in a quite different vein. His speech caused a sensation, as the speaker was a man of twenty-five who was previously unknown, and his tone, words and arguments were quite different from anything commonly heard.

> The sole aim of the committee was to persuade you that the king should be judged as a simple citizen, but I say that the king must be judged as an enemy: that we have not to judge him but to fight him, and that having no place in the contract that binds the French people, the forms of procedure are not to be found in civil law, but in the law of nations . . . The men who will judge Louis have a Republic to found; those who attach the least importance to the matter of a king's just punishment will never found a Republic. Among us, fineness of mind and character is a great obstacle to liberty . . . It is impossible to reign innocently, the folly of it is too clear . . . He is the murderer of the Bastille, of Nancy, of the Champ-de-Mars, of Tournai, of the Tuileries: what enemy or foreigner has done us greater harm? He is a kind of hostage kept by the *fripons*.[42]

A week later, the famous 'iron cabinet' was discovered in a wall of the Tuileries, containing documents that proved the collusion between Louis and the nation's enemies. It was no longer possible to delay the trial.

Robespierre, on 3 December, took up Saint-Just's argument:

> This assembly has been led, without realizing it, far from the real

42 Saint-Just, *Œuvres complètes*, pp. 476–84. ['*Fripon*', a rather general word meaning 'rogue', came to be particularly used in 1793–4 for rich capitalists suspected of political manipulations in their own interest. – Translator]

> question. There is no trial to be held here. Louis is not a defendant. You are not judges. You are not, you cannot be, anything but statesmen and representatives of the nation . . . Louis has been dethroned by his crimes; Louis denounced the French people as rebellious; to chastise them he called on the arms of his fellow tyrants; victory and the people decided that he was the rebellious one: therefore Louis cannot be judged; either he is already condemned, or the Republic is not acquitted . . . Peoples do not judge in the same way as courts of law; they do not hand down sentences, they throw thunderbolts; they do not condemn kings, they drop them back into the void; and this justice is worth just as much as that of the courts.[43]

The motion proposed by Robespierre signified execution without trial: 'Louis XVI, traitor to the nation, enemy of humanity, shall be punished by death in the place where the defenders of liberty perished on 10 August.'

This position was so radical that it did not attract unanimous support even among the Montagnards. Marat himself feared that it went against the grain of public sentiment: 'The ex-monarch must be judged, there is no doubt about it,' he wrote, presenting the trial as an educational tool: 'The gathering of evidence for his trial is the most certain means to finally deliver the nation from its most fearsome enemies, to terrify traitors, to root out every conspiracy, and to at last ensure the liberty, tranquillity, and felicity of the public.'

On 6 December, the Convention appointed a twenty-one-man commission charged with drawing up the indictment. It decided at the same time that voting at the trial would be by roll call. On 10 December, Robert Lindet handed over in the name of the commission 'the charge sheet of the crimes of Louis Capet', from the military preparations of July 1789 through to the shootings of 10 August 1792. The following day, Louis came to the bar of the Convention to hear the reading of this act and reply to the questions put by Barère. As Marat reported: 'Here was a completely new and sublime

---

43 Robespierre, *Virtue and Terror*, pp. 57–9.

spectacle for the philanthropist, that of a despot previously surrounded by the brilliance of his pomp and the formidable apparatus of his power, stripped of all the imposing signs of his former grandeur and brought like a criminal to the foot of a popular tribunal, to accept its judgement and pay the penalty for his misdeeds.'[44]

In actual fact, the atmosphere was muted. Louis replied in placid and cautious terms, blaming his ministers and denying the evidence of the iron cabinet. He appeared a second time on 26 December together with his three advocates, the old Malesherbes, Tronchet, and de Sèze who read a long plea on the theme that the whole trial was illegal: 'Louis would thus be the only Frenchman for whom there exists no law and no due process. He will have neither the rights of a citizen nor the prerogatives of a king. What a strange and unimaginable fate!'[45]

The Girondin deputies then attempted a diversion by calling for an appeal to the people – the primary assemblies – as embodying the direct sovereignty of the nation. The leaders of the Gironde spoke one after the other in favour of this referendum. Vergniaud: 'Any act emanating from the representatives of the people is an attack on its sovereignty if it is not subject to the people's formal or tacit ratification. Only the people, who promised Louis inviolability, can declare that it wishes to employ the right to punish that it had renounced.'[46]

Robespierre had answered this point already, on 28 December, denouncing the risk of civil war it involved:

> Can you not see that it is impossible for such a great multitude of assemblies to be entirely in agreement; and that this very division, at a moment when enemies are approaching, is the greatest of all calamities? In this way, the fury of civil war will combine with the plague of foreign war; and ambitious plotters will compromise with the enemies of the people over the ruins of the *patrie* and the bloody corpses of its defenders.[47]

44 *Journal de la République française*, 14 December 1792.

45 A. P., vol. 55, p. 617.

46 A. P., vol. 56, pp. 90–5.

47 Ibid., pp. 16–23.

After Buzot had proposed that the people be consulted not as to the appropriateness of the verdict but rather upon the sentence pronounced, and Pétion had argued for the king's imprisonment for reasons of foreign policy, voting began on 14 January.

The members of the Convention had to respond, one at a time and aloud, to three questions: 'Is Louis Capet guilty of conspiracy against liberty and offences against national safety? Shall there be an appeal to the nation as to the sentence passed? What punishment shall be inflicted on Louis?' The king's guilt was pronounced almost unanimously. The appeal to the people was rejected by 426 votes to 278. The death penalty was carried by 387 votes to 334, but as twenty-six of the former had also pronounced for a reprieve, a final vote was required, which rejected the reprieve by 380 votes to 310.

The execution took place on 21 January 1793. 'The tyrant has fallen under the sword of the law. This great act of justice has caused consternation to the aristocracy, destroyed the superstition around royalty and established the Republic. It has impressed a great character on the National Convention and made it worthy of the trust of the French people.'[48]

The trial and execution of the king represented a major defeat for the Gironde. On 23 January Roland resigned, to be replaced at the ministry by Garat, a prudent man who was always quick to side with the winners.

48 Robespierre, *Lettres à ses commettants*, second series, no. 3, 25 January 1793. *Œuvres complètes*, vol. 5, p. 226.

CHAPTER 9

October 1792 to June 1793

From victory to defeat, the declaration of war against England and Spain, the insurrection in the Vendée, the fall of the Gironde

> The extraordinary effects that the French Revolution had abroad arose less from the new methods and conceptions that the French introduced into the conduct of war than from changes in the state and civil administration, in the character of government, in the condition of the people, and so on.
>
> – Clausewitz, *On War*

Jemmapes, a series of victories

While these tremendous events were happening in Paris, the republican armies followed up Valmy with one victory after another. In the north, after the Austrians raised the siege of Lille, Dumouriez's army entered Belgium. The decisive battle took place on 6 November 1792. The Austrians had built a fortified position around the village of Jemmapes, a site that Michelet went to see:

> The position is not only strong and formidable, but imposing and solemn; it speaks to the imagination, and anyone passing

> would certainly stop there even if they did not know that its name was Jemmapes. It is a line of hills before Mons, an amphitheatre tipped at either end by two villages, Cuesmes on the right and Jemmapes on the left. Jemmapes rises onto the hill and covers a flank. Cuesmes is less easy to defend, and was supplemented by several ranks of redoubts in successive steps, and in these redoubts were the Hungarian grenadiers. These redoubts and the two villages formed to the right and left as many citadels that had first of all to be taken.[1]

Dumouriez reported to the Convention: 'At noon precisely, the whole infantry moved into battalion formation in the blink of an eye, and with great speed and good cheer advanced on the entrenched enemy.'[2] After a violent battle, towards two in the afternoon the Austrians 'retreated in the greatest disarray', the report says. They had lost 4,000 men and thirteen cannon.

Following the resounding victory of Jemmapes, Brussels, Liège, Antwerp and Namur were all conquered in the month of November. The whole of Belgium was occupied by the republican army.

On all the other fronts as well, victories came thick and fast. In late September, the entry of French troops into Savoy triggered great popular enthusiasm. 'The march of my army is a triumph. The people of both countryside and towns come running out to meet us, the tricolour cockade is everywhere', Montesquiou wrote to the Convention on 25 September. A few days later, the army of the Var entered Nice without a battle. On the Rhine, the army commanded by Custine also took the offensive: Speyer, Worms, Mainz and Frankfurt were conquered in the course of October.

1 Michelet, *Histoire*, vol. 2, p. 82.
2 A. P., vol. 53, p. 326.

Occupations and annexations

What to do with the territories occupied in this way? At the Jacobins, on 12 December, Prieur de la Marne expressed his doubts: 'The conquest of Brabant is not to our advantage. The Brabantine people are still encrusted with prejudice and fanaticism; so let us beware of continuing a foolish war, one that perhaps the executive power only wants to continue in order to hurl us over a precipice.'[3] On 18 November, however, Deutzel had brought to the Convention's attention a petition from the general council of Berg-Zabern, an enclave of the duchy of Deux-Ponts in the Palatinate: 'It would be impossible for us to endure any longer the character of slaves, and serve as watchdogs for our tyrant, among the free men by whom we are surrounded . . . Legislators, declare to the Universe that all peoples who shake off the yoke of despots and desire the protection of the French will be protected and assisted as if French.'[4] The next day, under the presidency of Grégoire, the Convention adopted the celebrated decree drafted by La Révellière-Lépeaux: 'The National Convention declares, in the name of the French nation, that it will extend fraternity and assistance to all peoples that seek to regain their liberty.'[5]

The first annexation was not long in coming. On 27 November, Grégoire proposed the union of Savoy to France: 'The National Convention decrees that Savoy will provisionally form an eighty-fourth department under the name of Mont-Blanc.'[6] And on 15 December, on Cambon's report, the assembly voted that: 'In countries that are or will be occupied by the armies of the Republic, generals shall proclaim there and then, in the name of the French nation, the sovereignty of the people, the suppression of all local authorities, existing taxes or contributions, . . . of corvées and in general of all privileges.'[7]

3 Aulard, *La Société des Jacobins*, vol. 4, p. 572.
4 A. P., vol. 53, p. 461.
5 Ibid., p. 474.
6 Ibid., p. 498.
7 A. P., vol. 55, p. 74.

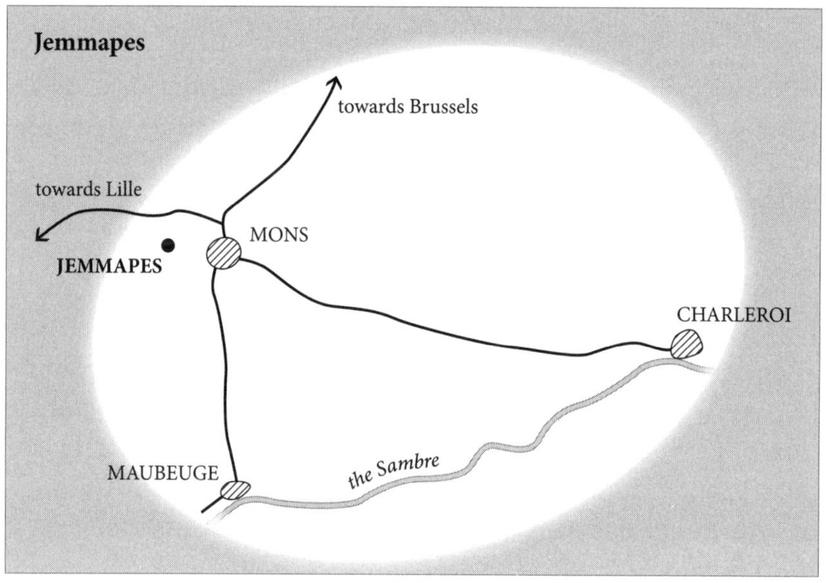

This was to forget that 'no one loves armed missionaries'. In one of his *Lettres à ses commettants*, Robespierre warned once more against a war of conquest, against exporting the revolution: 'We must not jeopardize the great interests that are common to all men by wounding too strongly the popular affections that cannot for the moment be uprooted.'[8] Marat spoke in similar vein: 'If, as the representatives of the French have declared, France does not want to make conquests, nor interfere in the government of the peoples where they go to bring liberty, what right have their generals to force the Belgians to accept laws they do not want, and that a handful of agitators want to give them?'[9]

But these voices were scarcely heeded. The attraction of giving France natural frontiers, combined with concern for oppressed peoples, led to enthusiastic acceptance of the expansionist policy of Dumouriez and the Girondins.

8 Robespierre, *Lettre à ses commettants*, 5 February 1793, *Œuvres complètes*, vol. 5, p. 265.

9 *Journal de la République française*, no. 77, 18 December 1792.

The wind changes: the Neerwinden disaster, the treason of Dumouriez, the declaration of war against England and Spain

This enthusiasm, however, would not last long. In just a few weeks (February to March 1793), victories and conquests gave way to disaster. The populations of the occupied territories became recalcitrant. In Belgium, popular assemblies could only be held with army protection, and the Convention's commissioners reported that, in the case of military reverses, 'a rebellion to rival the Sicilian vespers would break out against the French throughout Belgium, without Belgian patriots, fearful for themselves, being able to help in any way'. In the Rhineland, in Frankfurt, in the 'Rauracian republic' of the Swiss Jura,[10] even in Nice, opposition to annexation was expressed ever more openly in the form of attacks, the refusal of *assignats*, and popular revolts.

In the early months of 1793, the balance of military forces underwent a change. The republican army, which had hitherto enjoyed a numerical advantage, was almost halved when the volunteers, who had legally enlisted for a single campaign, upped and went home en masse. In Paris there was discord at the ministry of war, with Pache being replaced by Beurnonville, an intimate of Dumouriez. On 1 January 1793 a general defence committee had been established, but it was too large and thus ineffective – twenty-four members deliberating strategic questions in public. Soldiers were badly fed, badly dressed, badly led, and the year began with complete disorganization.

This did not prevent the defence committee and the executive council of the war ministry from approving the offensive plan proposed by Dumouriez. While the armies commanded by Miranda and Valence would defend a line on the Roer and the middle Meuse, Dumouriez himself, setting out from Antwerp, would enter Holland across the lower Meuse. To start with, this plan seemed successful. In February, the Dutch fortresses fell one by one without much

---

10 Where Le Porrentruy had been annexed, and turned into the department of Mont-Terrible.

resistance. But on 1 March, the Austrian troops commanded by Coburg attacked and routed the army of Belgium dispersed along the Roer. Aix-la-Chapelle and Liège were evacuated in terrible chaos, and the siege of Maastricht was hastily lifted. In order to defend Belgium, Dumouriez had to withdraw south and join up with the remaining fragments of Miranda and Valence's armies, but on 18 March he was crushed by the Austrians at Neerwinden, a disaster that led to the complete evacuation of Belgium. In the same weeks, the Prussians retook Worms and Speyer, and laid siege to Mainz. The left bank of the Rhine was lost, and the war would very soon move onto French territory.

After Neerwinden, Dumouriez – who had already sent a highly insolent letter to the Convention on 12 March – made contact with the enemy commander, Coburg. His plan was to dissolve the Convention, expel the Jacobins, and restore the monarchy according to the 1791 Constitution, with the former dauphin as Louis XVII. The Convention and the general defence committee prevaricated. Finally, on 29 March, four commissioners were dispatched, along with Beurnonville, the minister of war, to discharge and arrest Dumouriez. Instead Dumouriez had them arrested on arrival and handed them over to the Austrians, before trying to convince his army to march on Paris. The volunteers, however, refused to follow him, and, just like Lafayette in August 1792, he went over to the enemy to save his skin.

The critical military situation did not prevent the Gironde from pursuing their forward flight. On 1 February, Brissot detailed the hostile acts of the English and recommended war against them and their Dutch allies: 'It is the whole of Europe, or rather the tyrants of Europe, that you now have to combat on land and sea. You have no more allies, or rather, all the peoples are your allies; but these peoples can do nothing for you: they are in chains, and these chains must first of all fall.'[11] The Convention followed him and declared war on England and Holland. The vote for war on Spain followed on 7 March, on a boastful report by Barère: 'One more foe for France is just one more triumph for freedom.' The first coalition was born.

11 A. P., vol. 58, p. 112.

EXCURSUS: ENGLAND AND THE FRENCH REVOLUTION

In Germany, reactions to the Revolution can be summed up in a very simple contrast: general hostility on the part of the governing classes, but varying degrees of goodwill or even enthusiasm on the part of writers and philosophers such as Kant and Fichte, Hölderlin and Hegel.

The position in England is less well known to French people today, to the point of being sometimes reduced to a historical chauvinism that contrasts the good – the champions of the Revolution, from the chemist Priestley to the poet Wordsworth – and the bad, such as Burke and above all William Pitt, demonized in the phrase 'Pitt and Coburg'.

During the early phase of the Revolution, until the wars of conquest, the English reaction was largely favourable. Prints and leaflets hailing 'the overthrow of tyranny' or 'the triumph of freedom over despotism' were everywhere. In 1790, three theatres showed a play entitled *Taking the Bastille*. For Charles James Fox, the great Whig leader, the Revolution was 'how much the greatest event that has happened in the history of the world, and how much the best'; for the Welsh philosopher David Williams, it was 'the most beneficent event since the beginning of humankind'; for Thomas Christie, editor of the influential *Analytical Review*, 'the greatest revolution that has happened in the history of humanity'.[12] Keenest of all were the Dissenters and the radical Whigs, who had supported the American revolution.

On 4 November 1789, the Rev. Richard Price, a key figure among the Dissenters, delivered a highly political sermon before the members of the Society for the Commemoration of the Revolution of Great Britain (the revolution of 1688):

---

12 Gregory Claeys, *The French Revolution Debate in Britain*, London: Palgrave, 2007, p. 8.

> Behold all ye friends of freedom . . . behold the light you have struck out, after setting America free, reflected to France and there kindled into a blaze that lays despotism in ashes and warms and illuminates Europe. I see the ardour for liberty catching and spreading; the dominion of kings changed for the dominion of laws, and the dominion of priests giving way to the dominion of reason and conscience.[13]

It was these contentions that aroused such anger on the part of Edmund Burke, a Whig deputy formerly known for quite progressive positions in support of the American revolution, as well as the revolutions of the Irish and the Poles. His *Reflections on the Revolution in France*, published on 1 November 1790, was a bestseller, with 20,000 copies sold in six months. This work was above all an attack on the Declaration of Rights, and a warning to the English ruling class: what was happening in France could take place in England, if the members of the elite showed the same complacency as their French counterparts. Burke's tone was poetic, violently conservative, and sometimes crude:[14]

> In England we have not yet been completely embowelled of our natural entrails; we still feel within us, and we cherish and cultivate, those inbred sentiments which are the faithful guardians, the active monitors of our duty, the true supporters of all liberal and manly morals. We have not been drawn and trussed, with chaff and rags, and paltry blurred shreds of paper about the rights of man.[15]

Burke's book triggered an avalanche of hostile reactions, from popular societies such as the London Corresponding Society as well as

---

13 Cited by Mark Philip, 'Britain and the French Revolution', bbc.co.uk/history.

14 His abrupt change of political camp led to doubts about his mental health. Thomas Jefferson noted: 'The French Revolution astonishes me less than the revolution of Mr Burke.'

15 Edmund Burke, *Reflections on the Revolution in France* [1790], Oxford: Oxford University Press, 1999, p. 86.

intellectuals such as Mary Wollstonecraft, whose *A Vindication of the Rights of Woman* was one of the earliest attacks on Burke; above all from Thomas Paine, whose *Rights of Man* was also a bestseller and an inspiration for English popular movements for many years to come. In May 1792, however, the British government led by William Pitt struck back with a royal proclamation against seditious writings. Paine escaped prosecution by taking refuge in France, where four departments elected him as their deputy to the Convention (he opted for the Pas-de-Calais). The movement in support of the French Revolution was effectively repressed and had to go underground. The battle was lost, but it had decisively marked English intellectual and political life.

The reorganization of the army, the amalgame, the levy of 300,000 men

With a view to redressing the situation on the frontiers, the Convention took two far-reaching measures on 21 and 22 February 1793: the *amalgame*, and a levy of 300,000 men.

Until this time, as we have seen, the army was made up of two distinct kinds of unit: battalions of the line (the 'whites'), in which soldiers enlisted for a long period, and volunteer battalions (the 'blues'), who signed up for a single campaign. The volunteers received higher pay and elected their officers, whereas those of the troops of the line were appointed by the ministry. This situation made for frequent tension. Dubois-Crancé and the military committee pushed through a decree whose first article provided that 'there shall no longer be any distinction between the regime of the infantry corps known as regiments of the line and the national volunteers.' Article 2 said that 'the infantry shall form into half-brigades each made up of a battalion of former troops of the line and two battalions of volunteers. The uniform of the whole infantry shall be the same.' And Article 3, that 'the pay and the war bonus shall be the same for all individuals that make up the French infantry, each according to his rank, with the higher pay taken as the base for each rank.'[16] This radical reorganization needed time: the battles of spring 1793 were still fought under the old system, but the *amalgame* would be decisive for the victories of year II.

The levy of 300,000 men was more problematic. The total number was to be drawn from the departments in proportion to their population. Each departmental contingent was then divided between districts, and these between the communes, which were the actual point of recruitment. Initially, volunteers enrolled on a register. 'Should voluntary enrolment not produce the number of men set for each commune, citizens are to complement this without delay, and to this end they are to adopt the mode that a majority of them find most appropriate.'[17] This contained the germ of endless local squabbles. Furthermore, Article 16 stated: 'Any citizen called to march to the defence of the *patrie* . . . shall be entitled to have himself replaced by a citizen in fit state to bear arms' – to which was added, on Vergniaud's proposal, that those who had themselves replaced must arm, equip and clothe at their expense the citizens who replaced them. Later, this substitution option would lead to the decree of a tax on the rich, summoned to take part in defence with their money if not with their bodies.

Establishment of the Revolutionary Tribunal and the Committee of Public Safety; representatives 'on mission' to the front

The Convention did not confine itself to reorganizing the army. During the critical months of March and April 1793 it took three measures of great significance: the establishment of the Revolutionary Tribunal, the creation of the Committee of Public Safety, and the sending of representatives assigned to the armies.

The Revolutionary Tribunal was demanded by the most advanced Paris sections. On 9 March, the deputy for the Bas-Rhin, Bentabole, close at this time to Marat, returned from the Oratoire section to say:

16 A. P., vol. 59, p. 64.

17 Article 11 of the decree, A. P., vol. 59, p. 87.

'A general desire prevails in Paris to rush to the frontiers . . . We were told that citizens were only unwilling to leave because they perceived that there is no real justice in the Republic, and it was necessary for traitors and conspirators to be punished. They demanded a tribunal one could be sure of.'[18] David and Jean Bon Saint-André conveyed the same wish on the part of the Louvre section.

The following day, Vergniaud made clear the Girondin opposition to this project: it would be, he said, 'an inquisition a thousand times more fearsome than that of Venice. We will all die sooner than consent to it.'[19] The discussion became bogged down. At six in the evening, the session was about to adjourn when Danton suddenly took the floor:

> I summon all good citizens not to leave their posts! Let this assembly not depart without having pronounced on the public wellbeing! The safety of the people demands great methods, terrible measures . . . Since some have ventured in this Assembly to recall the bloody days that made any good citizen to groan aloud [someone had shouted: 'September!'], I will say, for myself, that if a tribunal had then existed, the people, who have been so cruelly reproached for those *journées*, would not have drenched them in blood; I will say, and I have the assent of all who were witness to those events, that no human power was in a position to stem the outpouring of national vengeance. Let us learn from the mistakes of our predecessors. Let us do what the Legislative Assembly failed to do, *let us be terrible so as to dispense the people from being so.* Let us organize a tribunal – not well, that is impossible, but the best we can, so that the sword of the Law may be poised over the heads of all its enemies.[20]

The law passed that evening set up an 'extraordinary tribunal' composed of a jury – twelve citizens from the Paris department and

18 A. P., vol. 69, p. 2.

19 Ibid., p. 60.

20 *Discours de Danton*, pp. 100–1. My emphasis.

the four adjacent ones – and five judges appointed by the Convention. 'The tribunal shall have a public prosecutor and two substitutes who shall be appointed by the National Convention' (Article 6). The prosecutor, elected three days later, would be Fouquier-Tinville. He was the key figure in this structure: he could have all those suspected of crimes against the safety of the Republic, except for deputies and generals, arrested and handed over to the tribunal.

The Committee of Public Safety was created on 6 April to replace the ineffectual general defence committee. The decree presented by Isnard detailed its composition: nine members of the Convention, elected by it for a month and re-eligible, deliberating in secret. Its decisions, 'signed by the majority of members taking part, which cannot be less than two-thirds, shall be implemented without delay by the provisional Executive Council [the ministers, thereby placed in a clearly subordinate position]. It shall deliver each week a general and written report of its operations and of the situation of the Republic.'[21]

The first Committee of Public Safety was made up of Dantonists (Delacroix, Bréard, Treilhard) around Danton himself, and men of the Plaine who had rallied to the Montagne (Cambon, Barère, Lindet).[22]

The representatives of the people on mission to the armies were established first on 9 April then on the 30th. Their job was to check on the operations of the Executive Council agents, the procurement teams, and especially the generals and officers, whom they could dismiss or detain. These full powers were supervised by the Convention and the Committee of Public Safety, to whom they had to send a daily list of their operations. They would be in the front rank – figuratively and often literally – in the campaigns and victories to come.

---

21 A. P., vol. 61, pp. 373–4.

22 The nine being completed by Delmas and Guyton-Morveau.

Start of the Vendée insurrection

The law on the recruitment of 300,000 men would detonate the terrible counter-revolutionary insurrection in the Vendée. It broke out on 11, 12 and 13 March at several points in a region stretching from the Atlantic coast inland towards Cholet and Bressuire. This was the culmination of four years of mounting tension, in which the rural regions south of the Loire had shown by several local revolts their hostility to the political changes, in particular the execution of the king and the deportation of refractory priests.

Peasants armed with farm tools and a few muskets occupied the towns of Montaigu, Mortagne, La Roche-sur-Yon and Cholet with little resistance, along with several smaller centres, disarming the National Guard, executing constitutional priests, massacring the most well-known patriots and then disappearing into the undergrowth. In Machecoul, the massacre continued for several days and left around fifty dead.

At the start of the uprising, the leaders were men of the people, smugglers, ex-soldiers, servants – such as the hawker Cathelineau, the game warden Stofflet, the wig-maker Gaston, the *gabelle* collector Souchu. The likes of Charette, Bonchamps, d'Elbée and La Rochejaquelein only came on the scene later: 'When they [the nobles] saw that the rebels fought with a fearlessness of which only fanaticism could render them capable, that they hurled themselves at the republicans' cannon and routed them, they no longer hesitated to accept the invitations of the peasants and to put themselves at their head.'[23]

As Charles Tilly has emphasized, this insurrection was not the massive reaction of a 'backward' region.[24] The towns, valleys and plains were quite favourable to the Revolution. The uprising broke out in the *bocage*, a landscape of enclosed fields and hedges, narrow sunken lanes, scattered hamlets and isolated farms. There was great tension between the peasants of this *bocage* and the inhabitants of the

---

23 Mercier du Rocher, administrator of the Vendée department, cited by Jaurès, *Histoire socialiste*, vol. 5, p. 348.

24 Charles Tilly, *The Vendée: A Sociological Analysis of the Counter-Revolution of 1793*, Chicago: University of Michigan Press, 1964.

towns, who successfully resisted along the coast – Girondins included, as they well knew that the 'brigands' did not make fine distinctions. Les Sables-d'Olonne, Pornic and Paimbæuf held their own against the attacks of the peasant insurgents: during the whole course of this war, the 'Catholic and royal' armies – as they would soon call themselves – never succeeded in taking a single port that would have allowed them to receive help from England.

As soon as the Convention was informed of the situation, it unanimously passed a law that prescribed the death penalty for anyone 'known to have taken part in the counter-revolutionary revolts and riots that have broken out or may break out over the question of recruitment, and for all those who have taken or kept the white cockade'.[25] But the situation on the frontiers was so critical that it was impossible to detach any substantial force for the Vendée. Against this victorious insurrection, the republican forces consisted essentially of National Guards hastily recruited in the adjacent departments. The Girondin majority on the defence committee did not take the matter seriously. When Mercier du Rocher 'described [to the committee] the civil war and all its horrors widespread on the territory of the Vendée', Gensonné replied that 'he should refrain from such reckless overstatement'.[26] This attitude would further weaken the position of the Girondins – already highly compromised by the failure of the war of conquest – in the decisive confrontation that was looming.

The popular movement of February 1793 in Paris

The Girondins' laissez-faire policy, their refusal to listen to the complaints of 'brigands' and 'anarchists', aroused the anger of the people, and not only in Paris. The month of February 1793 was marked by a strong movement against free-market economics, and

25 A. P., vol. 60, p. 331.

26 C. L. Chassin, *Études documentaires sur la Révolution française. La préparation de la guerre de Vendée, 1789–1793*, vol. 3, p. 515. Cited by Jaurès, *Histoire socialiste*, vol. 5, p. 363.

for the fixing of a maximum price on commodities – soon referred to simply as 'the maximum'.

Already on 13 January, delegates of the forty-eight Paris sections had come to the Convention to demand the compulsory acceptance of the *assignat* and a ban on exchanging it against gold or silver coin. A few days later, the Paris municipality[27] announced an increase in the price of bread, which had been held until then at three sous a pound – much cheaper than previously – thanks to a subsidy paid to the bakers: 'There is only one way to bring abundance to Paris, which is to pay for flour what it is worth, what our brothers in the departments pay.'[28] Immediately, threatening groups formed outside the bakeries, the sections marched to the Hôtel de Ville to protest, and the effervescence grew. On 4 February, the general council of the Commune decided that the price of bread would remain frozen thanks to a tax of 4 million on the rich, on which the Convention granted an advance.

Tension rose on 12 February when a delegation from the forty-eight sections presented itself at the bar of the Convention with a haughty and almost menacing petition:

> Citizen legislators, it is not enough to have declared that we are French republicans. The people must also be happy; there must be bread, for where there is no bread there can be no laws, no liberty, no Republic any longer . . . We have come, without fear of displeasing you, to *cast light on your errors* and show you the truth . . . You have been told that a just law on staple provisions is impossible.[29] That would be to say that it is impossible to govern states once tyrants are overthrown . . . No, a just law is not impossible; we have come to you to propose one, and *no doubt you will hasten to adopt it!*[30]

27 The municipality was the Paris executive, as distinct from the Commune's general council.

28 Mathiez, *La Vie chère*, p. 115.

29 This probably refers to Saint-Just's speech on provisions.

30 A. P., vol. 48, p. 475. My emphases. Mathiez detects here the hallmark of Jacques Roux.

The speaker concluded by demanding ten years in irons for any administrator engaging in trade in provisions; a uniform measure for grain across the whole territory of the Republic (the quintal of one hundred pounds), and the prohibition on pain of death of selling a 250-pound sack of wheat for more than twenty-five livres.

The Convention listened in silence, but lost all composure ('a violent muttering rose from every side of the hall') when one of the petitioners took the floor 'in the name of my electors, in the name of all our brothers in the departments . . .'[31] Louvet fumed: 'Are there two Conventions in France, two national representations? And if the petitioner is the representative of the departments, who then are we, and what are our powers?'

The Montagnards were as irritated as the Girondins, since the petition put all the representatives of the people in the same sack. Marat:

> The measures that have just been put to you at the bar are so excessive, so strange, so subversive of all good order, they tend so plainly to destroy the free circulation of grain and excite unrest in the Republic, that I am amazed they should have come from the mouths of men who claim to be reasonable beings and free citizens, friends of justice and peace . . . I demand that those who have imposed on the Convention in this way be prosecuted as disturbers of the public peace.[32]

Amid the general commotion on 22 February, women from the Quatre-Nations section, who had come to ask the Jacobins to lend them a hall, had their request rebuffed. The Jacobins were attacked from the platform. The women cried that there were merchants and hoarders among them who were growing rich from public destitution. Billaud-Varenne, in the chair, unable to appease the tumult,

---

31 The *fédérés* who had remained in Paris after 10 August, and those who had arrived in September to man the departmental guard, had formed themselves into a Comité des Défenseurs Réunis des Quatre-vingt-quatre Départements. This committee had sent delegates to bring the petition.

32 A. P., vol. 58, pp. 475–6.

was obliged to protect himself. The session was noisily adjourned. On Sunday 24 February, it was a delegation of laundrywomen who appeared at the Convention:

> Soon the less wealthy class of the people will no longer be able to afford the white linen that they cannot do without. It is not that the stuff is lacking, it is abundant; hoarding and speculation are what increase its price. Soap, which formerly cost 14 sous a pound, has risen now to 22 sous; what a difference! Legislators, you made the head of the tyrant fall beneath the sword; let the sword of the laws come down on the heads of these public leeches, these men who constantly call themselves friends of the people but who caress the people only the better to smother them.[33]

The laundrywomen left the hall, shouting: 'We've been adjourned until Tuesday, but we shall adjourn only until Monday. When our children ask us for milk, we don't adjourn them to the day after tomorrow.'[34]

Sure enough, the very next day, Monday 25 February, gangs of women, joined rapidly by men, invaded grocer's shops and helped themselves to soap, brown and white sugar, and candles, paying prices that they themselves fixed. Those grocers who balked at the arrangement were pillaged. The disturbances, which began in the morning in the quartier des Lombards, spread in the afternoon to the whole of the central districts, and flared up again over the next few days.

On the first day, those responsible for maintaining order in the capital were overwhelmed. Santerre, commander of the National Guard, was not in Paris. Pache, who had been elected city mayor a few days before, along with Chaumette, the Commune *procureur* and his deputies Hébert and Réal, attempted to harangue a crowd of women on the rue de la Vieille-Monnaie, but they could not make themselves heard. Pache tried hard to convince the general council of

33 A. P., vol. 59, p. 151.

34 *Les Révolutions de Paris*, no. 190, 23 February to 2 March 1793.

the Commune to sound the alarm and call in armed National Guards, but the council confined itself to sending a few of its members into the sections to restore calm.

The crackdown did not begin until the 26th. Santerre had 80,000 National Guards at his disposal when the alarm was finally sounded. His orders to them were clear: 'The provisional commander-general commands all citizens to take up arms and oppose the violation of property. That is the law and that is their oath. To arms, citizens! Defend the property of our brothers, those on the frontiers and those at home. Arrest any who betray their oath and deliver them to justice.'[35] The Jacobins, for their part, were much opposed to the fixing of prices and feared that the disturbances would hinder the sale of national properties[36] and drag the country into civil war. They played a major role in ending this Paris uprising that Robespierre portrayed as 'an intrigue hatched against the patriots themselves'.

For many historians, including Jaurès and Mathiez, the movement of February 1793 was led by 'a numerous and powerful party', that of the Enragés.[37] This view is no longer defensible today (see *Excursus*, p. 247 below). It now seems certain that the February events were a spontaneous popular movement in which some of the Enragés certainly played a role, but without having been its collective ringleaders.

A fight to the death between Gironde and Montagne

During the decisive months of spring 1793, when the defeats in Belgium, the treason of Dumouriez, the uprising in the Vendée and the food crisis threatened the very existence of the Republic, the confrontation between the Gironde and the Montagne ceased to be an an oratorical joust and became an implacable struggle.

On 1 April, in a dramatic session of the Convention, Lasource,

---

35 *Le Moniteur*, 1 March 1793, vol. 15, p. 575.

36 [These were properties confiscated from the clergy. See p. 108 above. – Translator]

37 Mathiez, *La Vie chère*, p. 145.

still riding high on the Girondin side, made very serious accusations against Danton. He attacked him for not having dismissed Dumouriez earlier, and for being part of a royalist conspiracy: 'If there was a plan to restore the monarchy, and Dumouriez was at the head of this plan, what was needed for its success? Dumouriez had to be kept on, as Dumouriez was necessary. Well then, I examine what your commissioners did. Danton arrives, and you will all remember that, far from speaking against this general, he praised him in no uncertain terms.'[38]

Danton counter-attacked as follows:

> You who proudly decreed the death of the tyrant, rally against the cowards (*gesturing to indicate the members of the right*) who wished to spare him; close your ranks, call on the people to gather in arms against the enemy abroad and to crush the enemy within, and by the firmness and constancy of your character confound all those wretches, aristocrats, Moderates (*still addressing the far left and sometimes indicating with a gesture the members on the right side*), all those who have slandered you in the departments. No further compromise with them . . . I have retrenched into the citadel of reason, I shall emerge with the cannon of truth, and I shall pulverize those wretches who have sought to accuse me.[39]

On 5 April, the Jacobins went on the offensive. In an address to the affiliated societies, they demanded that the Girondins' mandates be revoked: 'Yes, the counter-revolution is in the government, in the National Convention; it is here that criminal delegates hold the threads of the intrigue they have spun with the horde of despots who are coming to murder us.' The address called for petitions to be sent from all sides, manifesting 'the explicit wish for the instant recall of all the faithless members who betrayed their duties in not voting for the death of the tyrant, and above all those who led so

38 A. P., vol. 61, p. 52. It is true that Danton's role in this affair is unclear. For Mathiez, always anti-Danton, he was in league with Dumouriez. What is certain is that Danton supported Dumouriez for too long, no doubt convinced that only this general was capable of leading the army to victory.

39 Ibid., pp. 58–9.

many of their colleagues astray. Those delegates are traitors, royalists, or incompetents.'[40]

The first signature on the text was that of Marat, at this time president of the Jacobins club. On 12 April, at the Convention, during an unusually aggressive session in which Pétion demanded that Robespierre 'be branded with the hot iron that the ancients used to make imposters known', and Marat and Pétion called one another scoundrels, Guadet read the first lines of the Jacobins' address signed by Marat: 'Friends, we are betrayed! To arms, to arms!', which led to violent tumult on almost all the Assembly benches. Cries of '*À l'Abbaye! À l'Abbaye!*' were heard from all sides. The following day, an act of accusation against Marat was passed on a roll call by 226 votes to ninety-three, with forty-seven abstentions. Supported by the Paris Commune, by several sections, and by the clubs in the provinces, he was accompanied to the revolutionary tribunal by an immense crowd. Triumphantly acquitted on 24 April, he was crowned with flowers and carried back to his deputy's seat on the shoulders of sans-culottes.

The Paris sections did not wait for this verdict to strike a new blow against the Gironde. On 22 April, delegates from thirty-five of the forty-eight sections, accompanied by the municipality, accused twenty-two of the Girondin deputies before the Convention: 'The general assembly of the sections of Paris, after discussing at length the public conduct of the deputies of the Convention, has decreed that the following have openly betrayed the trust of their electors' – there followed the list of twenty-two deputies, whom the accusers called upon to 'withdraw from these precincts'.[41]

The Girondins responded by demanding the subjection of all Convention deputies to the verdict of the people meeting in the primary assemblies, but Vergniaud himself dismissed this idea, which risked leading to civil war. The Gironde based its counter-offensive on the more moderate Paris sections and the departmental

40 Aulard, *La Société des Jacobins*, vol. 5, p. 126.

41 A. P., vol. 62, p. 132. The twenty-two were Brissot, Guadet, Vergniaud, Gensonné, Grangeneuve, Buzot, Barbaroux, Salle, Birotteau, Pontécoulant, Pétion, Lanjuinais, Valazé, Lehardy, Hardy, Louvet, Gorsas, Fauchet, Lanthenas, Lasource, Valady and Chambon.

assemblies. In a *Lettre aux Parisiens* published towards the end of April, Pétion called on men of order to stand firm: 'War is being stirred up between those who have and those who have not, and you are doing nothing to prevent it. A few intriguers, a handful of factious men, are laying down the law to you, drawing you into violent and unconsidered measures, and you do not have the courage to resist . . . Parisians, emerge at last from your lethargy and make these noxious insects retreat into their lair.'[42] In Paris, however, the sections controlled by the sans-culottes were too many and well organized for this appeal to make much impression.

The Montagne heeds popular demands over provisions

These agitated weeks saw a steady evolution in the position of the Montagne, and particularly of the Jacobins, on the economic question. They had previously been very divided – several of them being opposed to authoritarian regulation and particularly the fixing of prices, presented as a measure inspired by Pitt – but they now drew nearer to the positions supported by the Paris sans-culottes. Their 'liberal' convictions were certainly undermined by the reports of commissioners sent to the provinces. One such, Bon Saint-André, on mission in the Lot and the Dordogne, wrote to Barère on 26 March:

> People everywhere are tired of the Revolution. The rich hate it; the poor lack bread, and are persuaded to direct their anger against us. Even the popular societies have entirely lost their energy . . . We spare no effort to replenish people's spirits, but we are speaking to corpses . . . It is absolutely imperative to give the poor the means to live, if you want them to help you complete the Revolution. We believe that a decree ordering a general requisition of all grain would be very useful, especially if it is supplemented by an arrangement establishing public granaries from the surplus held by individuals.[43]

42 Cited by Jaurès, *Histoire socialiste*, vol. 5, p. 419.
43 Ibid., pp. 159–60.

While waiting for the laws they demanded, the deputies posted in the provinces ordered inventories and requisitions to supply the markets, and prohibitions on removing grain from the departments in their charge.

Robespierre's speeches during the month of April 1793 reflect his growing radicalization.[44] On the 6th, he said at the Jacobins: 'Let us pass beneficent laws that will tend to bring food prices into line with the earnings of the poor.'[45] And on the 8th, again at the Jacobins:

> You have everything you need in the laws to exterminate our enemies legally. If there are aristocrats in the sections, expel them. If liberty needs rescuing, proclaim the rights of liberty and put your whole energy into it. You have an immense people of sans-culottes, utterly pure and vigorous, who cannot leave their work; have them be paid by the rich . . . I ask the sections to raise an army large enough to form the kernel of a Revolutionary Army that will draw all the sans-culottes from the departments to exterminate the rebels . . . I ask the Commune of Paris to support with all its power the revolutionary zeal of the people of Paris. I ask the Revolutionary Tribunal to do its duty, and punish those who in recent days have blasphemed against the Republic.[46]

Starting on 25 April, the Convention debated the principle of a maximum on grain prices, which was finally passed on 4 May on Thuriot's proposal. It was also decided to conduct a census of grain across the whole territory of the Republic. The administrative bodies were empowered to force cultivators and landowners to supply the markets. The measure was vigorously opposed by Vergniaud and Buzot, but Lullier, the *procureur-syndic* of the Paris department, received an ovation when he retorted: 'The choice is between the magistrates of the people and the rich hoarders, the dealers in grain,

44 It was not a complete U-turn: Robespierre had already supported Dolivier's 'anti-liberal' proposals in autumn 1792.

45 Robespierre, *Pour le bonheur et pour la liberté*, p. 221.

46 Aulard, *La Société des Jacobins*, vol. 5, p. 179.

who simply take advantage of the freedom of trade to snatch from the people their means of subsistence.'[47]

The approaching dénouement, the Commission of Twelve, Isnard's speech against Paris

Matters were coming to a head. On 17 May, Desmoulins presented at the Jacobins his 'Histoire des Brissotins ou Fragment de l'histoire secrète de la Révolution', in which he accused the Girondins of being 'almost all upholders of the monarchy, accomplices of the treasons of Dumouriez and Beurnonville, controlled by the agents of Pitt, d'Orléans and Prussia, and having sought to divide France into twenty or thirty federative republics, or rather to upset it so that there would no longer be a republic at all.'[48]

The following day, in the course of a stormy debate in the Convention, Guadet attacked the Paris authorities, 'greedy for both money and domination'. He proposed two measures: '1) The authorities of Paris shall be revoked. The municipality shall be temporarily replaced within twenty-four hours by the presidents of the sections. 2) The substitute deputies shall meet at Bourges as soon as can be arranged, but can only take up their functions on the certain news of the dissolution of the Convention.'[49] Barère disagreed ('If I wanted anarchy, I would support this proposal'), but he criticized the policies of the Commune, 'exaggerating or commuting laws as it pleases', and proposed the creation of a twelve-man commission 'charged with examining the decisions taken by the Commune in the last month'.[50]

The Girondins, who still held a majority in the Convention, had almost exclusively their own supporters chosen for this task. On 24 May, the Commission of Twelve, primed for combat, ordered the arrest of Hébert (for a virulent article that had appeared in *Le Père*

47 A. P., vol. 64, p. 598.
48 Aulard, *La Société des Jacobins*, vol. 5, p. 193.
49 A. P., vol. 65, p. 46.
50 Ibid., p. 47.

Duchesne the day before), Varlet,[51] and finally Dobsen, the president of the very active Cité section. It went on to demand the records of all decisions made in the last month by the Paris sections, as a prelude to legal action against section members. It ordered an investigation of Chaumette and Pache, and had a decree passed that gave it de facto control of the Paris armed forces.

These measures did not remain unchallenged. On 25 May, delegates from the general council of the Commune appeared before the Convention: 'We hereby denounce the assault committed by the Commission of Twelve on the person of Hébert, the substitute Commune *procureur* . . . The general council will defend his innocence to the death. It asks you to reinstate a magistrate who is estimable for his civic virtues and intellectual gifts.' Isnard, presiding, asserted that 'the Convention will not tolerate a citizen remaining in chains if he is not guilty', before launching into a diatribe that did much to inscribe his name in history:

> Listen to these truths I am telling you: France has placed the site of national representation in Paris, and Paris must respect this. If ever the Convention were debased; if ever, by one of those insurrections that have repeatedly surrounded the National Convention since 10 March, and of which we have always been the last to be warned by the magistrates – if, I say, by these ever recurring insurrections there should be an attack on the national representation, I declare to you in the name of France (*cries of 'No, no' from the far left*), I declare in the name of the whole of France, Paris would be destroyed; it would not be long before people were searching the banks of the Seine to see if this city had ever existed.[52]

The turmoil in Paris was racheted up by Isnard's speech. The following day, 26 May, the Club of Revolutionary Republican Women Citizens, led by Claire Lacombe, demonstrated in the streets to

51 On Varlet, see *Excursus*, p. 247 below.

52 *Le Moniteur*, vol. 16, p. 479.

demand the liberation of Hébert.[53] In the evening at the Jacobins, Robespierre, hitherto a supporter of stifling the Girondins by legal means, spoke up for insurrection: 'The moment has arrived: our enemies are openly oppressing the patriots; in the name of the law, they seek to plunge the people back into misery and slavery . . . I invite the people to rise in the National Convention in insurrection against all corrupt deputies.'[54] True, this proposal was ambiguous, as what precisely was an insurrection 'in the National Convention'? But the essential thing is that the word 'insurrection' was used.

On 27 May, Thuriot took aim at Isnard, who was still presiding: 'In what century are we living, then, if such a man presides; if the president of the National Convention, an incendiary rather than a regulator, appears to be grasping a torch designed to inflame the departments against Paris? . . . This is too much perfidy, I demand that the president step down.'[55]

The same evening, in fact, Isnard was replaced by Hérault de Séchelles. Delegations from the Paris sections followed one another to the bar, all demanding the release of the imprisoned patriots. The delegates and citizens in this procession gradually overflowed the benches reserved for petitioners and began to occupy the deputies' benches, until around midnight the Convention voted for the liberation of Hébert and the two other accused men, as well as the dissolution of the Commission of Twelve.[56]

On 28 May, the Cité section – whose president, Dobsen, had just been released from prison – summoned all the Paris sections to the Évêché. On the 30th, this revolutionary assembly organized the insurrection: it had the barriers of the customs wall closed, appointed Hanriot as general commander of the Paris armed forces, and established an insurrection committee of nine members including Varlet and Dobsen. The department joined the movement by organizing,

---

53 On this club, see below, p. 250.

54 Robespierre, *Œuvres complètes*, vol. 9, pp. 526–7.

55 *Le Moniteur*, vol. 16, p. 493.

56 The commission was re-established very temporarily the next day, the vote having been considered irregular: it was not clear whether the measures had been voted by the deputies alone, or whether petitioners had also taken part.

on Lullier's proposal, a general assembly of all the Paris authorities at the Jacobins. The insurrection committee decided to sound the tocsin at first light the following day.

31 May and 2 June 1793: fall of the Gironde

Around six in the morning, commissioners from thirty-three sections entered the Hôtel de Ville. Dobsen, who had chaired the revolutionary assembly at the Évêché, addressed the Commune as follows: 'The people of Paris, whose rights have been injured, have come to take the necessary measures to preserve their liberty. They rescind the powers of all the established authorities.'[57] The Commune accepted, aware that it was unable to lead the revolutionary action that was needed: Chaumette requested the general council to hand back its powers to the sovereign people. To unanimous shouts of *Vive la République!*, the dismissed council withdrew. Then Dobsen, still presiding, declared the reinstatement of the mayor, the Commune *procureur* and his deputies, as along with the general council, but in the name of the sovereign people. The reappointed Commune was thus released from its legal shackles, and the council became the revolutionary general council.[58]

At noon the alarm gun was fired, despite opposition from the Pont-Neuf section who pointed out that according to the law – since the September massacres – this required an order from the Convention. The Convention met in the afternoon, to the sound of the tocsin and the general alarm.

This was an agitated session, to say the least. Thuriot moved that the Commission of Twelve, 'which is the plague of France, be abolished immediately, that seals be affixed to its papers, and that the Committee of Public Safety should make a report on all of this.' Danton supported the proposal: 'Yes, your commission has merited

57 *Le Moniteur*, vol. 16, p. 517.

58 For Daniel Guérin, Dobsen's action was a manoeuvre designed to counter the influence of the Enragés on the insurrection movement (*La Lutte de classes*, vol. 1, pp. 120–1).

popular indignation. It has put magistrates of the people in chains simply because they combatted, in the press, that spirit of moderationism that France intends to kill in order to save the Republic.'[59]

In the tumult, and amid a hail of insults, a deputation from the Commune's provisional general council managed to make itself heard. It demanded: 1) the formation of a central Revolutionary Army made up of sans-culottes, funded by a tax on the wealthy at a rate of forty sous per day; 2) a decree of accusation against the twenty-two deputies designated by the Paris sections and by the great majority of the departments, as well as against the members of the Commission of Twelve (and the ministers Clavière and Lebrun); 3) that the price of bread be fixed at 3 sous a pound in every department, this reduction to be achieved by additional taxation of the rich; 4) the establishment throughout the Republic of workshops to make weapons, so that all sans-culottes might be armed, funded by a loan of a 1,000 million livres to be immediately apportioned; 5) the dismissal of all nobles occupying higher ranks in the armies of the Republic.[60]

Then a delegation from the Paris department came to the bar, with Lullier as its spokesman. 'We demand justice for a terrible insult directed at the nation. We are speaking of the political sacrilege proffered by Isnard in the sacred temple of the laws . . . You will avenge us for Isnard and Roland, and all impious men, against whom public opinion is clamouring.'

The petitioners, along with a crowd of citizens, entered the hall amid applause from the stands. They 'mingled fraternally with the members of the Montagne'. Vergniaud protested: 'The National Convention cannot deliberate in its present state. I ask it to go and join the armed force that is on the square and place itself under its protection.' He left, followed by a number of members, but returned a few minutes later.

Then it was Robespierre's turn to speak. He supported the dissolution of the Twelve, and criticized the Girondin project of protecting

---

59 A. P., vol. 65, p. 642.

60 Ibid., p. 652.

the assembly by an armed force. Vergniaud interrupted him: 'Conclude, then!'

Robespierre:

> Yes, I shall conclude, and against you; against you who, after the revolution of 10 August, sought to send those who made it to the scaffold; against you who have constantly called for the destruction of Paris; against you who tried to save the tyrant; against you who conspired with Dumouriez; against you who bitterly pursued the very patriots whose heads Dumouriez demanded; against you whose criminal vengeance has provoked the very cries of indignation that you want to make a crime on the part of your victims. Well! My conclusion is a decree of accusation against all the accomplices of Dumouriez, and all those designated by the petitioners.[61]

Finally, the Convention decreed the abolition of the Commission of Twelve, but took no position on the decree of accusation against the twenty-two.

In the evening, at the Jacobins, Billaud-Varenne reported as follows on a *journée* that had finished ambiguously:

> I have just come from the Convention . . . I believe, in view of the audacity of the conspirators, that the *patrie* has not been saved. I do not understand how the patriots were able to leave their posts without decreeing an act of accusation against the ministers Lebrun and Clavière. The insurrection was directed against the counter-revolutionaries on the right, and it follows that it should not end until they are all destroyed.[62]

During the night of 1–2 June, the insurrection committee and the Commune ordered Hanriot to 'surround the Convention with a respectable armed force, so that the leaders of the faction can be

---

61 Ibid., p. 655.

62 Aulard, *La Société des Jacobins*, vol. 5, p. 217.

arrested within the day should the Convention refuse to accept the demands of the citizens of Paris'. In the morning, the Tuileries were surrounded by National Guards, and by thousands of workers from the faubourgs. Cannon were aimed at the palace.

The atmosphere in the Convention was more than tense. At one point, Lanjuinais shouted out to Legendre: 'Come and throw me off the platform, then! (*Violent protests from the Montagne*) How can you ensure the freedom of the national representation, when a deputy comes up to me at this bar and says: "Until we put an end to scoundrels like you, this is how we shall continue to behave"?'[63]

Amid the cacophony, a deputation from the insurrectional Commune came to demand the arrest of the twenty-two members: 'The crimes of the factious members of the Convention are known to you, we have come one last time to denounce them. Decree right away that they are unworthy of the nation's trust. Place them under arrest.'[64] The petitioners marched out, shouting '*Aux armes!*'

Barère then suggested inviting the members in question to voluntarily resign from their posts for a set period. Isnard accepted, in fairly dignified language: 'I will not wait for the decree to be emitted, I hereby suspend myself, and return to the class of ordinary citizens.' Lanthenas and Fauchet echoed him, but Lanjuinais, with typical valiance, objected: 'A sacrifice must be freely made, and you are not free. The Convention is under siege; cannon are pointed at this palace; we are forbidden to stand at the windows; muskets are loaded. I therefore declare that I cannot emit an opinion at this moment, and shall remain silent.' Barbaroux agreed: 'Do not expect me to resign. I swore to die at my post, and I will keep my oath.'[65]

The discussion was interrupted by deputies protesting the order given by Hanriot not to let anyone leave the assembly precincts. Hérault de Séchelles, who was presiding, led a solemn exit from the Convention to try to break the encirclement. But all around the

63 A. P., vol. 65, p. 699.

64 Ibid., p. 700.

65 Ibid., p. 704.

palace they were met by bayonets. The only response Hérault received from Hanriot was 'Gunners, to your positions!'

The humiliated members returned to the hall to hear the closing words pronounced by Couthon, in a spirit of cruel irony:

> Citizens, all members of the Convention must now be reassured of their liberty. You have gone toward the people, and everywhere you have found them kind, generous, and incapable of infringing the safety of their mandatories, but indignant against the conspirators . . . I demand an act of accusation against the twenty-two denounced members, but given that opinion is so strongly against them, I propose they be placed under arrest in their own homes, along with the members of the Commission of Twelve and the ministers Clavière and Lebrun.[66]

The decree was passed, and the session adjourned at ten in the evening.

So ended the third great moment in the ascending phase of the Revolution, the third 'revolution in the revolution'. The elimination of the Girondins was necessary: even Michelet, whose sympathies were with them, recognized this: 'The Girondin policy, in the early months of 1793, was impotent and blind; it would have spelled the loss of France.'[67] But the events of 31 May to 2 June were different from the two previous revolutions, those of 14 July 1789 and 10 August 1792. The people had attacked the Bastille and the Tuileries in a spontaneous impulse, whereas this time the popular movement was encased in a parliamentary revolution with some of the features of a coup d'état. And indeed the fall of the Girondins was not greeted by great displays of popular joy, as the previous revolutions had been.

---

66 Ibid., p. 707.

67 Michelet, *Histoire de la Révolution française*, vol. 2, p. 443. He goes on: 'Personally, the Girondins were innocent. They never sought to dismember France. They did not have any dealings with the enemy.'

EXCURSUS: THE ENRAGÉS; WOMEN IN THE REVOLUTION

Enragés is a term of contempt, as used for example by Brissot in *Le Patriote français*; 'The character of these *enragés* [rabid ones] is to carry their popular doctrine to extremes . . . *Enragé*: False friend of the people, enemy of the Constitution.'[68]

Describing the popular movement of February 1793 in Paris, Mathiez and Jaurès, as we have seen, ascribe a major role to the 'party of the Enragés'. Jaurès: 'A kind of social party formed, seeking to bring economic problems to the fore'; Mathiez: 'The party that demanded the fixing of prices, the party of the Enragés, whose leaders were Varlet and Jacques Roux'.[69] It is quite odd that these great historians should have used the word 'party'; they were obviously aware that nothing existed at this time that could be properly described as a party. In my view, their use of the term signals a kind of hesitation as to what to call the Enragés. At all events, these did not form *a party*.[70] First of all, there were only three of them – Roux, Varlet and Leclerc – a bit short in terms of membership. And these three did not form any real group: they certainly knew one another, their paths crossed, they sometimes found themselves together in current struggles, but they did not start anything in common, whether a paper, a manifesto, or an organization. As Guillon writes, 'the Enragés did not form a group of conspirators

68 *Le Patriote français*, 10 May 1792, cited by Claude Guillon, *Notre patience est à bout, 1792–1793, les écrits des Enragé(e)s*, Paris: Éditions IMHO, 2009, p. 10. As well as this work, I have drawn here on Maurice Dommanget, *Enragés et curés rouges en 1793, Jacques Roux, Pierre Dolivier*, Paris: Éditions Spartacus, 1993; Morris Slavin, *The Left and the French Revolution*, Atlantic Highlands, NJ: Humanities Press, 1995, and Guérin, *La Lutte de classes*.

69 Jaurès, *Histoire socialiste*, vol. 5, p. 207; Mathiez, *La Vie chère*, vol. 1, p. 134. Marx was not far from the same idea when he wrote: 'The revolutionary movement which began in 1789 in the *Cercle social*, which in the middle of its course had as its chief representatives *Leclerc* and *Roux*, and which finally with *Babeuf's* conspiracy was temporarily defeated . . .' (*The Holy Family*, in *MECW*, vol. 4, p. 119).

70 Florence Gauthier, personal communication.

meeting to decide on actions to be undertaken.'[71] And when they left the political stage (to anticipate somewhat), they each left independently, rather than marching together to the scaffold like the 'factions' of year II.

The oldest of the trio was Jacques Roux (forty-one in 1793). Arriving in Paris in 1790, he became vicar of Saint-Nicolas-des-Champs, the main church in the Gravilliers, the section where a large part of his political life would be conducted, and he was also a member of the Cordeliers club. Varlet (twenty-nine in 1793) was a clerk with the postal service, which ensured him a regular income and enabled him to publish pamphlets at his own expense. After 10 August, as we have seen, he parked a platform on wheels outside the Tuileries on the Terrasse des Feuillants, from where he harangued passers-by and denounced the misdeeds of 'senatorial despotism' (today we would say 'parliamentarianism'). Leclerc (twenty-three in 1793) had travelled to Martinique at a very young age, where he saw slavery close up, then spent time in Lyon, where he undoubtedly met people of extreme views such as Lange and Hidins. Sent to Paris by the Lyon Jacobins, he addressed the Paris club on 13 May 1793, pressing it to establish 'a popular Machiavellianism'. In July he took up the old title of Marat's paper *L'Ami du peuple*, attacking in it the new Committee of Public Safety: 'It is a nine-headed Capet in place of the old one.'[72]

Notwithstanding the diversity of their characters and trajectories, and despite the absence of common action, the Enragés did display a convergence of ideas.[73] It was on the economy and the provisions question that they attacked first of all, demanding a clampdown on hoarding and speculation, and the setting of a maximum price on all

---

71 Guillon, *Notre patience est à bout*, p. 23.

72 *L'Ami du peuple*, no. 7, 4 August 1793. Cited after Guillon, *Notre patience est à bout*, p. 67.

73 And they were, too, generally reviled en bloc. Marat: 'These intriguers are not content to be the factotums of their representative sections, they busy themselves from morning to night introducing themselves into all the popular societies, influencing them and finally becoming the great doers. Such are the three noisy individuals who have taken over the Gravilliers section, the Fraternal Society and that of the Cordeliers: I mean little Leclerc, Varlet, and Abbé Renaudi who calls himself Jacques Roux' (*Le Publiciste de la République française*, 4 July 1793).

products of basic necessity. In the address that Jacques Roux delivered to the Cordeliers, then to the Convention, we read:

> Liberty is only a vain phantom when one class of men can starve the other with impunity. Equality is only a vain phantom when the rich use their monopoly to exercise a right of life and death over others. The republic is only a vain phantom when the counter-revolution is daily manipulating the price of food, which three-quarters of the citizens cannot afford without shedding tears.[74]

The Enragés – especially Varlet – were Rousseauians, champions of a radical democracy: a mandate was imperative, and deputies should be recallable at any time by their electors.

By way of these ideas, they were interpreters of the popular movement, sometimes its inspirers, but very rarely its leaders – only individually and at particular moments, such as Varlet with the insurrection committee at the Évêché. Their role was important but limited, which does not prevent them from being the darlings of today's far left and of that portion of revolutionary young people who take any interest in the French Revolution. This infatuation is easy to understand: direct democracy and the subordination of economics to politics are hotter topics today than the cult of virtue, and for many, the personalities of Roux, Varlet and Leclerc are more attractive than those of Robespierre and Saint-Just, tainted by the exercise of power.

Of all the women who came to the fore during the Revolution, the two who have inspired the most books, plays and films are Marie-Antoinette and Charlotte Corday. Next, but far behind, come certain women remarkable for their beauty or originality: Manon Roland, Olympe de Gouges, or Théroigne de Méricourt, the 'Liège amazon'. The rest, the women of the people, the anonymous ones, are often grouped under the term *tricoteuses*, almost as stigmatizing

---

74 Cited in Guillon, *Notre patience est à bout*, p. 96. This text deserves to be called the 'manifesto of the Enragés', since Roux, Varlet and Leclerc were all present for once at the 22 June session of the Cordeliers club, and spoke with common purpose.

as *pétroleuses* for the women of the 1871 Paris Commune. To be sure, everyone remembers that it was the women of Paris who went to Versailles in October 1789 to seek 'the baker, the baker's wife and the baker's boy'. Overall, however, the role of women in the Revolution remains vague, and is often dealt with in a few lines even by the best historians.

But women were present in the great revolutionary *journées*, and often in the front line. When Lafayette and Bailly fired on the people peacefully assembled on the Champ-de-Mars, on 17 July 1791, women were numerous among the victims. On 10 August, Claire Lacombe – the leading figure of the Club of Revolutionary Republican Women Citizens – distinguished herself so valiantly during the assault that the *fédérés* awarded her a civic crown. The agitation of sans-culotte women was an essential element in the popular movement that led to the insurrections of 31 May and 2 June 1793.[75]

As from 1791, women were admitted to the Société Fraternelle des Deux Sexes, which met at the Couvent des Jacobins in a hall situated beneath that of the famous Club. (Marat: 'the women's club that providence seems to have placed beneath that of the Jacobins to make up for its faults . . .'). They received membership cards, and took part in discussions and voting. Out of the six secretaries, the statutes laid down that two had to be women. This was where many women activists took their first steps – among them Pauline Léon and Claire Lacombe, who would soon go on to lead the Club of Revolutionary Republican Women Citizens. The Société Fraternelle was close to the Cordeliers club, where women could also speak. In May 1791, the two clubs jointly established a Comité Central des Sociétés Fraternelles, and after Varennes, Cordeliers and patriots of both sexes led a joint campaign for the abolition of the monarchy and the establishment of a republic.[76]

---

75 The following notes are based on Dominique Godineau, *Citoyennes tricoteuses, les femmes du peuple à Paris pendant la Révolution française*, Paris: Alinéa, 1988; Martine Lapied, 'Une absence de révolution pour les femmes?', in Biard (ed.), *La Révolution française, une histoire toujours vivante*; Marie Cerati, *Le Club des citoyennes républicaines révolutionnaires*, Paris: Éditions sociales, 1966; Guillon, *Notre patience est à bout*. The last of these contains biographical notes on the leading figures of the club, and on the Enragés with whom they were in contact.

76 Godineau, *Citoyennes tricoteuses*, pp. 116–7.

On 6 March 1792, women presented an 'Adresse individuelle à l'Assemblée nationale par des citoyennes de la capitale', written by Pauline Léon, that claimed the right for women to arm themselves with pikes, pistols and muskets, and to train in using them. This was a way of demanding citizenship for women:

> If, for reasons that we cannot conceive, you refuse our just demands, women whom you have raised to the rank of citizens by granting this title to their menfolk, women who have enjoyed the first fruits of liberty, who have conceived the hope of bringing free men into the world, and who have sworn to live free or die; such women will never consent to give birth to slaves, they will sooner die.[77]

Around this time, Pétronille Machefer, a street vendor who wrote tracts under the name La Mère Duchesne, exclaimed: 'Let us prove to men that we can equal them in politics. We shall denounce everything that is contrary to the Constitution and above all to *the rights of women*, and we shall teach them that there is more spirit and activity in a woman's little finger than in the whole body of a fat layabout like my very dear and faithful husband, Père Duchesne.'[78]

The Club of Revolutionary Republican Women Citizens was officially founded on 10 May 1793.[79] Two days later, its spokeswoman delivered an address at the Jacobins: 'We have decided that all women, from the age of eighteen to fifty, will form an army corps and sport the tricolour cockade. We shall make a collection to arm those sans-culotte women who do not have the means to equip themselves with weapons. We want the only bonnet worn by women to be that of

77 Guillon, *Notre patience est à bout*, p. 116.

78 Cerati, *Le Club des citoyennes*, pp. 12–13. My emphasis.

79 *Le Moniteur*, vol. 16, p. 362: 'Several women citizens presented themselves at the secretariat of the municipality and, to conform to the municipal police law, they declared their intention to meet together and form a society in which only women would be accepted. The aim of this society is to discuss the means of frustrating the plans of the enemies of the Republic. It will take the name Société Républicaine Révolutionnaire and will meet in the library of the Couvent des Jacobins, rue Saint-Honoré.' The club subsequently moved into an outbuilding (the 'charnel house') of Saint-Eustache.

liberty.'[80] Bentabole, from the chair, replied that 'the society is impressed by the heroic courage you display, and will engage all its brothers to second your generous efforts'.

The membership of this club – which varied from 150 to 200 – came from diverse backgrounds. The leaders had a good level of education, but members also included street vendors, poor wage-earners, genuine sans-culotte women who were often illiterate. Nor was the club politically homogeneous, though it was united in supporting the action that would end by eliminating the Girondins. There was a lively antagonism between those who supported Montagnard positions and others closer to the Enragés – the latter discernible in a petition read at the Jacobins on 19 May:

> Strike the speculators, the hoarders and the egoistic merchants. There is a terrible plot to have the people die of hunger by raising the price of food to frightful levels. At the head of this plot is the mercantile aristocracy of an insolent caste that seeks to equate itself with royalty and seize all wealth by raising the prices of basic necessities as high as its greed dictates. Exterminate all these scoundrels.[81]

There clearly were relations between the club and the Enragés, but the women were careful to maintain their independence. Their position towards Jacques Roux ranged from support to sharp criticism. Théophile Leclerc was the closest to the club, since he would marry Pauline Léon, one of its founders. On 26 August, he published an impassioned exhortation in his *L'Ami du peuple*: 'By your example and your speeches, arouse republican energy and reinvigorate patriotism in hearts that have grown lukewarm!'[82]

In the wake of some confused incidents, however, in which the revolutionary republican women were accused – not without reason – of seeking to impose the tricolour cockade and red bonnet on all

80 Guillon, *Notre patience est à bout*, p. 118.
81 Aulard, *La Société des Jacobins*, vol. 5, p. 198.
82 Guillon, *Notre patience est à bout*, p. 139.

women, the male revolutionary leaders eventually decided that the club had gone too far. On 9 Brumaire of year II (30 October 1793), Amar, in the name of the Committee of General Security, presented a decree forbidding 'clubs and popular societies [of women] under whatever name'. In his report, he maintained that 'women have little capacity for high conceptions and serious meditations . . . They are disposed, by their [biological] organization, to an exaltation that would be harmful in public affairs, and the interests of the state would soon be sacrificed to whatever the vivacity of passion might produce in the way of distraction and disorder.'[83] The decree was passed, at a moment coinciding with the loss of influence of the Enragés. The republican women citizens appeared before the Convention on 15 Brumaire to protest the decree, but had to withdraw precipitately 'amid booing and jeering'. The end of the Club of Revolutionary Republican Women Citizens was part and parcel of the restoration of order in the autumn and winter of 1793.

83 A. P., vol. 78, p. 51.

CHAPTER 10

June to October 1793

The 'federalist' uprisings, the Committee of Public Safety, the assassination of Marat, the Enragés and the popular movement, the general maximum

What has become of that ugliness that Death has so swiftly erased with the tip of its wing? Marat can henceforth challenge Apollo; Death has kissed him with loving lips and he rests in the peace of his transformation. There is in this work something both tender and poignant, a soul hovers in the chilled air of this room, on these cold walls, around the cold and funereal bath.

– Baudelaire, 'Le Musée classique du Bazar Bonne-Nouvelle'

The departmental uprisings: Lyon and Marseille

In the period that begins with the fall of the Gironde, everything combined to make the situation of the Republic almost desperate, far worse than a year before when the Prussians were besieging Verdun. The victories of the insurrection in the Vendée, disasters on the frontiers, the menace of famine – and on top of all this, the uprisings against the Convention in the departments.

This rebellion is often referred to as 'federalist', but the word does not denote any clear political position. It is more of a stigma, an insult or threat – which is somewhat curious, given the positive sense of the words '*fédération*' and '*fédérés*' at this time. None of the rebels, if I am not mistaken, aspired to a federal solution on American lines, still less to the secession of a part of the French territory. Two leaders of the rebellion put it as follows, in an address to the department of the Drôme:

> What are we proposing? Is it to fragment the Republic, to make you into a section of the French people and isolate you from the common interest, setting up several centres of power, action and movement in the state? It is by these features alone that federalism can be recognized. On the contrary, we want all the French to be subject to the same laws, inspired by the same principles, united by the same bond, led towards the same goal; to establish by their full power, by the indivisible exercise of their sovereignty, a government that is free and necessarily one, necessarily homogeneous, the Republic one and indivisible.[1]

The rebellion was certainly linked with the events of 31 May–2 June, but these were more of a trigger than an underlying cause. In many instances, moreover, and in many places, the rebellion had begun *before* the fall of the Gironde. That was the case in Lyon and Marseille, but not only there: in the last week of May, the departments of the Jura and the Ain invited the substitute deputies to Bourges, to form an assembly that would replace the Convention.

The great driver of the uprisings was resentment against Paris. Paris had abusively seized a dominant role; Paris was in the hands of extremists, anarchists, men without belief – Marat above all. Paris had taken control of the Convention:

1 Address of citizens Hallot, deputy for the Gironde, and Fontvielle, deputy for the Bouches-du-Rhône, to their brothers of the department of Drôme. Cited in Alan Forrest's excellent article, 'Federalism', in Peter Jones (ed.), *The French Revolution in Social and Political Perspective*, London: Arnold, 1996, pp. 358–79.

> The section [of Grande-Côte in Lyon] cannot but see that the National Convention is oppressed by the gallery, which, by its booing, shouts and cries, forces patriotic deputies to silence . . . that it is oppressed by a Commune of Paris more powerful than itself and which has allowed itself to infringe several decrees, in particular those relating to the freedom of the press.[2]

All the same, the Girondin leaders certainly played an important role in this affair. Of the twenty-nine placed under house arrest, several managed to escape, and returned to the provinces to drum up revolt. They were joined by some of the seventy-five deputies from the right who had signed a protest about the violence exercised against the Convention on 2 June. Buzot, who had fled Paris, roused his home department of the Eure, from where the movement spread to Calvados and almost the whole of Brittany, which joined with insurgent Normandy to form a general assembly of resistance at Caen. Bordeaux, after expelling the Convention's representatives, decided to raise a force of 1,200 men and to convene an assembly of the insurgent departments in Bourges. In Toulouse, Nîmes and Toulon – which the admirals surrendered to the English on 27 August – the prisons were now filled with 'Maratists' instead of Moderates and royalists.

But the scope of the rebellion was certainly overestimated, both at the time and by later historians:

> Pamphlets and leaflets printed in Bordeaux, Marseille and Caen reported between sixty and sixty-nine departments ready to take up arms against the Paris 'usurpers'. The leading Girondin politicians believed in the validity of these figures and repeated them in their writings, followed by a whole generation of historians . . . In actual fact, the number of departments really caught up in the movement remained limited. Out of the forty-nine departments that had protested against the proscription of the Girondins after 2 June, only thirteen continued to resist for more than a few days.[3]

---

2 Minutes of the section of Grande-Côte, 9 June 1793. Cited by Forrest, 'Federalism'.

3 Ibid., pp. 364–5. These departments were principally in the west (Calvados, Eure,

Popular participation in the uprisings – organized by the assemblies of departments and districts where the affluent classes were dominant – remained generally weak. The main threat came from Normandy, as the road to Paris would lie virtually open to a determined attack, but on 13 July, at Pacy-sur-Eure, a force of a few thousand men hastily recruited from the Paris sections routed the Girondin army. Buzot, Pétion and Barbaroux abandoned Caen for Bordeaux, and the uprising petered out almost of itself before the end of July, except in the two cities that each in its way played a very particular role in the 'federalist' revolt: Lyon and Marseille.

In Lyon, the struggle between the big merchants and the people went back to the first days of the Revolution. The silk industry, the main industrial activity, had been ruined by the emigration of its customers. Almost half of the workers and their families were reduced to public assistance, and the lot of those who still had jobs was scarcely any more enviable. Besides, the city had become a refuge for all kinds of counter-revolutionary elements, veterans of the struggles in Avignon, Arles, and the departments of Ardèche and Lozère. Lacombe Saint-Michel, the Convention deputy for the Tarn who was passing through Lyon, noted in a letter to Basire of 20 February 1793: 'Lyon is a hotbed of counter-revolution; it is dangerous at dinner to avow oneself a patriot; there are more than six hundred shop clerks who are actually former officers of the line, who emigrated and returned in this diminished capacity.'[4]

In 1790, the Lyon sans-culottes had formed thirty-two sectional clubs, the Sociétés Populaires des Amis de la Constitution, whose delegates met at a central Club. In 1793, this club was in the hands of the most advanced revolutionaries: Joseph Chalier, the 'Lyon Ezekiel' (Rancière), was backed by Manlius Dodier, Rousseau Hidins and Scevola Bursat. The club locked horns with the municipality led by the 'Rolandists', and on 9 March, Bertrand, who was close to Chalier, became mayor of Lyon: thus began the 'eighty days of

---

Finistère, Morbihan, Côtes-du-Nord, Ille-et-Vilaine, Mayenne) the centre (Rhône-et-Loire, Ain, Jura), the south-east (Bouches-du-Rhône, Gard – later joined by the Var) and the south-west (Gironde).

4 Cited by Jaurès, *Histoire socialiste*, vol. 5, p. 242.

Chalier'. The commune took measures akin to those demanded by the Enragés in Paris: it established a municipal bakery, fixed prices for subsistence goods, and set wage rates. The Club wanted to go further still and proposed the creation of a revolutionary tribunal, the permanent presence of the guillotine in the city, and the creation of a revolutionary army paid for by a tax on the rich to raise 6 million livres. This last measure, adopted by the commune on 14 May, triggered a counter-offensive by the sections, which had been overwhelmed by Moderates. After a few days, all but six sections came out in opposition to the municipal decree.

On 29 May, the balance of forces turned to the advantage of the Moderate sections. Chalier and his friends were arrested. The new authorities organized a *levée en masse* of 10,000 men under the command of a royalist officer, the comte de Précy. The Convention sent Robert Lindet on a mission of conciliation, but the Lyon leaders rejected any accommodation. Chalier was condemned to death, and guillotined on 16 July. Lyon would soon be under siege from the republican armies.

If the Lyon revolt was clearly counter-revolutionary, this was not the case in Marseille, where the movement opposed to the Convention was inspired, at least initially, by a difference in views over revolutionary action. Marseille had been at the forefront of the Revolution since its very beginnings. A series of riots and lootings had begun in spring 1789, showing the determination of the people of Marseille against an aristocracy of businessmen, shipbuilders and manufacturers. In April 1790, the National Guard – which had replaced the bourgeois militia – stormed the forts of Saint-Nicolas and Saint-Jean, held by royalist troops, and killed their commander. In 1791–92, volunteers from Marseille went to put down counter-revolutionary movements around the region, in Avignon, Aix, Apt and Sisteron. And we have seen the decisive role that the Marseille *fédérés* played in the taking of the Tuileries on 10 August.

April 1790 saw the creation of a new body, to counter a municipality in the hands of the 'elite': the Société Patriotique des Amis de la Constitution, which met on rue Thubaneau[5] and soon came to be

5 A small street close to the port, parallel to the Canebière. A popular quarter for

called simply 'the club'. Affiliated to the Paris Jacobins, it had a similar sociological composition: enlightened bourgeois, lawyers, independent professionals. Its members included Barbaroux, Rebecqui and Mouraille, the latter becoming mayor of the city in 1791.

The club was not the only representative of revolutionary Marseille. The thirty-three sections – one for each *quartier*, and eight for the areas around the city – began to intervene in public affairs, both local and national, from spring 1792.[6] On 17 January 1793, a message of the Marseillais to the National Convention, sent jointly by the club and the sections, rebuked those deputies who had requested an appeal against the death sentence on Louis XVI.[7] This address was violently criticized by Robespierre and Barère; they saw it as a sign of federalist tendencies. To regain control of the situation, the Convention sent Boisset and Moïse Bayle to Marseille, but their presence was less than helpful.

Discord now broke out between the club and the sections, which had so far seen eye to eye. On 17 March, the club organized an extraordinary meeting of the municipality, the district and the department, at which the decision was taken to establish a revolutionary committee of twelve members. The sections vigorously opposed this, deeming the measure 'impolitic and infringing the rights of the people'. They rejected the idea that executive power should be the exclusive preserve of administrative bodies, denying the club the leading role it was tending to assume in the city.[8]

In the sections – at least the most advanced of them, such as section 10 around the Hôtel de Ville, whose premises were used for general meetings[9] – a spirit of direct democracy prevailed. Section 18, for example, submitted to the citizens a project in favour of 'a democratic government in which the sovereign people would immutably retain

centuries, it has recently been 'normalized' by the present municipality.

6 On these points I have followed Alessi Dell'Umbria, *Histoire universelle de Marseille*, Marseille: Agone, 2006.

7 Among them Barbaroux and Rebecqui, who were expelled from the club.

8 Dell'Umbria, *Histoire universelle de Marseille*, p. 225.

9 For a detailed study of the sections, see Michel Vovelle, *Les Sans-culottes marseillais, le mouvement sectionnaire du jacobinisme au fédéralisme*, 1791–1793, Aix-en-Provence: Publications de l'Université de Provence, 2009.

the right and the action of its sovereignty', rejecting any delegation of power to 'representatives who arrogate unlimited powers to themselves'. The objective was to have no more than 'one single hierarchy of right, which the people will fully control, so that they can advance without fear of division'.[10] The implementation of these ideas would lead to a confrontation with the Jacobins of the club and the emissaries from the Convention, who took refuge in Montélimar in late April.

On 24 May, the general committee of the sections drafted a petition against the posting of Convention deputies to the armies, the unrestricted powers they disposed of, and 'the faculty they enjoy of transferring these powers to citizens who have not had the nomination of the people'. On 29 May, the committee declared that it refused to recognize the decrees of the Convention. On 3 June, it closed the club and replaced the municipality by a council of delegates of the sections. In early July, a dozen or so people connected with the club were guillotined. Marseille had now embarked on insurrection against the Paris authorities.[11]

It is hard to say at what precise moment the sections, up till then republican and revolutionary, were 'contaminated' by the Moderate and royalist elements who would eventually gain the upper hand, even seeking to open the city to the English. To put an end to this, regular troops commanded by Carteaux entered Marseille at the end of August 1793 and routed the forces of the sections.

Pacification measures

Faced with a country shaken by such serious disorders, the Convention was obliged to compromise. On 8 July, Saint-Just presented a 'Report on the thirty-two members of the Convention detained under the provisions of the decree of 2 June', in which, having demolished the Gironde leaders one by one, he concluded in a moderate tone:

10 Jacques Guilhaumou, 'Marseille et l'organisation "autonome" des pouvoirs pendant la Révolution française', *http://revolution-francaise.net.*

11 Dell'Umbria, *Histoire universelle de Marseille*, p. 227.

> You must make some distinction among the detainees: the great majority of them were deceived, and who can flatter themselves that they will never be so? The real culprits are those who fled, and you no longer owe them anything, since they harm their *patrie*. The fire of liberty has purified us, as the smelting of metals removes the impure scum from the crucible.[12]

In this conciliatory spirit, the Convention adopted three important measures to reassure the peasantry. As early as 3 June, it voted a law on the sale of national land, which would in future be divided into small plots that poorer buyers could pay for over ten years. On the 10th, it decided that municipal property would be divided on an equal basis per head.[13] On 17 July, it abolished without indemnity all feudal rights and duties, even if based on original title deeds, which were to be burned in order to prevent any future claim. The Montagnard Convention thus completed the work timidly embarked on by the Constituent Assembly in August 1789; after a number of intermediate steps, the seigniorial regime was at last definitively abolished.

The war in the Vendée

If the departmental uprisings were mere brush fires, with the exception of Lyon and Marseille, the same was not true of the Vendée, where the insurrection had spectacular successes in June 1793. It was waged by three armies, that of the Bocage, also known as the army of the Centre, that of the Marais, commanded by the famous Charette, and the most powerful, the army of the Mauges, which at times had a strength of more than 40,000, with such talented chiefs as D'Elbée, Stofflet, Lescure and La Rochejaquelein. The commanding general was

12 Saint-Just, *Œuvres complètes*, p. 618.

13 Up till then, 'the municipal regime to which the population were subject was absolutely oligarchic. Each inhabitant benefited in proportion to the extent of his own land, the wealth of his flocks; so it was the rich alone, or almost alone, who benefited' (Jaurès, *Histoire socialiste*, vol. 6, p. 142).

Cathelineau, a carriage-maker and sacristan of his native parish, Le Pin-en-Mauges. But 'there was never a good understanding between the "Catholic and royal" armies, which the needs of historiography amalgamate under the term "Vendéen", unknown to them.'[14]

In May, the Vendéens had taken Thouars, where General Quétineau had capitulated with 4,000 muskets and ten cannon, then Fontenay. On 9 June, the Mauges army captured Saumur, spreading panic throughout the Loire valley. La Rochejaquelein and Stofflet wanted to march on Paris, but the other leaders decided to head west and make for Nantes, where Charette was supposed to join them.

The republican forces were much smaller in number than the Vendéen army that was making ready to surround Nantes:

> Bonchamps, with his Bretons, was to attack from the Paris road and the château. The Poitevin division under Stofflet and Talmont approached by the Vannes road. The third and strongest army, that of Anjou [the Catholic and royal Grande Armée] took the central route from Rennes, under Cathelineau . . . As for Charette, he was left on the other bank of the Loire, the side from which Nantes was least open to capture.[15]

The soldiers, and particularly General Canclaux, were of the opinion that it was impossible to defend the city, and prepared for an evacuation to Rennes:

> If the defence had been only military, Nantes would have been lost. If it had been only bourgeois, by the National Guard dominated by merchants, business people, the well-off, etc., Nantes would have been lost. It would need the *bras nus*, rough workingmen, to move with violence against the brigands as an avant-garde. That is precisely what happened, and what saved the city.[16]

---

14 Jean-Clément Martin, *La Vendée et la Révolution*, Paris: Perrin, 2007, p. 170.

15 Michelet, *Histoire de la Révolution française*, vol. 2, p. 497.

16 Ibid., p. 494. Michelet emphasizes *bras nus*.

On the night of 28 June, the Vendéen attack was repelled, thanks in particular to the Paris gunners. Cathelineau was killed in the street fighting. 'Struck by this blow, the Vendée would not last much longer. They had believed him invulnerable, and were wounded to the quick, so deeply that they never recovered.'[17] The defeat outside Nantes did indeed mark a turning-point in the Vendée war, though the insurgents still won some major victories at Châtillon-sur-Sèvre on 5 July, at Vihiers on the 18th and Les Ponts-de-Cé on the 27th, which opened up for them the road to Angers.

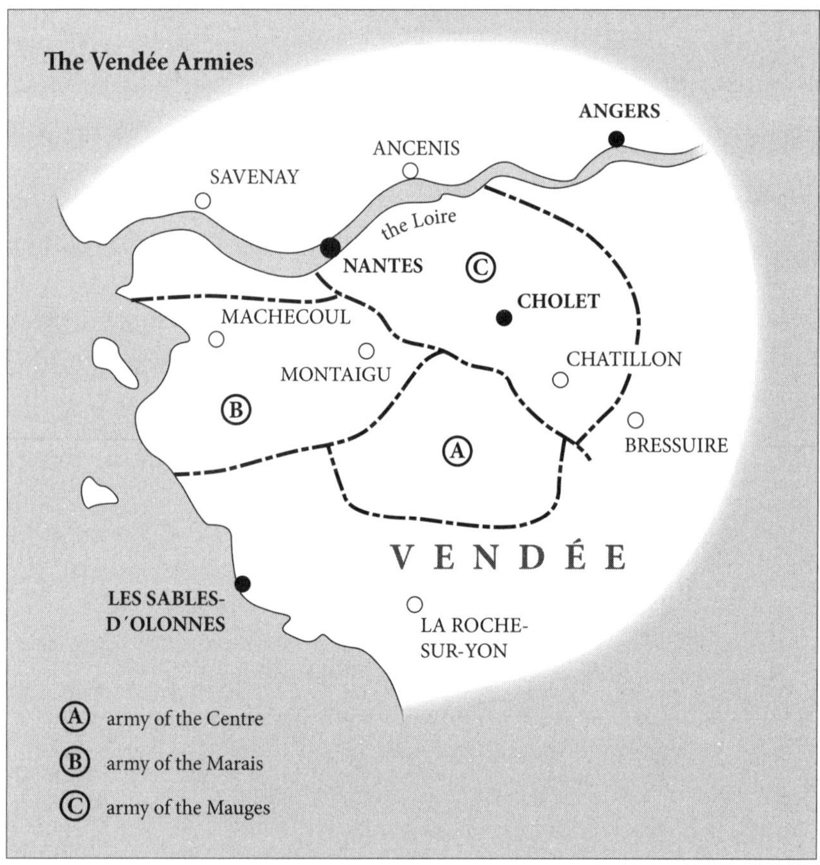

On 1 August, on a report by Barère, the Convention decreed the systematic destruction of the Vendée, 'measures with the object of exterminating this rebel breed, rooting out their lairs, burning their forests, destroying their harvests and combatting them with workers and pioneers as well as soldiers'.

17 Ibid., p. 501.

The assassination of Marat

During those critical months of June–July 1793, the armies on the frontiers experienced a string of disasters. The English entered the fray under the command of the duke of York, who prepared to lay siege to Dunkirk with a force of Hanoverians and Dutch. The Austrians, commanded by Coburg, occupied the strongholds in the north: Condé was taken on 10 July, Valenciennes on the 28th, then Le Quesnoy and Maubeuge were besieged and the road to Paris lay open. Mainz, which had been under siege by the Prussians since April, finally surrendered with military honours on 28 July. As a result, the armies of the Rhine and the Moselle had to fall back on the Lauter and the Saar.

The troops of the king of Sardinia invaded Savoy and threatened Nice. In the Pyrenees, the Spanish were advancing towards Perpignan and Bayonne. France was now little more than a great retrenched camp. The armies were demoralized, command was shifted from one person to another, there was discord between Bouchotte, his ministry where the Cordelier Vincent had brought in a number of sans-culottes, and the generals. Custine, who was appointed to head the army of the North despite his defeats in Alsace and the opposition of Bouchotte, found his plan of attack rejected and himself idle. He was recalled to Paris, indicted, and executed at the end of August. His successors, Kilmaine and then Houchard, failed to restore the cohesion and morale of the army.

On 13 July, just after Hérault de Séchelles had announced that Valenciennes was in danger, news came of the assassination of Marat by Charlotte Corday. This provoked tremendous outpourings of feeling among the people. Marat's violent death was like a symbol of all the impending dangers. The Convention attended his funeral en bloc. He was buried in an artificial grotto dug in the Tuileries gardens, his heart was suspended from the vault of the Cordeliers, and for several weeks the Paris sections held ceremonies in his honour, mingled with calls for vengeance. The Convention commissioned from David a painting that was exhibited opposite 'Lepeletier de Saint-Fargeau on his Deathbed'; this Marat dead in his bath, 'a gift to the weeping fatherland' (Baudelaire), expressed and concentrated the popular emotion.

EXCURSUS: MARAT

To understand the Parisians' intense grief at the death of Marat, it is necessary to free oneself – a difficult task – from the caricature image created by the Thermidoreans and reproduced by many historians. Michelet played a major part in crafting this image: 'He relieved his irate sensibility by horrid accusations, calling for massacre, advising murder. As his suspicions incessantly grew, and the numbers of guilty men, of necessary victims, increased in his mind, the Friend of the People would have ended up exterminating the people.' And further on:

> His unhealthy and irritable life, closed in on himself, preserved his fury intact. He ever saw the world through the narrow, slanting light of his cellar, through a peephole as livid and dark as those damp walls, as his own face, which seemed to have taken on their hues . . . His most frenetic transports were sacred; his bloody chatter, mixed too often with perfidious reports that he copied without judgement, was greeted as an oracle.[18]

To bolster the idea of Marat as a crime-monger, his poster '*C'en est fait de nous*' ('We've had it') is often cited; this was stuck on the walls of Paris on 26 July 1790, the day after the Fête de la Fédération: 'Five or six hundred severed heads would have ensured your rest, liberty and happiness. A false sense of humanity held back your arms and suspended your blows; it will cost the lives of millions of your brothers.' But only the most inveterate prejudice can take these figures literally – both the 'five or six hundred' and the 'millions' of brothers. This was clearly a manner of speaking, just as when someone says 'I'm light-years from thinking that . . .'

---

18 Michelet, *Histoire de la Révolution française*, vol. 1, pp. 397–425.

Marat did indeed *denounce* people, but we must bear in mind the meaning of the word at that time. Denunciation might certainly have the sense of informing, but more generally it meant attack or accusation. And whom did Marat denounce or attack? Right from the start, the powerful idols of the day: Necker ('But you, Monsieur, you notorious upstart, you first minister of finance, you whom the nation placed at the head of its defenders and who betrayed it so disgracefully . . .'); Mirabeau ('this hideous Proteus who only accepted the honour of becoming one of your representatives in order to sell your interests to the despot'); Lafayette ('that ghastly wretch and atrocious conspirator, the vile slave of the Court . . .').

At the great moments of consensus – the night of 4 August, the Fête de la Fédération – Marat exposed the mystification ('Don't you ever reflect? You are lulled by talk of peace and unity, at the very moment that stealthy preparations are being made for war.') He predicted the flight of the king, denounced the perils of war ('Here it is at last, the sinister plan that the infernal Riqueti [Mirabeau] has been machinating in the shadows'), and guessed at the treason of Dumouriez. In all those years, between imprisonment for debt, exile in London, illness and bankruptcy, what did Marat not predict, when was he mistaken? The people of Paris were right to mourn him – as were, closer to our own day, the Kronstadt sailors to give his name to one of their ships in 1918, and Abel Gance to have the role of Jean-Paul Marat played by Antonin Artaud in his *Napoléon*.

A new Committee of Public Safety

The Republic had no organized power that could deal with this situation. In the Executive Council the ministers were faded characters – except for Bouchotte at the ministry of war, but we have seen his fraught relations with the generals. The Convention was still smarting from the amputation of 2 June. The Committee of Public Safety formed in April, whose leading figures were Danton, Cambon and Barère, wasted time in secret negotiations with the Coalition powers. It proved as incapable of effectively curbing insurrection at home, as of marshalling troops at the frontiers. The Commune of Paris was riven by internal discord. It was as if every institution and all men in positions of responsibility had been wrong-footed: emerging from a bitter struggle, the victors had not had time to take stock and found a real government.

On 10 July, a new Committee of Public Safety was elected on a roll call vote. It was reduced to nine members,[19] with Lazare Carnot and Prieur de la Côte-d'Or, two 'soldiers', being co-opted in early August. Collot d'Herbois and Billaud-Varenne would also join the Committee after the *journées* of 4 and 5 September. On 27 July, Gasparin resigned and was replaced by Robespierre. Thuriot likewise resigned on 20 September. The Committee, from now on with twelve members,[20] held its meetings at the Tuileries, in the Pavillon de l'Égalité (Flore), not far from the hall in which the Convention sat.[21] It was not politically homogeneous: Robert Lindet, Carnot and Prieur de la Côte-d'Or were more moderate (in today's sense of the term – at that time, a 'Moderate' was a counter-revolutionary) than Robespierre, Saint-Just, Couthon, Prieur de la Marne and Saint-André. Billaud-Varenne and Collot d'Herbois represented the far left. In the centre were Hérault de Séchelles and Barère who, as an expert in tacking, leant either to one side of the Committee or the other according to circumstances.

During the autumn of 1793, the Committee of Public Safety organized and strengthened itself. Barère was in charge of relations with the Convention; Robespierre, Saint-Just and Couthon dealt with political matters; Billaud-Varenne and Collot d'Herbois were responsible for correspondence with the civil administrations and the Convention's representatives who were away on mission; Lindet headed the supply section, Carnot that of war, Prieur de la Côte-d'Or was assigned to armaments and Jean Bon Saint-André to the

19 These were Jean Bon Saint-André, Barère, Gasparin, Couthon, Hérault de Séchelles, Thuriot, Prieur de la Marne, Saint-Just and Lindet.

20 The number then remained unchanged until the arrest of Hérault de Séchelles on 26 Ventôse (16 March 1794), who was not replaced.

21 As we recall, this left the Salle du Manège in May 1793 for the Salle des Machines in the Tuileries.

navy. Structured in this way, the Committee of Public Safety trumped the Executive Council (the ministers) and administered the country over their heads. It exerted strong control over the generals whom it appointed, and in principle over the Committee of General Security, whose twelve members were appointed by the Convention on its proposal.[22] Only finance, where Cambon was the de facto minister, escaped its control.

The Committee of General Security, descended from the investigation committee established by the Constituent Assembly, sat in the Hôtel de Brionne, situated alongside the place du Carrousel and linked to the Tuileries by a wooden gallery. Its role was to thwart the plots of the enemies of the Revolution. It oversaw the execution of laws, and went after foreign agents and more generally all counter-revolutionaries. Its essentially policing functions did not prevent it from playing a growing political role throughout year II.

The Constitution of 1793

One task was particularly urgent in order to establish the irreversibility of the situation and reassure the country: to draft a new Constitution. The group in charge of this included Couthon, Saint-Just, and Hérault de Séchelles, who would be its main editor and present its report on 21 June. The Montagnards took as their starting point the draft Constitution written by Condorcet and put before the Convention on 15 February 1793. In this text, the direct sovereignty of the nation was proclaimed at every level. All elections were to be by direct (male) suffrage: two-level elections were abolished, so no more electoral assemblies. The primary assemblies would directly choose those responsible for representing the nation or administering in its name: the deputies and municipalities, but also the departmental administrators, judges, treasury commissioners and in particular

22 The number of members varied over time, but the twelve who made up the Committee of General Security from September 1793 to 9 Thermidor were: Vadier, Le Bas, David, Lavicomterie, Amar, Rühl, Vouland, Bayle, Dubarran, Jagot, Louis (from the Bas-Rhin) and Élie Lacoste.

ministers, elected by the people through a complicated system.[23] This manner of appointment made the executive very strong, and Saint-Just showed considerable perspicacity in saying: 'This council [the ministry] is appointed by the sovereign; its members are the only genuine representatives of the people. All the means of corruption are in their hands, the armies are under their control, public opinion is easily rallied to their attacks by the legal abuse that they make of the laws; the public mind is in their hands, with all the means of coercion and seduction.'[24] In contrast to this strong executive, the decisions of the legislative power would be constantly subjected to the judgement of the nation; it needed only the primary assemblies of two departments to demand it, and the legislative body was obliged to submit a law or decree to popular referendum.

Robespierre, for his part, had won the approval of the Jacobins on 21 April 1793 for a draft Declaration of the Rights of Man, which he elaborated before the Convention on 24 April. It reflected his concern to set limits to the notion of property, which, from a natural right in the 1789 Declaration, became a *social institution*:

> In defining liberty, the first of mankind's assets, the most sacred of the rights it receives from nature, you said, rightly, that its limits were the rights of others; why did you not apply that principle to property, which is a social institution? . . . You added more and more articles to ensure the greatest liberty for the exercise of property, but said not a single word to determine its legitimate character; so that your declaration appears to be made, not for men, but for the rich, for monopolists,[25] for speculators and tyrants.

---

23 The primary assembly of each department proposed a list of names. These lists were centralized by the legislative assembly, establishing a single list from which the primary assemblies made a definitive choice.

24 *Discours sur la Constitution de la France*, 24 April 1793, in Saint-Just, *Œuvres complètes*, p. 534. Saint-Just's *L'Essai de Constitution*, which followed on from this speech, began with the famous phrase: 'It is impossible to rule innocently.'

25 [The word *accapareur*, someone who corners supplies, came to be used at this time for both merchants and officials suspected of preventing adequate supplies of bread and other essentials from reaching the population. It is often translated as 'monopolist', although the sense is rather wider. – Translator]

Robespierre proposed to inscribe in the Declaration of Rights: '[The right to property] cannot prejudice either the security, or the liberty, or the life, or the property of our fellows', and that 'Any possession or any trade that violates that principle is illicit and immoral.' He went on to propose a progressive taxation: 'Citizens whose incomes do not exceed what is necessary for their subsistence should be exempted from contributing to public expenditure, others should contribute progressively in accordance with the extent of their wealth.'[26]

The final text of the 1793 Constitution maintained certain Girondin principles, and did not take on board all the proposals of Robespierre and Saint-Just (whose style can be recognized in the first article of the new Declaration: 'The purpose of society is the common happiness').

This constitution appears amazingly progressive, by today's standards, in its definition of a French citizen:

> Any man born or domiciled in France, having reached the age of twenty-one; any foreigner having reached twenty-one who, having resided for a year in France – either lives off his work – or acquires a property – or marries a Frenchwoman – or adopts a child – or feeds an elderly person; and any foreigner whom the legislative body deems to have deserved well of humanity – is admitted to the exercise of the rights of French citizenship (Art. 4).

For the election of deputies, the electoral constituencies were blocs with a population of 40,000 inhabitants, which meant that departments were divided, as a guard against federalist temptation.[27] Deputies were elected not by list, but by individual vote. If there was not an absolute majority in the first round, a second round would be held between the two candidates who were in the lead.

---

26 Robespierre, *Virtue and Terror*, pp. 67–9. The adopted Constitution, on the other hand, spelled out: 'No citizen is dispensed from the honourable obligation of contributing to the public expenditure' (art. 101). The 'poor' had replied to Robespierre that they wanted to pay tax, at least a low one, as this was the very expression of citizenship.

27 Jacques Godechot, *Les Institutions de la France sous la Révolution et l'Empire*, Paris: Presses Universitaires de France, 1951, p. 283.

The twenty-four ministers were appointed by a system with two levels. In each department, an electoral assembly chose a candidate. The legislative body then made its choice from among the eighty or so elected. True, these ministers were no longer directly elected by the nation, but the very principle of their election, which made them representatives for all that, remained a dangerous concession to Girondin conceptions.

As for the deputies, they were elected by primary assemblies made up of 'citizens of each canton domiciled there for six months' (Art. 11). The canton, instead of the usual seat of primary assembly, the commune: this was another anti-democratic measure, for everyone could go and vote in the commune but this was not so true of the canton, whose chief town might be quite a way off – and where in any case the popular political life of the communal assemblies was absent.[28]

The Convention did not adopt Robespierre's suggestions on the limitation of property. We could even say that article 19 of the Declaration of Rights actually went the other way and took up Condorcet's proposal: 'No one may be deprived of the least portion of his property without his consent, unless this is legally required by established public necessity, and on condition of a just and prior indemnity.' But the concerns that would today be called 'social' were not absent. The Declaration explicitly recognized the right to existence: 'Public aid is a sacred debt. Society owes its unfortunate citizens subsistence, either by providing them with work, or by ensuring the means of existence of those in no condition to work' (Art. 21). The right to education is also asserted: 'Instruction is the need of all. Society must promote with all its power the progress of public reason, and place education within reach of all citizens' (Art. 22).

On resistance to oppression, the Declaration of Rights took up in full Robespierre's famous formulation: 'There is oppression against the social body when a single one of its members is oppressed. There is oppression against each member of the social body when the social body is oppressed' (Art. 34). And especially: 'When the government

28 Florence Gauthier, personal communication.

violates the rights of the people, insurrection is for the people and for every part of the people the most sacred of rights and the most indispensable of duties' (Art. 35).

The Constitution was adopted on 24 June 1793, martial law being abolished at the same time. Its text would be placed in a 'sacred ark' of cedar wood in front of the desk of the Convention president. It would be ratified by a yes-no referendum, the results of which (around 1,800,000 in favour and 17,000 against) were published on 10 August 1793, the day of the Unity and Indivisibility of the Republic.[29]

Already on 25 June, however, Jacques Roux presented himself at the bar of the Convention, 'accompanied by several citizens and bearing an address from the sections of Gravilliers and Bonne-Nouvelle, and from the Cordeliers club'. He launched into a long critique of the Constitution that had been adopted the previous day, with brutal directness from the start:

> A hundred times this sacred precinct has echoed with the crimes of egoists and scoundrels; you have repeatedly promised to strike the blood-suckers of the people. The constitutional act is going to be presented for the sanction of the sovereign; and have you proscribed speculation? No. Have you pronounced the death sentence on hoarders? No. Have you determined what is freedom of trade? No. Have you prohibited the sale of coined silver? No. Well! We declare to you that you have not done everything for the happiness of the people.

As he developed his argument, Roux grew increasingly offensive towards the representatives of the people, calling them cowards ('Who can believe that the representatives of the French people, who have declared war on tyrants abroad, have been so cowardly as not to crush those at home?'), and merging hoarders and deputies in the

---

29 These figures indicate a very high number of abstentions, some 4 million, explained in part by the oral character of this vote.

same 'you': 'Accept then that out of pusillanimity you are authorizing the discredit of paper, you are preparing bankruptcy, by tolerating abuses at which despotism would have blushed in the last days of its barbarous power.' And finally, addressing the deputies of the Montagne, he rapped out: 'You must not leave your successors the terrible example of the barbarism of powerful men over the weak, of the rich over the poor; you must not end your careers ignominiously.'[30]

Throughout this long diatribe, Roux was interrupted by murmurs and protests, and the word 'ignominiously' triggered a ripple of indignation. Collot d'Herbois, in the chair, had to intervene on several occasions to let Roux speak. When he had finished, one of the members of the delegation, no doubt swayed by these reactions, declared out loud that 'this was not the petition to which the Gravilliers section gave its support'. The maligned deputies stood up in their turn. Thuriot began: 'You have just heard the monstrous principles of anarchy professed in this precinct . . . This man is a priest, a worthy emulator of the Vendée fanatics.' And yet – a strange fact that epitomizes the contradictions of this moment – he ended with a proposal that coincided with the popular movement and Roux's own speech, demanding 'that the committees of agriculture and trade be tasked with making a prompt report on his proposal to fix the price of food'. Robespierre also rose against 'a petition whose origin seemed to be popular but which was basically incendiary'. Léonard Bourdon, a member of the Gravilliers section, asserted that 'the section formally protests against the liberticidal principles developed in the petition'. Billaud-Varenne suggested that the speaker had not actually read the Constitution that he criticized. Charlier proposed Roux's arrest, but Legendre opposed it: 'I demand the expulsion of this man. There are patriots in his section, they will do justice themselves.'[31] Jacques Roux, as he would say a few days later, 'had drunk long draughts of the cup of bitterness'; he was expelled and disavowed by those who had accompanied him.

---

30 This speech became known as the 'Manifesto of the Enragés' – already cited above.

31 A. P., vol. 67, p. 420ff.

Jacques Roux and the 'manifesto of the Enragés'

In summer 1793, the popular movement was at its apogee. At no other time in the Revolution had the sans-culottes been so strong, in Paris especially,[32] or more capable of imposing a coherent programme. This combined national defence and defence of the Revolution: the purging of the army, in particular the expulsion of officers from the nobility, the formation of a Revolutionary Army that would ensure the provisioning of Paris, the application of the maximum to all essential goods, a compulsory loan from the rich, and 'the confiscation of all the goods of conspirators, to ensure a pension of 150 livres to every armed revolutionary'.[33]

The Montagnards who now dominated the Convention sought to block this movement. For them, the revolution of 2 June had achieved its purpose and the task now was to calm the departments, to reassure the deputies of the Plaine and the possessor classes, and to avoid measures of exception and terror.[34] The Commune supported their efforts, and Hébert, its deputy *procureur*, published in *Le Père Duchesne* words that seem astonishing from his pen: 'It is in the interest of the rich to sans-culottize themselves' (no. 243), or again: 'The sans-culottes do not resent the properties of the rich' (no. 245).

The balance of forces, however, was not in favour of order. The Committee of Public Safety had not yet been renewed. The Convention had no armed force at its disposal, and if the only effective power in Paris, the Commune, could not be relied on, it had no way of resisting a possible revolt. The Commune, for its part, commanded a National Guard that was not always docile, its popular and most

---

32 Albert Soboul, *Les Sans-Culottes parisiens en l'an II. Mouvement populaire et gouvernement révolutionnaire, 2 juin 1793 – 9 thermidor an II*, Paris: Librairie Clavreuil, 1958. The first chapter details the struggle between the Paris sections after 2 June, the most advanced of these being in the east and centre of the city, with the Moderates in the west.

33 This demand was issued by the sans-culottes of the Contrat-Social section, cited by Soboul, *Les Sans-Culottes parisiens*, p. 36.

34 The Plaine was far more numerous in the Convention than was the Montagne. Its deputies had previously supported the Girondins. It was important for the Montagne to ensure their support after 2 June.

numerous elements having been won to the ideas of requisition and the fixing of prices.

As a result of this situation, the disturbances that had continued throughout this time intensified from the end of June. The laundry-women on the Seine – clearly in the vanguard – emptied carriages and barges loaded with soap. Couthon reported to the Convention on 27 June:

> A few women, giving in to their fears, proceeded to the port of the Grenouillère and had four chests of soap distributed to them; from there to the port of Saint-Nicolas, where eight chests of soap, weighing some 200 pounds, were paid for at 3 livres 10 for a block of four or five pounds. The municipal officers managed to make them see reason and stop these excesses; today they are reported to be recommencing.[35]

The laundrywomen came to the Commune to ask that soap be sold at 20 sous a pound. Hébert replied: 'Paris would be doomed. With pillage of this kind, nothing will come into the city. If people push too far, the game is up, the counter-revolution will be accomplished and you will have a king.'[36]

There were more serious problems than soap. In this pre-harvest season wheat was scarce, the more so as the rebel departments in Normandy and the west had reduced their shipments, while drought was jeopardizing the operation of water mills. In July, queues and crowds once again formed outside the bakeries, which had to be protected by armed guards. Garin, the Paris administrator in charge of supplies, got the Commune to order a weekly check of the amount of flour held by bakers.

The Convention could not remain passive in the face of this mounting unrest. On 27 June, it instructed the Committee of Public Safety to report 'whether it might be advisable, in the circumstances, to provisionally authorize the departmental or

35 A. P., vol. 67, p. 543.

36 Cited by Mathiez, *La Vie chère*, vol. 1, p. 228.

district administrations to set a maximum price on foodstuffs and other basic commodities'. In the same session, the Convention decided to close the Bourse on rue Vivienne, thus meeting one of the popular demands: to prohibit the sale of gold and silver coin against *assignats*. The trade committee was tasked with reporting on 'ways of preventing or punishing gatherings of speculators on any premises they might choose instead of that of the Bourse'.[37] Thus the same Assembly that had booed Jacques Roux two days earlier was gradually advancing towards the realization of his programme.

That evening, Jacques Roux had a triumph at the Cordeliers. Received with shouts of '*Vive Jacques Roux! Vivent les sans-culottes!*', he lambasted those who had humiliated him in the Convention. *Le Courrier français* reported on 1 July: 'This speech was like an electric spark. It kindled the fire of enthusiasm in every heart. The society adopted the principles of Jacques Roux, decreeing that his address to the Convention be printed as a poster and sent to the Convention, the sections and the administrative bodies.' At the end of the session, Roussillon, who was presiding, embraced Roux amid general rejoicing.

Danger was scented at the Jacobins: Jacques Roux had roots among the Paris sans-culottes, while scarcity and economic crisis gave his words a worrying resonance. The day after the meeting at the Cordeliers, Robespierre spoke at considerable length. After praising Paris as 'worthy to complete a Revolution it had so gloriously begun', he attacked Jacques Roux by presenting him as a foreign agent: 'Do you believe that a priest who denounces the best patriots in concert with the Austrians could harbour genuinely pure ideas and legitimate intentions? . . . Do you believe it possible to overcome with one blow Austria, Spain, Pitt, the Brissotins and Jacques Roux?'[38] At the proposal of Collot d'Herbois, the club decided to send a delegation of twelve members to the Cordeliers to 'challenge the president on the accolade given to Jacques Roux and the club's decision to print his speech'.

37 A. P., vol. 67, p. 544.

38 Aulard, *La Société des Jacobins*, vol. 5, pp. 277–9; Robespierre, *Œuvres complètes*, vol. 9, pp. 601–3. Was Robespierre speaking in good faith? We may well wonder, but the foreign plot was a commonplace of political speeches at this time.

On 30 June, Robespierre, Collot d'Herbois, Hébert, Legendre, Thirion and Bentabole each spoke in turn at the Cordeliers, labelling Roux an 'agent of fanaticism, crime and perfidy'. Leclerc, who defended Roux, was called an 'escapee from Coblenz' and a 'paid agent of Pitt'. The hall had been well drilled, and made such a racket that neither Roux nor Leclerc could reply. At the end, the two men were expelled from the Cordeliers; the commando operation had succeeded. Marat, in his paper, gave Roux the coup de grâce by calling him a 'venal intriguer who had used the ploy of extreme positions, forcing up energies and carrying civic spirit beyond the bounds of wisdom'. He likewise denounced Roux's accomplices, Varlet, a 'brainless intriguer' and 'little Leclerc, a very clever rogue' who had been 'one of the main authors' of the disorders in Lyon.[39]

For the Enragés, this was the start of a long ordeal. Jacques Roux continued 'his harrowing adventure' (Dommanget), taking over *Le Publiciste de la République française* after the assassination of Marat, in which he wrote on 28 July that 'commerce and the right of property does not consist in making one's fellow men die of poverty and starvation'.[40] He was arrested on 22 August, released, but arrested a second time on 5 September and sent to the Revolutionary Tribunal, charged with incitement to looting. Convinced that he would be sentenced to death, he stabbed himself and died of his wounds on 10 February 1794.

Théophile Leclerc had to renounce all public activity, leave Paris and join the army. Jean Varlet, imprisoned on the order of the Committee of General Security for 'counter-revolutionary talk', was released on Hébert's intercession but politically neutralized. The Club of Revolutionary Republican Women Citizens was

---

39 *Le Publiciste de la République française*, no. 233, 4 July 1793. In 1792, when Marat was forced to go into hiding, he was put up by Jacques Roux in his small room on rue Au Maire. In July 1793, Roux replied to Marat in a pamphlet that contains these bitter sentences: 'Marat, men of great character have always been used to make revolutions. When they are no longer needed, they are broken like glass. It was natural, Marat, that I should experience such a fate' (cited by Dommanget, *Enragés et curés rouges*, p. 81). But by the time the pamphlet appeared, Marat was dead.

40 At the same time Leclerc took over *L'Ami du peuple*, which appeared until September.

definitively closed, as we saw, in autumn 1793. The various Enragés thus left the political stage at the very moment that their programme was at the point of being, if not applied, at least accepted under popular pressure.[41]

The popular movement and the elimination of the Enragés

Indeed, the movement was by no means abating. On 20 July, on place Maubert, 'the people, furious at the high price of eggs, threw themselves on this commodity and broke all the eggs that were there for sale'. The same day, the committees of Public Safety and General Security decreed in an emergency joint session that the Commune's administrator of supplies was to deliver to the bakeries, starting the next day, 2,400 325-pound sacks of flour. As Mathiez writes, fear of an uprising could be read between the lines of this decree.[42]

On 26 July, on the proposal of Collot d'Herbois, the Convention passed a decree against hoarders. The first article stipulated: 'Hoarding is a capital offence. Anyone is guilty of hoarding if they impede the circulation of goods or commodities of basic necessity, damage these or hold them in any place without putting them on sale daily and publicly.'[43] The municipalities appointed hoarding commissioners, to ensure that such commodities were put on sale 'in small quantities and for anyone'. Traders who did not make declarations of their stocks, or made false declarations, would be punished with death.

This terrible law was little applied: the crime was defined in too vague a way for such a radical penalty.[44] On 9 August, in the face of persistent scarcity, Barère sponsored a decree that established a *grenier*

41 Mathiez and Guérin see this as a manoeuvre by the Montagnards, who accepted the programme of the Enragés in order to cut them off from their popular base.

42 Mathiez, *La Vie chère*, vol. 1, p. 243.

43 A. P., vol. 69, pp. 551 and 594.

44 Out of forty-three cases tried, thirty ended in an acquittal and eight in a death sentence, lack of civic spirit figuring alongside hoarding in their indictment (Jaurès, *Histoire socialiste*, vol. 6, p. 245, note 42).

d'abondance (central grain store) in each district. Bakers were placed under the surveillance of the communes, who could requisition their ovens, but the decree remained a dead letter, as there was not enough grain to fill such granaries. Dubois-Crancé, for his part, proposed the nationwide establishment of stores selling bread at 2 sous a pound, but this extension of the Paris bread subsidy to the whole of the country was not accepted, as to meet the expense would have required issuing still more *assignats*, thus further inflating the price of all other goods.

The journées of 4 and 5 September

As in every serious crisis, it took a popular movement to sweep away hesitation and resistance. At dawn on 4 September a great gathering formed in the streets around the Hôtel de Ville. The majority were building workers, but there were also locksmiths, workers in the war industries, typographers from the Imprimerie Nationale – all paid in *assignats* whose value was constantly falling. The news spread that Toulon had surrendered to the English and, as so often, fear and hunger combined to explosive effect.

On the place de l'Hôtel de Ville, thick with people, a table was installed. A petition was written and a delegation appointed to present this to the municipal body. Its spokesman expressed himself in these terms:

> For the last two months we have suffered in silence, in the hope that it would come to an end, but on the contrary, the evil is increasing each day. We have come therefore to ask you to attend to the steps that public safety demands: act so that the labourer who has worked through the day, and needs to rest at night, is not obliged to stay awake for part of the night, and lose half of his day, in order to seek bread, and often without obtaining it.[45]

---

45 *Le Républicain français*, no. 244. Cited by Buchez and Roux, *Histoire parlementaire*, vol. 29, p. 26ff. My account of the events of 4 September at the Hôtel de Ville is drawn from this book.

The dialogue between the mayor and the workers grew tense. The deputation swelled, the hall was packed: '*Bread! Bread!*' was heard on all sides. Chaumette, the Commune *procureur*, arrived from the Convention and read the decree stating that a maximum price would be set on items of basic necessity. 'We don't want promises, we want bread, and right away,' was the response. Chaumette climbed on a table and finally obtained silence. 'I have been poor myself,' he said, 'and so I know what the life of the poor is like. We have an open war of the rich against the poor. They want to crush us; all right! we must forestall them, we must crush them ourselves, and we have the strength to do so!' He ordered sufficient flour to be brought to the Halle de Farine to provide bread for the following day; furthermore the Convention should be asked to establish a Revolutionary Army, 'to requisition wheat in the countryside, to promote deliveries, stop the manoeuvres of the selfish rich and deliver them to the vengeance of the laws'.

Hébert, the deputy *procureur*, followed on from Chaumette:

> Let the people proceed en masse to the Convention tomorrow and surround it as they did on 10 August and 31 May; let them not abandon this position until the national representation has adopted the measures required to save us. Let the revolutionary army depart the moment the decree has been accepted; but above all, let the guillotine follow every section and every column of this army.

Meanwhile, at the Jacobins, Robespierre called for unity between the sections, the Convention and the Commune: 'The Convention, the popular societies, the sections, the entire people of Paris must unite to prevent the blows that are being prepared against the established authorities.'[46] The club sent a delegation to the Hôtel de Ville led by Bourdon, to support the measures decided by the people.

In the morning of 5 September, a long procession of the sections advanced towards the Convention. Before the demonstrators arrived, the Assembly decreed that the Revolutionary Tribunal would be

---

46 Aulard, *La Société des Jacobins*, vol. 5, p. 388.

divided into four sections, the number of judges increased to sixteen and that of the jury to sixty, drawn from the sections by lot.

The people then peacefully entered the assembly. The Commune deputation, with mayor Pache and several municipal officers at its head, presented itself at the bar, followed by a crowd whose entrance was greeted by applause from the deputies and the stands. Chaumette took the floor, to enjoin the assembly to finish off the enemy within:

> And you, Montagne, forever celebrated in the pages of history, be the Sinai of the French people! Launch amid thunderbolts the eternal decrees of justice and the will of the people! Unshakeable in the midst of the gathered storms of the aristocracy, bestir yourselves, quivering at the voice of the people . . . Sacred Montagne! Become a volcano whose fiery lava destroys the hopes of the wicked for ever, calcifying those hearts in which the idea of monarchy still lives. No further quarter, no mercy for the traitors! If we do not forestall them, they will forestall us. Let us cast between them and us the barrier of eternity (*applause*).

Chaumette then proposed the creation of a revolutionary army, 'followed by an incorruptible and fearsome tribunal, and by the fatal instrument that with a single blow puts an end not only to conspiracies but also to the days of their authors'.[47]

In the wake of this speech, it was decided that the Committee of Public Safety would immediately draw up the project for the organization of a revolutionary army.

Danton supported the proposal: 'I know that when the people present their needs, when they offer to march against their enemies, no other measures need be taken than those which they propose themselves, as it is the national spirit that has dictated them.' A deputation from the Jacobins was then given the floor, accompanied by the commissioners of the forty-eight sections. Their speaker (who was not named) demanded the speedy judgement of Brissot and the Girondins:

47 A. P., vol. 73, p. 411ff.

> What, the likes of Vergniaud, Gensonné and other wretches, degraded by their treasons, are to have a palace for their prison, while humble sans-culottes tremble in dungeons under the daggers of the federalists? It is time for equality to parade its scythe over all these heads. It is time to terrify all conspirators. Well, legislators! *Place terror on the order of the day* (*stormy applause*)! Let the sword of the law fall on all the guilty parties.

The speaker ended by supporting the proposed revolutionary army and demanding the imprisonment of nobles until there was peace.[48]

Next, in this memorable session, Barère voiced the Committee of Public Safety's support for the measures desired by the assembly: he presented a decree that was passed immediately, establishing a paid armed force of 6,000 men and 1,000 gunners 'designed to crush the counter-revolutionaries, to execute wherever the need arises the revolutionary laws and the measures of public safety that are decreed by the National Convention, and to protect provisions'; this was the revolutionary army demanded by the people. The Commune, the Jacobins, the Convention and the Committee of Public Safety had been swept along by the irresistible Parisian movement.

The general maximum on prices and wages

During the weeks that followed, the Commune and the Convention shed ever more ballast under popular pressure, until they took the final step, the one most demanded by the sans-culottes but at the same time most contrary to the ideas of the majority of deputies, attached as they were to freedom of trade: the fixing of a 'general maximum' on items of basic necessity.

---

48 It is highly surprising that this speaker, delivering some of the most celebrated words of the period ('terror on the order of the day'), should have remained anonymous. Jean-Clément Martin believes it was Barère, which is unlikely, since Barère went on to express himself in the name of the Committee of Public Safety; he could hardly have spoken on behalf of the Jacobins too (Jean-Clément Martin, *Violence et Révolution, essai sur la naissance d'un mythe national*, Paris: Le Seuil, 2006, p. 188).

But before this, the Convention adopted a terrible measure, the law of suspects. Decreed on 17 September, on the report of Merlin de Douai, its first article provided that: 'All suspect people who are on the territory of the Republic and who are still at liberty shall be placed under arrest.' The next article defined these suspects in a very broad fashion: opinions, statements and writings were enough to put one into this category, which encompassed not only actual enemies of the Revolution, but also the indifferent and the timid.[49] It was up to the surveillance committees to draw up lists of suspects, deliver arrest warrants and place seals on their papers (Art. 3).

On the question of provisions, the Convention decreed on 11 September a general maximum on grain and flour: all millers were placed under requisition, with those who stopped milling or did not comply with the requisitions being liable to a fine of 3,000 livres. The price of a quintal of wheat was fixed at 14 livres over the whole territory of the Republic, but this measure was deemed inadequate and disturbances continued to spread. On 23 September, Coupé de l'Oise presented a report on the general maximum in the name of the provisions commission. He explained that

> in ordinary times, the price of goods is determined and formed naturally by the mutual interest of buyers and sellers . . . But when a general and unprecedented conspiracy of malevolence, perfidy and fury gathers to break this natural equilibrium, to starve and dispossess us, the welfare of the people becomes the supreme rule . . . By way of a necessary maximum we shall establish salutary and just limits, which it will not be permissible to trespass.[50]

---

49 'Suspect people include: 1) those who, by their conduct or by their relations, or by their statements or writings, have shown themselves supporters of tyranny or federalism, and enemies of liberty; 2) those who cannot justify . . . their means of existence and the performance of their civic duties; 3) those who have been refused certificates of good citizenship; 4) public officials who have been suspended or dismissed, and not reinstated; 5) those former nobles . . . who have not constantly manifested their attachment to the Revolution; 6) those who emigrated in the interval between 1 July 1789 and the publication of the law of 8 April 1792, whether they returned to France in the period set by this law or previously.'

50 A. P., vol. 75, p. 15.

On 29 September, chaired by Cambon, the Convention finally issued the great decree that would govern the whole economic life of the nation, in the form of a price tariff for commodities and a fixing of wages.[51] It was decided that the maximum price of items of basic necessity would be that of 1790 increased by a third.[52] At the same time, Article 8 consolidated working-class gains: the cap on wages was set at the level of 1790 increased by a half.

Despite the difficulties there would be in applying this text,[53] it marks – along with the law on suspects and the creation of the revolutionary army – the triumph of '*rabid*' ideas and the popular movement, at the very moment when the Enragés themselves, as we have seen, permanently abandoned the political stage.

---

51 Ibid., p. 321.

52 The items concerned were: fresh meat, salt meat and lard, butter, cooking oil, cattle, salt fish, wine, eau-de-vie, vinegar, cider, beer, firewood, charcoal, coal, candles, heating oil, salt, soap, potash, sugar, honey, white paper, leather goods, ironware, cast iron, lead, steel, copper, canvas, linen, wools, fabric, cloth, raw materials used for manufacture, clogs, shoes, colza and rapeseed, tobacco. For firewood and coal, the 1790 price was increased by only a twentieth. Fixed prices were set for certain items: a pound of tobacco would be 10 sous, a pound of salt 2 sous, and a pound of soap 25 sous.

53 Volume 2 of Mathiez's *La Vie chère* is largely devoted to the difficulties of applying the general maximum.

CHAPTER 11

October to December 1793

Trial and execution of the Girondins, the Wattignies victory, the end of the Vendée war, repression

> It had snowed so heavily all day long that the lady's footsteps were scarcely audible; the streets were deserted, and a feeling of dread, not unnatural amid the silence, was further increased by the whole extent of the terror beneath which France was groaning in those days.
>
> – Balzac, 'An Episode Under the Terror'

The 'revolutionary until peace' government

In the turmoil of autumn 1793, the Montagne and the Committee of Public Safety had an additional reason to bend to popular demands: they needed support to withstand an offensive from the other side, that of the moderate party known as the 'Indulgents'. What these wanted was normalization: a general amnesty and the application of the Constitution. Already on 11 August, Delacroix, who was close to Danton, had surprised a half-empty hall into voting for the election of a new Assembly, as the present one had accomplished its mission. Robespierre succeeded in having this vote reversed the next day ('The insidious proposal that has been put to you is designed only to replace the purged members of the Convention with the emissaries of Pitt and Coburg').[1]

On 25 September, Thuriot, who had resigned from the Committee of Public Safety on the 20th, attacked the Committee's policy, the purge and the economic controls:

> Be sure of one thing, citizens: for the people to be happy, trade needs to be vigourous; and those who seek to make the nation believe it can only attain happiness if all branches of its commerce are cut off are criminal indeed . . . There is now a move afoot throughout the Republic to persuade people that it can only survive by raising to all positions men of blood, men who from the start of the Revolution have stood out only by their love of carnage . . . This impetuous torrent leading us to barbarism must be stopped.[2]

Robespierre replied by defending the Committee of Public Safety:

> Eleven armies to direct, the weight of Europe to bear, everywhere traitors to unmask, emissaries bribed by foreign gold to undermine, disloyal administrators to keep under surveillance, to pursue . . . Do you think that without unity of action, without secrecy of operations, without the certainty of finding support in the Convention, the government will be able to triumph over so many obstacles and so many enemies?[3]

At the end of his speech, 'in a spontaneous movement, the whole Assembly rose and declared that the Committee of Public Safety enjoyed its full confidence', and on Billaud-Varenne's proposal, it approved 'unanimously and amid universal applause' the measures taken by the Committee.

---

1 Aulard, *La Société des Jacobins*, vol. 5, p. 342.

2 A. P., vol. 75, p. 123. Thuriot, a deputy from the Marne, was an ambiguous character: a violent opponent of the Girondins who often took advanced positions, but resigned from the Committee of Public Safety and became its adversary. Some believe he was later involved in the Conspiracy of Equals.

3 Ibid., p. 131.

In a major speech 'On revolutionary government', delivered on 10 October in the name of the Committee of Public Safety, Saint-Just explained: 'In the Republic's present circumstances, the Constitution cannot be established: this would lead to its own immolation. It would become the guarantee of attacks on liberty, since it would lack the violence necessary to stamp them out.' He then turned on the ministry: 'A people has only one dangerous foe, that is, its government. Yours has constantly made war on you with impunity . . . The government is a hierarchy of errors and assaults.' He went on to reject any idea of amnesty or clemency: 'You have not only traitors to chastise, but also the indifferent; you have to punish anyone who is passive in the Republic and does nothing for it . . . The sword of the laws must move everywhere with rapidity, and your arm be raised everywhere to stop crime.'[4] The first article of the proposed decree contained just one line: 'The provisional government of France is revolutionary until there is peace', meaning that the Convention would not be renewed before that time.

Trial and execution of the Girondins, Marie-Antoinette and Philippe-Égalité

Rather than amnesty, popular pressure forced an acceleration in the holding of political trials, particularly that of the Girondins. The Committee of Public Safety seemed in no hurry to send them to the Revolutionary Tribunal, but the sections – and especially Hébert, who bore a grudge against those who had had him arrested in May 1793 – campaigned for them to be judged. On 30 August, Hébert addressed the Cordeliers as follows: 'Brissot, that monster who made the blood of a million men flow by forcing us to declare war, Brissot still breathes, and patriots boast of having mettle! . . . Brissot must perish, the perjured deputies must fall beneath the sword of justice; the people wish it, and their will is law.'[5] On 3 October, on a report

4 Saint-Just, *Œuvres complètes*, pp. 628–45. This speech contains some of Saint-Just's most famous sayings: 'Those who make revolutions in the world, those who seek to do good, can only sleep in the tomb', and, 'It is impossible to govern except severely.'

5 *Journal historique et politique*, 31 August 1793.

from Amar, the Convention voted an act of accusation against twenty-one of the Girondin deputies,[6] accused of conspiracy against the unity and indivisibility of the Republic, and against the liberty and security of the French people.

The trial opened on 24 October. Pache, Chaumette, Hébert, Fabre d'Églantine and Chabot were among the witnesses – all for the prosecution. Reading the transcript of the hearing,[7] it appears that the accused defended themselves well – especially Vergniaud – and that the trial respected certain legal forms. But the advocate for the defence, Chauveau-Lagarde, was scarcely heard, and on 29 October, deeming the debate too prolonged, the Convention decreed on Robespierre's proposal that 'after three days of debate, the president of the tribunal shall be authorized to ask the jurors if their minds are sufficiently enlightened; if they reply in the negative, the hearing shall be continued until they declare that they are in a position to pronounce.' On the morning of the next day, Antonelle, the spokesman of the jury, indicated that their conscience was not sufficiently enlightened. The debate resumed, and at the end of the day, the jury declared that it was now in a position to deliver a verdict. The twenty-one defendants were condemned to death, and guillotined the following day. The body of Valazé, who killed himself with a dagger on hearing the verdict, was taken along with his friends in the tumbril to the place de la Révolution.

Marie-Antoinette had been guillotined on 16 October, Philippe-Égalité would follow on 6 November, Madame Roland on the 8th, Bailly on the 10th, and 'the infamous Barnave', as Hébert called him, on the 28th of the same month.

---

6 Brissot, Vergniaud, Gensonné, Duperret, Carra, Gardien, Dufriche-Valazé, Duprat, Brulart-Sillery, Fauchet, Ducos, Boyer-Fonfrède, Lasource, Lesterpt-Beauvais, Duchastel, Mainvielle, Lacaze, Lehardy, Boileau, Antiboul and Viger. In the Convention, Osselin proposed to add to the list the names of 73 (75?) deputies who had publicly protested against the *journée* of 2 June. Robespierre opposed this: 'the National Convention must not attempt to multiply the guilty. It is the leaders of this faction who must be singled out.'

7 Gérard Walter, *Actes du tribunal révolutionnaire*, Paris: Mercure de France, 1968/1986, pp. 236–41.

A new strategy, the levée en masse, scientists at work

During these early months of year II, the Committee of Public Safety gained in authority, as the measures it took – the reorganization of the army, the purging of the general staffs and the *levée en masse* – would finally improve the situation on the frontiers.

Saint-Just, in his speech of 10 October, had stated the necessity of a new strategy:

> Everything that is not new in a time of innovation is pernicious . . . Our nation already has a character: its military system must be different from that of its enemies. Now, since the French nation is terrible in its verve and its adroitness, while its enemies are sluggish, cold and tardy, its military system must be impetuous . . . The system of war of French arms must be the order of the shock impact.[8]

This meant new men to replace the old heads of the army who had learned their warcraft under the Ancien Régime. Houchard was dismissed and dispatched to the Revolutionary Tribunal, for having failed to exploit his advantage after the battle of Hondschoote (his indictment led to a fierce struggle in the Convention, and prompted Thuriot's resignation from the Committee of Public Safety). He was replaced by a thirty-one-year-old general, Jean-Baptiste Jourdan. Pichegru (thirty-two) was appointed to head the army of the Rhine, and Hoche (twenty-five) the army of the Moselle.[9] The overall organizer was Carnot, theorist of the offensive strategy.[10] All that remained of the division between the regulars and the volunteers also

---

8 Saint-Just, *Œuvres complètes*, p. 640.

9 These young generals were spotted by the representatives on mission. 'The commissioners who had lived among the general staffs were able to discover talents so far unknown, and with the scarcity of leaders being so palpable, bring forth, from the lowest ranks of the army, generals devoted to the Republic. Hoche, Marceau, Kléber, Jourdan, Masséna, Brune, Macdonald and even Bonaparte owed their good fortune to the representatives on mission' (*Mémoires de R. Levasseur de la Sarthe*, Paris: Rapilly, 1829).

10 Carnot's leading role as 'organizer of victory' was exaggerated by the Thermidorians (Carnot was to be a major figure in the post-Thermidor Convention, subsequently becoming a member of the Directory in place of Sieyès, who had refused nomination).

disappeared: the white uniform inherited from the Ancien Régime was replaced wholesale by the blue of the volunteers.

The idea of the *levée en masse*, for its part, was launched not by the Committee of Public Safety but rather by the popular movement. On 12 August, one of the commissioners delegated by the primary assemblies to the festival of the 10th addressed the Convention as follows: 'A great example must finally be given to the Earth, a terrible lesson to the tyrants of the Coalition. Appeal to the people, let them rise up en masse; only they can smite so many enemies, only they can ensure the triumph of liberty.' Hérault de Séchelles, presiding, replied: 'Let the words you have just uttered echo throughout the land, as the thunder of vengeance and destruction'.[11]

On 23 August, Barère, in the name of the Committee of Public Safety, presented a report on 'the civic requisition of young citizens for the defence of the *patrie*'. His conclusion has become famous:

> From this moment until the time that the enemies have been expelled from the territory of the Republic, all French people are on permanent requisition for the service of the armies. The young will go into combat; married men will forge weapons and transport supplies; women will make tents and serve in hospitals; children will shred old linen for lint; the old will be brought to the public squares to excite the courage of the warriors, preach hatred of kings and the unity of the Republic.[12]

If only young men of eighteen to twenty-five were actually requisitioned, this was because what the army lacked was not men but powder, muskets, cannon, clothing, all the equipment needed for a great army on campaign. To establish and operate factories and arsenals, Carnot and Prieur de la Côte-d'Or appealed to technicians and the best scientists of the day. The chemist Guyton de Morveau, also a deputy for the Côte-d'Or, had the idea of establishing a commission of scientists attached to the Committee of Public Safety. He proposed the

11 A. P., p. 101.
12 Ibid., vol. 72, p. 262ff.

application of Chappe's telegraph (the first line, built between Lille and Paris, would inform the Convention of the recapture of Le Quesnoy), and founded the first company of balloonists tasked with following enemy movements from the air. To tackle the shortage of powder, with the encouragement of Chaptal, director-general of powder, a revolutionary manufacturing process was perfected by Carny. Monge, engineer-adviser to the Committee of Public Safety, exclaimed: 'Give us saltpetre, and three days later we shall load the cannon.'[13]

In September, Monge and Berthollet were commissioned to write 'a practical work with plates explaining the manufacture of steel', 15,000 copies of which were distributed in the country's factories and workshops. On 11 October, Hassenfratz announced at the Jacobins club the commencement of weapons manufacture in Paris. On the 20th, the Committee of Public Safety decided to establish at Meudon a national institution for 'researching the experiences of war'. A school of fast-track professional training was created, attended by 800 students and with instructors who included Guyton, the great Fourcroy (who invented a process for separating copper and bronze from church bells), Berthollet, Carny, Monge and Périer. The first students were fêted at the Jacobins, and received with great ceremony at the Convention, one of them astride a newly cast cannon.[14]

The Wattignies victory, crushing of the Vendée army, recapture of Toulon

After the disasters of spring and summer 1793, after so much chaos and demoralization, this great movement would have spectacular results on all fronts.

---

13 Joseph Fayet, *La Révolution française et la science*, Paris: Libraire Marcel Rivière, 1960, p. 241. The following section draws substantially from this work.

14 One major absentee among these illustrious figures was Lavoisier, convicted and guillotined for his role in the Ferme-Générale. The idea of the wall of the Farmers-General, so hated by the people of Paris, was not implausibly ascribed to him. At his trial, the remark of the Tribunal's president, Coffinhal, that 'the Republic has no need for scientists or chemists', is probably apocryphal.

In the North, the incomplete victory of Hondschoote was rapidly followed by another victory at Wattignies, the joint achievement of Jourdan and Carnot (15–16 October). Carnot took 50,000 men from the army of the Rhine, assembled them at Guise and then marched them at full speed towards the besieged town of Maubeuge. Coburg, after crossing the Sambre,

> left thirty thousand men to guard the starving people of Maubeuge and took up position two leagues away on a chain of hills and wooded villages, blocking all the roads with felled trees and crowning the heights with proud breastwork between which cannon showed their maw to the enemy. Below, his massed Hungarian infantry guarded the approach. Behind were the Austrians and Croats. To the side, on the plain, a tremendous cavalry, the finest in the world, stretched away under the sun, ready to cut down the battalions that their artillery had shaken. This was another Jemmapes, but on a far larger scale, with a victorious army three times the size and in a far more fearsome position.[15]

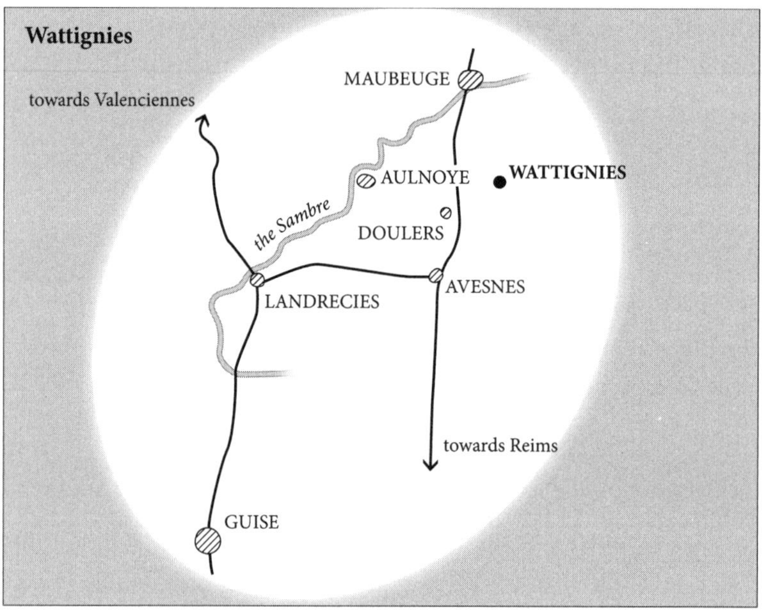

15 Michelet, *Histoire de la Révolution française*, vol. 2, p. 601.

Carnot gave the signal for attack, first on the flanks and then at the centre.

> For four hours, our troops in the centre, climbing towards Doulers, fought with their bayonets, led by Jourdan in person . . . Our men arrived breathless at the foot of the slopes, to find themselves facing the cannon and met by a hail of bullets . . . At the point when our men, under the torrent of gunfire, hesitated and drifted, the Austrian cavalry arrived on our flank and the infantry which had given way came back at us. Nightfall brought an end to this terrible execution.

The following day,

> Despair gave Carnot and Jourdan inspiration. They did an incredible thing. Out of the forty-five thousand men that they had, they took twenty-four thousand and led them forward on the left, leaving on the right flank lines that were weak, thin, and sure to be defeated. On 16 October 1793, at midday (the exact hour at which the queen's head fell on the place de la Révolution), Carnot and Jourdan marched in silence with half of their army (leaving an empty space behind them!) towards the plateau of Wattignies.[16]

The 'incredible thing' was successful: the columns climbed the hill to attack and seized the position. Three Austrian regiments were destroyed, Coburg retreated across the Sambre, Maubeuge was relieved. Chancel, the commander there who had not stirred during the fighting, was dismissed and sent to the guillotine. The victory of Wattignies, without being decisive, had immense repercussions across the country. 'Carnot, who had won this victory, returned and shut himself in his office in the Tuileries, leaving the celebration to his colleagues.'

In the Vendée, the republican forces that had been led up to then by Ronsin and Rossignol, authentic sans-culottes but not very

---

16 Ibid., p. 603.

effective as generals, were united by the Committee of Public Safety and placed under the command of the inept Léchelle, fortunately seconded by young generals who would soon be spoken of: Marceau and Kléber, one of the defenders of Mainz – the Mainz garrison played an important role in the victories that would soon follow.[17] Two columns, one leaving from Niort and the other from Nantes, crossed the Vendée and joined forces at Cholet, where the Vendéens were defeated on 17 October. The rump of the Vendée army, led by Stofflet and La Rochejaquelein, crossed to the right bank of the Loire after the battle of Ancenis in which Bonchamps was killed. In a long march in search of a haven where the English might rescue them, they managed to reach Granville, but failed to take the town, which was held by the Convention deputy Le Carpentier. Returning south, they reached Le Mans, where they were once again crushed in a terrible street battle by the army commanded by Marceau and Kléber (13–14 December). What remained of the Vendéen army was destroyed at Savenay on the Loire estuary on 23 December; this was the end of the great Vendée war.

In Lyon, the siege stretched on interminably, the city resisting despite bombardments. Kellermann, held responsible for the slow pace of events, was replaced by Doppet, and Couthon, sent to replace Dubois-Crancé, decided to attack the city: 'I understand nothing of military tactics,' he wrote on 3 October, 'but what I do know is that the army of the people is here, that this army intends to take Lyon, and that living might is the only means appropriate to the all-powerful people.'[18] The attack was launched on 8 October, the republican army entered the city on the 9th, and resistance collapsed the next day.

Toulon was also attacked under the leadership of Barras, the representative on mission. The troops were commanded by Dugommier, but Barras soon noted the qualities of a young artillery captain named Bonaparte, whose actions would be decisive in forcing the city to surrender. 'We reported to the Committee of Public Safety that the

17 Emerging with honours of war, this garrison could no longer fight on the same front. It was then transferred to the Vendée.

18 Martine Braconnier, *Couthon*, Polignac: Éditions du Roure, 1996, p. 182.

army of the Republic entered Toulon on 29 Frimaire [19 December]. The National Convention decreed that the name of Toulon would be replaced by that of Port-de-la-Montagne, and that the houses within this town be razed.'[19]

On 23 October, the Committee of Public Safety was able to address a triumphal proclamation to the armies:

> The cowardly satellites of tyranny have fled before you. They abandoned Dunkirk and their artillery, they hastened to escape utter ruin by putting the Sambre between them and your victorious columns. Federalism was struck down in Lyon. The republican army entered Bordeaux to deal it a final blow. The Piedmontese and Spaniards have been chased from your territory. The defenders of the Republic have just destroyed the rebels of the Vendée.[20]

Repression – Nantes, Lyon, Toulon, Marseille

The crackdown that followed was most merciless where the rebellion had been most deadly and aroused most disquiet.

In the Vendée, General Turreau, appointed to head the army of the West in December 1793, began by proposing to the Convention a general amnesty for the rebels, but he did not receive a reply. He rejected Kléber's plan, which was to encircle the region and dot it with a series of strongholds. In January 1794 he launched the famous mobile columns to criss-cross the region and lay waste the land of the insurgents, who no longer formed an army but were continuing guerrilla actions. Some of these columns indiscriminately killed everyone they met, others first evacuated any inhabitants viewed as patriots, but in general this was a massacre – as well as militarily ineffectual, since the Vendéens even proved capable of retaking Cholet for a while. It would be a long time before the countryside of this region could be regarded as pacified.

---

19 *Mémoires de Barras*, Paris: Éditions littéraires et artistiques, 1946, p. 129.

20 Cited by Mathiez, *La Révolution française*, vol. 3, p. 64.

Meanwhile Carrier, the representative on mission who arrived in Nantes in October 1793, was conducting the repression in that city. Vendéen prisoners were brought in by the thousand. As the guillotine was too slow, and typhus threatened the prisons, he initially resorted to mass shootings, then used boats whose bottoms opened to discharge their human cargo in the middle of the Loire, turned for this purpose into a 'national bath'. In parallel with this, local revolutionary tribunals kept firing squads and guillotines busy in Angers and La Rochelle.

All these horrors were made possible by the lack of clear directives from the revolutionary government, by the indiscipline of the troops, and by rivalries between the generals. As Jean-Clément Martin has shown, 'it is impossible to find revolutionary unanimity with regard to Turreau's columns' (and the same could be said of the drownings at Nantes). The Thermidorians exploited these tragic events to discredit Robespierre, and, nearer our own day, counter-revolutionary historians speak of a 'Vendéen genocide', but making the Vendée into a symbol in this way smacks more of propaganda than of genuine history.[21]

After the fall of Lyon, the Convention decreed on 12 October: 'The city of Lyon is to be destroyed; all the dwelling-places of the rich shall be demolished; there shall remain only the houses of the poor.' In addition, 'the name of Lyon shall be erased from the list of towns of the Republic. The collection of houses remaining shall henceforth bear the name of Ville-Affranchie.'[22]

As long as the repression was directed by Couthon, it was not very terrible. To respect the decree of 12 October, he proceeded to the place Bellecour and chipped at a few of the buildings earmarked for demolition with a small hammer. But in November he was replaced by Collot d'Herbois and Fouché, accompanied by a unit of the revolutionary army under Ronsin. A revolutionary commission was

21 See chapter 3 of Jean-Clément Martin, *La Vendée et la Révolution*: 'À propos du "genocide vendéen"'.

22 Articles 3 and 4 of the decree, *Le Moniteur*, vol. 18, p. 104.

established and rained down death sentences. Here again, the guillotine was too slow for mass executions: the condemned were killed by cannon loaded with shot in front of pits dug to receive their bodies. In November, Collot planned a massive deportation of Lyon workers: 'You spoke to me of the patriots of this town,' he wrote in December to Couthon. 'Do you believe that there are any such people? I think it impossible. There are sixty thousand individuals who will never be republicans. What has to be done is to expel them and scatter them carefully across the surface of the Republic . . . Thus dispersed, they will at least follow the steps of those who march before or alongside them.' And Ronsin wrote to Vincent: 'There are not fifteen hundred Lyonnais who deserve to live.'[23] The shootings continued through to February 1794.

Barras and Fréron in Toulon and Marseille (renamed 'Ville Sans-nom'), and Tallien in Bordeaux, likewise set up revolutionary commissions that handed down hundreds of death sentences. These proconsuls, who lived in grand style into the bargain, would be recalled in Germinal of year II and questioned over their excesses, but this was a little late in the day.

EXCURSUS: THE NOTION OF TERROR

There is general agreement that from summer 1793 to summer 1794 things took place that were genuinely terrifying. The mass shootings in Lyon, the drownings in Nantes, are so monstrous as to be hard to imagine, but simply reading aloud the list of fifteen or twenty men and women guillotined on a random day in Paris, with their names, ages, occupations and addresses, makes the horror palpable enough. I have no intention of prettifying this horror, or comparing it – to its advantage? – with other butcheries in France or elsewhere. I simply venture the hypothesis that 'the Terror' with a capital T was a creation of the Thermidorians, with the aim of demonizing what they

23 Cited by Jaurès, *Histoire socialiste*, vol. 6, pp. 320–1.

had just overthrown. The notion of Terror was then taken up by celebrated historians and thinkers of all persuasions, from Edgar Quinet to Claude Lefort, by way of Hannah Arendt, François Furet and David Andress.[24] (The list could be much longer.)

The Terror is often presented as a compact segment of history, with a beginning and an end that can be precisely dated. The beginning is generally identified as 5 September 1793, with the session of the Convention at which, as we saw, the anonymous spokesman of the Jacobin delegation enjoined the deputies to 'place terror on the order of the day'. This famous phrase, however, was not followed up: no law or decree gave it concrete embodiment. 'Contrary to what is regularly assumed by historians, terror, in a sense that was not, moreover, made precise, was not placed on the order of the day on 5 September, nor on the agenda of the Convention, nor less precisely on any agenda of national life whatsoever.'[25] Moreover, Jacques Guilhaumou has shown that the phrase had already been uttered by Claude Royer, spokesman for the *fédérés* who gathered in Paris for the festival of 10 August 1793. On 30 August, at the Jacobins club, he exclaimed: 'Let us place terror on the order of the day, it is the only way to wake up the people and force them to save themselves.' And in the weeks that followed, this phrase became a regular trope in addresses to the Convention and the reports of its representatives on missions outside the capital.[26]

It does not make much sense, then, to fix the start of the Terror on 5 September 1793, no more than to see it as ending on 9 Thermidor of year II. The guillotine did not stop working on that day, quite the contrary: the White Terror of the Thermidorians was a

---

24 Edgar Quinet, *La Révolution* [1865], Paris: Belin, 1987, in particular book 17, 'Théorie de la Terreur'; Claude Lefort, 'La Terreur révolutionnaire', in *Essais sur le politique*, Paris: Le Seuil, 2001, pp. 81–119; Hannah Arendt, *On Revolution*, New York: Viking Press, 1963; Furet, *Interpreting the French Revolution*; David Andress, *The Terror*, New York: Farrar, Straus and Giroux, 2005, and 'La violence populaire durant la Révolution française', in Michel Biard (ed.), *Les Politiques de la Terreur*, Rennes: Presses Universitaires de Rennes, 2008 (Actes du colloque international de Rouen, 2007).

25 Martin, *Violence et Révolution*, p. 188.

26 Jacques Guilhaumou, '"La terreur à l'ordre du jour': un parcours en révolution (1793–1794)', *revolution-francaise.net*, 2007.

massacre that rivalled anything carried out by the guillotine in the previous months.

The notion of Terror remains equally vague when considered in terms of space rather than time. Historians seem to have followed those novelists – Balzac, Dickens – for whom the whole of France *lived in terror*. But outside the areas of 'federalist revolt', nothing happened with any resemblance to 'the Terror'. Even in Normandy, a centre of insurrection, there were no executions, thanks to the reconciliatory action of the representative on mission, Robert Lindet, a member of the Committee of Public Safety. In Paris, the citizens enjoyed themselves hugely (provided they were not hungry): the theatres were full, new buildings were constructed, and new streets under the direction of a 'jury of the arts' made up of artists and representatives of the population.[27]

The notion of Terror with a capital T leads to equating the repressive action of the Revolutionary Tribunal in Paris with the massacres in the departments. But if the former was indeed due to the initiative of the revolutionary government, the latter were episodes in a civil war with casualties on both sides. And the figures are in no way commensurate: the war in the Vendée, the insurrections in the Midi and their repression, cost tens of thousands of lives. The Paris Tribunal, out of 4,021 verdicts delivered between 6 April 1793 and 9 Thermidor year II, pronounced 2,585 condemnations to death versus 1,306 acquittals.[28] The notion of Terror appears in this light as the artificial conflation of very different events.

It can be historically convenient to refer to a certain period of time as 'the Terror'; thus volume 3 of Mathiez's *Histoire de la Révolution française* is entitled 'La Terreur'. But what is much more debatable is to view the Terror as a theory of government, a system deliberately chosen and proclaimed.

At the famous session of 5 September 1793, Drouet challenged his fellow deputies:

---

27 See Allan Potofsky, *Constructing Paris in the Age of Revolution*, London: Palgrave Macmillan, 2009, p. 164.

28 Walter, *Actes du tribunal révolutionnaire*, p. 33.

> Are you not called scoundrels, brigands, murderers, from every side? Well, then! Since our virtue, our moderation, our philosophical ideas, have been of no use, let us be brigands in the service of the people, let us be brigands . . . (*angry murmurs, calls for the speaker to be brought to order*) . . . I would like you to declare to these guilty men [the suspects] that if, impossibly, liberty were imperilled, you would massacre them without pity (*heckling drowns the speaker's voice*).

And Thuriot, in a heated response, was greatly applauded when he exclaimed: 'Far from us the idea that France should be tainted by blood; it is only being tainted by justice.'[29]

On 4 Germinal of year II (4 April 1794), a deputation from the popular society of Cette (Sète) came to the bar of the Convention. 'Treason is once more somersaulting around the people; it wants to be hoisted with the monarchy; well! Let us hoist it to the scaffold! Legislators, make death the order of the day!' The hall protested, and Tallien replied from the president's chair: 'It is not death that is the order of the day, but justice . . . The language you have just used in this precinct is unworthy of a republican.' The deputation was dismissed and referred to the Committee of General Security.[30]

Saint-Just, in his report of 8 July 1793 'on the thirty-two members of the Convention detained by virtue of the decree of 2 June', used the term 'terror' more than once, *always in a negative sense* ('the attempt has been made to dominate the National Convention by disorder and terror'; 'the plan to stifle Paris . . . had been attempted by means of armed force, then they thought to succeed by means of terror'; 'the plan of Valazé, that of assembling citizens through terror'; 'to confound the government with terror and declamations').[31] In his report of 8 Ventôse year II (26 February 1794) 'on persons incarcerated', he contrasted the effectiveness of justice with the garrulousness of terror: 'Justice is more fearsome for the enemies of the Republic

29 A. P., vol. 73, p. 423.
30 Ibid., vol. 88, p. 145.
31 Saint-Just, *Œuvres complètes*, pp. 602–19.

than mere terror. How many traitors have escaped terror, which talks, and would not escape justice, which weighs crimes in its hand! . . . Justice makes the people happy and consolidates the new order of things. Terror is a double-edged weapon, which some have used to avenge the people, and others to serve tyranny.'[32]

Robespierre himself, in a famous passage in his speech of 17 Pluviôse year II (5 February 1794), related the notion of terror to that of justice: 'Terror is nothing but prompt, severe, inflexible justice; it is therefore an emanation of virtue; it is not so much a specific principle as a consequence of the general principle of democracy applied to the homeland's most pressing needs.'[33]

Terror with a capital T is a historically inconsistent notion, and it is an ideological artifice to superimpose a theory of Terror on the events of this time. As Haim Burstin has written, 'the stereotype [of the Terror] has been increasingly distanced from its concrete origin, its actual materiality, to serve all kinds of political reflections on the history of France, eventually symbolizing by metonymy the Revolution itself.'[34]

---

32 Ibid., p. 669.

33 Robespierre, *Virtue and Terror*, p. 115.

34 Burstin, 'Entre théorie et pratique de la Terreur: un essai de balisage', in *Les Politiques de la Terreur*, p. 39.

CHAPTER 12

Autumn 1793

Dechristianization, the cultural revolution of year II, the Frimaire reversal

In a moment, the moment it became possible to speak, priests fell into the most profound disrepute.

– Restif de la Bretonne, *Vingt nuits de Paris*

Dechristianization: political manoeuvre or popular movement? Notre-Dame becomes a temple of Reason; the cult of martyrs

In October 1793, just when the situation on every front had recovered, a movement broke out across France which contemporaries – Robespierre, Danton, Chaumette – described as a *torrent*, an *explosion*, a *volcanic eruption*. This was dechristianization.

Historians differ as to what triggered it. Some see it as a political manoeuvre: for both Jaurès and Daniel Guérin,[1] responsibility lay with the Hébertistes seeking to mobilize their popular clientele. For Mathiez, rather, it was the Indulgents who 'unleashed the movement of dechristianization, cunning overbidders who sought to create new

1 Jaurès, *Histoire socialiste*, vol. 6, pp. 304-7; Guérin, *La Lutte de classes*, vol. 1, chapter 6: 'A diversion that became a groundswell'.

forms of patriotic service'.[2] For Soboul, on the other hand, the movement had a popular origin: 'Dechristianization followed a current whose manifestations can be seen right from the entry of the sans-culottes into political life at the start of 1792.'[3] Likewise, for Serge Bianchi, dechristianization 'lay in the straight line of a popular impulse'.[4]

The most plausible explanation is that the movement had a popular base made up of the most advanced activists, while 'politicians' supported it and sometimes used it, only rarely preceding or instigating it. This was however the case in the department of the Nièvre. In September 1793, Fouché, as the representative on mission, hosted Chaumette who was visiting his family at Nevers. The anti-religious campaign then took a strong upturn: on 25 September, it was decreed that 'any minister of the Catholic faith or other priest paid by the nation' was obliged 'to marry or adopt a child, or to keep and feed at his table an indigent old person', failing which he would be removed from his position. On 10 October, Fouché issued a decree prohibiting the exercise of all forms of religious worship 'outside of their respective temples', ordering the destruction of 'all religious signs' in public places, and instructing that the gates of cemeteries should bear the notice: 'Death is an eternal sleep'.[5] A few days later he wrote to Chaumette, who had returned to Paris: 'Things have reached the point where this most superstitious of regions no longer offers the traveller a single sign that recalls a dominant religion, priestly ceremonies have all returned inside the temples. The aristocracy of manufacturers and forge-masters is crushed, everything is working and the rich are paying up.'[6] This is certainly one instance in which the action of politicians played a predominant role in triggering the movement.

---

2 Albert Mathiez, *Robespierre et la déchristianisation*, Le Puy: Imprimerie Peyriller, Rouchon et Gamon, 1909, p. 17.

3 Soboul, *Les Sans-Culottes parisiens*, p. 287.

4 Serge Bianchi, 'La déchristianisation de l'an II, essai d'interprétation', *AHRF*, no. 233, July–September 1978. This gives a summary of the historiographical controversies over dechristianization, arguing the case for a popular origin of the movement.

5 Albert Mathiez, *Contribution à l'histoire religieuse de la Révolution française*, 1907, cited in Guérin, *La Lutte de classes*, vol. 1, p. 268.

6 Cited by Soboul, *Les Sans-Culottes parisiens*, p. 287.

But there are abundant examples showing how dechristianization was a movement of genuine popular initiative. On 12 September, the Panthéon-Français section demanded the opening in all sections or cantons of the Republic of a 'school of liberty', which would preach the 'horror of fanaticism' on Sundays and holidays. On 2 October, the Croix-Rouge section asked for its name to be changed to 'Bonnet-Rouge', fearing that 'the present name [Red Cross] perpetuates the ferment of fanaticism'.[7]

In the Brie, on 10 Brumaire (31 October), the commune of Ris adopted Brutus as its patron in place of Saint Blaise, and expelled its parish priest. And on 16 Brumaire, delegates from the commune of Mennecy, also in the region of Brie, presented themselves at the bar of the Convention 'decked in cassocks and chasubles, some carrying pennants and banners, others crosses, censers and chalices'.[8] Their demands were:

1. that from this day on the commune of Mennecy should dispense with a parish priest;
2. that the presbytery be put on sale as national property;
3. that the building formerly used as a church should become the meeting-place of the popular society; as a consequence, busts of Marat and Lepeletier should replace the statues of Saint Peter and Saint Denis, their former patrons, the statue of liberty be placed at the centre of the altar, and every sign of fanaticism disappear before that of liberty;
4. that the commune of Mennecy-Villeroy should from now on be known as the commune of Mennecy-Marat.

The petitioners presented to the nation the 1,500 livres that the parish priest received, along with the church's silverware and precious cloths.

---

7 Soboul, *Les Sans-Culottes parisiens*, pp. 284–5. In the article cited above ('La déchristianisation de l'an II'), Serge Bianchi emphasizes the role of 'day-labourers, apprentices, builders, foresters, poor peasants . . . social categories that were little or poorly Christianized' and had long escaped regimentation by the Church (p. 363).

8 A. P., vol. 78, pp. 465–7.

At the same memorable session, the Convention voted on Thuriot's proposal a decree legalizing dechristianization: 'Departmental administrations are authorized to decide the suppression, combination and boundaries of parishes without recourse to the National Convention.' The Mennecy proposal was written into the *Bulletin* as a kind of appendix, a model for the application of this decree.

Each commune, therefore, could abandon Catholic worship and allocate its church to other activities. Churches were soon transformed into temples of Reason, meeting halls, schools or hospitals. Cemeteries were secularized, the marriage of priests encouraged, and ecclesiastics banned from public education.

In Paris, the central committee of popular societies, based at the Évêché, demanded the abolition of priests' salaries, so that their survival would in future depend solely on the generosity of their congregations. On 17 Brumaire (7 November), the Convention opened with a long series of letters and delegations from communes donating their church's silverware to the nation, announcing their decision to change their names, or reporting the marriage of their priest. Next came a delegation from the department and commune of Paris, led by Momoro, Chaumette, Lullier and Pache. Momoro: 'The bishop of Paris and several other priests, guided by reason, have come before you to cast off the character imposed on them by superstition.' Bishop Gobel now stepped up:

> Born a plebeian, I learned early on the principles of liberty and equality . . . Now that the Revolution is striding forward to a happy outcome, there must no longer be any other public and national religion than that of liberty and holy equality, as this is what the sovereign wishes; consistent with my principles, I bow to its will and have come proudly to declare that from this day forth, I renounce the exercise of my functions as minister of the Catholic religion, joined in this by my citizen vicars present here.[9]

9 Ibid., p. 550ff.

The erstwhile bishop, with the liberty bonnet on his head, was embraced by the session's president (Laloy) amid the cheers of the people. Several members of the Convention who had once been ecclesiastics, including Coupé de l'Oise, former *curé* of Sermaize, Robert Lindet, former bishop of the department of Eure, Gay-Vernon, former bishop of Limoges, and Julien de Toulouse, a Protestant minister, likewise renounced 'all religious duties'.

Over the following days, various sections paraded before the Convention:

> The Gravilliers section was introduced, with a body of men at its head dressed in priestly and pontifical robes . . . The citizens all shed these simultaneously, and beneath the travesties of fanaticism there emerged defenders of the *patrie* dressed in national uniform. Each threw away the garment he had doffed, and stoles, mitres and chasubles went flying through the air, to the sound of instruments and repeated cries of '*Vive la liberté! Vive la République!*'[10]

On 20 Brumaire (10 November), the Paris Commune held a great civic festival in the former cathedral of Notre-Dame, now a temple of Reason. In the centre of the nave a mountain had been constructed – in homage to the Montagne of the Convention – topped by a small temple bearing the inscription: 'To Philosophy'. From this temple emerged Liberty, represented by a young female actor draped in the tricolour, 'in lieu and stead of the former Blessed Virgin'.[11] After the ceremony, a large crowd accompanied the general council to the Convention.

> An immense host of musicians made the vaults resound with the cherished airs of the Revolution; a procession of republican girls, dressed in white with tricolour sashes and flowers in their hair, preceded and surrounded Reason. This was a faithful image of

---

10 *Le Moniteur*, vol. 18, p. 401.

11 See the detailed description and relevant engraving in Lynn Hunt, *Politics, Culture and Class in the French Revolution*, Berkeley: University of California Press, 2004, pp. 63–5.

> beauty, with the liberty bonnet on her head. Today the whole people of Paris thronged beneath the Gothic vaults, for so long stricken by the voice of error, and that now for the first time echoed to the cry of liberty . . . The people have said: 'No more priests, no gods but those bestowed on us by nature.' They led Reason to the president, who gave her the fraternal kiss to the sound of applause.[12]

The Convention then proceeded in a body towards the temple of Reason, acclaimed by the crowd. On arrival, deputies and people together sang a hymn composed by Gossec to lyrics by M. J. Chénier.[13]

This *journée* of 20 Brumaire quickened the pace of dechristianization. The popular societies and revolutionary committees gave the movement an irresistible momentum.[14] The committee of the Marat section decided to remove from the church of Saint-André-des-Arts 'its baubles and other objects of charlatanism, and to give this national building the name of Temple of the Revolution'. The section committees of Arsenal, Droits-de-l'homme and Indivisibilité announced to the Commune their decision to bring the Convention all the decorations and silverware of the church of Saint-Paul. The sections of Faubourg-du-Nord, Brutus and Unité took similar decisions.[15] By the end of Brumaire year II, Catholic worship had practically ceased in the churches of Paris.

However, this unbridled dechristianization created a vacuum which would be spontaneously filled by the cult of revolutionary martyrs, including the 'young martyrs' (Bara, the thirteen-year-old drummer killed at Cholet, and Viala, the twelve-year-old from

---

12 A. P., vol. 78, p. 710.

13 The first verse was: 'Descend, Liberty, daughter of nature/The people have regained their immortal power/Over the pompous debris of the old imposture/Their hands raise your altar once more.'

14 The popular societies had been formed to get around the ruling of 5 September 1793 that restricted the general assemblies of sections to two weekly sessions. The revolutionary committees had been instructed from September to draw up lists of suspects and see to the application of revolutionary laws.

15 Soboul, *Les Sans-Culottes parisiens*, p. 295.

Avignon killed in a battle against the Marseille insurgents), with a certain continuity of rituals and practices. The revolutionary cults were celebrated in the temples of Reason, and clearly emulated traditional worship in their setting, liturgy and practices. Statues of Marat, Lepeletier and Chalier replaced those of Catholic saints, and the revolutionary colours supplanted the black of the detested priests. 'Impelled in each section by a few men brought up on the philosophy of the eighteenth century, this republican cult firmly established itself in the winter of year II, giving a large fraction of the sans-culottes, now severed from Catholicism, the religious sustenance that they seemed unable to do without.'[16]

The cultural revolution of year II: names, the republican calendar, the family, the universal 'tu'

Dechristianization, initially so surprising, is more understandable when placed in a broader configuration, which Serge Bianchi has dubbed the 'cultural revolution' of year II.[17] This is a legitimate label, as between the revolution of 2 June 1793 and the counter-revolution of 9 Thermidor great upheavals took place in the life of the country, some launched by the Montagnards in government, others produced by the inventiveness of the popular movement, but together aiming to make a clean slate of the past and found a 'regenerated' society – the word used at the time.

A clean slate meant first of all getting rid of all images of kings. The statue of Louis XIV on the place des Victoires was pulled down, and there was a plan to replace that of Henri IV on the Pont-Neuf with an immense effigy of Hercules sculpted by David, the base of which would be made of the heads of the statues from the façade of Notre-Dame: 'a monument to the glory of the French people, erected over the double tyranny of kings and priests'.[18] The royal tombs at

16 Ibid., p. 309.

17 Serge Bianchi, *La révolution culturelle de l'an II, élites et peuple, 1789–1799*, Paris: Aubier, 1982.

18 On Hercules as a symbol of the people, see Lynn Hunt, *Politics, Culture and Class*

Saint-Denis were partly destroyed. Bronze statues were melted down for cannon. The entire country was expunging the traces of monarchy.

In order to throw off the past, names were changed, above all those of towns, from which saints, nobles and kings all vanished. Three thousand communes changed their names, with 'Montagnes' becoming widespread – Villeneuve-Saint-Georges was now Villeneuve-la-Montagne, and Saint-Germain-en-Laye renamed Montagne-Bon-Air. Montmartre became Montmarat, and Soisy Soisy-Marat. The sans-culotte influence was felt even in remote departments, for example with Han-les-Sans-Culottes (formerly Han-les-Moines, in the Ardennes), or Rocher-de-la-Sansculotterie (Port-Breton in the Vendée).[19] Streets were likewise given new names. In Paris, besides the saint-shedding faubourgs Antoine and Marcel, the rue Michel-le-Comte became Michel-le-Peletier; the place Royale (today place des Vosges) became place des Fédérés; the place Vendôme, place des Piques; the place du Carrousel, place de la Fraternité; the rue Princesse, rue Révolutionnaire; the rue Dauphine, rue de Thionville; and the quai des Théatins, quai Voltaire (as it still is today).

Children born at this time might be given first names like Bara, Rousseau, Brutus or Mucius Scaevola, and adults could change their names, becoming Gracchus Babeuf or Anaxagoras Chaumette.

In September 1793, the Convention decided to replace the traditional calendar with its Sundays and saints. The adoption of the republican calendar was a political measure, but went hand in hand with the impulse to rationalize national life by the decimal system: as early as August 1793, the new units of metre and gram were created to put an end to the diversity of measures in different provinces. On 20 September, Gilbert Romme delivered a long report in the name of the Committee of Public Instruction.[20] Criticizing the traditional calendar as a 'monument of servitude and ignorance', he proposed to divide the year into twelve months of thirty days, each made up of three *décades*. The names he

---

in the French Revolution, pp. 98–110, which has an interesting iconography. The statues from the façade of Notre-Dame were beheaded in the (mistaken) belief that they represented kings.

19 Bianchi, *La Révolution culturelle*, p. 216.

20 A. P., vol. 74, p. 553. Romme was a scientist who had studied both mathematics and medicine. He was later one of the 'Prairial martyrs'.

chose recalled the great episodes of the Revolution (Jeu de paume, Bastille) and revolutionary virtues (Unity, Fraternity).[21] Sunday, an essential day in Catholic life, thus disappeared – leading Aulard to see this as the most anti-Christian measure of the Revolution.

Calendars would be printed in thousands of copies to be sent throughout the country, indicating for the first year the equivalent days and months of the Gregorian calendar. They were illustrated with etchings by the best artists of the day, with revolutionary mottoes on the frontispiece and medallions of revolutionary martyrs around the edge.[22]

Convincing and educating the people: press, posters, almanacs, public instruction

The popular societies demanded recognition of social categories that had been marginalized and shut out by the Church: unmarried mothers, illegitimate children, foundlings. On these points, and the rejection of traditional patriarchy as a whole, the Convention adopted measures that were astonishing for a country until recently subject to a generalized patriarchal system. In October 1793, the law established equal rights of inheritance for sons and daughters, extending this also to children born out of wedlock. It became impossible to favour one child in particular or to disinherit them. Within marriage, each spouse acquired equal right of control over common property, and a common contract for the whole of France was created to enshrine this equality.[23] Foundlings, who made up a third of all births in Paris, became 'natural children of the *patrie*'.

---

21 [On 24 October the months would be given the beautiful names created by Fabre d'Églantine: Vendémiaire (from the Latin *vindemia*, grape harvest), Brumaire (*brume* or fog), Frimaire (*frimas*, frost), Nivôse (Latin *nivosus*, snowy), Pluviôse (Latin *pluvius*, rainy), Ventôse (Latin *ventosus*, windy), Germinal (Latin *germen*, germination), Floréal (Latin *flos*, flower), Prairial (*prairie*, pasture), Messidor (Latin *messis*, harvest), Thermidor (Greek *thermon*, summer heat), Fructidor (Latin *fructus*, fruit). [Year I of the new calendar opened with 1 Vendémaire on what by the Gregorian calendar was 22 September 1792. – Translator]

22 Bianchi, *La Révolution culturelle*, p. 200.

23 Divorce had already been legalized by the Legislative Assembly in 1792.

The forty-eight Paris sections in year II (1790 names in parentheses)

1. Tuileries
2. Champs-Élysées
3. République (Roule)
4. Montagne (Palais-Royal)
5. Piques (Place Vendôme)
6. Le Peletier (Bibliothèque)
7. Mont-Blanc (Grange-Batelière)
8. Muséum (Louvre)
9. Gardes-Françaises (Oratoire)
10. Halle-au-Blé
11. Contrat-Social (Postes)
12. Guillaume-Tell (Place Louis-XIV)
13. Brutus (Fontaine-Montmorency)
14. Bonne-Nouvelle
15. Amis-de-la-Patrie (Ponceau)
16. Bon-Conseil
17. Marchés (Marché-des-Innocents)
18. Lombards
19. Arcis
20. Faubourg-Mont-Marat (Faubourg Montmartre)
21. Poissonnière
22. Bondy
23. Temple
24. Popincourt
25. Montreuil
26. Quinze-Vingts
27. Gravilliers
28. Faubourg-du-Nord (Faubourg-Saint-Denis)
29. Réunion (Beaubourg)
30. Homme-Armé (Enfants-Rouges)
31. Droits-de-l'homme (Roi-de-Sicile)
32. Maison-Commune (Hôtel de Ville)
33. Indivisibilité (Place-Royale)
34. Arsenal
35. Fraternité (Île-Saint-Louis)
36. Cité (Notre-Dame)
37. Révolutionnaire (Henri-IV)
38. Invalides
39. Fontaine-de-Grenelle
40. Unité (Quatre-Nations)
41. Marat (Théâtre-Français)
42. Bonnet-Rouge (Croix-Rouge)
43. Mutius-Scaevola
44. Chalier (Thermes-de-Julien)
45. Panthéon-Français (Sainte-Geneviève)
46. Observatoire
47. Sans-Culottes (Jardin-des-Plantes)
48. Finistère (Gobelins)

The concern for equality that lay at the heart of the collective thinking of the sans-culottes was expressed among other things by the generalized use of the familiar '*tu*'. On 10 Brumaire (31 October), a deputation from all the Paris popular societies addressed the Convention as follows: 'This abuse [the use of '*vous*'] perpetuates the arrogance of the perverse and their adulation.' The sans-culottes demanded a law to impose the informal *tu*, which would give 'greater visible familiarity, a greater inclination to fraternity, and consequently greater equality'. The Convention proceeded to debate this. Thuriot wondered: 'Is it not contrary to liberty to prescribe to citizens the way in which they should express themselves?'[24] Nonetheless, on 22 Brumaire, the directorate of the Paris department decreed that *tutoiement* would be used in offices and in correspondence. The *tu* form spread rapidly in all the popular organizations, then to the Convention itself: by the end of autumn 1793, *vous* had disappeared from its speeches. A play was performed in Paris entitled *La Parfaite Égalité ou les tu et les toi*. As in every cultural revolution, change can also happen from the bottom up.

To 'regenerate' society it was not enough to obliterate the signs of the past; it was also necessary to act constructively, and above all to convince and educate the people. Newspapers such as Hébert's *Le Père Duchesne*, the Jacobins' *Journal de la Montagne*, the *Journal des hommes libres* and Desmoulins's ephemeral *Le Vieux Cordelier*, were read in the evenings at the popular societies, and during the day in the workplace and the public square: workers and passers-by gathered around public readers. In October 1793, the Arsenal section and the popular society of l'Harmonie demanded 'the organization of spoken publicity by means of a newspaper expressly made for the people, and read out even in the villages by public officials and publicists'.[25]

The press, therefore, was not enough, and new modes of information flourished in year II: posters, which could issue a challenge to a deputy as well as announce the decrees of the Convention or the decisions of its representatives on mission; almanacs, which popularized the principles of the Revolution – such as Collot d'Herbois's

24 A. P., vol. 78, p. 85. On *tutoiement*, see Soboul, *Les Sans-Culottes parisiens*, p. 656.
25 Soboul, *Les Sans-Culottes parisiens*, p. 671.

L'Almanach du Père Gérard or Sylvain Maréchal's *L'Almanach des Républicains*.[26] Hundreds of revolutionary songs were written and sung, many composed by celebrated musicians such as Grétry, Gossec, Cherubini, Méhul (*Chant du Départ*), with lyrics by Chénier, Maréchal and a host of others now forgotten. They were sung in the solemn processions of civic festivals, or in carnival-type masquerades in which the participants, often disguised as priests, pulled carts full of ciboria and stoups that would be burned while they danced the farandole around the bonfire.

The sans-culottes demanded the organization of public instruction. On 14 July, the Droits-de-l'homme section demanded 'a public instruction that teaches citizens the rules of duty and the practice of the virtues'. It was not just moral principles that required to be instilled: the section of Faubourg-Montmartre wanted 'an instruction designed to perfect the arts and crafts, to give a great boost to national industry and the activity of our manufactures, and to destroy tyranny for ever'.[27]

On 13 July, Robespierre had read to the Convention the report of Lepeletier de Saint-Fargeau on public instruction; on the 29th, he proposed a decree that adopted it almost word for word.[28] This long text, rather more in the tradition of Sparta than of Rousseau, stipulated in its first article that 'all children shall be brought up at the expense of the Republic, from the age of five until twelve for boys, and eleven for girls'. (None of the texts discussed by the Convention called for gender equality: 'girls shall learn spinning, sewing and laundering'.) Since national education was 'a debt of the Republic to everyone', it would be free and compulsory (Art. 3). When children had 'completed their national education, they shall be returned to the hands of their parents or guardians' (Art. 5), which evidently meant, without saying so outright, that children would be removed from their parents for the duration of their schooling. The decree provided for strict moral and civic education, work in factories or in the fields, and sanctions for breaches of discipline: 'Any child of

---

26 On posters and almanacs, see Bianchi, *La Révolution culturelle*, pp. 173–8.

27 Soboul, *Les Sans-Culottes parisiens*, p. 498.

28 A. P., vol. 69, pp. 659–64.

either sex, aged more than eight years, who has not performed a task equivalent to his or her meal, will only eat after the other children have finished, and will bear the shame of eating alone' (Art. 16).

The Committee of Public Instruction, in whose name Robespierre spoke, was divided over this decree.[29] Only two of its six members supported it, Robespierre himself and Bourdon. Grégoire and Coupé de l'Oise were opposed. Grégoire: 'We all agree as to the necessity of a common education, but need it be common in the sense that all the children residing in national homes are to be brought up at the expense of the Republic? . . . It is not enough that a system comes surrounded by illustrious names, that it has Minos, Plato, Lycurgus and Lepeletier as its patrons.'[30] In the end, no decision was taken, and when the Convention debated the question in Frimaire of year II, the decree adopted was short and vague, providing only that school was free and compulsory from the age of six and for a minimum of three years.

The slowness of the law's application led to popular recriminations. In no. 349 of *Le Père Duchesne*, Hébert expressed 'Père Duchesne's great anger at seeing how lame is the progress of public instruction, and that there are monopolists of the mind who do not wish the people to be instructed, so that beggars may continue to beg'.

In the field of the arts, on the other hand, the cultural revolution obtained a marked success. The old academies were suppressed; painters and Opéra performers publicly burned their qualifications and diplomas. The Republic employed and subsidized revolutionary artists: thousands of statues of its martyrs and the great names of antiquity were commissioned for public buildings. At the 1793 Salon, a thousand paintings were exhibited, and the most honoured painters included Girodet, Van Loo, Carle Vernet, Boilly and David. The National Museum (the Louvre), established under the

---

29 Ibid., note to p. 659.

30 A. P., vol. 70, p. 19. Rühl and Lakanal did not speak. As for Coupé, he proposed a far more Rousseauian project: 'It might well be a misfortune for humanity were all men to become philosophers. Do not teach man this reasoned apathy, let him obey all the impulses of nature, and remain of the people.'

Legislative Assembly, opened its rooms to the public. Alexandre Lenoir founded a Museum of French Monuments in the Couvent des Petits-Augustins,[31] to display many of the statues and paintings confiscated from churches and châteaux. The Convention decided to organize in each department a museum for 'the paintings, statues, engravings and other artistic monuments found in national buildings and the homes of émigrés'.[32] Topino-Lebrun, a politically committed painter (also a juror on the Revolutionary Tribunal) declared: 'Republicans, let us seize hold of the arts, or rather, restore them to their original dignity. Only then will they have the right to be public and free of charge. Servile and cringing under despotism, they will obey the omnipotence of the sovereign people: they will adopt the people's sublime stance.'[33]

Robespierre against dechristianization

This festive moment, when the leaders were overwhelmed by popular enthusiasm and the 'torrent' of dechristianization seemed to break through every dyke, lasted less than two months. The ebb began in late November, its spectacular turning-point being Robespierre's speech of 1 Frimaire year II (21 November 1793).

The Jacobins had been the scene of concerted attacks against the dechristianizers. The first skirmish took place on 18 Brumaire (8 November). Hébert accused Laveaux, editor of the *Journal de la Montagne*, of having published the day before an article against atheism, in which he had 'opened on the subject of God, an unknown and abstract entity, disputes more fitted to a theologically-inclined friar'. Laveaux replied: 'I believed this view [atheism] to be dangerous, I refuted it; that is my opinion and I am proud of it.'[34]

The next day, Robespierre went on the offensive against the popular societies, the uncontrolled motors of dechristianization: 'The

31 This chapel now forms part of the École des Beaux-Arts on quai Malaquais.

32 Bianchi, *La Révolution culturelle*, p. 172.

33 Ibid., p. 191.

34 Aulard, *La Société des Jacobins*, vol. 5, pp. 500–1.

aristocrats,' he said, 'awaiting the favourable moment for a counter-revolutionary movement, gather together in clubs that they are careful to call popular societies.' And he demanded that 'patriots proceed to the purging of all the popular societies in the sections, the number of which is increasing daily'.[35]

On 1 Frimaire, Robespierre, who played a major personal role in this matter, launched a frontal attack on the dechristianizers:

> Is it still true that the chief cause of our ills is fanaticism? Fanaticism! It is dying; I could even say it is dead. By fixing all our attention on it in recent days, are we not looking away from our genuine dangers? . . . By what right do men, unknown until now in the course of the Revolution, come to seek amid all these events the means of usurping a false popularity, leading even patriots into taking false measures, and loosing trouble and discord among us? By what right do they disturb freedom of worship in the name of freedom, and attack fanaticism with a new fanaticism? . . . Why should we permit the dignity of the people to be trifled with in this way, and the bells of folly to be attached to the sceptre of philosophy itself?
>
> It was believed that by accepting civic offerings, the Convention had proscribed the Catholic cult. No, the Convention had in no way taken such a bold step. The Convention will never do so. Its intention was to maintain the freedom of worship that it proclaimed, and at the same time to repress all those who would abuse this to disturb public order . . . I may perhaps be called narrow-minded, a man of prejudices, even, who knows, a fanatic. I have already said that I speak neither as an individual nor as a systematic philosopher, but as a representative of the people. Atheism is *aristocratic*; the idea of a great being that watches over oppressed innocence and punishes triumphant crime is completely of the people. The people, the unfortunate, will applaud me; if I should find critics, it would be among the rich and among the

35 Robespierre, *Œuvres complètes*, vol. 10, p. 165.

> guilty. I have been, since my schooldays, a poor enough Catholic; I have never been a cold friend or faithless defender of humanity. I am only the more attached to the moral and political ideas that I have just expounded before you. If God did not exist, it would be necessary to invent him.[36]

At the end of this long speech, Robespierre attacked some 'foreign agents' by name, shady characters involved in all kinds of financial swindles, and moreover active dechristianizers: he had Dubuisson, Desfieux, Proli and Pereira expelled from the Jacobins.[37] Three days later, Danton called for 'no more anti-religious masquerades in the precinct of this Convention'.

In the wake of these attacks, the Convention, on Robespierre's proposal, recalled by a solemn decree of 16 Frimaire (6 December) its commitment to freedom of worship. Article 1 spelled out that: 'All acts of violence and measures contrary to freedom of worship are prohibited.' However, on Barère's proposal, an additional article clarified that: 'The Convention does not intend to undo what has been done up to this day by virtue of the decrees of the people's representatives', meaning that the churches that had been closed would remain so.[38]

The leaders of the Commune, who had been wholeheartedly involved in dechristianization, put up only a weak defence and were soon backing down. In the Jacobins, Hébert, criticized for attacking Laveaux who had spoken in favour of the Supreme Being, replied: 'I am accused of atheism, I flatly deny the accusation . . . As for the religious opinions I am accused of having emitted in my

---

36 Ibid., pp. 195–7. The last sentence was of course borrowed from Voltaire.

37 Pereira, along with Cloots, was part of the group that had convinced Bishop Gobel to announce his abjuration.

38 A. P., vol. 81, p. 120. What is revealing here is that in the same session when this decree was voted, several societies from provincial towns came to the bar to proudly assert acts of dechristianization. The popular society of Mugron, for example: 'Citizen representatives, you have opened the book of universal morality, you have lit the torch of philosophy, you have enlightened us. We want no other worship than that of liberty, our church will be called the Temple of Virtue. We no longer need a *curé*, the church silverware will be sent to Bayonne and the bells to the administration. *Vive la République, vive la Montagne!*'

paper, I flatly deny the fact and declare that I preach to the rural population that they should read the Gospel. This book of morals seems to me excellent, and by following its every maxim one may become a perfect Jacobin. I regard Christ as the founder of the popular societies.'[39] Chaumette, for his part, spoke to the Commune in praise of tolerance, albeit ambiguously: 'It matters little whether someone is theist or atheist, Catholic or Greek, whether someone believes in the Koran, in miracles, in werewolves or in fairy tales, that is not our concern . . . We need not inquire whether he goes to Mass, to the synagogue or the preacher; we need only inquire whether he is a republican.'[40]

Few voices were raised to criticize the retreat on dechristianization. Lequinio, a deputy for the Morbihan and representative on mission at Rochefort, wrote to the Committee of Public Safety: 'You speak to me of the decree of 16 Frimaire; well, I have to tell you that this decree nearly brought about great evils in the surrounding departments; the patriots did not understand the spirit behind it and became dejected, while it so greatly emboldened the aristocrats that it was necessary to use armed force in many places to stifle insurrections.'[41] At the popular society of Moulins, an anonymous sans-culotte proposed sending an address to the Committee of Public Safety inviting it to acknowledge its mistake: 'You will have as much satisfaction in retracting as regret at having been mistaken.'[42] Certain representatives on mission – Javogues in the Saône-et-Loire, Albitte in the Mont-Blanc, Lanot in the Corrèze – sent letters to the Committee of Public Safety explaining the risks of the new policy. They were recalled. 'I shall leave,' wrote Lanot to the Committee, 'satisfied of taking as my reward the hatred of plotters, priests and Moderates, which I have applied myself to deserving.'[43]

---

39 Aulard, *La Société des Jacobins*, vol. 5, p. 549.

40 Cited by Guérin, *La Lutte de classes*, vol. 1, p. 445.

41 Ibid., p. 460. Lequinio had published in 1792 a book entitled *Les Préjugés détruits*, in which he argued for equality between men and women, the abolition of the death penalty and slavery, radical atheism and the condemnation of war.

42 Ibid., p. 461.

43 Ibid., p. 464.

How can we explain Robespierre's reversal on the question of worship? ('Reversal' is not too strong a word: on 18 June 1793, in the discussion on the draft Constitution, he had said: 'I fear that conspirators will draw from the constitutional act confirming the freedom of worship the means for annihilating public liberty; I fear that men who wish to form counter-revolutionary associations will disguise them in religious forms.')

Robespierre explained his reasons himself. Some of these bore on foreign policy: he feared that dechristianization would shock the neutral countries, and particularly Switzerland, which he counted on to act as intermediary when negotiations with the Coalition opened.[44] Others arose from the concern to avoid trouble in the departments. On 15 Frimaire (5 December), at the Convention, he explained that 'there are communes that are not fanatical, but where nonetheless it is seen as deplorable for the authorities, backed by armed force, to order churches to be vacated and ministers of the cloth to be arrested simply because of their occupation.'

Robespierre's turnaround reflected his personal philosophy. As a good disciple of Rousseau, he detested the materialist philosophers. 'Helvétius', he declared to the Jacobins, 'was a brigand, a wretched smooth talker, an immoral individual, one of the cruellest persecutors of the good Jean-Jacques, who most deserves our homage. Had Helvétius lived in our day, do not believe that he would have embraced the cause of liberty; he would have joined the crowd of smooth-talking intriguers who are a curse to the *patrie* today.'[45] He was no more tender towards the Encyclopédie, 'that sect which, in matters of politics, always failed to accept the rights of the people'. Robespierre was a deist, and thus opposed to atheism. However,

---

44 In a dispatch to the Committee of Public Safety, Soulavie, the French representative in Geneva, reported on a conversation with the baron de Staël, the Swedish minister, who said that it was imperative 'to destroy absolutely the bad impression that the new form of worship has made in Europe' (cited by Guérin, *La Lutte de classes*, vol. 1, p. 407).

45 Aulard, *La Société des Jacobins*, vol. 4, p. 550. 'Two ladders were brought in amidst applause, and the busts of Mirabeau and Helvétius were taken down. Soon they were broken, with everyone jostling for the glory of crushing them underfoot.'

there were numerous atheists among the dechristianizers; one was Sylvain Maréchal, whose hit philosophical poem, 'Dieu et les prêtres', dedicated to Chaumette, was quite explicit: 'That God whom you feared was but a false giant/Born from your ignorance and nourished by the priests . . .'[46] Whatever the case, the position now adopted – in which Robespierre played, as we have said, a very prominent role – marked a distance from the sans-culotte movement, all the greater inasmuch as the Committee of Public Safety was simultaneously moving to control the popular organizations.

Curbing the popular movement: the law of 14 Frimaire year II

In his report 'on provisional and revolutionary government', a prelude to the law of 14 Frimaire, Billaud-Varenne explained: 'As soon as the centrality of the legislature ceases to be the linchpin of government, the edifice lacks its main foundation and inevitably crumbles.'[47] During the discussion, Merlin de Thionville suggested renaming the Committee of Public Safety as the Committee of Government. Billaud opposed this, as did Barère: 'Only the Convention governs, and it alone must govern. The Committee of Public Safety is not the only instrument that it uses; it also uses the Committee of General Security and the Executive Council [the ministers]. We are the advance post of the Convention, we are the arm that it moves, but we are not the government.'[48] And yet it was indeed in the hands of the Committee of Public Safety that this law would concentrate the fundamentals of power.

The decree passed on 14 Frimaire[49] dealt first of all with the execution of laws. It established a commission charged with the daily publication of every new law and decree, and with conveying these immediately to all the officials and authorities affected by their application.

---

46 Cited by Guérin, *La Lutte de classes*, vol. 1, p. 421.

47 A. P., vol. 79, 28 Brumaire year II, pp. 451–60.

48 A. P., vol. 80, p. 360.

49 Ibid., pp. 629–35.

In the departments, districts and communes, all elected positions (general councillors, departmental presidents, *procureurs généraux*, *procureurs syndics*) were suppressed. In their place, a national agent in each district and each municipality, appointed by the government, would supervise the execution of the laws. He was to render an account to the government Committees every ten days.[50]

It was the district administrations that were responsible for the application of revolutionary laws and measures of public safety. The departmental administrations now dealt only with the allocation of contributions, and the maintenance of manufactures, roads and canals: their role became secondary.

The popular organizations were more than reined in:

> Any congress or central meeting established either by representatives of the people or by the popular societies, under any name whatsoever, even the name of central surveillance committee or revolutionary or military central commission, is revoked and expressly prohibited, as subversive of the unity of action of the government and tending toward federalism. Those existing will be dissolved within twenty-four hours of the date of publication of the present decree.

The local revolutionary armies were likewise dissolved. ('Any army other than that established by the Convention and common to the whole Republic is dismissed by the present decree.')

The representatives on mission were invested with full powers to propose the purging and reorganization of existing authorities. To those who asked for the new administrators to be appointed by the electoral assemblies, Couthon replied that 'in the extraordinary government it is from the centre that all impulses must spring, it is

50 In fact, the existing *procureurs syndics* were usually appointed as national agents (Art. 15), except in the case of a purge decided locally. In this case, they were replaced by individuals 'appointed to the post'. The list of persons 'retained' or new 'appointees' was then sent to the Convention, 'so that the members of the Convention may offer information on individuals who might be known to them'.

from the Convention that elections must come. I ask for the purging of administrations to be conducted here, and for the Convention to make the appointments to replace the administrators who will be removed.' Adopted.

Thus all elections were suppressed and all powers concentrated in the hands of the government Committees, the arms of the Convention in both senses. Legislative centralization was maximal. The Executive Council no longer had any *raison d'être*. It was finally abolished on 12 Germinal (1 April 1794) and replaced by twelve executive commissions attached to the Committee of Public Safety.

Was the curbing of the popular movement in Frimaire of year II, as Daniel Guérin believes, a victory of the revolutionary bourgeoisie united against those whom it called the *bras nus*? This view, in keeping with Guérin's thesis of the class struggle during the Revolution, is unconvincing. The hypothesis of a kind of *union sacrée* of the 'Montagnard bourgeoisie' against the people does not take account of the divergences separating Robespierre and his friends both from the liberal-Voltairean members of the Convention, in the Plaine, and, in the other direction, from the turbulent Cordeliers whose base was in the Commune and the ministry of war. There could be no unity between such contrary currents, as indeed the course of events would show. Robespierre and the Committee of Public Safety – which it makes no sense at all to call 'bourgeois' – took alone the decision to halt dechristianization and cut short the popular ferment. Robespierre said: 'Democracy is not a state in which the people rule by themselves on all public affairs.' For him, order was necessary to straighten out the country and win the war. It would seem that he no longer remembered what he had asserted in spring 1793: 'The Montagne needs the people; the people are supported by the Montagne.'[51] He did not see – no doubt he could not – that his volte-face would cut him off from his main support, without which things would rapidly take a turn for the worse.

---

51 Robespierre, *Œuvres complètes*, vol. 9, p. 492.

CHAPTER 13

Brumaire to Germinal year II/ November 1793 to April 1794

The 'foreign plot', the fall of the 'factions': trial and execution of the Cordeliers and Dantonists

> Robespierre, alone: 'Oh, my Camille! They are all abandoning me. How empty and barren everything is . . . I am alone.'
>
> – Büchner, *Danton's Death*

Why a struggle to the death?

The halt to dechristianization and the law of 14 Frimaire formed part of a triangular struggle between the revolutionary government, the Indulgents and the Exagérés.

This confrontation would become a struggle to the death. But why? If we ignore the commonplace about the Revolution being, like Chronos, doomed to devour its children, there are at least two possible answers, one bearing on the political culture of the time, the other on the conjuncture.

The first of these is suggested by the contrast with the American Revolution, which, despite its violent beginnings, ended up with a pacified system inspired by England. For the American historian Lynn Hunt:

> [In] France there was no 'Whig science of politics', no familiarity with the ins and outs of ministerial turnovers, no practice with patronage systems and interest group formations . . . The struggle between the regenerated French nation and her presumed enemies was particularly divisive, thanks to the combination of the novelty of political mobilization, the intensity of social antagonism (as exemplified in talk of famine plots), and the unparalleled emphasis on doing something entirely new in the world. If Americans and Englishmen found it difficult to accept the emergence of party politics and factional competition, then the French refusal to sanction such developments was all the more determined. And the consequences of such a refusal were all the more disastrous.[1]

The second answer is bound up with the fact that France was at war with the coalition of European powers. The men in government were obsessed by the idea of collusion between their opponents and the enemy abroad. It is easy to wax ironic over this fear today, to see it as a kind of collective paranoia, and believe that: 'Like the people's will, the plot was the figment of a frenzied preoccupation with power; they were the two facets of what one might call the collectively held image of democratic power.'[2] It is easy, because we know that no such plot existed. But in autumn 1793, everyone was mindful of recent betrayals (Mirabeau, Louis XVI, Lafayette, Dumouriez). That new plots might be being spun in the shadows hardly seemed improbable.

The conflict that began in October–November 1793 ended in Germinal of year II (March–April 1794) with the fall of the so-called 'factions'. (This term was highly pejorative at the time, when 'factious' was tantamount to 'criminal'.[3] To use the word without scare quotes is to give credence to that accusation.) It was essentially a Parisian battle, and waged above all in the Convention and the Jacobins club. The popular movement, if it continued to be noisy and even

---

1 Hunt, *Politics, Culture and Class in the French Revolution*, p. 43.

2 Furet, *Interpreting the French Revolution*, p. 54.

3 Saint-Just, 'Any faction is criminal, since it tends to divide the citizens', in 'Rapport sur les factions de l'étranger', *Œuvres complètes*, p. 695.

deafening at times, no longer played the decisive role that it had done in the previous power struggles.

The standard story of these six months posits a linear process, Robespierre starting with the elimination of the Exagérés, helped by the Indulgents, then turning against these very Indulgents and sending them too to the guillotine. This kind of simplification masks the entanglement of interests and destinies, the human and political complexity of the moment, everything that lends it tragic force and gives it a general significance, even beyond its own era.

The forces at play: the Committee of Public Safety, Exagérés, Hébertistes and Cordeliers, Indulgents and Dantonists

The first force here was the revolutionary government – chiefly the Committee of Public Safety, an emanation of the Convention that had elected it and regularly confirmed it unchanged throughout the period.[4] If the Committee spoke for a long time with a single voice, this did not mean it was homogeneous, as we have seen: internal differences would harden as difficulties mounted. The central bloc, formed by Robespierre, Saint-Just and Couthon, was usually reinforced by Saint-André and Lindet when they were not out on mission. Billaud-Varenne and Collot d'Herbois, elected to the Committee in the wake of the quasi-insurrectional *journées* of 4 and 5 September 1793, had links with the popular movement. We shall see how on several occasions Collot sought to steer the revolutionary government towards Cordelier policies. On the other side, Carnot was more representative of the 'right', though without being close to Danton and the Indulgents. Opposed to a radical application of democracy in the army, he was surrounded by career officers, often former nobles, and stood for expansion to France's natural borders – hence his frequent altercations with Saint-Just, much opposed to a war of conquest.

The Committee of Public Safety was not all-powerful vis-à-vis

4 Apart from the elimination of Hérault de Séchelles, who was not replaced.

the Convention, which remained largely 'centrist' even after the elimination of the Girondins. The Plaine did not always follow it: after rowdy sessions, the Committee's recommendations might be amended or even rejected. Finally, as the second element in the government, the Committee of General Security, statutorily subject to the Committee of Public Safety, gained increased independence over time. It would be decisive in the fall of the Robespierrists in Thermidor.

After the Enragés had left the stage, the 'left' opposition is often described as 'Hébertiste' – scarcely an appropriate term, since while Hébert was very influential as a journalist, he was not a party leader. In fact the word '*hébertiste*' rarely appears in texts of the time, which more commonly speak of '*exagérés*' or '*ultra-révolutionnaires*'. In the reports of interior ministry informants, which retain the language of the street, Hébert is often mentioned, but not '*hébertistes*'. Soboul, in one of his notes to Jaurès's *Histoire*, wrote: 'We put "*hébertistes*" in apostrophes. Cordeliers would be the better word',[5] which is quite correct, and certainly better than the 'plebeians' proposed by Daniel Guérin.

Whatever the name they are given, this group is poorly regarded by most historians. Those whose heroes are the Enragés see the Cordeliers/Hébertistes as opportunists: 'They had become knowledgeable about the people, they were marvellously skilled at pastiche of their language; they were experts in the art of manipulating and making use of them . . . The plebeians served the bourgeois revolution at the same time as serving themselves', writes Guérin.[6] For Jaurès, 'the Hébertiste party, which had neither a social programme, a religious programme, a military tactic, an administrative system, or indeed humanity, represented no more than an overbidding of blood and the boundless promotion of military officialdom and exhausting war.'[7] Nor were they more highly esteemed by Mathiez: 'The

5 Jaurès, *Histoire socialiste*, p. 281.

6 Daniel Guérin, *Bourgeois et bras nus, la guerre sociale sous la Révolution (1793–1795)*, Paris: Les Nuits rouges, 1998, pp. 132–3.

7 Jaurès, *Histoire socialiste*, vol. 6, p. 327.

majority were less desirous of realizing a social programme than impatient to satisfy their own ambitions and grudges. They had no social policy to speak of.'[8] The only historian to praise the Hébertistes, to my knowledge, was Gustave Tridon, the right hand of Blanqui, who wrote in 1864:

> Through them, the human spirit, the spirit of Greece and Rome, came close to eternal triumph. At their voice, bastilles, monasteries and parliaments crumbled, and in the regenerated Notre-Dame, on the sacrificial altar, Reason – the heretic of the Middle Ages, the friend of Voltaire and Diderot – was enthroned! We salute those pure and noble citizens, Hébert and Pache; Chaumette, whom the people loved as a father; Momoro, with his burning pen and generous spirit; Ronsin, the intrepid general; and you, gentle and melancholic figure in whom German pantheism joined hands with French naturalism, Anacharsis Cloots![9]

In less lyrical vein, Morris Slavin's judgement seems to me the most well-founded:

> Despite their verbal extremism, the Hébertistes constantly pressed the sans-culottes to lead a more democratic politics, to conduct a social program to the benefit of themselves and their allies, to limit the power of the possessors and the new bureaucracy, to create new institutions. They helped to educate the people politically and restore them their dignity. In this sense, they deserve to be treated sympathetically by historians.[10]

---

8 Mathiez, *La Révolution française*, vol. 3, p. 150.

9 Gustave Tridon, *Les Hébertistes, plainte contre une calomnie de l'histoire*, 1864. Thanks to Dominique Le Nuz, Blanquist emeritus, for having drawn my attention to this pamphlet. It is cited by Mathieu Léonard, *L'Émancipation des travailleurs, une histoire de la Première Internationale*, Paris: La Fabrique, 2011.

10 Morris Slavin, *The Hébertistes to the Guillotine*, Baton Rouge: Louisiana State University Press, 1994, p. 8. Thanks to Sebastian Budgen for having brought this excellent work to my attention.

The Cordeliers, while their base was primarily Parisian, were also influential in the departments through the committees of popular societies, which organized congresses at Marseille, Valence and Dunkirk – the embryonic organization of a local executive power, absolutely incompatible with the legislative centralism imposed by the law of 14 Frimaire.[11]

The Indulgents, the 'right opposition' around Danton, Desmoulins and Fabre d'Églantine, maintained that the bloodshed had to stop. Desmoulins proposed the creation of a clemency committee that would gradually take over from the other committees. *Le Vieux Cordelier*, his newspaper whose first issue appeared on 15 Frimaire of year II (5 December 1793), disseminated this idea together with a critique of economic regulation (the maximum) and a suggestion of compromise with the foreign enemy. But rumours of corruption gradually enveloped the Indulgents. Already in September, Chabot, Basire, Julien de Toulouse and Osselin – 'business deputies', Robespierre called them – were accused of involvement in fraudulent deals and favouring dubious suppliers, and were dismissed from the Committee of General Security. Among the scandals of this time, the most serious was that of the liquidation of the Compagnie des Indes, which would divide the Montagne and precipitate the fall of the Indulgents.

The Compagnie des Indes affair, the 'foreign plot'

Two affairs provide the backdrop to this period, the scandal of the Compagnie des Indes[12] and the foreign plot – although in reality

11 See Françoise Brunel, *Thermidor, la chute de Robespierre*, Brussels: Complexe, 1989, pp. 14–16. A remarkable volume in every way, despite its slimness.

12 The Compagnie des Indes affair was very complicated. To sum up: joint stock companies had been suppressed by a decree of 24 August 1793, in the wake of attacks from 'business deputies' who prospered by frightening companies and speculating on a fall in their shares. On 8 October 1793, Delaunay presented a draft decree on the liquidation of the Compagnie des Indes, which Fabre had amended more strictly by providing that this liquidation be carried out by the state rather than by the company itself. But when the text

there was only one, as the foreign plot was an invention of Fabre d'Églantine who, being at the centre of the Compagnie scam, dreamed it up to create a diversion and discredit his opponents.

On 19 Vendémiaire of year II (10 October 1793), Fabre read a long memorandum about the plot at a meeting attended by Robespierre and Saint-Just, for the Committee of Public Safety, and Le Bas, Vadier, Amar, David and Guffroy for the Committee of General Security.[13] Fabre pointed the finger at Proli, Dubuisson ('another cunning fellow and a subject of the emperor'), and Pereira ('both Spaniard and Jew by nation, a protégé of Beaumarchais and in his debt'). He raised the spectre of espionage:

> How can it be that these men I have named and their cabal know all the secrets of the government two weeks before the National Convention? . . . How is it that Desfieux and Proli, being great patriots, are inseparable companions of the most dangerous foreign bankers? . . . These suspect characters have managed to win faithful supporters in every milieu, particularly in the Convention, and even in the Jacobins.

Fabre was so convincing that the speeches of Saint-Just and Robespierre in the days that followed sound like echoes of his denunciation.

The sensation caused by this 'plot' was not simply due to Fabre d'Églantine's fertile mind; the idea came just at the time when the Revolution's attitude towards foreigners was undergoing a total change. The situation in the autumn of 1793 was a far cry from the internationalism of the previous year, when the Legislative Assembly

---

of the law was published, the original draft had been restored; the company was to conduct its own liquidation. The text of the falsified decree, which carried Fabre's signature, appeared in the *Bulletin des lois* without anyone noticing this serious alteration. The '*fripons*' (rogues) had extracted 500,000 livres from the Compagnie for changing its liquidation conditions. The 'foreign plot' was invented by Fabre d'Églantine in order to divert suspicions. See Albert Mathiez, *Un procès de corruption sous la Terreur: l'affaire de la Compagnie des Indes*, Paris: Alcan, 1922.

13 See on this meeting Louis Jacob, *Fabre d'Églantine, chef des 'fripons'*, Paris: Hachette, 1946, chapter 10.

decided to give French citizenship to a series of eminent foreigners, including Joseph Priestley, Thomas Paine, Jeremy Bentham, Anacharsis Cloots, George Washington, Friedrich Schiller and Tadeusz Kościuszko.[14] With the war, this generous universalism gave way to distrust and even explicit hostility towards foreigners. On 5 April 1793, at the Jacobins, Augustin Robespierre (Maximilien's younger brother) had demanded the expulsion of all the foreign generals 'to whom we have foolishly entrusted the command of our armies'.[15] On 11 July, in the Convention, Barère proposed that 'all Englishmen not domiciled in France before 14 July 1789 be held to leave within a week'. Cambon, finding the measure too lenient, suggested arresting all suspect foreigners, and eventually (1 August) the Assembly decreed that 'foreigners from countries with which the Republic is at war, and who were not domiciled in France before 14 July 1789, shall be immediately arrested and seals placed on their papers, files and effects.'[16]

In this climate, the foreign plot was all the more credible in that Paris was indeed full of 'suspect' foreigners, particularly political refugees and bankers: Walter Boyd, an English banker who had opened a Paris office and was protected by Chabot; Perrégaux, a banker from Neuchâtel (and so a Prussian subject); Proli, a Belgian banker (so an Austrian subject); the Frey brothers, originally from Moravia, who had been suppliers to Joseph II at the time of the Turkish war; Pereira, a businessman established in Bordeaux; and many others. In his denunciation, Fabre cleverly mingled truth and falsehood: it is perfectly possible that these individuals were engaged in shady financial activities, and they may well have used their fortunes to corrupt

14 Three of these would be elected deputies to the Convention: Priestley (who refused, pleading his bad French), Thomas Paine, and Anacharsis Cloots, who were deputies for the Pas-de-Calais and the Oise respectively. The decree of 26 August 1792 began as follows: 'Considering that the men who, by their writings and their courage, have served the cause of liberty and prepared the emancipation of peoples, cannot be regarded as foreigners by a nation that their enlightenment and courage has made free, the Assembly . . .'

15 Aulard, *La Société des Jacobins*, vol. 5, p. 125.

16 See on this question Albert Mathiez, *La Révolution et les étrangers, cosmopolitisme et défense nationale*, Paris: La Renaissance du livre, 1918, and Sophie Wahnich, *L'Impossible Citoyen, l'étranger dans le discours de la Révolution française*, Paris: Albin Michel, 1997.

the political milieu and advance their own interests; but they are thoroughly unlikely to have been agents of foreign powers, or to have acted together to foment any real plot.

However this may be, the 'plot' served as a weapon in the struggle between Indulgents and Exagérés; the former, accused of trafficking with foreign financiers and protecting aristocrats and royalists, replied by accusing the latter of being pawns of foreign plotters, who were whipping up popular fury and pressing for extreme measures in order to undermine the Republic. Indeed, foreigners could be found on both sides, and some would also show up in the tumbrils taking the various 'factions' one after the other to the guillotine in Germinal of year II.

The Indulgents' offensive, Camille Desmoulins and Le Vieux Cordelier

The dramatic confrontation during the autumn and winter of year II had two successive phases. In the first phase, from Frimaire to Ventôse (November–December 1793 to February–March 1794), the Indulgents and Exagérés were at each other's throats, while the revolutionary government played the role of arbiter: on several occasions, Robespierre took a position above the mêlée and dismissed the pleas of both 'factions'. In the second phase, however, from Ventôse to Germinal (March–April 1794), the deepening crisis impelled the revolutionary government to take the initiative that would end with the elimination of the factions.

Even before Robespierre turned against against dechristianization, the Indulgents had moved to the offensive. On 20 Brumaire (10 November), Basire and Chabot pushed through a decree that limited the powers of the Committees to arrest deputies. The following day, the counter-offensive at the Jacobins was led by Hébert: 'The guilty must perish, even those within the Convention itself, for they are even guiltier than the rest . . . I demand the expulsion of Thuriot from the Société des Jacobins, the investigation of the conduct of

Chabot and Basire, and the prompt judgement of the deputies who were accomplices of Brissot and his faction.'[17] On 22 Brumaire, in the Convention, Barère and Billaud-Varenne had the decree of the 20th unanimously rejected.

A few days later (25 Brumaire), the same Basire and Chabot each separately denounced, in the Committee of General Security, the great foreign plot: they explained that the baron de Batz, a royalist agent, had used the money of the Compagnie des Indes to pay '*exagéré* patriots', all friends of Hébert, grouped behind Anacharsis Cloots. The revolutionary army, the war ministry and the popular societies were preparing a new 31 May that would lead to the dissolution of the Convention. Chabot maintained that he had joined the plot the better to denounce it. The Committees let themselves be convinced by the denunciations of Chabot and Basire, which in their eyes corroborated those of Fabre d'Églantine the previous month, but the tale-tellers themselves seemed so suspicious that they were arrested on 27 Brumaire, at the same time as the deputies whom they had denounced, Julien de Toulouse and Delaunay d'Angers. Only Fabre d'Églantine was left in peace, and was even asked by the Committee of General Security to assist with the investigation of the plot.

Danton, who had returned in haste from Arcis-sur-Aube, relaunched the Indulgents' offensive. On 11 Frimaire (1 December), Cambon proposed the demonetizing of gold and silver coin. Danton spoke against the decree, adding a sideswipe at the Exagérés: 'Any man who takes an ultra-revolutionary stance will bring results as dangerous as the most decided counter-revolutionaries could bring . . . Let us remember that if the pike is the weapon of overthrow, it is with the compass of reason and talent that the social edifice must be raised and consolidated.'[18]

On 13 Frimaire (3 December), at the Jacobins, Danton replied

---

17 Aulard, *La Société des Jacobins*, vol. 5, pp. 507-8. The supposed 'accomplices of Brissot' were the seventy-five members of the Convention who had protested against the purge of 31 May–2 June. Robespierre had always (and successfully) opposed their indictment.

18 A. P., vol. 80, p. 454.

to a member of the Le Havre society who had asked for a detachment of the revolutionary army, complete with guillotine, to be sent to the Seine-Inférieure to arrest and punish the rebels who had escaped from the Vendée, and for the Le Havre church to be placed at the disposal of the local society: 'I say we should beware of those who seek to carry the people beyond the limits of the Revolution, and who propose ultra-revolutionary measures.' Danton was violently attacked by Coupé de l'Oise, who taunted him with 'diminishing the vigour of the revolutionary movement', and booed by other members. He defended himself with some difficulty: 'Am I not the same man who was at your side in moments of crisis? Am I not he whom you often embraced as your friend and who is ready to die with you? . . . I shall remain standing with the people.'

Robespierre sped to his aid: 'Does no one raise their voice? Well! I shall do so . . . Danton! Do you not know that the more courage and patriotism a man has, the more the enemies of the public cause pursue his downfall? Do you not know, do you not all know, citizens, that this method is infallible?'[19]

It was at this critical moment that Camille Desmoulins launched his new paper, *Le Vieux Cordelier*. The first number, composed in haste, contained, besides blatant flattery of Robespierre, the repeated theme of the Exagérés as foreign agents and a defence of Danton: 'Already fortified by the ground gained during Danton's illness and absence, this party, insolent and dominant in the Society, amid the most touching and persuasive passages of his [Danton's] justification, booed him from the galleries, whilst in the Assembly they shook their heads and smiled with pity, as if hearing the speech of a man whom all votes had condemned.'[20]

The manoeuvre was followed up over the next few days by Thuriot, who proposed to the Convention on 17 Frimaire (7 December) that patriots detained under the law of suspects should be released: 'It has

19 Aulard, *La Société des Jacobins*, vol. 5, pp. 541–2. Robespierre's outburst shows the friendship he felt for Danton, to whom he had written very affectionate letters at the time of the loss of his first wife.

20 Camille Desmoulins, *Le Vieux Cordelier*, Paris: Armand Colin, 1936, p. 43.

clearly been shown that men who have served the Republic well are languishing in the dungeons. An authority is needed that is strong enough, and vested with sufficient trust, to return them to the freedom for which they fought.'[21]

The third number of *Le Vieux Cordelier*, which appeared on 25 Frimaire (15 December), was devoted to the subject of clemency. This critique of the law of suspects and revolutionary violence was constructed on a paraphrase of Tacitus. After taking the reader 'to Les Brotteaux [in Lyon] and the place de la Révolution, and [showing] him these places drowned in the blood that flowed there for six months, for the eternal emancipation of a people of 25 million men, and not yet washed down by liberty and public happiness,' Desmoulins imagined what Pitt might say:

> Although the patriot Pitt, having become a Jacobin, in his order to the invisible army that he funds in our midst, had told it to demand, like the marquis de Montaud, *five hundred heads in the Convention*, and that *the army of the Rhine should execute the Mainz garrison*; to demand, like a certain petition, that *900 thousand heads should fall*; like a certain requisition, that *half the French people should be imprisoned as suspect*; and, like a certain motion, that *barrels of powder be placed beneath these countless prisons, with a fuse permanently alongside . . .* [22]

This was very well received by the Paris public, and boosted the energy of the Indulgents. In the Convention on 27 Frimaire (17 December), Fabre attacked Bouchotte and the ministry of war, the stronghold of the Exagérés: 'There is a ministry whose influence

---

21 A. P., vol. 81, p. 90. In the wake of this intervention, Couthon had a vote passed that the revolutionary Committees were held to account within twenty-four hours for arrests of individuals not included *stricto sensu* in the law of suspects.

22 Desmoulins, *Le Vieux Cordelier*, pp. 81–2. The author's emphases. Les Brotteaux was the square in Lyon where the shootings ordered by Collot d'Herbois were carried out; Montaud had denounced in the Jacobins all the friends of Desmoulins, Danton, Thuriot, Chabot, etc.; the 'imprisonment of half the people' was an allusion to Chaumette's charge-sheet against the suspects of 5 September 1793; 'powder barrels beneath the prisons' was a proposal made to the Convention on 17 September by Collot d'Herbois.

equals that of Roland, which has peopled the Republic with its agents and commissioners, which has appointed those mustachioed men with their big sabres trailing on the ground and striking the cobbles, who frighten the children.'[23] And Fabre demanded the arrest of Vincent, the powerful general-secretary of the ministry of war, of Maillard and of Ronsin, a general of the revolutionary army. That same evening, Bourdon de l'Oise had Ronsin expelled from the Jacobins. A few days later, Fabre obtained the arrest of Mazuel, head of cavalry in the revolutionary army. The Indulgents were victorious all along the line, while Robespierre and the Committee of Public Safety, still under Fabre's influence, remained convinced of the dangers of the foreign plot.

Three days later (30 Frimaire / 20 December), the Convention was invaded by a crowd of women demanding the release of their relatives and husbands. The pressure was so strong that Robespierre had to speak. He began with recriminations: 'Is this how republicans demand the liberty of the oppressed? . . . Why come here with such a great show? Is the idea of appearing with such fracas at the bar not to force the Convention to reconsider?' But he was obliged to tack, and ended by proposing a decree to the effect that 'the Committees of Public Safety and General Security shall appoint commissioners to find ways of freeing any patriots who might have been imprisoned.'[24] This was not so different from the clemency committee demanded by Desmoulins, and the Indulgents had won another point.

Counter-attack by the Montagnards and Exagérés, rout of the Indulgents

At the end of Frimaire, however, the wind would change under the impact of two events. The first was a discovery in the investigation Amar was conducting on Chabot's denunciation: the original of the false decree of liquidation of the Compagnie des Indes bore the

23 A. P., vol. 81, p. 605.

24 Robespierre, *Œuvres complètes*, vol. 10, pp. 263–4.

signature of Fabre, who had thus accepted a text contrary to his own amendment. Robespierre – as shown by his notes – began to wonder if he had not been deceived by a cunning swindler.

The second event was the return to Paris of Collot d'Herbois. He felt threatened by the arrest of Ronsin, on top of which a petition from the inhabitants of Lyon had appealed to the Convention to put an end to the punishment of Commune-Affranchie.[25] On 1 Nivôse (21 December), escorted from the Bastille to the Tuileries by a great popular procession and a delegation of Lyon sans-culottes carrying the head and ashes of Chalier, Collot appeared before the Convention, justifying his actions in Lyon and denouncing the unhappy effects of Ronsin's arrest:

> Energetic men were paralysed by the news that the Convention disapproved of all strict measures. To you were ascribed traits of weakness and pusillanimity such as you are not capable of . . . The general of the revolutionary army [Ronsin] left Commune-Affranchie to consult with the Committee of Public Safety . . . Before his departure, the aristocrats were already spreading the story that he had been summoned to your bar – and two hours after arriving here he was placed under arrest. Imagine what hay the ill-disposed will be able to make from this circumstance.[26]

Hébert's comment, in no. 326 of *Le Père Duchesne*: 'Fortunately – damnation! – Collot d'Herbois, the intrepid defender of the sans-culottes, has arrived to disentangle the whole plot. The giant has appeared, and all the dwarves who were plaguing the best patriots have retreated a hundred feet under the ground.'

That same evening at the Jacobins, the Montagnards and Exagérés laid into Desmoulins. Nicolas: 'I accuse Camille Desmoulins of having published a libel with criminal and counter-revolutionary intentions. Camille Desmoulins has long been flirting with the guillotine.' He demanded Desmoulins's expulsion from the society.

25 Slavin, *The Hébertistes to the Guillotine*, pp. 77–8.

26 A. P., vol. 82, p. 94.

Hébert: 'Ever since he married a rich woman, he has frequented only aristocrats and has often been their protector.' He violently attacked Fabre d'Églantine:

> A man who is the kingpin of every plot: a man forever busy with exaggerating our perils and sowing discord among the patriots, getting each to accuse the other in order to destroy them: this man is Fabre d'Églantine . . . I demand that Camille Desmoulins, Bourdon [de l'Oise], Philippeaux and Fabre d'Églantine be expelled from the Society . . . and that the Society finally declare that Vincent and Ronsin have not forfeited its trust.[27]

Two days later, at the Jacobins, Collot attacked the Indulgents and their policy of clemency:

> What! The Committee of Public Safety is being attacked in the press! It is accused of having spilled the blood of patriots! Blamed for the death of fifty thousand men! And do you believe that the authors of these tracts have acted in good faith? That men who translate the ancient historians for you [an allusion to Desmoulins] are patriots? They want to moderate the revolutionary movement. Well! Does one direct a storm? Let us cast far behind us any thought of moderation. Let us remain Jacobins, let us remain Montagnards, let us save liberty.

Philippeaux replied by once again attacking Ronsin and Rossignol, 'who were never at the head of their troops. Just once, Ronsin led his own forces; that was the day he had forty thousand men beaten by three thousand rebels.' The session grew stormy, and Robespierre intervened to restore calm, placing himself above the parties and against divisions:

> Citizens, where does all this agitation come from that has been tormenting you in recent days? Do you know that foreign powers have here encircled you? They have placed you between two reefs:

27 Aulard, *La Société des Jacobins*, vol. 5, p. 569ff.

> between moderation, which has been eternally defeated, and the Prussian perfidy of those men who want a universal republic, or rather universal conflagration. You may be sure of this, that the tactic of our enemies, an unfailing one, is to divide us; they want us to tear ourselves apart in close combat with our own hands.[28]

On 6 Nivôse (26 December) in the Convention, Barère presented on behalf of the Committee of Public Safety his report on the implementation of the law on suspects. This was a long charge-sheet against a policy of clemency:

> So, I shall say with better reason and policy than certain writers in newspapers who, without knowing it and perhaps without wishing it, have favoured counter-revolutionaries and rekindled the ashes of the aristocracy, I shall say: nobles, *suspect*; priests, men of the court, men of law, *suspect*; bankers, foreigners, known speculators, *suspect*; citizens who disguise their condition or outward form, *suspect*; men who complain of everything required to make a revolution, *suspect*; men afflicted by our successes at Dunkirk, at Maubeuge and in the Vendée, *suspect*. Oh! What a fine law it would have been to declare suspect those who, at the news of the taking of Toulon, did not feel their heart beat for the *patrie* . . . Arrests like these would not have motivated a new translation of Tacitus, who wrote only for tyrants without revolution, and not against revolutionary republicans.[29]

On 15 Nivôse, the seals on Delaunay's house were removed, and Fabre's false declaration came dreadfully to light. On 18 and 19 Nivôse (7 and 8 January), a dramatic sequence of events took place at the Jacobins, heralding the end of Fabre d'Églantine and the rout of the Indulgents.[30]

---

28 Ibid., pp. 573–6. The 'Prussians' who want a 'universal republic' is clearly an allusion to Anacharsis Cloots.

29 A. P., vol. 82, pp. 365-6. The 'translation of Tacitus' was a veiled attack on Desmoulins.

30 Aulard, *La Société des Jacobins*, vol. 5, p. 595ff.

At the start of the session of the 18th, Philippeaux, Bourdon de l'Oise, Camille Desmoulins and Fabre d'Églantine were called three times to explain themselves before the Society. None of them appeared. Robespierre confined himself to asking that the meeting not concern itself overmuch with Philippeaux, but rather with the crimes of the English government. When Camille appeared, he admitted his mistake, and Robespierre reproved him in a firm but friendly manner:[31]

> I consent for liberty to treat Desmoulins like a foolish child who has a pleasant disposition but was led astray by bad company; but we must require him to prove his repentance for all his follies by abandoning the company that misled him . . . I shall end by demanding that these numbers [of Desmoulins's paper] be treated like the aristocrats who buy them, with the contempt that the blasphemies they contain deserve. I move that the Society burn them in the centre of the hall.[32]

Camille was offended: 'Robespierre was good enough to reproach me in a language of friendship; I am disposed to reply to him in the same tone. I shall start with the first line. Robespierre said that my numbers should be burned; I reply, like Rousseau, "Burning is not an answer." ' Robespierre's tone then became more threatening: 'Learn, Camille, that were you not Camille, it would not be possible to be so indulgent towards you. The manner in which you seek to justify yourself proves to me that you have bad intentions.'

The next day, the order of the day included a public reading of numbers 3 and 5 of *Le Vieux Cordelier*. Momoro started off with number 3, but when it came to number 5, Hébert asked to refute it: 'It is particularly directed against me. Not that I think myself wounded by it: this man is so covered with mud that he can no longer touch a true patriot.' Robespierre opposed this: 'It is

31 Robespierre had been a friend of Desmoulins since they were students together at the lycée Louis-le-Grand. He had been a witness at Camille's marriage to Lucile.

32 Robespierre, *Œuvres complètes*, vol. 10, pp. 308–9.

pointless to read the fifth number of *Le Vieux Cordelier*, the opinions on Camille must already be settled . . . I am not espousing the quarrel of either man. Camille and Hébert have committed equal wrongs in my view.'

At the end of this speech, Fabre d'Églantine stood up to move towards the rostrum. Robespierre 'invited the Society to beg Fabre to remain'. Fabre continued, but Robespierre stopped him in his tracks:

> If Fabre d'Églantine has his subject all prepared, mine is not yet finished. I beg him to wait. There are two plots, one of which has the object of frightening the Convention, and the other of troubling the people. The conspirators who lie behind these hateful schemes seem to be fighting one another, and yet they work together in defending the cause of the tyrants . . . I ask this man, who is never seen without a lorgnette in his hand, and who is so very skilled at explicating plots in theatrical works, to be so kind as to explain himself here: we shall see how he acquits himself with this one.[33]

The attack left Fabre speechless. He was expelled from the Jacobins and on 23 Nivôse (12 January 1794) the Committees of Public Safety and General Security issued an arrest warrant for him that was executed the following day. Amar gave a report to the Convention, recapping the whole affair and justifying Fabre's arrest. Danton attempted a sideways defence of Fabre: 'I demand that the Convention confirm the arrest of Fabre d'Églantine, that the Committee of General Security take all necessary measures, and that those charged be then brought to the bar to be tried before the whole people, so that these know who still deserves their esteem.' This brought a menacing riposte from Billaud-Varenne: 'Woe to him who sat alongside Fabre d'Églantine and who is still his dupe.'[34] That was the end of it, the Indulgents were more than discredited; they would continue their efforts but their days were now numbered.

---

33 Aulard, *La Société des Jacobins*, vol. 5, p. 603.

34 A. P., vol. 83, pp. 291–2.

Outside of the clubs and assemblies, the popular movement incessantly demanded the liberation of Ronsin and Vincent who, from prison, had posters in his defence put up throughout Paris. The Guillaume-Tell section presented themselves en masse at the Convention on 11 Nivôse (31 December): the petition of the 'so-called Lyonnais' had been written in Paris 'to inveigle pity'; the requests of the prisoners' wives were 'one of the cogs in this hellish machinery'. It was 'the product of the aristocracy of priests, nobles, parliamentarians, financiers, bourgeois'. In conclusion: 'Chains for the suspects, axes for the guilty heads.'[35] On 12 Pluviôse (31 January), it was the sections of Mutius Scaevola, Bonnet-Rouge, Unité and Marat – those most in the van at this period – who demanded that Ronsin and Vincent be either released or judged by the Revolutionary Tribunal. On 14 Pluviôse, faced with popular pressure and the initiatives of the Cordeliers, and given the lack of any material evidence against them, the Committee of General Security proposed – with Danton's support – the liberation of Ronsin and Vincent, which the Convention decreed without debate.

The abolition of slavery

One moment of light in this dismal time was on 16 Pluviôse year II (4 February 1794), when the Convention voted the abolition of slavery in the colonies. We recall how in May 1791, a decree of the Constituent Assembly on 'unfree persons' had amounted to making slavery constitutional. Since then, however, the slave uprising in Saint-Domingue, which began on the night of 22 August 1791, had changed everything. In France, the Société des Citoyens de Couleur led by Julien Raimond[36] had helped to inform the Jacobins about the situation, counterbalancing the influence of the colonial lobby.

35 *Journal de la Montagne*, 7 Nivôse year II, cited by Soboul, *Les Sans-Culottes parisiens*, p. 343.

36 On Julien Raimond and the Société des Citoyens de Couleur, see Florence Gauthier, *L'Aristocratie de l'épiderme*, Paris: CRNS Éditions, 2007. On the course of the revolution in Saint-Domingue, see Gauthier, *Triomphe et mort du droit naturel en révolution*.

In April 1792, the Legislative Assembly had voted to recognize the political rights of free men of colour and to dispatch two civil commissioners to restore order. The task fell to Polverel and Sonthonax, who took measures against the slave-owning colonists and reorganized the administration, incorporating free men of colour. They conducted a policy of appeasement towards the insurgents, going so far as to free runaway or abandoned slaves. But in France the Convention under the Girondins declared war, as we saw, on England and Spain, and appointed a governor of Saint-Domingue by the name of Galbaud, who disembarked with his troops at Cap-Français in May 1793. He took the side of the colonists against the commissioners, but on 23 June the insurgent slaves crushed the expeditionary force and its colonist supporters. Galbaud fled to Canada. This was the end of the rule of the slave-owners in Saint-Domingue.[37]

In August 1793, the Cap-Français municipality voted the abolition of slavery, which was ratified by Sonthonax. The *nouveaux libres* elected a deputation sent to inform revolutionary France of all these happenings. Three of these deputies appeared at the bar of the Convention on 18 Pluviôse.[38] Their spokesman, Dufaÿ, related this turbulent history at length. 'The blood of Frenchmen flowed. The torch of civil war was lit in Saint-Domingue by counter-revolutionaries with Galbaud at their head, the traitor Dumouriez's friend and second-in-command.'[39] He told how the slaves had come to the aid of the commissioners, saying: 'We are blacks, Frenchmen, we are going to fight for France, but in return we want liberty – they even added *the rights of man*.' And Dufaÿ concluded: 'Legislators, the blacks are slandered, all their actions depicted in a poisonous light, because they can no longer be oppressed. We place them under your safeguard.'

One deputy exclaimed: 'Any further discussion would dishonour

---

37 For an overall presentation of these events, Florence Gauthier, '1793–94: la Révolution abolit l'esclavage. 1802: Bonaparte rétablit l'esclavage', *revolution-francaise.net.*

38 They were arrested on arrival on the order of the Committee of General Security, then released.

39 A. P., vol. 84, pp. 276–85. Yves Bénot ('Comment la Convention a-t-elle voté l'abolition de l'esclavage en l'an II?', in *Révolutions aux colonies, AHRF*, special issue, 1993) has studied this session and the next day's in detail, showing the resistance put up by remnants of the colonial party.

this assembly', and Delacroix proposed a resolution that 'The National Convention decrees that slavery is abolished throughout all the territory of the Republic; in consequence, all men without distinction of colour shall enjoy the rights of French citizens.' Some members protested that the very word 'slavery' risked sullying a decree of the Convention, and that liberty was 'a right of nature'. Grégoire opposed this attempt to derail the resolution: 'The word slavery must be included; without it, some would claim that you intended something else.'

The president (Vadier) pronounced the abolition of slavery 'amid applause and shouts of *Vive la République, vive la Convention, vive la Montagne!*'

Popular agitation: Saint-Just and the Ventôse decrees

While these events were unfolding in the foreground of the winter stage, popular discontent was becoming increasingly noisy. Paris was supplied fairly adequately with bread, but other essential items – meat, butter, eggs, soap, candles – were either lacking or priced out of reach. Early in Ventôse (February 1794), interior ministry observers described the tension in the streets:

> The difficulty that there is in obtaining the most common and essential things is already giving rise to angry murmurs. The spectacle of several injured women in the groups that cluster round the door of every shop has caused unruliness in several neighbourhoods. In the distribution of the least items it is force that decides, and this morning several women nearly lost their lives trying to obtain a little butter.[40]

The word on the street was that only the guillotine could sort matters out. As one observer, Pourvoyeur, reported:

40 Report of Latour-Lamontagne, 13 Ventôse, in C. A. Dauban, *1794, Histoire de la rue, du club, de la famine*, Paris: Plon, 1869, p. 143.

> What struck me most was the situation in the Saint-Jean market, where at least three thousand women stood in line, grumbling loudly about having spent four hours there without obtaining anything; they made remarks that were far from patriotic; there were many guards, both mounted and on foot. 'Is this how we are fed?' they said. 'They must want to see us starve, since they take no forceful measures to supply Paris! Of what use is the revolutionary army?'[41]

Unrest spread through the war manufactures and cotton-spinning workshops, where women workers, advised by Hébert, wrote a petition that they circulated with the aid of the popular society of the Marat section. 'When reproved for the uncivic character of their demands, these workers replied that "they didn't give a f . . ., they had Père Duchesne at their head".'[42] The assembly of the Finistère section contended that the revolutionary army's powers had been 'castrated, by not attaching to each of its divisions some revolutionary judges and a guillotine, the terror of our enemies'.[43]

It was in this climate that Saint-Just presented to the Convention, on 8 Ventôse (26 February), his report on persons imprisoned. This was a response to *Le Vieux Cordelier* and the attempts of the Indulgents to challenge the law on suspects, free the detainees and terminate the Terror:

> Those who demand the freedom of aristocrats do not want the Republic at all, and they fear for them. It is a flagrant sign of treason, this pity displayed towards crime, in a Republic that can only be based on inflexibility . . . It is enough for them to be virtuous in writing; they exempt themselves from probity; they grow fat on the spoils of the people, glutted with it, they insult the people, and they march in triumph on the coattails of crime for which crime they seek to excite your compassion; surely it is impossible to

41 Ibid., p. 171.

42 Soboul, *Les Sans-Culottes parisiens*, p. 685.

43 Ibid., p. 689. The Finistère section was that of the faubourg Saint-Martin, which had renamed itself in honour of the Breton *fédérés*.

> remain silent about the impunity of these great offenders, who wish to do away with the scaffold because they fear mounting it themselves . . . It would seem that every one of them, appalled by his own conscience and by the inflexibility of the laws, has said to himself: 'We are not sufficiently virtuous to be so ruthless; philosopher legislators, take pity on my weakness; I dare not tell you that I am rotten, I would rather say that you are cruel.'[44]

The audience waited for precise accusations, but Saint-Just, with one of those leaps that are a feature of his speeches, moved on to something else: 'No man who has proved himself the enemy of his country can be a possessor . . . Let us abolish begging, which dishonours a free state; the properties of patriots are sacred, but the assets of conspirators are there for the unfortunate. The unfortunate are the powers of the Earth; they have the right to speak as masters to the governments that neglect them.'

The brief final decree centred on this famous paragraph: 'The goods of persons recognized as enemies of the Revolution are confiscated to the benefit of the Republic; these persons shall be detained until peace, and then banished in perpetuity.' A few days later (13 Ventôse), Saint-Just explained how this decree would be applied: every commune in the Republic would draw up a list of the indigent on their territory; the Committee of Public Safety would then make a report on the best way of compensating these unfortunates with the confiscated assets; the surveillance committees would be charged with conveying to the Committee of General Security 'the names and the conduct of all those detained since 1 May 1789'.

Were these famous Ventôse decrees the prelude to 'a whole future development of social equality' (Jaurès)? Were they 'a formidable attempt to extract a social programme from the confused aspirations of Hébertism' (Mathiez)? Or was this rather a 'demagogic manoeuvre' to draw the masses away from the Hébertistes' (Guérin), a 'tactical manoeuvre to counteract advanced propaganda' (Soboul)? There can be no doubt of Saint-Just's sincerity: in Ventôse, he was working on

44 Saint-Just, *Œuvres complètes*, p. 656ff.

the manuscript that has become known under the name of *Institutions républicaines*, and these decrees would not have looked amiss in the context of this wide social project. But at this particular moment, it was tempting to use them to wrong-foot the popular 'agitators'.

'The effect produced was immense', wrote Jaurès, 'and it was indeed, to use Saint-Just's own expression, a stroke of genius.'[45] That is saying too much. It is true that on 14 Ventôse the observer Latour-Lamontagne reported: 'In every group and in all the cafés, the talk is only of the decree that orders the distribution of the goods of aristocrats to the sans-culottes; this popular law has excited universal joy, citizens are congratulating and embracing one another. Here is a decree, one of them said, that is worth more than ten battles won against the enemy.'[46] But this joy was short-lived, as the measures would obviously bear fruit only in the long term, and could not bring immediate relief to a people in difficulty. Hence the melancholy remark with which Mathiez closes his chapter: 'Strangely enough, and bewilderingly for [Saint-Just], he was neither understood nor supported by the very men he sought to satisfy.'[47]

The Cordeliers' 'offensive'

One indication that Saint-Just was not understood is that the day following the publication of these decrees, the Cordeliers launched what historians call their 'offensive'. The cascade of events that would climax on the scaffold three weeks later began with a session at the Cordeliers on 14 Ventôse (7 March).[48] The president started by reading the prospectus of the newspaper *L'Ami du peuple*, which, following Marat's original, 'would espouse the principles of that martyr of liberty' under the guarantee of the Cordeliers. The tablet of the Rights of Man was then covered with black crepe, 'and will remain veiled until the people recover their sacred rights through the

45 Jaurès, *Histoire socialiste*, vol. 6, p. 362.
46 Dauban, *Paris en 1794*, p. 151.
47 Mathiez, *La Révolution française*, vol. 3, p. 149.
48 *Le Moniteur*, vol. 19, p. 629ff.

annihilation of the faction'.[49] What faction was this? Vincent denounced Basire, Bourdon de l'Oise and Philippeaux, whose conspiracy, 'more to be feared than that of Brissot', would overthrow liberty 'if the full terror that the guillotine inspires in the enemies of the people is not deployed'.

Carrier, back from the Vendée, then took the floor:

> I was dismayed, on my arrival at the Convention, by the new faces that I saw on the Montagne, and the whispered utterances there. The aim, I can see, is to make the Revolution retreat . . . The monsters! They want to break the scaffolds; but never forget, citizens, that those who want no more guillotine feel that they deserve it themselves. Cordeliers! You want to produce a *maratiste* paper; I applaud your enterprise; but this dyke against the efforts of those who seek to kill the republic is scarcely robust; insurrection, a holy insurrection, that is what you must confront the scoundrels with.

Hébert then denounced 'the ambitious men who usher others forward and themselves stay behind the curtain; who the more power that they have, the less they can be satisfied, who want to reign. But the Cordeliers will not tolerate this (*several voices: No, no, no!*). I shall name the men who have shut the mouths of patriots in the popular societies; for the last two months I have held back . . .' Boulanger, Momoro and Vincent pressed him to speak. He resumed, making a clear allusion to Robespierre:

> Remember that [Camille Desmoulins] was expelled and struck off by the patriots, and that one man, who was no doubt misled . . . otherwise I should not know what to call it, was conveniently there to have him reinstated despite the wishes of the people, who had expressed themselves on this traitor very well . . . When sixty-one guilty men[50] and their companions remain unpunished and do not

49 It had already been covered up once, during the imprisonment of Vincent and Ronsin.

50 These were the Convention members who had protested against 31 May, whose prosecution Robespierre had prevented.

> fall beneath the sword, can you still doubt that a faction exists that wants to destroy the rights of the people? Well then! Since it exists, since we can see it, what are the means of delivering ourselves from it? Insurrection. Yes, insurrection; and the Cordeliers will not be the last to give the signal that will strike the oppressors dead.

The session rose at ten in the evening without mooting any practical measures to follow up what was more or less a declaration of war. Likewise in the next few days, apart from an initiative by the Marat section that proceeded en masse to the general council of the Commune on 16 Ventôse to call for insurrection, after itself covering the tablet of the Declaration of Rights. But Chaumette prudently pointed out to the delegation the dangers of provoking disturbances in Paris just when the spring military campaign was about to begin. The same day, Barère denounced in the Convention the manoeuvres of those who were agitating the people over provisions. The public prosecutor of the Revolutionary Tribunal was charged with informing against 'the authors of the distrust inspired towards those bringing goods and provisions into Paris'.[51]

That evening in the Jacobins,[52] Collot d'Herbois declared, after a long defence of the Committee of Public Safety:

> The Cordeliers society, of which I shall never speak without respect, will not long remain the dupe of the intriguers who have manipulated it. This is not the first time it has been led astray; it has always returned; it has done so openly. Jacques Roux, too, attempted to seduce it; it brought him to justice. These ambitious men, who want to start insurrections only to profit from them, what have they done for the public cause? Can we recall a single sign of devotion to duty? We would have rushed to celebrate it. Do they think it enough to cover the walls with bad posters in order to prove their patriotism?

51 *Le Moniteur*, vol. 19, p. 635.
52 Ibid., p. 647.

Momoro, followed by Carrier, protested these accusations against the Cordeliers. Carrier: 'We said nothing about starting insurrections, except in the case of being forced to it by circumstances. If we thereby made any motion against the Convention, I shall lay down my head.' Several members 'upheld Carrier's objection and complained that several passages in Hébert's speech of 14 Ventôse had been misreported in the public broadsheets'.[53]

Both Jaurès and Mathiez view this as a retraction, a pitiful climbdown. Yet what the Cordeliers were saying was true. It is impossible to follow Jaurès when he maintains: 'It was therefore a kind of military coup d'état that the Hébertistes were preparing, a demagogic 18 Brumaire that would have dishonoured, bloodied and ruined France.'[54] What the Cordeliers were preparing, however, was not an *armed* insurrection: it is scarcely likely that hardened revolutionaries would have envisaged an armed action without any groundwork – and they knew that the revolutionary energy of the sections was more than restrained by the work of the bureaucratized revolutionary Committees. The Cordeliers' insurrection was what would today be called a symbolic gesture. Soboul recalls the earlier cases when assemblies or sections declared themselves 'in insurrection', meaning thereby to signal 'the resistance of a people that rises up, refuses to obey laws that it does not accept, takes back the exercise of its sovereign rights, holds its mandatories to account and dictates to them its wishes'.[55] Robespierre himself, we recall, had declared himself in a state of insurrection before 31 May, and he certainly did not mean by this that he had any intention of taking up a pike or a musket.

The next day, 17 Ventôse, a delegation from the Jacobins proceeded to the Cordeliers, 'introduced amid lively applause'.[56] It was led by Collot d'Herbois, who played the role of conciliator throughout this period. He emphasized the need for unity: it was time 'to close ranks

53 This is highly likely, and *Le Moniteur* published a kind of apology: 'We will promptly rectify the mistakes that are pointed out to us, by publishing the authentic minutes of the Society as soon as we have cognizance of them' (vol. 19, p. 648).

54 Jaurès, *Histoire socialiste*, vol. 6, p. 375.

55 *Le Moniteur*, vol. 19, p. 663ff.

56 Soboul, *Les Sans-Culottes parisiens*, p. 542.

to fight en masse, and by the force of opinion, the scoundrels who seek to divide [us]'. But this was soon followed by a reprimand: 'Deceived by individuals more attentive to cries of revenge than to the voice of the *patrie*, you have uttered the word insurrection. But in what circumstance does one speak of this?' And he evoked 'Pitt and Coburg hovering over France like birds of prey', before concluding with a tribute to the Convention.

Momoro, Ronsin and Hébert replied with a kind of honourable amends. Hébert explained that what had been meant by insurrection was 'a closer union with the true Montagnards of the Convention, with the Jacobins and all good patriots, to obtain justice against unpunished traitors and persecutors'. The black cloth covering the Rights of Man was torn down and handed to the Jacobins as a mark of fraternity: the deputation was embraced to shouts of *Vive la République*.

But this reconciliation was only superficial. Collot had not succeeded in isolating the leaders from the mass of the Cordeliers. Over the days that followed, the turmoil in Paris continued. Anonymous posters appeared on walls, and there were threatening rumours of imminent revolt. In no. 355 of *Le Père Duchesne*, published on 23 Ventôse, Hébert called for the general unity of patriots around a Convention 'purged of all the traitors who are conspiring against liberty', which clearly sounded like an appeal for a new 31 May.

Arrest, trial and execution of the Cordelier leaders

On the previous evening, the Committee of Public Safety had resolved to put an end to the Cordelier movement, approving the report drawn up by Saint-Just 'against foreign factions'. It is unlikely that the Committee had genuinely been shaken by the posters and rumours: its informers regularly reported the lack of any insurrectionary preparations, and the isolation of the Cordeliers from a large part of the sans-culottes. But the moment doubtless seemed ripe for strengthening the central power by liquidating a movement that was decidedly uncontrollable.

The report presented to the Convention by Saint-Just on 23 Ventôse denounced 'a conspiracy led from abroad, preparing famine and new fetters for the people'.[57] This reprise of the foreign theme was aimed as much against the Indulgents as against those who were to be arrested that night: he inveighed against 'the faction of Indulgents, who want to save the criminals, and the foreigners' faction, which makes a great noise because it cannot do otherwise without revealing itself, but which turns severity against the defenders of the people'. It was a long and rather confused speech, but the final decree that was unanimously adopted ordered the Revolutionary Tribunal to inform 'against the authors and accomplices of the conspiracy being hatched against the French people and its liberty'. In the night of 23–24 Ventôse, the main Cordelier leaders, Hébert, Ronsin, Vincent, Momoro and Ducroquet, were arrested.

'Amid general indifference', writes Mathiez.[58] It is true that news of the arrests was not followed by any great upset in the streets, and some of the ministry's observers even noted that it was greeted here and there with satisfaction. The few overt protests came from the most advanced sans-culottes, such as those of the Marat section where, on 26 Ventôse, the observer Pourvoyeur reported: 'Several argued for a mass procession to the Convention to demand the release of the oppressed.' By and large, the people of Paris kept their trust in the Committees, Robespierre, and the Convention. The reality of the 'horrible plot' was not questioned.

The trial opened on 1 Germinal (21 March), presided over by Dumas and with Fouquier-Tinville as public prosecutor. The twenty-one accused were a mixture of groups and individuals whose selection was calculated to justify the different charges. For the appeal to insurrection, the Cordelier leaders, Hébert, Momoro, Ronsin and Vincent, the latter supplemented by agents of the war ministry, Mazuel, Leclerc and Bourgeois; for the attempt to starve Paris, Ducroquet, supplies commissioner for the Marat section, Descombes, responsible for purchases of provisions at the

57 Saint-Just, *Œuvres complètes*, p. 675ff.

58 Mathiez, *La Vie chère*, vol. 2, p. 190.

Commune, and Ancard, who had defended the arrested leaders at the Cordeliers; for the foreign plot, Anacharsis Cloots – who had no connection with the Cordeliers, but advocated a universal republic, 'a deeply thought-out treachery that supplied a pretext for the coalition of crowned heads against France',[59] according to Renaudin, one of the thirteen jurors; also the banker Kock, Proli, and the group of agents at the foreign affairs ministry, Desfieux, Dubuisson and Pereira. A few other individuals had been thrown in, alleged to have made subversive statements.

After four days of debate, all the defendants were condemned to death except for one, Laboureau, who was an agent provocateur. They were guillotined on 4 Germinal of year II. 'It is impossible to say', noted Pourvoyeur, 'the number of persons that there were to see the conspirators pass and be guillotined. Wherever they passed, there were shouts of *Vive la République*, with hats in the air and everyone calling out some injurious epithet, especially to Hébert.'[60]

The elimination of the Cordeliers by the governing Committees was such a serious turning-point in the course of the Revolution that we must dwell a moment on its interpretations (leaving aside the formidable question as to why all revolutions, from the great English Revolution through to the Cultural Revolution in China, ended up eliminating the far left).

The simplest explanation, and the one I would call Robespierrist, presents the Cordeliers as self-seeking arrivistes moved by the desire for revenge, who risked making France into 'a demagogic, incoherent Poland, soon delivered to the European counter-revolution' (Jaurès). The guillotine, for them, was 'the alpha and omega of politics' (Mathiez). Robespierre and the Committee of Public Safety were models of patience up until the moment when they were forced to act. With all due respect for Jaurès and Mathiez, this explanation does not hold up. Robespierre and the Committees were well informed as to the situation, they therefore knew that

59 See Walter, *Actes du tribunal révolutionnaire*, pp. 426–529.

60 Caron, *Paris pendant la Terreur*, vol. 6, p. 85.

there was neither a call for armed insurrection nor a foreign plot (for several weeks they had known that this was an invention of Fabre d'Églantine). Nor could they believe that the Cordeliers were *manoeuvring* to starve Paris (exploiting the discontent caused by shortages is quite another matter).

A different explanation is offered by Soboul: there was a social confrontation between the Committees and the Cordeliers. This was 'one episode in the struggle embarked on by the Committees, from September 1793, against the popular movement, to integrate it into the Jacobin framework of bourgeois revolution'.[61] For Soboul, not the most orthodox of Marxist historians, the bourgeoisie (in this case, the Committees) was the driving force of the Revolution, and those who opposed it (the Cordeliers, the popular movement) went against the current and were therefore crushed. Soboul seems ill at ease between his genuine empathy with the sans-culottes and his 'Marxist' conception of the bourgeois revolution.

However, this interpretation also fails to convince – at least me. Robespierre, Collot d'Herbois, Saint-Just, Vadier and Le Bas were no more bourgeois than Hébert, Momoro or Carrier. If there were differences in education and trajectory, these are found equally within the two groups, and above all, none of the individuals on either side belonged to the possessor class.[62] Nor can their supporters be divided between bourgeois and sans-culottes: in Ventôse of year II, the governing Committees still enjoyed the trust of the great mass of the sans-culottes, even the 'pronounced patriots'. And the Committees were far from being supported by the 'Moderates' (who could, in a strict sense, qualify as bourgeois) who worked openly against the revolutionary government. The confrontation between Committees and Cordeliers as an episode in a class struggle is a very fragile historical construct.

What seems to me more likely is that this confrontation was *a matter of strategic priorities*, compounded by antagonisms of persons

61 Soboul, *Les Sans-Culottes parisiens*, p. 779.

62 The sole exception being Amar, who possessed a fortune. Later he was the financial backer of Babeuf's Conspiracy of Equals.

and style (it would be an idealist view of history to neglect such questions).

The strategy of Robespierre and the Committees was completely focused on the war against the foreign coalition: it had to be won before the Constitution of 1793 could be applied, and a democratic and egalitarian republic constructed. But to win the war, all forces had to be united, all centrifugal movements controlled and if necessary repressed. The strategy of the Cordeliers, on the contrary, and of the whole leading wing of the popular movement, was to advance the revolution *at home* by putting the Moderates and Indulgents out of action, failing which the counter-revolution would triumph, with consequences that would include losing the war. The two strategies were irreconcilable. The first required a central grip, a brutal one if need be, the second relied on the autonomy of the popular societies and distrust towards any government, even a revolutionary one. The clash was inevitable.

Arrest, trial and execution of Danton and his friends

No more than a week went by between the execution of the Cordeliers and the arrest of Danton, demonstrating how the government Committees saw the two affairs as connected – 'all plots are united; they are waves that seem to separate, and yet they mingle', Saint-Just had said. It is quite possible that some members of the Committees – Billaud-Varenne, Collot d'Herbois, Amar – had only agreed to send the Cordeliers to the guillotine on condition of seeing the Indulgents follow them without delay.

Danton was aware of the danger, but despite the advice of his friends (to escape, to attempt a coup against the Committees . . .) he did nothing. He was no longer the Danton of summer 1792, the man who had personified energy and boldness. Though just thirty-four years old, he was tired, almost resigned. 'In this struggle, despite the threat to his life, he seemed no more than the shadow of himself. The giant of the rostrum resembled a mere flimsy lawyer.'[63]

---

63 *Mémoires de R. Levasseur*, vol. 3, pp. 29–30.

On the night of 10 Germinal (30 March), the two Committees in joint session ordered the arrest of Danton, Philippeaux, Delacroix and Desmoulins, who would join in prison the accused in the Compagnie des Indes affair, Chabot and Fabre d'Églantine. On the morning of the 11th, the session of the Convention was stormy.[64] Legendre, a hero of the Bastille and 10 August, took the floor: 'Citizens, four members of this assembly were arrested last night; I know that Danton is among them . . . I am here to demand that the arrested members be brought to the bar, where you will hear them out, and where they will be either accused or absolved by you. I believe Danton to be as pure as I am. He has been in irons since last night; there was a fear no doubt that his answers would destroy the accusations made against him.' Loud applause, shouts of '*Vote, vote!*' Fayau, a Montagnard deputy from the Vendée, opposed Legendre's motion: 'It seems to me that the Convention can never have two weights and measures. Is there a decree stipulating that detainees must be brought to the bar to be heard? No.' He asked the Committees to make a report, on which the Convention would then pronounce.

Amid the tumult, Robespierre asked to speak:

> The question is to know whether the self-interest of a few ambitious hypocrites is to prevail over the interest of the French people . . . He [Legendre] has spoken of Danton, because he believes no doubt that a privilege attaches to this name; no, we do not want any privileges; we do not want any idols. We shall see today whether the Convention will be able to break a supposed idol that long ago turned rotten, or whether in its fall it will crush the Convention and the French people.

Robespierre recalled his own connections with Danton:

> They [the friends of Danton] believed that the memory of an old connection, an ancient faith in false virtues, would lead me to

64 A. P., vol. 87, p. 626ff.

> restrain my zeal and my passion for liberty . . . I, too, was Pétion's friend; as soon as he was unmasked, I abandoned him. I also had connections with Roland; he betrayed, and I denounced him. Danton wants to take their place, and he is no longer in my eyes anything but an enemy of the people.[65]

Saint-Just then entered the hall, and a deep silence fell. He read a long report 'on the conspiracy hatched over several years by criminal factions to absorb the French Revolution into a change of dynasty', beginning with the words: 'The revolution is in the people, and not in the renown of some individuals.'[66] In this text, which he wrote based on some notes of Robespierre's,[67] Saint-Just attacked first of all Fabre and his friends, a party 'lacking in courage, [which] conducted revolution like a theatrical plot'. It was then the turn of Danton, whom he painted as the accomplice of Mirabeau, the Lameth brothers, Philippe d'Orléans, Brissot and Dumouriez . . . all those who were or became enemies of the Revolution. He accused Danton of having slept through the night of 9–10 August [1792],[68] of having always avoided taking sides: 'In tempestuous debates, your absence and silence were a subject of indignation; you, you spoke of the countryside, the joys of solitude and idleness; but you were able to emerge from your torpor to defend Dumouriez,

65 How did Robespierre come round to treating as a 'rotten idol' the same Danton whom he had defended at the Jacobins, as we saw, only a few weeks before? How could he accept sending his dear Camille to the guillotine? To these questions, unless I am mistaken, no answers have been given.

66 Saint-Just, *Œuvres complètes*, p. 706.

67 Albert Mathiez, 'Les notes de Robespierre contre les Dantonistes' [1918], in *Études sur Robespierre*, Paris: Éditions sociales, 1958, p. 121. Mathiez shows that these notes were written by Robespierre in order to correct and improve the initial report made by Saint-Just before the two Committees met in joint session on the night of 10 Germinal; the original report has been lost. Saint-Just took up many ideas from Robespierre, and even expressions, except on Desmoulins, whom Robespierre presented as having strayed, whereas Saint-Just blamed him squarely.

68 Robespierre in these notes: 'On that fatal night, he planned to go to bed, if those around him had not forced him to report to his section, where the Marseille battalion had assembled. He spoke there energetically: insurrection was already decided and inevitable', which is rather different and probably more accurate as to what happened that night (ibid., p. 141). See on this point Lucile Desmoulins's testimony (p. 72 above).

Westermann, and the generals who were his accomplices.' Saint-Just pilloried Danton with extreme violence: 'A bad citizen, you conspired; a false friend, you spoke evil of Camille Desmoulins two days ago, an instrument that you have lost. A bad man, you compared public opinion to a woman of ill-repute; you said that honour was ridiculous, that glory and posterity were folly: maxims that were bound to reconcile the aristocracy to you; they were the maxims of Catiline.'[69]

The Convention decreed unanimously, 'and amid the most vigorous applause', the arrest of Camille Desmoulins, Hérault de Séchelles, Danton, Philippeaux and Lacroix.

Their trial began on 13 Germinal (2 April 1794). Once again, the list of the accused was an amalgam of political figures, rogues involved in financial scandals (Fabre d'Églantine, Chabot, Basire, Delaunay d'Angers, d'Espagnac), and foreigners (the Frey brothers, Gusman, Diederichsen). At the hearing of the 14th, Danton found a new verve to defend himself and counter-attack: 'I demand to measure myself against my accusers. Let them be produced for me, and I will plunge them back into the nothingness from which they should never have emerged! Vile impostors, show yourselves and I will tear off the masks that protect you from public condemnation!'[70] The audience in the hall applauded. Through the open windows, Danton's voice could be heard as far away as the quays, a crowd gathered and the jurors grew uneasy. The Committees then took the emergency decision to send Saint-Just to the Convention to obtain a decree allowing the trial to continue in the absence of the accused. 'Miserable creatures,' he said, 'they admit to their crimes by resisting the law; only criminals are afraid of an awful justice.' All the accused were condemned to death, and guillotined on 16 Germinal (5 April).

Whatever one thinks of Danton in his last phase, his dodgy friends and his political contortions, the accusation of having been a traitor from the start of the Revolution, and the emergency law voted to

69 It would seem that Saint-Just's report made no allusion to Danton's venality, a subject to which Mathiez devoted several works (in particular *La Corruption parlementaire sous la Terreur*, Paris: Armand Colin, 1927).

70 Walter, *Actes du Tribunal révolutionnaire*, p. 564.

stifle his resounding voice, make this one of the blackest moments in the whole history of the Revolution.

At the time of the Cordelier group's arrest, there was talk of adding Pache, the mayor of Paris, Bouchotte, the war minister, and Hanriot, commander of the National Guard. The Committees decided against this, but they did have Chaumette arrested on 28 Ventôse. His trial – the 'prison conspiracy' – opened on 21 Germinal (10 April). A batch of twenty-three other defendants was put together around him, some of whom might have fitted just as well into the trial of the Cordeliers, or that of the Dantonists – among them Lucile Desmoulins and Françoise Hébert, Godel (the ex-bishop of Paris), General Dillon . . . The charge against Chaumette was that he had tried to make the Commune – of which he was, to recall, *procureur général*, with Hébert as deputy – a rival to the Convention, to have used the revolutionary army to intimidate those supplying Paris, and to have propagated atheism to the point of making it an official position. After a trial of three days, Chaumette and sixteen of his fellow accused were condemned to death. Seven others, simple sans-culotte activists who had done nothing wrong, were acquitted.

CHAPTER 14

April to July 1794

The dramas of Germinal and Thermidor

It is only the victorious faction that calls itself a government, and precisely in the fact that it is a faction there immediately lies the necessity of its decline.

– Hegel, 'Absolute Liberty and Terror', *Phenomenology of Spirit*

The purge

Following the elimination of the Cordelier leaders, the revolutionary government took over the hubs of the Parisian popular movement. Pache was replaced as mayor of Paris by Fleuriot-Lescot, devoted to Robespierre. In the Commune, the citadel of the advanced patriots, another Robespierrist, Payan, was appointed national agent, and worked with the committees to purge the general council. On 15 Prairial, to fill the gaps created by dismissals, the Committee of Public Safety appointed sixteen new members, without bothering to draw them from the sections they were supposed to represent.[1]

The revolutionary army, which had recruited many sans-culottes

1 On the repression and purge, see Soboul, *Les Sans-Culottes parisiens*, pp. 823–916. Both Fleuriot-Lescot and Payan would join the Robespierrists in the tumbril the day after 9 Thermidor.

both in Paris and in the provinces, was weakened by the elimination of Ronsin. On 7 Germinal (27 March), Barère asked the Convention to vote its disbandment: 'Is it not an injury to the heroic work of the Republic's fourteen armies to give a new army the exclusive name of revolutionary army?'[2]

The war ministry, headed by Vincent with the support of Bouchotte, had been a stronghold of the sans-culottes, as we have seen. The minister was dismissed, and then, on Carnot's proposal, all other ministries were suppressed on 12 Germinal (1 April): 'I have come to propose the abolition of the entire executive council, whose existence you have felt on many an occasion to be incompatible with the republican regime.' The aim was 'to divide the exercise of particular powers in such a way that by confining the scope of each of its agents within the strictest limits, unity of leadership may be preserved'.[3] The ministries were replaced by twelve commissions, each composed of two members and a deputy minister, appointed by the Convention on the proposal of the Committee of Public Safety. These commissions were subordinate to the Committee, and had to account to it every day.[4]

Saint-Just's report 'on the general police'[5] (26 Germinal/15 April), showed once again the concern for centralization. Its first article stipulated: 'Persons detained on suspicion of conspiracy shall be transferred from all points of the Republic to the Revolutionary Tribunal of Paris'; and Article 13: 'The representatives of the people shall resort to the established authorities and may not delegate powers', that is, establish tribunals or exceptional revolutionary commissions. And, unprecedentedly, twenty-one representatives on mission were recalled at a stroke on 30 Germinal, a move that would entail heavy consequences.

During this time, the popular societies of Paris – which had been

2 A. P., vol. 87, p. 486.

3 Ibid., p. 694.

4 The twelve commissions were: civil administration, police and tribunals; public instruction; agriculture; trade and supplies; public works; public assistance; transport; finance; army; navy and colonies; arms and explosives; foreign relations.

5 Saint-Just, *Œuvres complètes*, p. 742.

created to circumvent the restrictions imposed on the sections[6] – saw their role steadily reduced. Saint-Just had already castigated them in his report of 23 Ventôse, before the arrest of the Cordeliers: 'Ever since the popular societies became filled with deceitful individuals who loudly demand their elevation to the legislature, the ministry or the general staff; ever since these societies began to contain too many government employees and too few citizens, the people have had no place in them.'[7] Under pressure, several societies decided to dissolve themselves. Others were dissolved by the local revolutionary committees – which had become, as we saw, a salaried instrument of the government. Some revolutionary commissioners in the most advanced sections – the Révolutionnaire section, the Marat section that had campaigned for insurrection, the section of Les Arcis – were sacked by the Committee of Public Safety. The Jacobins enjoined their members to resign from the sectional societies, on pain of expulsion.

It was around this time that Saint-Just wrote, in solitude, the famous note: 'The revolution is frozen; all principles have weakened; all that remains are the red bonnets worn by plotters. The exercise of terror has jaded crime, as strong liquor jades the palate.'[8]

An end to the Revolution?

Once the popular movement had been controlled and the Moderates brought to heel, the revolutionary government had its hands free to wage external war and apply its political and social ideas. In his great speech of 18 Pluviôse (5 February), 'on the principles of political morality that should guide the National Convention', Robespierre recognized the need to define these ideas: 'We have been guided, in such stormy circumstances, by a love of good and a feeling of the needs of the *patrie*, rather than by an exact theory

6 This demobilization in the sections was also the result of the most patriotic elements leaving for the armies.

7 Saint-Just, *Œuvres complètes*, p. 685.

8 Ibid., p. 1141.

and precise rules of conduct, which we had not even the leisure to draw up. *It is time to state clearly the goal of the revolution, and the conclusion we want to reach.*'[9]

For Robespierre, republic and democracy were synonymous, and democracy could only be understood as representative. He distanced himself somewhat from the thought of his beloved Rousseau: 'Democracy is a state in which the sovereign people, guided by laws which are its own work, does for itself all that it can do properly, and through delegates all that it cannot do for itself.'

'The essence of the republic or of democracy,' Robespierre continued, 'is equality.' But this equality, for him, was bound up with a notion that today strikes us as belonging to a quite different register: virtue. 'Since the soul of the Republic is virtue, equality . . ., the first rule of your political conduct should be to relate all your operations to the maintenance of equality and the development of virtue.' What kind of equality and virtue did Robespierre have in mind?

Equality clearly meant above all equality of rights ('The French are the first people in the world to have established true democracy, by calling all men to equality and the plenitude of citizens' rights'). But what about equality of condition? This question is naturally bound up with that of property. In his draft Declaration of Rights, as we noted, Robespierre had proposed a restrictive definition of the right of property, which 'can prejudice neither the safety, nor the liberty, nor the existence, nor the property of our fellows' – a formulation that did not find a place in the final Declaration, which was far more 'liberal' ('the right to enjoy and dispose freely of one's goods, revenues, the fruit of one's labour and industry').

By decreeing the confiscation of the goods of suspects to the benefit of the poor, the Ventôse decrees moved towards a certain equalization of conditions. But Saint-Just was not a leveller, and opposed any 'agrarian law' (the dividing up of land). 'I do not mean that the land of the republic should be divided up among its members; these physical means of self-government are suited only to brigands.'

---

9 Robespierre, *Virtue and Terror*, p. 109ff. My emphasis. Subsequent quotations are drawn from the same speech.

He preferred 'to determine the maximum and minimum of property, so that there is land for all'.[10] To that end, he suggested limiting the effects of inheritance and establishing a *public domain* with the estates of those who did not have direct heirs: 'The public domain is established in order to repair the misfortune of members of the social body . . . It will perhaps be said that the public domain will not suffice for the unfortunate, but they will not exist in so sincere a *patrie.*'[11] What Saint-Just and Robespierre were aiming for was the disappearance of 'disgraceful' opulence, the establishment of a public domain 'to relieve the people of the weight of taxation in times of hardship', and, more generally, the replacement of material ownership by the right to existence.

As for virtue – which stood directly in the tradition of Montesquieu's *The Spirit of the Laws*, where it chiefly meant love of equality – this has to be understood in a very different sense from that of today. It obviously did not mean petty-bourgeois virtue: among the revolutionaries, whose great model was the Roman republic, it meant *virtus*, that is, strength of mind, courage, public spirit. 'A republican government has virtue as its principle; otherwise, terror. What do they want who want neither virtue nor terror?'[12] Saint-Just asked. In Robespierre's words, 'the republican body must begin by subjecting within its own ranks all private passions to the general passion of the public good', that is, to virtue. The opposite of republican virtue was not debauchery but opportunism, selfishness, 'the abjection of the personal ego'.

In the spring of year II, the leading members of the Committee of Public Safety were determined to put an end to internal strife. 'In order to found and consolidate among us democracy, to arrive at the peaceful reign of constitutional laws, the war of liberty against tyranny must be ended, with a happy outcome to the storms of revolution', Robespierre had said on 18 Pluviôse. And Saint-Just, at the

10 Saint-Just, 'Fragments sur les Institutions républicaines', *Œuvres complètes*, pp. 1130–1. This text was not made public during Saint-Just's lifetime.

11 Ibid., pp. 1120–1.

12 Ibid., p. 1139.

end of his report 'on the general police' of 26 Germinal (15 April): 'Form civil institutions, institutions which have not been thought up yet; there is no lasting liberty without these. They sustain love of the *patrie* and the revolutionary spirit, *even when the revolution is over*.'[13]

Billaud-Varenne, early on in his report of 1 Floréal (20 April) 'on the war and the means to support it', also mentioned the end of the revolution: 'If naught but courage or an excess of despair are needed to undertake a revolution, both perseverance and wisdom are needed to conduct it well; greatness of soul and genius are also needed in order to bring it to an end.' After a long development evoking the great men of antiquity, from Coriolanus to Aemilius Paullus, Lycurgus to Themistocles, he underlined the need to educate the people by means of 'institutions apt to familiarize every citizen with the simple truths that form the elements of social happiness'. This permanent education 'is in the dignity of your deliberations; it is in the zeal and enlightened discussions of the popular societies; it is in all the places where the nation gathers; it is in the armies; it is in the example of private virtues that a father gives to his children'. And, to conclude: 'Citizens, we have promised to honour misfortune, it would be finer by far to make it disappear. Thus beggary will find its extinction in national munificence.'[14] Françoise Brunel notes how close the themes and terms used by Billaud-Varenne were to those of Saint-Just at the same time: institutions, doing good, the honour due to the unfortunate, and even the final phrase cited here, which clearly alludes to the Ventôse decrees.[15] There was indeed, at this time, political agreement at the top. But all hopes of a democratic, egalitarian and fraternal republic remained suspended until the outcome of the war on the frontiers.

13 Ibid., p. 263. My emphasis.

14 A. P., vol. 89, p. 94.

15 Brunel, *Thermidor*.

Fleurus

By the time the spring campaign began, the army was no longer the heterogeneous and poorly commanded force it had still been a year before. The unit now was the half-brigade, corresponding to the traditional regiment and made up of two battalions of volunteers and one battalion of the line, all with the same uniform and led by officers of the same rank. This army of year II, commanded, as we have seen, by generals who were very young and had in most cases risen from the ranks – Jourdan, Pichegru, Marceau, Kléber, Macdonald[16] – was larger than the armies of the Coalition, in which, moreover, as often in such cases, there was both rivalry among leaders and distrust between nations. This meant that the bulk of the Coalition forces was made up of the Austrian army commanded by Coburg, while the English and Dutch remained inactive in the north, and the Prussians were encamped in the Palatinate.

Despite this, the campaign started badly for the republicans. The Austrians broke through between the Sambre and the Escaut, between the army of the North and that of the Ardennes. At the beginning of Floréal, the besieged small town of Landrecies surrendered after four days of bombardment. The Oise gap, leading to Paris via Compiègne, lay almost open to the Imperial troops. Carnot hurriedly sent Saint-Just and Le Bas to organize an entrenched camp at Guise to block their route. Then he drew a large contingent from the Moselle army (commanded by Jourdan) to reinforce that of the Ardennes (which Pichegru commanded along with that of the North). He ordered a general offensive on two axes, a southern one towards Charleroi and a northern one towards Courtrai. The republicans reached Courtrai and defeated the Imperial forces at Tourcoing. On the Charleroi side there was bitter fighting. Led by Saint-Just, the Ardennes army crossed and recrossed the Sambre on five occasions. Finally, when Jourdan arrived with reinforcements, Charleroi capitulated. Coburg made a final effort to drive the republicans from their positions on the Sambre, but without success. Between Charleroi

16 Hoche, suspected of Hébertisme, was in prison.

and Namur, on 8 Messidor (26 June), the republican army won a decisive victory at Fleurus, opening the way to Belgium. Pichegru and Jourdan's two armies converged on Brussels, which they entered on 20 Messidor. Antwerp and Liège were taken in the first week of Thermidor. And at the same time, on all other fronts, the Rhine, the Alps and the Pyrenees, a series of victories took the war beyond the Republic's territory.

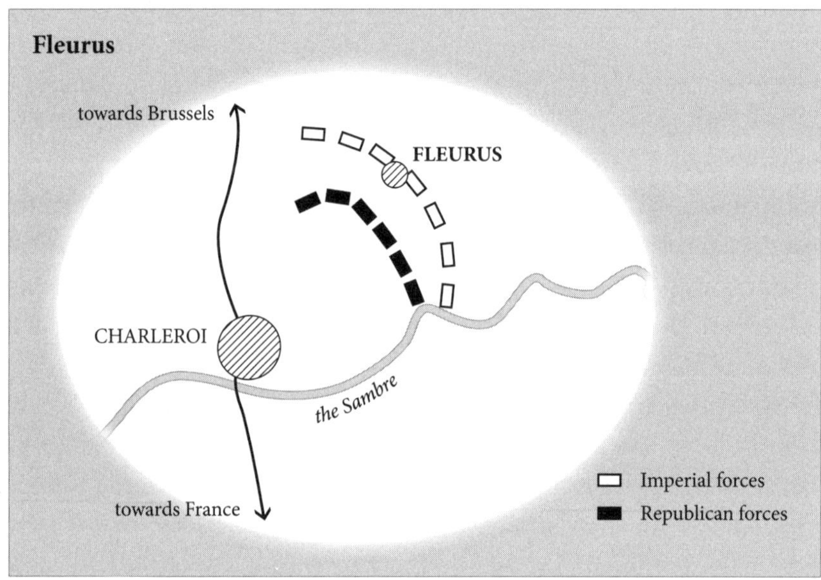

The cult of the Supreme Being; the Catherine Théot affair

Victories on the frontiers, a clearer domestic situation: in this spring of year II, one might have thought that 'the peaceful reign of constitutional laws' and 'the peaceful enjoyment of liberty and equality' were coming within reach. Instead of which, two initiatives were taken that would poison the political atmosphere, sharpen antagonisms and pave the way for the Thermidor drama: the institutionalization of the cult of the Supreme Being, and the reform of the Revolutionary Tribunal by the law of 22 Prairial.

On 18 Floréal (7 May), Robespierre delivered a long presentation to the Convention 'on the relation of religious and moral ideas to republican principles, and on national festivals'.[17] After exalting 'all the movements of the glorious revolution', he put forward the idea that 'the only foundation of civil society is morality'. This morality had been travestied by those who preached atheism: 'The same rascals that appealed to the sovereignty of the people so as to slay the National Convention, invoked hatred of superstition to bring us civil war and atheism.' Robespierre then sought to show that by breaking 'the sacred bond that unites men to the author of their being', the bases of morality are undermined: 'One must only ever attack an established religion with caution and a certain delicacy, for fear that a sudden and violent change may appear as an assault upon morality, and a dispensation from honesty itself.'

Robespierre then turned to defining the cult of the Supreme Being, distinguishing this from 'fanaticism':

> Recalling men to the pure cult of the Supreme Being means dealing a mortal blow to fanaticism. All fictions disappear before Truth, and all madness falls away before Reason. Without constraint or persecution, all sects must fuse of themselves into the universal religion of Nature . . . The true priest of the Supreme Being is Nature: his temple is the universe, his cult is virtue, his feast days, the joy of a great people gathered before his eyes to strengthen the gentle ties of universal brotherhood.

At the end of this report, the two first articles of the decree laid down: 'The French people recognizes the existence of the Supreme Being and the immortality of the soul', and 'recognizes that worship worthy of the Supreme Being consists in the practice of man's duties'.[18] Article 7 was a long list of festivals to celebrate each *décade*, honouring the Human Race, Truth, Justice, Modesty, Heroism, Maternal Tenderness, Posterity and Happiness.

---

17 Robespierre, *Œuvres complètes*, vol. 10, pp. 442–65.

18 Chief among these were: 'to detest bad faith and tyranny, punish tyrants and traitors, succour the unfortunate, respect the weak, defend the oppressed, do to others all the good that one can, and be unjust towards no one' (Article 3).

Couthon proposed to have the report not only printed (in 200,000 copies) and sent to the armies, all public bodies and all popular societies, but also reproduced on posters to be put up in the streets,[19] 'translated into every language and distributed throughout the universe'. That same evening at the Jacobins, Lequinio, an avowed atheist as we recall, praised Robespierre's report to the skies: 'One of the finest reports that has ever been delivered at the rostrum of the Convention was presented in today's session by Robespierre. Each sentence he spoke was applauded; we would have wished to applaud him each time he impressed on our souls lofty sentiments worthy of liberty.'[20] He asked for the text to be read out to the Society, which received it with rapture.

However, the move to impose the cult of the Supreme Being led to a convergence of attacks against Robespierre as a 'new pontiff'. Yet there was nothing very new about all this in Floréal year II: the June 1793 Declaration of the Rights of Man had been placed under the auspices of the Supreme Being, and even the actual cult, as defined in Robespierre's report, differed very little from the cult of Reason promoted by the dechristianizers since autumn 1793.[21] It goes without saying that the cult of the Supreme Being was not invented by Robespierre; this sort of pantheism was in the air throughout the revolutionary period. Saint-Just likewise wrote around the same time: 'The French people recognize the Supreme Being and the immortality of the soul . . . The immortal souls of those who died for the *patrie*, of those who were good citizens, who cherished their mother and father and never deserted them, lie in the breast of the Eternal.'[22]

---

19 'Thus in Clermont-Ferrand, on the façade of a lateral door to the nave of the cathedral, [it is still possible to read] "The French People recognize the Supreme Being and the immortality of the soul",' in Jean-Christophe Bailly, *Le Dépaysement*, Paris: Le Seuil, 2011, p. 339.

20 Aulard, *La Société des Jacobins*, vol. 6, p. 114.

21 Mathiez, 'Robespierre et le culte de l'Être suprême' [1910], in *Études sur Robespierre*, p. 157. Mathiez also establishes that the list of festivals every ten days (which may raise a smile today) was drawn up in full by Mathieu, deputy for the Oise, on behalf of the Committee of Public Instruction.

22 Saint-Just, 'Fragments . . .', p. 1103. It is true that he adds: 'In no civil commitment are religious considerations permitted, and any act that refers to these is null and void'.

Despite all this, Robespierre saw fit to deliver this report in a very personal fashion, which left him more exposed. Why did someone like him, who never left anything to chance, choose to do so? We can dismiss the idea of a 'pontificate', which corresponds neither to his character nor to this particular speech. The reason was rather a political one. Robespierre was aware of the risk of glaciation that threatened the revolution, expressing this in his speech of 18 Pluviôse: 'The greatest reef that we have to avoid, perhaps, is not the fervour of zeal, but rather *the lassitude of the good*, and the fear of our own courage' (my emphasis). It may be that he saw the theatrical launch of the cult of the Supreme Being as a grand design capable of concentrating revolutionary energies and galvanizing them once more.

The highpoint of this launch was the Festival of the Supreme Being on 20 Prairial (8 June). Organized by Jean-Louis David, who was a member of the Committee of General Security, this immense celebration took place in radiant sunshine. It began at the Tuileries, where representatives from the forty-eight sections were gathered, the men holding oak branches and the women flowers. At midday, the Convention appeared in a body, headed by Robespierre who had been elected to its presidency four days earlier. He delivered a first speech, then set fire to an effigy depicting Atheism that had been erected in the Grand Basin of the Tuileries gardens. A statue of Wisdom emerged from its ashes, and Robespierre, in a second speech, proclaimed: 'It has returned to nothing, that monster which the spirit of the kings spewed over France. Let all the crimes and misfortunes of the world vanish with it!'[23] A great procession then moved towards the Champ-de-Mars, where a tall symbolic Mountain had been erected. The Convention, preceded by Robespierre, climbed to the summit, where a liberty tree had been planted. The crowd chorused the refrain of an anthem composed by Gossec to words by Chénier: 'Before laying down our swords triumphant/Let us swear to annihilate crime and tyrants.' The celebration ended with a tremendous artillery barrage, and 'all the citizens, men and women'

23 A detailed description of the festival is given by Mathiez, 'Robespierre et le culte de l'Être suprême', pp. 175–80.

– according to the official account – 'mingling their sentiments in fraternal embrace, ended the festival by raising to heaven the cry of humanity and civic spirit: *Vive la République!*'

It has often been noted that even while the festival was under way, some members of the Convention voiced their irritation aloud, commenting that Robespierre walked too far in front of the other deputies and seemed transported, in a kind of ecstasy. But unless I am mistaken, there is no reliable contemporary source to confirm that Lecointre or Bourdon de l'Oise sniped at Robespierre loudly enough to be heard by him. Testimonies alleging this come from people trying to whitewash themselves after Thermidor, or to show off the courage they had displayed towards Robespierre.

What does seem well established, however, is that the 'Supreme Being' operation was poorly received by a good part of the Committee of General Security, in which there were numerous atheists and anti-clericals – Vadier, Amar, and Lavicomterie, the author of a book entitled *Les Crimes des papes depuis saint Pierre jusqu'à Pie-VI*, or Rühl, who had shattered the holy ampulla outside Reims cathedral. They feared that Robespierre, for all his sallies against priests, might engineer a resurgence of 'fanaticism' under cover of a general reconciliation.

The conflict broke out on 27 Prairial (15 June), when Vadier presented a report to the Convention, in the name of the two Committees, 'on the discovery of a new conspiracy that . . . had established a primary school of fanaticism in the rue Contrescarpe, in the Observatoire section'.[24] Vadier, one of the few leading characters in this phase of the Revolution to be more than fifty years old (he was born in 1736), remembered the days of Voltaire and Diderot. He delivered a kind of parody, making fun of religion and conspiracy-mongering at once, based on the rumpus around Catherine Théot, a poor old woman with messianic delusions:

> [Rue Contrescarpe] is the home of a sixty-nine-year-old maid named Catherine Théos [*sic*], who dares to call her religion

24 A. P., vol. 91, p. 639ff.

> Christian and herself the Mother of God. Her den attracts a swarm of bigots and fools who crowd around this ridiculous shrine. Here are hypnotists, illuminati, truculent and vaporous wretches with a cold heart for the *patrie* but a hot head, ready to upset or to betray it.

Vadier described in detail the mystery rituals around this woman, the kisses in a circle on her venerable face, 'two on the forehead, two on the temple, two on the cheeks, but the seventh, which completes the seven gifts of the Holy Spirit, is respectfully applied to her chin, on which her disciples suck with a sensuous delight'. The assembly roared with laughter, which was bound to annoy Robespierre, its recently appointed president. 'The police,' writes Mathiez, 'who had Catherine's meetings under surveillance, made her say that Robespierre was the regenerating Messiah whose advent she announced'.[25] To put an end to the whole business, Robespierre obtained a reprieve from his colleagues on the Committee of Public Safety, in the course of a session marked by violent clashes – particularly with Billaud-Varenne, who refused to go against the Convention's decree calling for prosecution of this 'Mother of God'. Thus the religious question wormed its way even into the Committee of Public Safety.

EXCURSUS: ROBESPIERRE AGAINST THE WORLD?

The cult of the Supreme Being has done much to alienate a large part of the revolutionary far left from Robespierre. For Blanqui, Robespierre was 'a perpetual and monotonous declaimer, ceaselessly intoning the words justice, virtue, reason, morality, mingled with sighs over Brutus, Cicero, Catiline, Caesar, etc.' Blanqui believed that 'the people no longer existed on 9 Thermidor, so demoralized and numbed were they by Robespierre's projects of reactionary

25 Mathiez, *La Révolution française*, vol. 3, p. 206.

dictatorship and religious reconstitution'.[26] For Daniel Guérin, Robespierre, 'a little provincial lawyer with no cases, was deeply embittered on the eve of the 1789 Revolution. And he saw the Revolution as an unhoped-for opportunity to take his revenge . . . He corresponded very well to the definition that Marx gave of the petty bourgeois.'[27] Similar verdicts are offered by those for whom the movement of the Enragés represents the high point of the Revolution, and who cannot forgive Robespierre for having managed their fall.

Let us briefly recap. Under the Constituent Assembly, as we have seen, Robespierre took up positions that were remarkably coherent and courageous – positions in which he was always in a minority and sometimes completely alone: against the property restriction on suffrage (his extraordinary speech on the silver *marc*), for the civil rights of actors and Jews, against martial law, against slavery in the colonies, against the death penalty, for the right of petition and the freedom of the press. In what country, and in what assembly, has anyone rowed so consistently against the current, and with such strength of conviction? In the first sessions of the Constituent Assembly, he was mocked for his reedy voice and his shyness, but by the end his stature was such that he was able to get the Assembly to make a sacrifice unique in history, by ruling that its members would not be eligible for the next legislature.

Under the Legislative Assembly, it was still alone that Robespierre waged his struggle against the war: even Marat, the far-seeing Marat, did not support him at first. And on 2 January 1792, in a great premonitory speech, Robespierre rehearsed one by one the disasters that the war would bring in its wake, through to military dictatorship.

Some will say that Robespierre forgot all these fine principles once

---

26 Cited by Maurice Dommanget, *Les idées politiques et sociales d'Auguste Blanqui*, Paris: Éditions Rivière, 1957, p. 310ff. My thanks to Dominique Le Nuz for pointing out to me this reference. See also Albert Mathiez, 'Notes inédites de Blanqui sur Robespierre', in *Girondins et Montagnards* [1930], Paris; Les Éditions de la Passion, 1988, p. 220ff. It has to be said that, writing these notes in the Doullens prison in 1850, Blanqui only had available to him the *Histoire des Girondins* by Lamartine – a personal enemy of his into the bargain.

27 Guérin, *La Lutte de classes*, vol. 1, p. 362.

he became the most influential figure on the Committee of Public Safety; that the apostle of liberty got rid of everyone who did not think the same as him, and that the opponent of the death penalty chopped off thousands of heads. These are old charges, raised immediately after Thermidor, when it was necessary to legitimize the elimination of a man who personified the Revolution.

'A blood-drenched tyrant', we often read. The two terms merit examination. As far as 'tyrant' goes, Robespierre was never a dictator. All the major decisions of the Committee of Public Safety were taken collectively. Even those in which Robespierre's personal role is most conspicuous bear the signatures of those members of the Committee who were present.[28] When Robespierre found himself in a minority on the Committee, he withdrew his proposal (for example with the justice committee that he proposed against Camille Desmoulins's clemency committee). One could say that within the Committee Robespierre exercised a moral leadership, but can he be reproached for what was simply his elevated perspective?

The proof that Robespierre was not a dictator is his end (to anticipate slightly). Isolated and at bay, he let himself be brought down – it could even be said that he went to the slaughter. A dictator, a Bonaparte, would have behaved rather differently.

As for 'blood-drenched', there are many instances when Robespierre intervened to save lives. He was opposed, as we saw, to the prosecution of the sixty-three Convention members who had protested against 31 May ('The National Convention must not seek to multiply the guilty'). His tenacity on this point, and others, led to his being accused of *modérantisme* on many occasions.

It remains true that he contributed greatly to sending the Cordeliers group and the Dantonists to the guillotine. But many indirect signs suggest that he found it deeply painful to stand at the centre of that death-dealing vortex – a pain that led to his illness, fatigue and

28 After Thermidor, some members of the Committee of Public Safety, seeking to defend themselves against the accusation of Robespierrism, maintained that they had not been party to this decision or that (Billaud-Varenne and Barère, for example, claimed that they had had nothing to do with the Prairial laws, whereas they had actually championed these in the Convention).

absences. (After he defended Boulanger at the Jacobins, the account of proceedings indicates that 'Robespierre was obliged to stop speaking, his physical resources did not permit him to continue.')[29] How could it have been otherwise in the case of Danton, to whom he had sent such affectionate letters at the time of the death of his first wife, or of Camille, his fellow pupil at Louis-le-Grand and whose marriage he had attended as a witness?

Neither a dictator nor a cruel man, Robespierre did however play a major role in bringing the popular movement to heel in the winter and spring of year II. He worked to dissolve the Enragés group, he put a decisive brake on dechristianization and, along with other members of the Committee of Public Safety, sent the Cordeliers group to the guillotine. By these actions, he contributed to 'freezing' the Revolution. If there were a court of History, that would be the main charge against him.

Robespierre was certainly not the infallible leader described by Mathiez, but he was still an impressive and tragic figure. Revolutionary posterity, as we have seen, has not always understood him. Yet in no. 40 of his *Tribun du peuple*, Babeuf wrote: 'It is not for me to proudly compete with the claim of Maximilien Robespierre to having initiated, during the Revolution, the project of real Equality, which he showed a hundred times was the goal of all his desires. Such is the fair due I believe is owed to that *tyrant*, whose remains and effects the State has just sold for a sum of 300 livres.'[30]

The Prairial law

The Festival of the Supreme Being was held on 20 Prairial; the Prairial law that reorganized the Revolutionary Tribunal dates from the 22nd

29 Aulard, *La Société des Jacobins*, vol. 5, p. 686. Boulanger was accused of having backed the idea of insurrection at the Cordeliers. Robespierre replied that 'the greatest danger would be to confuse patriots with the cause of the conspirators.'

30 5 Ventôse year IV (24 February 1796). Cited by Mathiez, 'Babeuf et Robespierre', in *Études sur Robespierre*, p. 247. For a while, Babeuf rejoiced in the fall of Robespierre, but he rapidly changed his mind.

(10 June). If these two events are described here separately, this is only in the interest of a clear account, as they were almost simultaneous in the accelerated pace of the spring of year II.

The Prairial law and what is generally accepted as its consequence, the 'great Terror', are at once very well known and very hard to comprehend. What is certain is that on 22 Prairial, Couthon presented a report to the Convention in which he began by listing the operational defects of the existing system of repression: 'Counter-revolutionary perfidy has hidden beneath a veil of hypocritical delicacy its plan to ensure the impunity of conspirators; it has been murdering the people with false humanity, and betraying the *patrie* by its scruples.' He went on to explain the principles of the reorganization of the Revolutionary Tribunal: 'The delay in punishing the enemies of the *patrie* must be no more than the time needed to recognize them; it is less a matter of punishing than of annihilating them . . . Indulgence towards them is an atrocity, clemency is parricide.'[31]

The lengthy final decree spelled out the composition of the new tribunal, divided into four sections, with twelve judges and fifty jurors. It was 'established to punish the enemies of the people', ten varieties of whom were listed. Some of these were clear enough (those who 'called for the restoration of the monarchy, or sought to debase or dissolve the Convention'); others sound more abusive to our ears ('those who have sought to mislead public opinion and prevent the instruction of the people, to deprave manners and corrupt public consciousness . . .'). The evidence required was 'documents of any kind, whether material, moral, or written . . . The rule for verdicts is the conscience of the jurors, enlightened by love of the *patrie*.' There would be no defenders or witnesses, 'unless this formality should appear necessary'. If the accused was not acquitted, the only penalty was death.

This bill triggered a stormy debate. Ruamps, a deputy for the Charente and a convinced Montagnard, exclaimed: 'This decree is important, I demand its printing and a postponement. If it were adopted without postponement, I would blow my brains out.' The

31 *Le Moniteur*, vol. 20, p. 694ff.; A. P., vol. 91, p. 483.

postponement was supported by several votes, and Robespierre was obliged to leave the president's chair for the rostrum: 'Two strongly pronounced opinions are held in the Republic, citizens; one aspires to punish severely and inescapably the crimes committed against liberty . . . The other is the cowardly and criminal opinion of the aristocracy, which, since the start of the Revolution, had not ceased to demand, whether directly or indirectly, an amnesty for the conspirators and the enemies of the *patrie*.' The decree was adopted.

The following day, however, Bourdon de l'Oise, a leading figure of the 'right opposition', expressed his disquiet concerning Article 10, according to which 'No individual may be brought to the Revolutionary Tribunal except by the National Convention, the Committee of Public Safety, the Committee of General Security, the representatives of the people serving as commissioners of the Convention, and the public prosecutor.' He proposed decreeing that the Convention 'did not intend to infringe the laws that prevent any representative of the people from being brought before the Revolutionary Tribunal without a warrant against him having first being issued by the Convention'.[32] On 24 Prairial, first Delacroix and then Mallarmé criticized, quite sensibly, the vagueness of certain formulations: 'It is necessary in a republican government,' said Mallarmé, 'that [the laws] can be understood even by children. I ask the Committee of Public Safety to tell us what it understands by the words conspirators, defenders, and patriotic jurors.' A testy exchange between Bourdon and Robespierre ensued. Bourdon: 'The Committee of Public Safety has reproached me for my speech yesterday, and in giving me this reprimand told me I talked like Pitt and Coburg. If I were to take the same liberty in replying to them, where would we then be?' Robespierre denounced 'the hypocrites who seek to draw off a section of the Montagne and make themselves leaders of the party'. When Bourdon defended himself in personal terms, he attracted a thundering reply: 'I did not name Bourdon. Woe to him who names himself!' In the end, the decree was adopted with minor amendments.

32 A. P., vol. 91, p. 528.

The great unknown, which divides historians, is the reason that impelled Robespierre and the Committee of Public Safety to take the initiative of such a dreadful law, at a time when the horizon was actually growing brighter.[33] The explanation most often advanced – by Mathiez and Lefebvre in particular[34] – takes as its starting point an attempted assassination: on 1 Prairial (20 May), a certain Admirat, armed with two pistols, had lain fruitlessly in wait for Robespierre. Finally deciding to return home, he ran into Collot d'Herbois, shot at him and missed. Three days later, a girl by the name of Cécile Renault called at the Duplays' house and insisted on seeing Robespierre. Two small knives were found on her. Before the Committee of General Security, she declared: 'I desire a king, because I would rather one than fifty thousand, and I only went to see Robespierre in order to see how a tyrant was made.'

For Georges Lefebvre, 'emotional reaction . . . makes it possible to explain the chain of events. The [assassination] attempts at the beginning of Prairial fuelled a fresh flare-up of punitive excitation among supporters of the revolutionary government.' In Robespierre's eyes and those of the government, 'the attacks seemed to herald a general offensive against the Committees, in which what still remained of the suppressed "factions" joined forces with the counter-revolution: the "foreign plot" was reborn.'[35]

But Admirat and Cécile Renault were only poor wretches, pitiful *déclassés*. The government could not seriously see them as agents of an international conspiracy, the armed hirelings of Pitt, that 'enemy of the human race'. Besides, when one Rousselin proposed at the Jacobins club to provide the members of the Committee of Public Safety with personal bodyguards (which would have been effective

---

33 It is sometimes claimed that the Prairial laws were promulgated when the Fleurus victory had already transformed the situation on the northern front. This is incorrect: Fleurus dates from 8 Messidor (28 June), and so eight days after 22 Prairial (20 June), when the outcome of the campaign was still uncertain. It was no more certain at the time of the tumbrils of the 'great Terror'.

34 Mathiez, *La Révolution française*, vol. 3, p. 197ff.; Georges Lefebvre, 'Sur la loi de prairial an II' [1951], in *Études sur la Révolution française*, Paris: Presses Universitaires de France, 1963, pp. 108–37.

35 Ibid., pp. 120 and 123.

against further attacks), Robespierre strongly opposed any such measure, 'which tends to cast disfavour on them [the members of the Committee], to attract envy and slander by showering honours on them, isolating them in order to make them lose esteem and to turn against them everything that hatred can invent'.[36]

The difficulty in understanding the Prairial law results above all from the manner in which it is presented: a connection is implicitly accepted between the *intentions* of those who proposed it and the *consequences* it is supposed to have brought in its train, that is, an accelerated repression. As if, by proposing the reorganization of the Revolutionary Tribunal, Robespierre and the Committee of Public Safety had programmed the 'great Terror'. But in fact there are many reasons to treat the law as one thing and its consequences as another, if not separate then at least distinct.

The Prairial law reinforced the centralization of power, which had steadily increased since the great law of 14 Frimaire. The essential point is that it must be situated in a logical continuity with the Ventôse decrees and Saint-Just's report on the general police of 26 Germinal (15 April), in which, as we saw, the Paris Revolutionary Tribunal was charged with judging suspects from all over the country, with the result that the provincial revolutionary tribunals were suppressed. In the interim, the Committee of Public Safety had made one exception to this decree: on 10 Floréal (10 May), to avoid transferring to Paris the enormous number of suspects from the Midi, a decree established a 'popular commission' in Orange, whose operation prefigured the Prairial law[37] – which decidedly did not come about as an emergency law voted under the sway of emotion.

Certain aspects of the law itself did not necessarily imply an accentuation of the Terror. It did lay down that the Tribunal had no other choice than acquittal or death, but the suspects whom it was to judge had to be *screened in advance* by six commissions, with the power to have the prosecution dropped if the charges seemed insufficiently

36 Aulard, *La Société des Jacobins*, vol. 6, p. 153.

37 The only penalty was death, the evidence required being 'any information, of whatsoever kind, that may convince a reasonable man and a friend of liberty'.

well-founded.[38] As for the two aspects of the law that strike us today as particularly unacceptable, the absence of a defence lawyer and the suppression of witnesses, this was no great change from the earlier situation, when defenders were scarcely listened to and witnesses were almost always for the prosecution.

It remains the case that, in the weeks following the passage of this law, executions were stepped up in a properly terrifying way: from 23 Prairial to 8 Thermidor, the Revolutionary Tribunal pronounced 1,284 death sentences and acquitted only 278 of the accused, whereas in the forty-five previous days it had pronounced 577 condemnations against 182 acquittals. (To interpret these figures correctly, however, it should be taken into account that the Paris Revolutionary Tribunal was now the only one of its kind; we should subtract from the number of Paris condemnations, therefore, those that would have been pronounced during the same period by the provincial tribunals – something that is clearly impossible.)

On 29 Prairial (17 June), a heterogeneous group of fifty-four prisoners, including Admirat and Cécile Renault, mounted the scaffold. They were dressed in the red smock of the parricide, a theatrical gesture that, in Thermidor propaganda, referred obliquely to Robespierre, the 'father of the *patrie*'. Following this, allegations of prison plots, escape attempts and the misdeeds of the elusive baron de Batz were the excuse to send vast numbers to the guillotine: seventy-three Bicêtre inmates were executed on 28 Prairial and 8 Messidor, 146 prisoners from the Luxembourg between 19 and 22 Messidor (10 July), forty-six from the Carmes on 5 Thermidor, and seventy-six from Saint-Lazare over the three following days.[39] The guillotine had been moved from the place de la Révolution (now Concorde) to the barrière du Trône Renversé (now place de la Nation). The almost daily passage of tumbrils through the faubourg Antoine aroused pity and despair. 'There were murmurs on all side', wrote a traveller from Lyon, 'and above all in the faubourg

38 Out of the six commissions, only two were established in Paris, and these only began operation in the first days of Thermidor.

39 Brunel, *Thermidor*, p. 71.

Saint-Antoine, which was not pleased to see fifty heads fall each day from the class of unfortunate sans-culottes.'[40]

How can this hecatomb be explained? For Georges Lefebvre, a 'punitive excitation', like that of September 1792, 'turned against the prisons; this time it did not lead to a massacre: the Committees would not have allowed it, and official repression pre-empted it'[41] – an update of Danton's formula: 'Let us be terrible, to prevent the people from being so.' For Mathiez, as for Jean-Clément Martin, the great Terror was due to the sabotaging of the law of 22 Prairial, organized by the Committee of General Security to discredit Robespierre once and for all. 'This "scaffold nausea" rebounded on Robespierre at that moment – and for the rest of history.'[42] To both these explanations, which certainly contain a part of truth, we might also add the momentum of a judicial machine that got wildly carried away, egged on by a pair of activists, the public prosecutor Fouquier-Tinville and Dumas, the president of the Revolutionary Tribunal.

Tension over wages

As well as this 'nausea', there were problems with provisions and wages, particularly sensitive subjects in Paris, where the popular movement, no matter how supervised, had not completely lost its vitality.

There was no absolute shortage like the previous year, even if soap and meat were scarce. But the measures taken by the government to make the maximum more flexible led to a rise in prices.[43] Pourvo-

---

40 Cited by Lefebvre, 'Sur la loi de prairial an II', p. 130.

41 Ibid., p. 126.

42 Martin, *Violence et Révolution*, pp. 229–30. Among recent examples that make Robespierre responsible for the 'bloodbath', see one of the most recent biographies, that by Ruth Scurr, *Fatal Purity, Robespierre and the French Revolution*, New York: Metropolitan Books, 2006: 'He bears direct responsibility for the Law of 22 Prairial, which was designed to both speed up and expand the Revolutionary Tribunal's work. In this simple, technical, legal sense, his hands are covered in blood. It does not matter which, or how many, individuals he intervened personally to save at the eleventh hour' (p. 297).

43 On 1 Germinal, the municipality posted a new list of maximums, with higher

yeur, whom we quoted before, noted that 'the people are murmuring: "Ah! Things can't go on like this! It's just us poor devils who suffer from all this; as for the rich, what do they care if everything is so dear, they lack for nothing!"'[44]

The effects of the price rise were aggravated by the question of wages. During the winter, the maximum wage (which, we recall, was set at the level of 1790 increased by half) had been very widely breached under popular pressure. The observer Grivel noted in a report of 28 Nivôse that 'objects of basic necessity for [workers] have only slightly increased in price, whereas their wages have tripled or quadrupled. A worker or clerk who used to earn only four or five livres a day now earns twenty or twenty-four livres and sometimes more.'[45] At the beginning of Floréal (end of April), the Commune tried to bring wages back to the legal maximum. The municipality sent in the police against the workers who were causing trouble or even going on strike. After the tobacco grinders, the 'united' workers' leaders at the Paris ports were arrested on the orders of the Commune (9 Floréal/28 April), which equated their organization with a reconstitution of the banned corporations. On 19 Prairial (7 June), the Committee of Public Safety had the workers' leaders in the war factories imprisoned; these were subject to a quasi-military regime, and particularly disgruntled as their wages had been held by decree to the legal minimum. On a report from Barère (22 Prairial), the Convention directed the public prosecutor to pursue 'counter-revolutionaries engaged in criminal manoeuvres in the workshops manufacturing *assignats*, arms, gunpowder and saltpetre'.[46] Finally, on 5 Thermidor, the municipality set a maximum wage to apply throughout the commune of Paris, a measure that infuriated the salaried population as it meant a reduction that was in many cases substantial. This wage cap would have a major influence on the behaviour of the sections on the night of 9 Thermidor.

---

prices than those set earlier.

44 Caron, *Paris pendant la Terreur*, vol. 3, p. 65.

45 Cited by Mathiez, *La Vie chère*, p. 221.

46 Soboul, *Les Sans-Culottes parisiens*, p. 948.

Dissension between the two Committees and within the Committee of Public Safety

It was against this backdrop that the final struggle was played out that would culminate in the drama of 9 Thermidor. Many points remain obscure because, as Françoise Brunel emphasizes, the sources are hardly reliable.[47] We do have the newspapers, the reports of the Convention's sessions – written up after the event – and those of the Jacobins, but not those of meetings of the governing Committees, which did not keep formal records. And no more than doubtful fragments remain of discussions and confrontations in private rooms or in the corridors of the Convention. What has come down to us is chiefly from post-Thermidor, and thus biased, sources: denunciations of the most visible members of the former Committee of Public Safety – Barère, Billaud-Varenne, Collot d'Herbois; their efforts to save their skins by showing how they resisted the 'tyrant'; the bragging of those who, like Lecointre, played up their valiance vis-à-vis Robespierre; and finally, memoirs written long after the events.[48] In these documents the cowardice of some, the dignity of certain others, fear and the desire for revenge all transpire; but as to what actually happened, interpretation has to be cautious.

On the Convention after the fall of the 'factions', Levasseur wrote:

> Weakened by its dissensions, the Montagne no longer enjoyed a strong majority within the Convention, and this majority was itself fractured into a large number of shades of opinion, each of which had victims to mourn. The revolutionary government was

---

47 Brunel, *Thermidor*, p. 44.

48 Among the post-Thermidor documents most often cited, the majority date from year III and were published by order of the Convention: L. Lecointre, *Les Crimes de sept membres des anciens comités de Salut public et de Sûreté générale, ou dénonciation formelle à la Convention nationale contre Billaud-Varenne, Barère, Collot d'Herbois, Vadier, Vouland, Amar et David* (BHVP, 950217); *Réponse des membres de l'ancien Comité de Salut public dénoncés, aux pièces communiquées par la Commission des vingt et un* (BHVP, 955817); C. Duval, *Projet de procès-verbal des séances des 9, 10 et 11 thermidor* (BHVP, 600446); E. M. Courtois, *Rapport sur les événements du 9 thermidor an II* (BHVP, 603651); J. Vilate, *Causes secrètes de la Révolution du 9 au 10 thermidor*, Paris: Langlois, vendémiaire an III.

> thus no longer supported by anything but the divisions of its enemies; it was strong only on account of the irrevocable hatreds that separated the friends of Danton from the former supporters of Hébert, and the Montagne from the debris of the Gironde.[49]

Among the enemies of the revolutionary government, a first group was comprised of former Dantonists, who had been heard to protest against the Prairial law and defend what today would be called the 'parliamentary immunity' of the Convention deputies. The most vocal among them were Bourdon de l'Oise, Lecointre, Thuriot and Legendre. These future 'right-wing Thermidorians' demanded the reform of the Revolutionary Tribunal and an end to the Terror.

The representatives on mission, recalled en masse, did not form a group in the strict sense; what united them was fear. Robespierre had criticized some of them for their brutality in the repression of 'federalism', others for their complacency towards atheism, and others again for a lifestyle of corrupt and debauched proconsuls – certain individuals combined several of these grounds for reproach. For Mathiez, 'little by little a subterranean opposition formed, with fear as its motive and mortar . . . Fréron, Barras, Tallien and Fouché, who would become [Robespierre's] most redoubtable adversaries, visited him and wrote him imploring letters. He could, by reassuring them, have had them at his feet. But he spurned them with contempt. What is more, he made no secret of the fact that he intended to have them punished.'[50]

But these two oppositions would have been powerless if the Committees had remained homogeneous and united among themselves. Instead, as Sénart wrote,

---

49 *Mémoires de R. Levasseur*, vol. 3, p. 71. Despite being written thirty-five years after the events, Levasseur's memoirs offer a valuable testimony. The honest Levasseur seeks neither to allot himself a fine role nor to excuse himself. He was a 'critical Robespierrist', a rarity at this time.

50 Mathiez, *La Révolution française*, vol. 3, p. 196. The particular case of Tallien is well known: what mattered for him was to save the life of his mistress, Thérésa Cabarrus, in prison since 3 Prairial on a warrant from the Committee of Public Safety signed by Robespierre.

> These two committees were both opposed to each other, and internally divided . . . In the Committee of Public Safety, Robespierre, Couthon and Saint-Just formed one group, Barère, Billaud and Collot d'Herbois another, and Carnot, Prieur and Lindet a third group again. In the Committee of General Security, Vadier, Amar, Jagot and Louis (of the Bas-Rhin) formed one group, David and Le Bas another, Moïse Bayle, Lavicomterie, Élie Lacoste and Dubarran a third. Each group had a name: Robespierre's set was known as 'the people in charge', Vadier's as 'the energetic ones', Billaud's as 'the revolutionaries', Lindet's as 'the examiners', David's as 'the listeners' and that of Moïse Bayle as 'the counterweights'. These somewhat peculiar monikers were common currency.[51]

Even though the antagonisms cut across one another, the key point is the increasing hostility of the Committee of General Security towards the Committee of Public Safety, to which it was legally subordinate.[52] The anti-clericals and atheists, who were in a strong position in General Security, were dismayed by the officializing of the cult of the Supreme Being, and it was from their ranks, as we saw, that the Catherine Théot affair emerged, a device mounted against Robespierre.[53] A further important grievance was that the Committee

---

51 G. J. Sénart, *Révélations puisées dans les cartons des comités de salut public et de sûreté générale*, Paris: Dumesnil, 1824, cited by Buchez and Roux, vol. 33, p. 8. Sénart relates what he heard in the milieu of the members of the Committee of General Security, for which he was an agent.

52 See on this point Michel Eude, 'Le Comité de sûreté générale en 1793–1794', *AHRF*, 1985, no. 261, p. 295.

53 In 'The 9 Thermidor: motives and effects' (in Jones (ed.), *The French Revolution in Social and Political Perspective*, Martyn Lyons makes the interesting remark that many of Robespierre's enemies on the Committee of General Security were from the Midi: Moïse Bayle from Marseille, Vadier and Barère from the Pyrenees, Amar from Grenoble, Voulland from Uzès, Jagot from the Ain, Lacoste from Dordogne, and Dubarran from the Gers. 'The southern origins of the Thermidorians is in striking contrast to the predominantly northern Robespierrists (the Auvergnat Couthon provides the exception). This is of more than academic interest. Robespierre, who had never been south of the Loire, had no experience of the situation in the Midi. He did not know the strength of popular Catholicism in the South-West, or of counter-revolutionary Royalism in Marseille, except at second hand. For the Thermidorians [the members of the Committee of General Security who acted against

of General Security had not been involved with drafting the law of 22 Prairial – its members, moreover, kept a significant silence during the rowdy sessions of 23 and 24 Prairial.

Robespierre and his supporters, for their part, criticized the way in which the Committee of General Security exercised its police functions, not hesitating to use agents of doubtful republican loyalty to infiltrate counter-revolutionary milieus. For Robespierre, 'any informer who acts only from a motive of self-interest, in hopes of a reward, is a false republican.'[54] In his speech of 8 Thermidor, he would say: 'I tremble when I think that enemies of the Republic, and former professors of monarchy, and ex-nobles, émigrés perhaps, have suddenly turned into revolutionaries and made themselves into agents of the Committee of General Security to take revenge on the friends of the *patrie* for the birth and success of the Republic.'[55]

It was perhaps this mistrust that lay at the root of another contentious issue between the Committees: the creation on 27 Germinal, following Saint-Just's report on the police, of a Bureau of Administrative Surveillance and General Policing, responsible to the Committee of Public Safety. True, its role was simply to 'inspect the authorities and public agents charged with cooperating with the administration' (Article 5 of the decree), but the Committee of General Security could only interpret it as an encroachment on its terrain, a dispossession.

Even within the Committee of Public Safety there was discord. Violent quarrels over military tactics broke out between Saint-Just and Carnot. After the battle of Fleurus, from which he had just returned, Saint-Just criticized Carnot for having ordered, without consulting him, 18,000 men to be detached from the army of Sambre-et-Meuse for an expedition to the Atlantic coast. According

---

Robespierre], Robespierre's policy of religious conciliation was a surrender in the face of the enormous strength of the counter-revolution in the Midi . . . In their opinion, . . . Robespierre did not realize that vigorous measures against the clergy were essential to the defence of the Republic in the Ariège, the Gers, and the Gard' (pp. 408–9).

54 *Papiers trouvés chez Robespierre*, cited by Lyons, 'The 9 Thermidor', note 13.

55 Robespierre, *Œuvres complètes*, vol. 10, p. 557.

to him, had the order been carried out Jourdan could never have won his great victory at Fleurus.[56]

Stranger than this, and more serious for the course of events, was the growing friction between Billaud-Varenne and Robespierre. Strange, as their positions were fundamentally close. On the origin of this quarrel we have, unless I am mistaken, no really trustworthy source. Billaud-Varenne had never forgiven Robespierre for his hesitation in sending Danton before the Revolutionary Tribunal. It would have been hard for him to swallow his exclusion from drafting the law of 22 Prairial.[57] He reputedly criticized Robespierre for violating the Convention decree that accused Catherine Théot. All this is quite probable, but what emerges most clearly from the accounts of their altercations and from Billaud's defence after Thermidor, I believe, is the personal dislike between the two characters – both of them dour, plain-spoken, abrupt and haughty. And Billaud, as we saw, would play a key role in the drama of Thermidor, enabling Martyn Lyons to see this as actually *a revolution from the left* – a paradoxical view, but not altogether unreasonable.[58]

Rumours and 'plot'

From late Prairial to the beginning of Messidor (throughout June, that is), successive episodes betrayed a hardening of antagonisms.

---

56 Aside from personal antipathies, they were opposed on a basic question: Carnot wanted a war of conquest in Flanders, waged by a professionalized army, whereas for Saint-Just the war should only be defensive.

57 'The day after 22 Prairial, in the morning session [of the Committee of Public Safety], Billaud-Varenne accused Robespierre aloud as soon as he entered the session, reproaching him for having taken to the Convention, alone with Couthon, the abominable decree that terrified patriots. It was, he said, against all principles and the regular course of the Committee to present a draft decree without communicating it to the Committee . . . "I see clearly that I am alone, and that no one supports me," said Robespierre, and immediately flew into a rage . . . He shouted so loud that several citizens gathered on the Tuileries terraces. The window was closed, and the discussion continued as hotly as before' (*Réponse des membres de l'ancien Comité de salut public*, note 8).

58 '9 Thermidor, seen so often as the work of reactionaries, was interpreted by the Comité de Sûreté Générale and by its main authors as a revolution of the Left' (Lyons, 'The 9 Thermidor', p. 397).

The Théot affair was followed by that of the Indivisibilité section, in the context of the quelling of the Paris sections by the purged municipality. The commissioners of this section were denounced by the president of the general assembly for preaching atheism and announcing the imminent restoration of the section societies. In the margin of the report from the police bureau to the Committee of Public Safety, Robespierre noted on 6 Messidor: 'Arrest all those named in this article.' The twelve commissioners were arrested on 9 Messidor, and the warrant for the order of their arrest was signed by Robespierre alone. This affair led to serious altercations between the governing Committees, until eventually, on 21 Messidor (9 July), a joint decree by the two Committees freed the Indivisibilité commissioners. The same day, to complete its revenge, the Committee of General Security had that section's president arrested for slanderous denunciation.[59]

The affair of the Paris gunners would further envenom the political atmosphere. These had always been ardent sans-culottes, devoted to Hanriot, the commander-in-chief of the National Guard and a loyal supporter of Robespierre. When Carnot ordered six companies of these gunners to be sent to the army of the North, it was perceived as a bid to strip Paris of its most determined and effective popular militants.

As of 15 Messidor (3 July), Robespierre ceased attending the Committee of Public Safety, which went down badly with most of his colleagues. He did not reappear until 5 Thermidor, after twenty days of absence. In his speech of 8 Thermidor he explained the reasons for this retreat: 'I shall confine myself to saying that for more than six weeks, the nature and force of calumny, the impossibility of doing good and stopping harm, forced me to absolutely desist from my functions as a member of the Committee of Public Safety, and I swear that in this I consulted only my reason and my *patrie*.'[60]

---

59 Soboul, *Les Sans-Culottes parisiens*, pp. 973–4. On 9 Thermidor, Billaud-Varenne criticized Robespierre for the arrest of 'the best revolutionary committee in Paris, that of the Indivisibilité section'.

60 Robespierre, *Œuvres complètes*, vol. 10, p. 565. Robespierre spoke of 'six weeks', which was inexact.

It was at the Jacobins that he chose to express himself from then on, with his offensive vigour intact. Already on 13 Messidor, he almost openly attacked his hostile colleagues: 'In London I am denounced to the French army as a dictator; the same slanders have been repeated in Paris: *you would tremble if I told you where* . . . In Paris it is said that it was I who organized the Revolutionary Tribunal, that this tribunal was organized to murder patriots and members of the Convention; I am depicted as a tyrant and an oppressor of the national representation.'[61]

Ten days later, the session of the Jacobins was devoted to a homage to the Lyon friends of Chalier. Robespierre laid into Dubois-Crancé: 'They [the conspirators] left by the gate where the army corps commanded by Dubois-Crancé was stationed, but it remained immobile.' Dubois-Crancé was expelled from the Jacobins on a motion from Couthon, and Fouché, likewise challenged, was summoned to 'vindicate himself before the Society of the reproaches addressed to him'.[62] On 26 Messidor, when Fouché had failed to respond to this summons, Robespierre spoke: 'I begin by declaring that Fouché as an individual is of no interest to me. I did once associate with him, because I believed him a patriot; when I denounced him here, it was less on account of his past crimes than because he is committing others out of sight, and because I regard him as the leader of the conspiracy that we have to foil.'[63] With that, Fouché too was expelled from the Jacobins.

During these highly tense weeks, public life in Paris is described in many contemporary (and Thermidorian) accounts as a time of generalized fear and suspicion. There were said to be lists of proscriptions drawn up by Robespierre, including both the most compromised representatives on mission and the most visible ex-Dantonists.[64]

---

61 Buchez and Roux, *Histoire parlementaire*, vol. 33. My emphasis.

62 Ibid., pp. 341–2.

63 Ibid., p. 345.

64 Robespierre alluded to this on 8 Thermidor: 'Is it true that hateful lists have been presented, naming a number of members of the Convention, which are claimed to be the work of the Committee of Public Safety, and subsequently to be my work?' In his *Mémoires*, the Convention deputy Levasseur from the Sarthe wrote: 'The enemies of this famous man carefully nourished this unfounded belief; they circulated lists of proscribed men, including

> No deputy dared to go out unarmed. All carried a pair of pistols, or, more discreetly, a dagger like Tallien, or, if they had not entirely lost the habits of a *grand seigneur*, a sword-stick like Amar. Robespierre never left his house unless accompanied by a body-guard, usually composed of the jury of the Revolutionary Tribunal . . . Robespierre's spy followed Thuriot and Bourdon of the Oise during Messidor, and Tallien, too, was followed. According to one of his acquaintance, Fouché slept at a different address every night to escape arrest. Vadier, President of the *Comité de Sûreté Générale*, put his own spy Taschereau on Robespierre, but Taschereau betrayed him, preferring to report to Robespierre on Vadier's movements.[65]

Since primary sources for this period are rare, or have still been little studied, one may well wonder, with Françoise Brunel,[66] whether this background noise was not strongly amplified after Thermidor, with a twofold intent: to stress the dangers incurred by the Thermidorians and the courage they had displayed, and to legitimize the fall of the 'tyrant', as the only possible way out of such an intolerable situation.

This period also invites a further question: was there really a *plot* to get rid of Robespierre, or is this again a post-Thermidorian story? For Mathiez, there was no doubt that Thermidor was prepared by an understanding between those whom he calls 'the leading Montagnards', led by Tallien and Fouché, and the floating mass of the Convention, the Marais or marsh. Gérard Walter is so sure of it that he entitled his book *La Conjuration du Neuf Thermidor*.[67] Martyn Lyons believes that there were enough common interests among Robespierre's opponents to explain their union against him – and many other examples could also be cited in support of the plot theory.

This theory rests largely on the memoirs of Fouché and Barras,

---

figures from all parties, and these lists were always presented as the work of Robespierre' (*Mémoires de R. Levasseur*, vol. 3, p. 77).

65 Lyons, 'The 9 Thermidor', p. 399.

66 Brunel, *Thermidor*, p. 81.

67 Gérard Walter, *La Conjuration du Neuf Thermidor*, Paris: Gallimard, 1974.

which are a tissue of fabrications – especially when covering this particular period – as well as on the boastings of Lecointre and Tallien. To anticipate a little, it is certainly possible that, on the evening of 8 Thermidor, the most implicated of the proconsuls agreed together on the line they would take the next day; but does this really add up to a plot? The hypothesis of a broad conspiracy involving the proconsuls, members of the Committees and deputies of the Plaine, has the support of prestigious historians,[68] but it rests on sources that are after the event and of debatable reliability. Hostilities were opened by Tallien during the session of 9 Thermidor, and immediately taken up by Billaud-Varenne. Yet in the preceding weeks Billaud had expressed publicly and in a threatening way his utter contempt for the dubious character that was Tallien; a prior understanding between these two men is more than unlikely.[69]

The attempt at reconciliation

Over and above these reservations as to the truth of *rumours* and the existence of a *plot*, several witnesses do report a situation too tense to last. The noisy rifts within the revolutionary government spread into the provinces, arousing an alarm that became general. Barère, an expert in reconciliation, now sought to bring the Committees and Robespierre together. It was probably at his instigation that the two Committees met in plenary session on 4 Thermidor, still in the absence of Robespierre.[70] Their decree, drafted by Barère, was a notable surety

68 Including Mathiez and Soboul ('The plot was hatched during the night, between the members of the Committees, the Plaine, and the deputies who had long been planning the downfall of Robespierre,' Soboul, *Les Sans-Culottes parisiens*, p. 996).

69 The only possible 'collusion' between the proconsuls and Robespierre's opponents in the governing Committees was that between Fouché and Collot d'Herbois, bound together by their atrocities during the repression of Lyon.

70 For the sessions of the two committees on 4 and 5 Thermidor, the essential text is that of Mathiez, who magisterially unravelled the skein of post-Thermidor documents ('Les séances des 4 and 5 thermidor an II aux deux comités de salut public et de sûrete générale', in Albert Mathiez, *Girondins et Montagnards* [1930], Paris: Les Éditions de la Passion, 1988, pp. 139–70.

extended to Robespierre and Saint-Just, since it involved finally applying the laws of Ventôse: four popular commissions were to be established, charged with screening suspects in the departments, as should have been in operation for a long time already.[71] Besides this, it was decided to establish four peripatetic sections of the Paris Revolutionary Tribunal to judge those detainees in the departments whom the popular commissions had designated after their checks.

Robespierre agreed to participate in the session envisaged for the next day. The assembled deputies started off by staring silently at one another. 'The next day,' wrote Saint-Just in the speech he was unable to deliver on 9 Thermidor, 'we met together again. Everyone kept a deep silence, both sides were present. I rose and said: "You seem to be upset: everyone here should explain themselves openly, and I shall begin, if you will permit." '[72] In a scathing passage of this account of the proceedings, Saint-Just denounced the hypocrisy of Billaud-Varenne: '[He] said to Robespierre: "We are your friends, we have always marched together." This disguise made my heart shiver. The day before he had called Robespierre a Pisistratus, and outlined an act of accusation against him.'

Accordingly, though there was far from total reconciliation, and it is quite possible that Robespierre 'set himself up as denouncer and reproached [the Committee members] for being the first bulwark of the counter-revolutionaries',[73] it remains the case that concessions were made on both sides: on the one hand, the previous day's decree was revised in a way that made it more efficient;[74] on the other, Saint-Just agreed to sign the decree sending a large contingent of Paris gunners to the army of the North. It was decided that Saint-Just should give a report to the Convention in the name of the two Committees, to show that they were no longer at loggerheads.

---

71 Only the two Paris commissions had been set up, and the first two lists of detainees were only approved by the Committees in the first days of Thermidor.

72 Saint-Just, *Œuvres complètes*, pp. 769–85.

73 *Réponse des membres de l'ancien comité de salut public*, p. 89.

74 The new text read as follows: 'Revolutionary Commissions shall be appointed as appears necessary for the judgement of the detainees sent to the Tribunal', obviating any need to apply to the Convention to form the four mobile sections (Mathiez, 'Les séances des 4 et 5 thermidor', p. 149).

A parenthesis. We might discern at this point a gap between Robespierre and Saint-Just, the former not believing in reconciliation and the latter doing his best for it, as proved by the genuinely 'ecumenical' decree proposed at the end of his undelivered speech of 9 Thermidor[75] – in this sense, moreover, it is possible to agree with Dionys Mascolo when he writes: 'If [Saint-Just] had been allowed to deliver his speech of 9 Thermidor, the [counter-revolution] would probably not have taken place.'[76] In this speech, Saint-Just showed that he understood his friend ('His distancing and the bitterness of his soul may excuse him somewhat: he does not know the story of his persecution, he only knows his own misfortune'). But he sought to avoid the imminent disaster. Instead of demanding the punishment of those whom he had just denounced at length (Billaud-Varenne and Collot d'Herbois), he ended on a gentler note: 'I make no conclusion against those whom I have named; I desire them to justify themselves, and for us to become wiser.'

There was widespread relief at the news of the understanding re-established within the Committees. Barère hailed this at the Convention on 5 Thermidor (22 July), as did Couthon at the Jacobins the day after. Voulland, an important member of the Committee of General Security, wrote to his fellow-citizens in Uzès: 'It seemed that the horizon surrounding the two Committees was a little befogged; this fog, which the malevolent tried to point to and make consistent, was seen only by them; the storm . . . was spirited away and dissolved even before it had formed.'[77]

75 'The National Convention decrees that the institutions, which will be constantly amended, shall provide the means to prevent the government, while losing none of its revolutionary energy, from tending towards arbitrariness, favouring ambition, and oppressing or usurping the national representation.'

76 Dionys Mascolo, 'Si la lecture de Saint-Just est possible' [1946], in *À la recherche d'un communisme de pensée*, Paris: Éditions Fourbis, 1993, p. 37.

77 Mathiez, 'Trois lettres de Voulland sur la crise de thermidor', in *Girondins et Montagnards*, p. 175. This letter is dated 8 Thermidor, but was written before Robespierre's speech of that date.

8 Thermidor, Robespierre defeated by the Convention

In the republican calendar, each ten-day *décade* had a particular name: the first *décade* of Thermidor was dedicated to Misfortune. This misfortune began to take shape in the Convention on 8 Thermidor, when Robespierre, in a very long speech, declared that for him it was not a time for reconciliation. 'I need to unburden my heart', he began, before defending himself vigorously against his 'slanderers' on the question of 'these plans for dictatorship and attacks on the national representation, imputed first of all to the Committee of Public Safety in general. By what fatality has this grand accusation been suddenly shifted onto the head of just one of its members? It is a strange project for a man to get the National Convention to murder itself by its own hands, so as to clear his path to absolute power! Let others perceive the ridiculous side of these charges, for my part I see only their atrocity.'[78] He cast onto his opponents the responsibility for the blood that had been shed: 'Is it we who threw patriots into dungeons, and carried terror to all conditions of men? It is the monsters who have accused us.' He repeatedly returned to the accusation of tyranny: 'They call me a tyrant . . . If I were one, they would grovel at my feet, I would stuff them with gold and guarantee them the right to commit any and every crime, and they would be grateful.'[79]

This part of the speech was infused by anger, with words of pain at times whose sincerity went far beyond the customary rhetoric of the day. 'Who am I, who stand here accused? A slave of liberty, a living martyr of the Republic, as much the victim of crime as its enemy. All rogues offend me; . . . my zeal is labelled a crime. Take my consciousness away, *I am the most unhappy of men*' (my emphasis).

Robespierre then moved on to accusation. 'It is at this point that I

78 Buchez and Roux, *Histoire parlementaire*, vol. 33. Françoise Brunel emphasizes that the official account of this dramatic session was belated, and of doubtful reliability: 'It was not the least original feature of the *journées* from 2 to 18 Thermidor that they were reconstructed in year IV or even year V by the editors of the *Conseils du Directoire*, many of whom had an interest in "forgetting" ' (Françoise Brunel, *Thermidor*, p. 89).

79 Robespierre, *Virtue and Terror*, pp. 130–1.

have to let out the truth, and reveal the genuine wounds of the Republic.' He turned first of all to the Committee of General Security, to 'the excessive perversity of the subaltern agents of a respectable authority established in your midst . . . I cannot respect rogues; less still do I adopt the royal maxim that it is useful to employ them.' Then he attacked those in charge of finance: 'Who are the supreme administrators of our finances? Brissotins, Feuillants, aristocrats and known rogues; people like Cambon, Mallarmé, Ramel . . .' Without mentioning them by name, he attacked Vadier, for his role in the Catherine Théot affair; Billaud-Varenne ('Why do those who used to say to you, "I declare that we are walking on volcanoes" [a phrase often used by Billaud], believe that today we are walking only on roses?'); Barère ('You have been told much about our victories . . ., they would appear greater if recounted with less pomp'), and Carnot ('Division has been sown among the generals; the military aristocracy is protected; the military administration shrouds itself in a suspect authority; your decrees have been violated in order to shake off the yoke of a necessary surveillance').

Robespierre's conclusion, delivered with an icy violence, deserves to be quoted in full:[80]

> So let us say that there exists a conspiracy against public liberty; that it owes its strength to a criminal coalition that intrigues inside the Convention itself; that this coalition has accomplices in the Committee of General Security and in the offices of that Committee, where they predominate; that the enemies of the Republic set that committee up against the Committee of Public Safety, thus constituting two governments; that some members of the Committee of Public Safety are in this plot; that the coalition thus formed seeks to ruin patriots and the homeland [*patrie*]. What is the remedy to this ill? Punish the traitors, replace the staff of the Committee of General Security, purge the committee itself, constitute government unity under the supreme authority of the National Convention, which is the centre and the judge, and in this way

80 Ibid., pp. 140–1.

> crush all the factions with the weight of the national authority, to raise on their ruins the power of justice and liberty; such are the principles. If it is impossible to pronounce them without appearing ambitious, I would conclude that principles are proscribed and that tyranny reigns among us, but not that I should silence them; for what can they hold against a man who is right and who knows how to die for his country?
>
> I was born to fight crime, not to control it. The time has not arrived for men of substance to be able to serve the homeland with impunity; defenders of liberty will just be outlaws, for as long as the horde of scoundrels predominates.

This amazing harangue aroused such great emotion that Lecointre, despite being a sworn enemy of Robespierre, was the first to demand its printing. It was on this very question that a highly serious confrontation then began, in which for the first time Robespierre had the worst of it in the Convention. Bourdon de l'Oise opposed the immediate printing of Robespierre's speech, proposing to refer it to the two Committees for examination. Couthon obtained a vote that, on the contrary, it not only be printed, but also sent to every commune in the Republic. Vadier then spoke up to defend himself over the Théot affair ('one of the most extensive conspiracies') and maintained that 'the operations of the Committee of General Security have always been characterized by the stamp of the justice and severity required to repress the aristocracy.'

Cambon, violently challenged in Robespierre's speech, began by justifying his financial measures, but his conclusion marked the turning-point of the session: 'It is time to speak the whole truth: a single man paralysed the will of the National Convention; it is the man who has just delivered the speech, it is Robespierre; so, make your judgement *(applause)*.'

Voices hostile to Robespierre were then heard from all sides. Billaud-Varenne: 'The more that Robespierre's speech inculpates the Committee, the more scrupulously must the Convention examine it before deciding to send it to the communes . . . I prefer my corpse to serve as a throne to an ambitious man than to become, by my silence, the accomplice of his misdeeds. I ask for it to be sent back to the two Committees.' Panis: 'I criticize Robespierre for having expelled from the Jacobins whomever he likes. I do not want him to have more influence than anyone else.'

Charlier: 'When a man boasts of having the courage of virtue, he must have that of truth. Name those whom you accuse. (*Applause. Several voices: 'Yes! Yes! Name them!'*) Robespierre refused: 'I stand by what I have said, and declare that I will take no part in any decision to prevent the dispatch of my speech.'

After interventions opposed to the printing of the speech, as much from the left as from the right (Amar, Thirion and Barère, who sensed the wind changing), the Convention voted to refer the printing to the Committees. Robespierre had lost. The events of the next two days would be only the sequel to this unprecedented disavowal.

We often read that this speech of Robespierre's was a form of political suicide, and that his refusal to name the deputies whom he accused was a fatal mistake: 'Robespierre refused to reply, and by this move he lost. All those who had something to reproach themselves for felt threatened.'[81] The tone of Robespierre's speech, however, was not that of a man wilfully courting disaster. And we may doubt that Robespierre, always so swift to sense the currents of the Convention, took a false step by refusing to name the 'rogues'. As I see it, what he was after, in a kind of double or quits, was what would today be called a vote of confidence, an endorsement of his past conduct and a general consensus on his proposal to reorganize the revolutionary government. If he was unwilling to name names, it was to avoid going into detail. He even said as much: 'People speak to me of Fouché! I do not intend to deal with this now; I distance myself from all that.' The elimination of the corrupt was only one step on the path he was mapping out.

That evening at the Jacobins, Robespierre read his speech again, meeting with lively applause.[82] 'It is said that after he read his speech,

81 Mathiez, *La Révolution française*, vol. 3, p. 217.

82 Buchez and Roux (*Histoire parlementaire*, vol. 34, pp. 2–3) make the point that 'no document of the time that might help towards a history of the Jacobins club on the stormy evenings of 8 and 9 Thermidor has been preserved. No journalist stenographed the debates,

Robespierre addressed the Jacobins with these words: "The speech that you have just heard is my last testament. I have seen it today: the league of the ill-willed is so strong that I cannot hope to escape it. I succumb without regret; I leave you my memory, it will be dear to you, and you will defend it."' He spoke of drinking hemlock, and David cried out: 'I will drink it with you.' At which point Couthon called for a vote, passed by unanimous acclaim, for the immediate expulsion of the deputies who had voted against the printing and dispatch of Robespierre's speech. 'Billaud and Collot were at the club; they were driven out amid insults and threats',[83] a humiliation which doubtless influenced their actions the next day.

On his return to the Committee of Public Safety, Collot apparently delivered a violent attack against Saint-Just, but later that night it seems an agreement was reached: Saint-Just would prepare a report on the institutions, which he would read to his colleagues before submitting it to the Convention – but he did not do so, which deepened the distrust of the Committee members when they arrived at the session of the Convention on the morning of 9 Thermidor (27 July).

9 Thermidor

The sitting opened in the late morning, presided by Collot d'Herbois, who had been elected to the chair on 2 Thermidor – one of the many chance factors that would play a part in the unfolding of these days' events.[84] It began, as usual, with the reading of letters, then Saint-Just came to the rostrum to present the report envisaged the previous day. His speech, which began with the famous words: 'I am not of any faction, I shall combat them all,' was very soon interrupted by

---

and the minutes drawn up by the club's bureau were confiscated by the Thermidorians and removed from the reach of posterity.' The account of the session rests on 'tradition', on the testimony of Billaud-Varenne, and on the report by Courtois in year III. Thus everything has to be taken with a pinch of salt.

83 Ibid., p. 3.

84 A. P., vol. 93, p. 550ff.

Tallien, who asked to speak on a point of order, but instead violently assailed both the speaker and Robespierre: 'Yesterday a member of the government isolated himself from it, delivered a speech in his own name, and today another does the same. Once more there are attacks, aggravation of the ills of the *patrie* that are casting it into the abyss. I demand the curtain be completely torn away *(very loud applause on three separate occasions).*'

Billaud-Varenne interrupted Tallien on a further point of order, with equal virulence. After reporting in his way on the last evening's session at the Jacobins ('Yesterday the intention was proclaimed in that Society of killing off the National Convention'), he moved to the offensive: 'The moment has come to speak the truth . . . The assembly would be misjudging events and its own position, were it to conceal from itself that it stands between two deaths. It will perish if it is weak.' 'No! No!' shouted the deputies, jumping up and waving their hats. The spectators responded with shouts of '*Vive la Convention, vive le Comité de salut public!*' Saint-Just remained motionless and mute throughout the session.

Le Bas then asked to speak. The president refused him, and when Le Bas insisted, the assembly had him called to order. In an electric atmosphere, Billaud continued his onslaught, punctuated by murmurs of indignation. He attacked Hanriot ('the head of the National Guard, accomplice of Hébert, an infamous conspirator'), Dumas ('the president of the Revolutionary Tribunal, [who] openly proposed at the Jacobins to expel from the Convention all impure men, that is, all those that they want to put to death'), and above all Robespierre. He accused Robespierre of having 'brought about single-handed the decree of 22 Prairial, that decree which, in the impure hands that he chose, could be deadly to patriots', of having defended Danton, of having organized 'spying on the representatives of the people that he wanted dead'. And he concluded: 'It is iniquitous to speak of justice and virtue when these are flouted, and to become exalted only when stopped or contradicted.'

Robespierre moved eagerly to speak, but the whole hall echoed with shouts of 'Down with the tyrant!' He fell silent, and slumped on the bench next to the rostrum. Tallien spoke again, demanding the arrest of Hanriot, and lambasting Robespierre who 'wanted to attack and isolate us by turns, so that he would remain alone in the end with the villainous and debauched men who serve him. I ask for this session to be declared permanent until the sword of the law has safeguarded the Revolution and we order the arrest of his creatures.' Billaud instantly proposed and obtained the arrest of Hanriot, his general staff, and Dumas.

Barère then launched into a long report, in which he carefully avoided siding with anyone. The final decree suppressed the post of commander of the National Guard: the head of each legion would command it in turn.

The discussions resumed in the greatest confusion. Vadier, after once again recounting the Théot affair, also turned on the 'tyrant': 'To listen to Robespierre, he is the sole defender of liberty: this drives him to despair, he will abandon everything, he is of rare modesty (*laughter*) and his constant refrain is: I am oppressed, I am forbidden to speak; and it is only he who speaks usefully, as his will is always done.'

Tallien again: 'I request the floor in order to bring the discussion back to its real point.' Robespierre replied: 'I shall certainly be able to do so.' He tried again to intervene, but the shouts from the assembly prevented him from making himself heard. Tallien continued his diatribe, but when he asserted that 'it was while Robespierre was in charge of the general police that they [these acts of oppression] were committed; that the patriots of the revolutionary committee of the Indivisibilité section were arrested', Robespierre exclaimed: 'That is a lie! I . . .' His voice was drowned out by yells. 'It is to you, pure men, that I speak, and not to the brigands (*violent interruption*).' 'For the last time, president of assassins, I ask you to let me speak.' Thuriot, who had replaced Collot in the president's chair: 'You will speak in your turn.' Shouts of 'No! no!' from all sides. The din continued, Robespierre exhausted himself in efforts to make himself heard, and his voice faded away.

It was two in the afternoon when the obscure Louchet, a deputy for the Aveyron, proposed the decree to arrest Robespierre, which was passed unanimously. Augustin Robespierre asked to share the fate of his brother, which was similarly passed, and followed by a third decree that placed Saint-Just, Couthon and Le Bas under arrest. Amid uproar, under a barrage of invective, the arrested deputies finally made their exit to the bar of the hall, from where they were conducted to the Committee of General Security.[85] In the course of the evening, each was taken to a different place of detention: Robespierre was brought first to the Luxembourg prison, where the guards refused to accept him, then to the police administration building on the quai des Orfèvres, where he remained until late in the night; Augustin Robespierre was locked up in Saint-Lazare, Saint-Just in the former Collège des Écossais which had been converted into a jail, and Couthon in the prison of Port-Libre, established in the former abbey of Port-Royal.[86]

Defeat of the Commune insurrection

While this drama was playing out in the Tuileries, the Commune's general council had met in ordinary session at the Maison-Commune (the Hôtel de Ville). Towards two o'clock, spectators arriving from the Convention brought the news of the arrest warrant for Hanriot.[87] Fleuriot-Lescot, the mayor, and Payan, the national agent, reacted without delay, sending members of the general council to their sections to sound the general alarm. Hanriot urged the heads of the six legions of the National Guard[88] to each send 400 men to the Maison-Commune, and organized a concentration of gunners with their ordnance on the Place de Grève.

---

85 The Committee of General Security sat at the Hôtel de Brionne, on the river side of the Tuileries (off the Pavillon de l'Égalité, now Flore, to which it was connected by a wooden corridor).

86 The Collège des Écossais still exists, on 65, rue du Cardinal-Lemoine (then Fossés-Saint-Victor); the abbey of Port-Royal is today part of the maternity hospital of that name.

87 The official account of the session (Buchez and Roux, *Histoire parlementaire*, vol. 34, pp. 47–56) is very confused. The Communal insurrection is described in great detail in Soboul, *Les Sans-Culottes parisiens*, pp. 997–1024.

88 The six legions of the National Guard each comprised the National Guards from eight sections.

The heads of four of the six legions, however, refused to assemble their men. They were summoned to the Convention around three o'clock, where Thuriot, acting as president, forbade them to obey Hanriot – whose position, of course, had just been abolished. The result was that out of forty-eight sections, only sixteen sent detachments to the Maison-Commune.[89] But since some of these – the section of the Panthéon-Français and, from around the Halles, the sections of Les Amis-de-la-Patrie, Les Arcis and Réunion – provided more men than requested, it is estimated that by seven in the evening, an armed force of some 3,000 Guards had been mobilized by the Commune on the place de Grève. This force was all the stronger for the presence of most of the gunners' companies, manned by volunteers with a strong revolutionary consciousness, their cannon arrayed in front of the Maison-Commune.[90]

In the early evening, the general council asked the section chiefs to come to the Commune and take an oath to save the *patrie*. A *Proclamation au peuple* was issued: 'Citizens, the *patrie* is more endangered than ever; scoundrels have dictated laws to the Convention that they are oppressing . . . People, rise up, do not lose the fruits of 10 August and 31 May, let us cast all the traitors into the grave.'[91] Two envoys went to the Jacobins to request their support: the Society declared itself in permanent session, and sent a deputation to take an oath 'to die rather than live under crime'.

The general council appointed the same evening a nine-man executive committee 'for the salvation of the Republic'[92] – but there was

---

89 Almost all these sections were in eastern Paris, whereas the west, beyond rue d'Enfer and rue de la Harpe on the left bank (more or less the line of the boulevard Saint-Michel), and beyond the rue and faubourg Saint-Denis on the right bank, were loyal to the Convention.

90 We should remember that twelve companies had been sent to the front by Carnot, but their guns remained in Paris. Soboul notes that 'there were volunteers among the citizens competent enough to operate the cannon' (*Les Sans-Culottes parisiens*, p. 1003).

91 Buchez and Roux, *Histoire parlementaire*, vol. 34, p. 46.

92 These were: Payan, Coffinhal, vice-president of the Revolutionary Tribunal; Louvet, administrator of provisions; Lerebours, commissioner for public assistance; Legrand, from the Cité section; Chatenay, a juror on the Revolutionary Tribunal; Desboisseaux, from the Fraternité section; Arthur, from the Piques sections, and Bernard, from the Montreuil section.

little that this committee could do, and the lack of a competent military leader rapidly made itself felt.

Its first idea was an improvisation that backfired. Around five o'clock, Hanriot set out on horseback with an escort of a few gendarmes to rescue the arrested deputies, who at that point were still at the Committee of General Security. When he reached the courtyard of the Hôtel de Brionne, he tried to break down the door of the room in which the Committee was sitting. Old Rühl came out and ordered the gendarmes on duty there to seize Hanriot, explaining that he had been dismissed from his post and was under arrest. The general was tied up, with the help of his own escort.

Around eight o'clock, Coffinhal left the place de Grève bound for the Tuileries, to rescue Hanriot and the arrested deputies. With him went 400 men from the Amis-de-la-Patrie section and several companies of gunners, joined en route by some 1,200 men from the section of Panthéon-Français. The column reached the place du Carrousel and the guns were pointed at the Hôtel de Brionne, whose door had been broken down, but the building was almost empty: the members of the Committee of General Security were in session at the Convention, and the arrested deputies had already been moved. Hanriot, however, was freed, and carried triumphantly into the courtyard.

Now came the turning-point of this *journée*: instead of taking advantage of its superiority, in both guns and men, to invade the nearby hall where the Convention was sitting, the column, lacking orders or leaders, returned to the Maison-Commune.

The Convention had had a narrow escape. In the evening's extraordinary session,[93] the assembly unanimously passed decrees placing outside the law Hanriot, the mayor Fleuriot-Lescot, and all the members of the Commune who had risen in rebellion, as well as Robespierre and the other deputies, who had meanwhile been liberated by a force sent by the Commune, and thus 'evaded the arrest warrants against them'. On Voulland's proposal, Barras was appointed

93 A. P., vol. 93, pp. 562–95.

commander-in-chief of the armed force, and seven deputies chosen to be his aides.[94]

Meanwhile the Commune was trying to get organized. The liberated Augustin Robespierre appeared to great applause, followed by Le Bas. Around ten in the evening, the mayor appointed a delegation to go and convince Robespierre to join the Commune movement: 'He does not belong to himself, he must belong wholly to the *patrie*, to the people.' After a first refusal – Robespierre wanted, like Marat, to be brought before the Revolutionary Tribunal – he agreed to proceed to the Maison-Commune, where he was joined shortly after by Saint-Just and Dumas, and later Couthon.

Throughout these long hours, however, the National Guards and gunners were left on the place de Grève without supplies or instructions. News of the outlawing circulated with devastating effect. At eleven in the evening, the section members began to return home. By one in the morning, the last battalion, that of Finistère (faubourg Saint-Marceau) had left the deserted square.

When Léonard Bourdon broke into the Maison-Commune at the head of a hastily recruited column, boosted by the battalion of his own Gravilliers section, Le Bas shot himself in the head and died, Augustin Robespierre threw himself out of the window and broke his leg, and Couthon, in his wheelchair, hurled himself down the grand staircase and survived. Maximilien Robespierre tried to kill himself but managed only to smash his jaw,[95] while Saint-Just let himself be taken without resistance, stoical and silent as he had been since his interrupted speech the previous day.

Such was the end of the Communal insurrection, defeated without putting up a fight. The responsibility clearly lies with those who failed to lead it – Hanriot, and the leaders of the general council. The legalistic scruples of Robespierre also played a part, along with the

94 These were Fréron, Féraud, Bourdon de l'Oise, Rovère, Bollet, Delmas and Léonard Bourdon.

95 Or else he was shot by a gendarme by the name of Merda, who broke his jaw. Both versions have their champions, and both are plausible, an uncertainty that is indicative of the vagueness surrounding all these events.

silence of Saint-Just, once so valiant in the face of gunfire, but this evening seemingly broken.

Yet if only a third of the sections marched with the Commune that day, if the *sectionnaires* so readily dispersed into the night, this is because the Parisian popular movement, brought to heel by the very men it was supposed to defend that evening, was no longer what it had been on 10 August or 31 May. The proclamation of the maximum wage, *just four days previous*, was the last straw in dividing it from the Robespierrists in the Commune. Its relative passivity was no more than the decree absolute of a divorce begun during the winter of year II.

The guillotining of the Robespierrists

The following morning, 10 Thermidor, the outlawed prisoners were brought to the Conciergerie. The assembled Convention ruled 'that the Revolutionary Tribunal shall carry out without delay the decrees passed yesterday against the deputies declared traitors to the *patrie* and placed outside the law, against the mayor and national agent of Paris, against Dumas, Hanriot, Lavalette and Boulanger. Their execution will take place today on the place de la Révolution.'[96]

The hearing at the Revolutionary Tribunal, which opened at one in the afternoon, was confined to verifying the identity of the prisoners, as their outlaw status made any regular trial pointless. The verdict was delivered at four o'clock: twenty-two death sentences.[97] The executions took place the same evening: Couthon died first, Robespierre last but one, Fleuriot-Lescot the last. The bodies were thrown into the common grave of Les Errancis, behind Parc Monceau, and sprinkled with quicklime.

The following day, the tribunal pronounced seventy-one further

96 A. P., vol. 93, pp. 596–618.

97 Maximilien and Augustin Robespierre, Saint-Just, Couthon, Dumas (who had presided this very tribunal two days before), Payan, Fleuriot-Lescot, Hanriot, Lavalette, Vivier (who chaired the Jacobins session on the night of 9 Thermidor), and twelve members of the Commune's general council.

death sentences – chiefly members of the Commune's general council – and a further twelve the day after. Out of the ninety-five members of the council present at the Maison-Commune on 9 and 10 Thermidor, eighty-seven were guillotined.[98] A new Terror had begun.

98 This is the number given by Françoise Brunel (*Thermidor*, p. 109). Gérard Walter gives the lower but still impressive figure of seventy-five (*La Conjuration du Neuf Thermidor*, p. 158).

Epilogue:

The meaning of 9 Thermidor

A slandered creek, not so deep, death

– Mallarmé, 'Tombeau de Verlaine'

From that moment all was lost! To justify their crime, those who had cooperated in the events of that day were obliged to change into heads of accusations the very principles, conduct, and virtues of their victims. The interested professors of democracy, and the ancient partisans of aristocracy, were found to accord once more. Certain rallying cries that recalled the doctrines and institutions of equality, were now regarded as the impure howls of anarchy, brigandism, and terrorism. Those that in Robespierre's time had been wisely kept in check for the nation's safety, seized upon authority again; and to revenge themselves for the humiliation they had been reduced to, they involved in a long and sanguinary proscription, together with the sincere friends of equality, those also who had preached it from self-interest, and even the very factionists who by reason, jealousy, or blindness, had so largely and fatally cooperated in the counter-revolution of the 9th Thermidor.[1]

---

1 Filippo Buonarroti, *Buonarroti's History of Babeuf's Conspiracy for Equality*, London: Hetherington, 1836, p. 37.

The name of the man who explains the meaning of 9 Thermidor in this way was Filippo Buonarroti, a friend of Robespierre who for a long time defended his memory and spread his ideas. At the start of his book on the Conspiracy of Equals, he presents the event as a radical break, or at least a disastrous turn: 'From the moment that the Revolutionary Government had passed into the hands of the Egoists it became a veritable public scourge.'[2]

Major historians have also given credit to the idea of a Thermidorian break, by ending their histories of the Revolution at this date. The most prestigious example is that of Michelet. In the closing lines of his great book, a child, taken by his parents to the theatre soon after Thermidor, is amazed to see on the way out 'men in jackets, their hats doffed, asking the spectators as they leave: "Do you need a carriage, *master*?" The child does not understand these new words. He asks for an explanation, and is simply told that there has been a great change with the death of Robespierre.'

Jaurès breaks off his contribution to the *Histoire socialiste de la Révolution française* after Thermidor, at the end of volume 6, leaving 'in the hands of our friends the torch whose flame has already been buffeted by such stormy winds'. Mathiez similarly ends the third and final volume of his *Histoire de la Révolution française* with Thermidor, 'a memorable example of the limits of human will grappling with the resistance of things' – a nod, perhaps, to Saint-Just's expression, 'the force of things'.[3]

Alongside these venerable writers of the past, it is unsettling to see some present-day historians, even among the most interesting,

2 Ibid.

3 Mathiez's 1929 book *La Réaction thermidorienne* (Paris: La Fabrique, 2010) is different from the three volumes of his *Histoire*, and cannot readily be viewed as a continuation. François Furet's interpretation of Thermidor also evolved between *La Révolution française*, written together with Denis Richet in 1963, and *Penser la Révolution française* in 1978. In the first of these books, he wrote: 'Not only did the revolutionary movement continue to advance; it went beyond itself in seeking to consolidate its conquests – the fundamental liberties and property-ownership without privilege' (François Furet and Denis Richet, *The French Revolution*, London: Weidenfeld & Nicolson, 1970, p. 215). In the second: '[Robespierre] may have put the Revolution "on ice" when he silenced the Parisian *sections* and instigated the trials of the spring of 1794; but it was when he died, in Thermidor, that the Revolution died' (p. 57).

interpret Thermidor in a very different way. For Martyn Lyons, 'in regarding 9 Thermidor as the end of the Revolution, we have taken for granted an interpretation of the Revolution which has perhaps overstated the role of Robespierre and the Terror'. Lyons arrives, as we have seen, at the rather paradoxical conclusion that '9 Thermidor, seen so often as the work of reactionaries, was interpreted by the *Comité de Sûreté Générale* and by its main authors as a revolution of the Left.' Neither Barère, nor Billaud, nor Collot, he continues, 'imagined that the overthrow of Robespierre would necessarily mean the end of the Terror . . . The Thermidorean regime of the Year 3 became a perversion of their original intentions.'[4]

Françoise Brunel goes further, writing that 9 Thermidor appears to her a 'non-event', apart from the number of victims. For her, the end of the Revolution is located not in Thermidor of year II but in Germinal–Prairial of year III (April–May 1795), when, after the final Paris uprising was crushed, the 'last Montagnards' were arrested and either deported or condemned to death. 'None of this [the closing of the Jacobins club, the abrogation of the maximum, the Constitution of year III] was inevitable on 9 Thermidor.'[5] It is true that the Roman-style suicide of the 'Prairial martyrs',[6] the throwing of Marat's ashes into the sewer, and the return of the Girondins to the Convention, all these events of year III, may well appear as an ending. For Yannick Bosc, it is the new Constitution of that year that marks the real break.[7]

But is it possible to argue, for all that, that there was a *continuity in the Revolution* beyond 9 Thermidor?

On 10 Thermidor, in the evening session,[8] the Convention decided on Lecointre's proposal to purge the popular commissions – set up,

4 Lyons, 'The 9 Thermidor', pp. 395, 397, 411.

5 Brunel, *Thermidor*, pp. 127–8.

6 Bourbotte, Duquesnoy, Duroy, Goujon, Romme and Soubrany, condemned to death by a military commission after 4 Prairial, all tried to commit suicide. Some of them succeeded, others were taken to the scaffold wounded or dying.

7 Yannick Bosc, *Le Conflit des libertés. Thomas Paine et le débat sur la Déclaration et la Constitution de l'an III*, Université Aix-Marseille I – Université de Provence, 2000.

8 A. P., vol. 93, pp. 616–8.

we recall, to screen suspects and distribute their assets to the poor. This operation would be conducted under the auspices of the Committees of Public Safety and General Security, but the final decision would be taken by the Convention itself. This was a major step towards the de facto annulment of the Ventôse decrees.[9]

The following day, on Thuriot's proposal, the Revolutionary Tribunal, 'peopled by Robespierre's creatures', was suspended and replaced by a temporary commission. In the evening, as proposed by Tallien, the Convention decreed that all the Committees would be renewed by a quarter each month. Delmas requested successfully that 'no member shall be able to return to a committee within a month of leaving it'.[10]

On 14 Thermidor (1 August), the Prairial law, a 'veritable martial law', was abolished.[11] Fouquier-Tinville was placed under arrest at Fréron's proposal ('I demand that Fouquier-Tinville go and expiate in hell the blood that he has spilled').

On 7 Fructidor (24 August), *less than a month after the fall of Robespierre*, a series of laws were passed that completely reorganized the revolutionary government and administration. The revolutionary committees were reduced to one per local administrative capital – Paris would have twelve, and 'the arrondissement of each of these committees shall include four sections': this put an end to the autonomy of the sections, and was the origin of the ordering of Paris into twelve arrondissements, which lasted until 1860.

The government was now divided into sixteen committees,[12] with twelve principal ones to which twelve executive commissions were attached. The Committee of Public Safety saw its brief reduced to the

---

9 For the events of Thermidor and Fructidor of year II, see Mathiez, *La Réaction thermidorienne*, chapter 1.

10 A. P., vol. 93, pp. 619–44 and 645–51.

11 Official martial law, abolished by the Montagnard Convention, would be re-established by the Constitution of 1798.

12 The Committees of public safety, general security, finance, legislation, public instruction, agriculture and arts, trade and supplies, public works, transport and post, army, navy and colonies, public assistance, administrative divisions, minutes and archives, petitions and correspondence, and inspectors of the national palace (A. P., vol. 95, pp. 396–420).

direction of diplomacy and military operations, the manufacture of war materiel, and the importation and circulation of goods. Domestic administration and tribunals were removed from it and assigned to the Legislation Committee, which became the third Committee of government.

In parallel with this legislative overhaul, the leading personnel were massively purged. On 13 Thermidor, the Convention chose the men who would fill the vacancies on the Committee of Public Safety: only Dantonists and representatives of the Plaine were elected, plus Tallien.[13] For the Committee of General Security, the gaps were filled by Legendre, a close friend of Danton; Goupilleau de Fontenay, whose altercations with Rossignol in the Vendée had made his reputation; Merlin de Thionville, an associate of Chabot and Basire; André Dumont, famous for his repressive ferocity in the Somme; Bernard de Saintes, and Jean Debry, a Girondin who had signed the protest against 31 May (he would resign the same day): here again, Moderates, corrupt men discredited before Thermidor.

It took only a few days, therefore, three or four weeks at the most, to destroy the foundations of the revolutionary government and lay down those of what would soon become the *Thermidorian reaction*.[14] Any who thought they could continue the work of the great Committee, once Robespierre was got rid of, were soon carried away in the great reactionary current.[15]

So 9 Thermidor does indeed constitute a rupture; but since this date clearly does not mark the 'end' of the Revolution, what other moment should be chosen as the final curtain? It is not very convincing to end with the last session of the Convention, nor with the pitiful exit of the Directory on 18 Brumaire of year VIII, nor again with the transition from the Consulate to the Empire. Did the

13 These were Bréard, Eschasseriaux the elder, Laloi, Thuriot, Treilhard and Tallien.

14 Furet and Richet note that the political use of this term appears for the first time in the *Dictionnaire de l'Académie* (1798): 'Reaction. Applied figuratively to a party that takes revenge and acts in turn.'

15 On 7 Nivôse year III, a parliamentary commission was formed to examine the behaviour during the Terror of Billaud-Varenne, Collot d'Herbois, Barère and Vadier, 'Robespierre's tail'. After the Germinal uprising, they were sentenced to deportation.

Revolution end with the departure for St Helena of the man in the little hat, whom Mme de Staël saw as a 'Robespierre on horseback'?

What was brutally concluded with Thermidor is the incandescent phase of the Revolution, in which men of government, sometimes followed and sometimes driven forward by the most conscious section of the people, sought to change material inequities, social relations and ways of life. They did not succeed, to be sure. Their failure and their tragic end were not fundamentally due to the coalition of *fripons*, but far more to the social fear aroused by their programme, and the contradictions between the realism of the revolutionary government and the demands of the popular movement.

The heirs of the Thermidorians, who have governed and taught us continuously ever since, seek to travesty this history. Against them, let us keep memory alive, and never lose the inspiration of a time when one heard tell that 'the unfortunate are the powers of the Earth', that 'the essence of the Republic or of democracy is equality', and that 'the purpose of society is the common happiness'.

Index

Page numbers in **bold** refer to maps